Psychic Reality and Psychoanalytic Knowing

ADVANCES IN PSYCHOANALYSIS: THEORY, RESEARCH, AND PRACTICE

A series of volumes edited by Joseph Reppen, Ph.D.

REPPEN ● *Beyond Freud: A Study of Modern Psychoanalytic Theorists*

FAST ● *Gender Identity: A Differentiation Model*

BARRATT ● *Psychic Reality and Psychoanalytic Knowing*

REPPEN ● *Analysts at Work: Contemporary Psychoanalysts Describe Their Practice, Principles, and Techniques*

REPPEN ● *Psychoanalysis: Future Directions*

Advances in Psychoanalysis:
Theory, Research, and Practice
Volume 3

Psychic Reality and Psychoanalytic Knowing

Barnaby B. Barratt, Ph.D.

 THE ANALYTIC PRESS
1984

Distributed by
LAWRENCE ERLBAUM ASSOCIATES, PUBLISHERS
Hillsdale, New Jersey   London

The Analytic Press

Distributed solely by

Lawrence Erlbaum Associates, Inc., Publishers
365 Broadway
Hillsdale, New Jersey 07642

Library of Congress Cataloging in Publication Data

Barratt, Barnaby B., 1950–
  Psychic reality and psychoanalytic knowing.

  (Advances in psychoanalysis : theory, research, and
practice)
  Bibliography: p.
  Includes indexes.
  1. Psychoanalysis.   2. Psychology—Philosophy.
I. Title.   II. Series: Advances in psychoanalysis.
BF175.B28   1984   150.19′5   84-6353

ISBN 0-88163-013-6

Printed in the United States of America
10   9   8   7   6   5   4   3   2   1

CONTENTS

Foreword by Merton M. Gill, M.D. . . . .   **vii**

1. **Psychology and Psychic Reality** **1**
    Psychic Reality   1
    A System of Representations   8
        Psychoanalysis as the Study of Representational
            Worlds   11
        Terminology and Classification in the
            Study of Representations   14
        The Question of the Subject   23
        The Question of Science   27

2. **Psychoanalytic Disputation and
    Psychoanalytic Misapprehension** **50**
    Why is Freud's Psychology so Controversial?   50
    The Problem of "Metapsychology"   57
    Ego Psychology as Cul-de-Sac   62
    "Eine Psychologie der Verdrängung"—
        "A Psychology of Repression"   65
    Psychoanalysis and the Subject   76
    Psychoanalysis as Science   85

3. **"Analytic" Epistemology** **89**
    Psychoanalytic Knowing Is Not Subjectivistic   91

Notes on Psychoanalysis and Transcendental Subjectivism
  ("Phenomenology")   98
Psychoanalytic Knowing Is Not Objectivistic   121
Freud's Psychology and "Analytic" Cooptations   134
  Against Psychologies of "Selfhood" and
    Subjectivity   138
  Against Psychologies of "Ego Objectivity"   141
Psychoanalysis as a Different Kind of Science   166

4. **Hermeneutic Ontology and the
    Dialectics of Deconstruction** **171**
  Psychoanalysis Is Not Hermeneutic in the Traditional
    Mentalist Sense   173
  Psychoanalysis Is Not Hermeneutic in the Contemporary
    Ontological Sense   183
  Against the Lacanian Reformation   212
  Dialectics and Deconstruction   239
  Psychoanalytic Negativity, Therapeutic Discourses,
    and the Question of Ideology   256

References **275**

Name Index **287**

Subject Index **293**

FOREWORD

by Merton M. Gill, M.D.

Barnaby B. Barratt would be called a purist by some. He believes that Freud's central message has been adulterated, and he polemically and passionately argues for the reinstatement of the pure vision. He summarizes it thus:

> Psychoanalysis is indeed *eine entscheidende Neuorientierung in Welt und Wissenschaft*. In this book, I have tried to demonstrate the validity of this claim, first by disposing of all ideological variants of psychoanalysis (the world-views of subjectivistic or objectivistic epistemology and of hermeneutic ontology), and then by showing that the uniquely scientific and emancipatory quality of genuine psychoanalytic praxis, as the psychic pursuit of the repressed, is due to its movement as the discourse of dialectical negativity within and through the limits and conditions of semiotic construction.

The statement is not quite comprehensive because Barratt deals not only with ideological variants of psychoanalysis, but also with certain epistemological and ontological views which do not represent themselves as variants of psychoanalysis. But that is a small matter. What is important is that to many analysts this summary statement will seem to be an abstract and philosophical statement, employing terms that sound quite strange and are presumably distant from their real concerns. Strange and seemingly distant they are, but I believe they should be of crucial concern to all analysts who aspire to be anything more than technicians. They would have important repercussions for technicians, too, if they were taken seriously by the theoreticians whose models and world-views ultimately determine how technique is construed and taught.

Barratt promises future work in which the implications of his thesis will be developed, first, on a "more practical, clinical level" and, second, through "a consideration of the general issues of ideology, with an eye to the semiotic and material formation of human subjectivity." He gives us a few tantalizing hints about this future work when he tells us that "implied in this discussion of the negativity of psychoanalytic discourse is an odyssey wherein the psychoanalyst is moved as much as the patient. For, above and beyond all else, the discourse cannot function without their relatedness, the psychoanalyst's 'care' in the Heideggerian sense. And it is a profoundly dialectical engagement— conatively, affectively, and cognitively." I especially look forward to how the author will relate the present study to how he believes psychoanalysis should be practiced, because I felt that in an earlier essay in the *Annual of Psychoanalysis* (see Barratt, 1978; and the accompanying discussion by Louis Fourcher) he incorrectly concluded that Roy Schafer's position necessarily leads to a trivialization of psychoanalysis into psychotherapy.

Hegel, Husserl, Heidegger, Schleiermacher, Dilthey and Gadamer, Descartes and Kant march through these pages, but so do Hartmann and Rapaport, Lacan, and briefly the interpersonalists and the object relations theorists. But mainly the discussion is what many would consider an essentially philosophical discourse. The words "epistemology" and "ontology" must rival "and" and "the" in frequency. Can this really be pertinent to psychoanalysis?

I believe it is—indeed, crucially so. To me one of the most heartening and promising shafts of light in the generally dark and discouraging stasis in psychoanalytic literature is the growing controversy about the basic character of psychoanalysis as a scientific discipline. I myself have joined those who argue that psychoanalysis should be a hermeneutic and not a natural science. Those bare bones of slogans have acquired significantly more flesh and blood for me through reading this work. I have long been embarrassed by the gap between the ardor with which I have taken the stand for psychoanalysis as a hermeneutic discipline and my naiveté about the psycho-philosophical basis for such a conviction. I cannot claim to know whether Barratt's reading of the philosophical authors I have mentioned is correct, but I do believe that he gives us a remarkably coherent account of their views, and he provides me with a framework for reading them should I ever come to do so.

Some of the issues that have been illuminated for me are these: how Descartes and Kant stand in relation to a positivist world–view and why their understanding of the relation between subject and object will not do for psychoanalysis; how the phenomenology of Husserl was an advance and yet how it clashes with the fact that psychoanalytic knowing is not subjectivistic; how Heideggerian-Gadamerian hermeneutics is a "romantic and traditionalist totalization" and how "psychoanalytic discourse proves the falsity of this totalization, concretely disclosing its ultimate emptiness and immobility, as well as the pseudo-concreteness of its ideological operations"—the last in the chapter which I found the most difficult to follow despite the reiteration of the thesis.

As for the reiteration, I was somewhat troubled by it in my first, fairly rapid run-through of the monograph (I call it a monograph rather than a book because of its relatively simple and straightforward design and logical line). But now I find it an asset because all major points become clearer as they are reiterated in varying nuances. The very fact that the language and concepts are foreign to most psychoanalysts makes this repetition all the more desirable because I hope that analysts will be prominent among its readers.

I was most taken aback by, and ready to quarrel with, the slashing attack on Heinz Hartmann and my mentor David Rapaport as the leading figures of ego psychology, despite a bow to Rapaport's honesty and concern for logical thought. I still think the attack is somewhat one-sided and does not give enough credit to the advances of ego psychology, especially in its effort to expand psychoanalysis into more than a psychology of psychopathology. I also did not find very persuasive Barratt's disagreement with what he considers to be two of the faults of ego psychology—namely, its contentions that the ego must be partly unconscious not only in the descriptive sense but also in some systematic sense and that the repression barrier must be within the ego. But even so, I do find compelling Barratt's argument that in ego psychology "the 'ego' either loses its denotation as subject of conscious, unconscious, and preconscious representational activity or is totalized in a manner that portends to bring ego psychology into alignment with subjectivistic psychologies proclaiming the unified, identitarian nature of mental activity." I also believe that his rather perfunctory criticisms of interpersonal and object relations theorists fail to acknowledge their virtues and their struggle against the same perversion of Freud's clinical model against which he inveighs—but again I see the cogency of his argument. Indeed, one of the central virtues of this passionate work is how single-mindedly it hews to the line of Barratt's conviction that he knows Freud's central message and will brook no beclouding of it, no matter how sophisticated or valuable in some respect it may be.

Who is it who presumes to write with such conviction and authority? Dr. Barratt, a psychologist, is a research candidate at the Michigan Psychoanalytic Institute, as well as admittedly an autodidact in philosophy. But of course it is not his credentials that matter but the merit of the book. My estimate of the latter is that I urge you to read, indeed, to study it.

". . . doch kann ich Ihnen versichern, dass mit der Annahme unbewusster Seelenvorgänge eine entscheidende Neuorientierung in Welt und Wissenschaft angebahnt ist."

". . . yet I can assure you that, through the supposition of unconscious mental processes, a critical new direction in the world and in science is open to us."

Sigmund Freud,
Vienna, 1915,
*Vorlesungen zur Einführung in die Psychoanalyse,
Gesammelte Werke,* 11:15,
(1916–1917).

1 Psychology and Psychic Reality

How do we know our mental life, and how is our mental life altered by our efforts to know it better? This book attempts an epistemological and ontological discourse concerning the understanding of human mental processes, and it aims toward a definitive thesis on the dialectics of knowing and being in this work of psychological understanding.

My argument concerns issues of subject, "object," being, and method in psychological knowledge. It is perhaps a rather complex argument, which needs to be apprehended as a whole. By and large, its import lies not so much in its particular components, as in their assemblage. What this work reconfronts are questions pertaining to all psychology and, for that matter, to all human sciences. Yet much of its focus is on the understanding of unconscious mental contents, on the question of knowing and being in Freud's psychology. To set the stage for this inquiry, we need to reexamine our ideas about reality, representation, subject, and science.

PSYCHIC REALITY

In a remarkable yet somewhat elusive chapter in his *Principles of Psychology*, William James (1890) discusses the psychological sources of our sense of reality. He argues that "reality" necessarily entails a relation to our practical and emotional life: *"the fons et origo of all reality, whether from the absolute or the practical point of view, is thus subjective, is ourselves"* (Vol. 2, pp. 296–297). Attempting to forge a pragmatist's solution to the dilemma of realist and idealist philosophies, he refers to the multiple worlds in which we live and proposes a rudimentary categorization of them. James suggests that for each of us, these worlds attain the status of "real" when they are invested with our interest. In other words, our active life is guided by a practical sense of reality, contingent upon the excitement, frustration, and satisfaction of our desires. Although James consistently shies away from the more radical implications of his ideas, he does at least set forward the problem of *personal realities*—the possibility of an understanding of human individuality, and of the idiographic craft of living in the world.

"As the cosmologist is," to paraphrase Heraclitus' pre-Socratic doctrine, "so will the cosmology be." An understanding of the world is conditioned by the inner order and disorder of the one who understands. Each person is, in a certain sense, his or her own cosmologist. Although the history of philosophical reflection, particularly in Europe, has tended toward serious consideration of this aphorism, the dominant tradition of Anglo-American psychology, despite the promise of James' leadership, has generally obscured the issue, often ignoring it.

In medieval times it could be believed that the world simply is as it is, given to us purely in experience. It could be believed that objects simply present themselves as they are; that truth is a matter of correspondence or adequate resemblance. The naiveté of this faith is now unarguable. Modern thinkers have had to reexamine the processes and presumptions of their knowledge. This shift from medievalist theological preoccupations toward the epistemological concerns of modern philosophy can be seen as a response to the "revolution" of Copernicus, Kepler, Galileo, and Newton. It is heralded by the developments of Continental rationalism from René Descartes to G. W. von Leibniz, and of British empiricism from Thomas Hobbes to David Hume. Descartes' work—his mentalization of representational knowledge and his method of doubt in his search for mental procedures by which certainty may be secured—marks the beginning of the transition to modern problems. Immanuel Kant's systematic, syncretic formulations, with their central thesis that *experiences of the world conform to the structures and functions of the mind*, represent the culmination of this transitional period.

Since the insights of this "Age of Reason" from Descartes to Kant, it has become impossible to assume that the human mind is a passive imitation of an external, independent universe, somehow given to us in the purity of experience. Accordingly, we must relinquish the assumption that "reality" is experienced or otherwise apprehended apart from the mind's representational activity. As Goethe said, "We see only what we know." We may still conceive abstractly of an absolute reality, of an independent, outer domain of things-in-themselves, the existence and nature of which are derived by collective agreement about observed phenomena. But in pausing to consider what is entailed by "collective agreement about observed phenomena," the constructive activity of the mind persistently asserts itself.

Epistemology—as the study of the conditions of possibility for human experience and understanding—and *psychology*—in its proper etymological sense, not as a technology of behavior, but as a study of the inner ordering of experience and understanding—would not be of such interest to us were it not for the foundation of all human pursuits in the constructive activity of subjectivity and intersubjectivity. If experience in the world is conditioned by mental structures and functions, and understanding of the world is similarly formed by the mind's representational activity, then these structures and functions of the mind effectively determine the "reality" in which we live. Epistemologically, this leads us to further examination of general statements about reality and the universally constitutive life of the mind. And psychologically, this raises important questions about *reality in relation to the individuality of mental processes.*

It is Sigmund Freud who offers us the indispensable notion of *psychic reality*, connoting the individualization of reality relative to the person's mental processes. Freud first coined this term in a 1913 publication, although the same idea, designated "thought-reality," appears once in his unpublished writings as early as 1895.[1] Prior to Freud's work, I am not aware of the use of this notion anywhere in the literature of Continental philosophy. The term seems without immediate or direct precedent, even though, in a certain sense, it was presaged in the writings of Friedrich Schiller, Friedrich Nietzsche, Wilhelm Dilthey, and others. After Freud's introduction of this notion, however, several similar ideas were deployed throughout European scholarship for diverse purposes. The ethologist Jacob von Uexküll, for instance, distinguished the *Umwelt* as the organism's biological world or habitat, the *Mitwelt* as the organism's world of relations to others, and the *Eigenwelt* as the organism's world of internal or self-relations. From a different perspective, various existential, phenomenological, and hermeneutic philosophies developed Edmund Husserl's idea of the *Lebenswelt*, as the intersubjective ground of all experience and understanding.

Psychic reality is necessarily defined in terms of the particular person's psychological processes; it comprises *all that is real for the individual subject.* It is an interiority of personal experiences and

---

[1] Throughout this book, most references to Freud's writings are to the original German, and quotations have been translated by me from the original. Readers wishing to move from citations in the *Gesammelte Werke* to the *Standard Edition* translation should consult George Klumpner and Ernest Wolf's useful "pagination converter" (1971).

understandings, an *Innenwelt*, as Freud sometimes called it. In Freud's writings, this psychic reality is contraposed to "external" (1895a), "factual" (1912–1913), or "material" reality (1916–1917), corresponding to what in contemporary parlance would be called "objectivity"—the conventions of general agreement about the way the world is. By contrast, psychic reality defines the world as it is experienced and understood by the individual subject. It is the private sense of reality, in which the person effectively lives.

Unfortunately, in some post-Freudian literature, under the auspices of an ideology of adaptation and following some precedent in Freud's own writings, the term "psychic reality" has acquired a more restricted usage, connoting pathology. The "neurotic" supposedly lives in psychic reality, whereas the "normal" is clear-sightedly at home in "external" or "objective" reality. Here "psychic reality" refers to some partial sphere of a person's mental functioning, a maladaptive aspect counterposed to a "conflict-free sphere." Against this more restricted usage, it must be said that "normality," as Freud suggested, is nothing but an idealization, a fiction based on certain cultural conventions. "Conflict-free functioning" is at best a relative notion, concocted for the convenience of the clinician. And "external" or "objective" reality, as will be argued throughout this book, is a matter of intersubjectivity, of general agreement concerning the way things are. Thus, for our purposes, "psychic reality" retains its broader and philosophically more cogent usage, denoting all that is real for any individual subject.

Psychic reality, then, includes not only the individual's accession to the normative ordering of experience, to the conventions of understanding and the authority of nomothetic mentation, but also, and more especially, the individual's transgressions from or personalizations of this normativity. The latter should not be dismissed as mere "failures" to meet the collective standard of "reality testing," for they concern the particular truth of each person's sense of reality, the idiographic character of all experience and understanding. Moreover, psychic reality refers not only to the world as the subject readily apprehends and articulates it, to all that is descriptively available to consciousness and preconsciousness, but also to the unconscious constituents of the individual's sense of reality. Freud's work, more than any other impulse of modern thought, potentiates our awareness of the full richness of the content and particularity of this inner world. Since Freud, psychotherapeutic, literary, and artistic discourse has become newly available to us in a manner that intimates the desirousness, creativity, loneliness, and terror of the personal reality underlying manifestations of "objective" or "rational" thought. Psychoanalysis consistently discovers that the individual's particular grasp of the world is infused with wishes, memories, fantasies, and dreams, in a manner that cannot be immediately or fully apparent to the subject of conscious and preconscious mentation. This infusion—the idiographic quality of all experience and understanding—testifies to the vitality of unconscious mental activity in constituting the reality in which the person effectively lives. Comprehended from this perspective, Freud's psychology ushers in an extraordinarily radical notion of human individuality.

In the history of Western thought, we might distinguish four phases in the notion of individuality. This is a crude distinction, not to be regarded as a chronological or necessarily sequential scheme, nor as an adequate analysis of the range of perspectives from which individuality might be conceptualized. These "phases" are suggested solely for heuristic purposes, in order to delineate one aspect of the position of Freud's psychology within the history of humanistic ideas.

To begin with, we might point to cultures or historical periods in which no strongly operative sense of individuality is discernible. The person is not meaningfully differentiated, but identified with some extrapersonal entity that governs individual destiny. Just as slaves appear in the mind of the master as a populace without personhood, so too may there be moments in a society's system of thinking in which individuals have no distinctive conception of their individuality. Documentation provided by classical scholars and by cognitive anthropologists—such as evidence of judicial principles in which the child is liable for the crimes of ancestors, or of name-giving procedures in which there is no form of personal designation—points to ways of thinking in which individuality, even if recognizable as such, is at best a nugatory matter.[2]

Individuality is assigned greater value in the next, typological con-

---

[2] Following the current decline of free-market structures in Western society, with their attendant liberal philosophies, a Huxleyan resurgence of such ways of thinking is neither impossible nor improbable. As Theodor Adorno and others have suggested, such a resurgence would follow from the monopolization of capital, the consolidation or increasing pervasiveness of the state or corporate apparatus, and the escalating administration of interests formerly consigned to the "private" sphere of life. Given the current conditions of our society, further research on ideological processes in the formation of subjectivity is exigent.

ception, which differentiates the person in answer to the question: *What* am I? Here individuality is defined *externalistically* or *objectivistically*—contingent not upon the individual's own experiences and self-understanding, but upon general agreement by others about the person's observably distinctive qualities. The person's "distinctiveness" is thus grounded extrinsically and behaviorally, referring to an outer unity rather than an inner theme. Such typological notions of individuality may initially be expressed in terms of social roles or cultural ideals; later, as generic attributes or traits. Hence individuality is comprehended as a categorization of persons along some ostensible, fixed dimension. Distinctions between persons in the same category are irrelevant, excoriated as so much "error variance." To determine individual differences "objectively" in this manner is to deny individuality as subject, and to obscure questions about personal reality, its formation and transformation, in favor of a fixed, "external" frame of reference. Biography or life history, in this mode of thinking, appears merely as fortuitous sequence, an adventitious chronicle of deeds done.

Against this view of biography as mere chronicle, the writing of autobiography—a genre that has burgeoned since Rousseau's and Goethe's work at the end of the eighteenth and beginning of the nineteenth centuries—marks a shift from an extrinsic to an intrinsic notion of individuality. It implies a "self-consciousness" in the sense of G. W. F. Hegel, Friedrich Schleiermacher, or Arthur Schopenhauer—an attempt to express the personal meaning and constructivity of life experiences. This conception asserts the *individual as subject*, asking the inwardly posed question: *Who* am I? The development of this view since the Enlightenment seems related to changes in the market structure of capitalism, the educational opportunities of the bourgeoisie, the erosion of religious authority and dogma, and the shifts in the epistemological horizon to which I have already alluded. For example, from the Kantian thesis that experiences of the world conform to the (universal) structures and functions of the mind, it is the shortest of steps to Friedrich Jacobi's subjective idealism or *Lebensphilosophie*, to Johann Fichte's self-posited ego, or to Friedrich Schelling's meditations on the "I" principle. And from there readily follows the idea that individuals may *uniquely* construct themselves and their worlds. To write or speak autobiographically, the subject differentiates the self and its experiences from those of all other persons. This differentiation is made not so much in terms of the exteriority of social identity and cultural ascription as inwardly, in terms of the person's experiences of the world as having idiographic history and meaning. The autobiographical mode thus implies an *interiority of personal experience and understanding*. It connotes an individuality that is necessarily *self-reflective;* typically it implies a person's claim to a life history that is, in some sense, self-formative.

The notion of the individuality highlights the intrinsic nature and history of the person as a self-reflective and self-formative subject. For the moment, we shall retain the Hegelian term "self-consciousness" to encompass all that is psychic. Elaboration of these ideas about self-reflection and self-formation leads us to a final notion of individuality, which not only recognizes the constructive, self-formative quality of the person's self-consciousness, but also insists on the *transformative potential of the subject's reflection and interrogation*. First prescribed by Hegelian philosophy, this conception is epitomized by Freud's method of psychological inquiry. Freud does not, of course, suggest that all mental formation requires reflection in a deliberate sense, nor that self-reflection necessarily entails transformation. Yet Freudian discourse does establish a view of the individual in which the subject's experiences and understandings may be transformed through a particular reflective and interrogative praxis. We are not yet ready for a detailed discussion of this notion of individuality, concerning as it does the *dialectical locus of the human subject*. For the moment, it returns us to Freud's notion of psychic reality, as the grounds of a psychological praxis which claims that for the subject to inquire upon this reality within a particular mode of discourse is necessarily to transform it.

Psychoanalysis is the study of the individuality of the psychic subject as a reality—a discipline *sui generis*. It is an inquiry upon the particular subject's psychic reality. Without this notion of psychic reality, there would be no such distinctive discipline as Freud's psychology. As we shall see, it is the only *adequate* psychology that is methodologically directed to scientific inquiry upon the idiographic nature and history of reality relative to the person's mental processes. Moreover, whereas other psychologies typically foreclose this individualization of reality by their epistemological and ontological presuppositions, the discourse of psychoanalytic interrogation gives credence to the subject of mental processes as formative, reflective, and transformative. In my opinion, psychoanalysis is, first and foremost, a disciplined study of the vicissitudes of personal meaning, an inquiry upon the interiority of representation and desire by which the individual human subject articulates itself and its world. This definition leads us into fundamental questions concerning psychic reality as a system of representations, the subject of this system, and the character of science as an inquiry upon this interiority of personal meaning.

A SYSTEM OF REPRESENTATIONS

What is the "reality" psychoanalysis inquires upon and from which its inquiry proceeds? Although it is irreducibly anchored in the material conditions of existence, the reality in which we each live is the reality of our representations, and the meanings by which we live inhere to this representational world. If psychic reality is the legitimate domain of any scientific psychology, then—without lapsing into an untenable idealism—the mind (individual or collective) must be conceived as a system of representations.

The notion of the mind as a system of representations implies the proposition that *mental processes are constructive and significational.* That is, the conditions of possibility for all human experiences and understandings are constituted by the structures and functions of the mind. In no sense is the world known to us apart from the activity and creativity of this representational system.

Since the Kantian revolution, with its insight that all experiences conform to the structures and functions of the mind, modern philosophy has been unable to appeal to the evidence of sensation and perception as the pure primordium of our experiences of the world. Such experience is constructed, signified or represented, not given to us in some untrammeled form. "Realism" has become at best an article of faith, to be treated *critically.* Yet Kant's philosophy does not lapse into some arbitrary idealism. It establishes with great rigor a synchronic, architectonic epistemology, specifying a two-tier construction of knowledge. This supposedly universal epistemology admits both the noumenal—*things as they are,* determined by transcendental deduction of the categories of synthetic *a priori* judgment—and the phenomenal—*things as they appear,* which is the realism of empirical-synthetic experience in time and space, of that which seems given to self-consciousness yet does involve *a priori* representational laws comprising the conditions under which "objects"[3] can appear. The point

---

[3] It is with hesitation that the term "object" is employed in this book. The term is a source of considerable confusion in both the psychoanalytic and the philosophical literature. Later in this chapter, in the section on terminology and classification in the study of representations, part of what I advocate is a

here is that the conditions of all possible experience are established in terms of mental structures and functions. Following Kant, *things-in-themselves* are neither directly attainable nor merely given. Reality, as an exteriority, is not concretely presented to us, but represented by us. What we know is what we represent.

A serious psychology, responsive to the critical contributions of epistemological reflection, must take account of several further propositions entailed by the tenet that the mind is a system of representations. The very idea of a *system* of representations denotes a totality of internal relations. In other words, *representations are determined by their interrelationship.* The possibility of any particular experience is formatively conditioned by the totality of experiences and understandings. Meaning is thus sustained by a network of meanings. What, then, is the nature of this totality? More speculatively, what is its relation to the material conditions of existence, and what are the "origins" of the representational process?

The representational process must, in a certain sense, be taken as a system of signs unto itself, for the implicit proposition is that *representations are built upon one another.* That is, the possibility of "new" experiences and understandings is conditioned by prior representations. The representational world thus has a transformative, developmental, or *historicized* quality,[4] with the present and future created from the fabric of the past. This diachronic aspect of mental processes is one which the Kantian tradition of epistemological reflection and the psychologies that conform to it embrace uneasily, despite Kant's emphasis on the temporality of mental life. It raises questions

---

discussion of the psyche as the subject's construction of a system of self- and other-representations, and this entails some modification of the clinical jargon of "object relations." Philosophically, the term "object" has been used and abused in several different ways. As "that which is known," it may denote the thing standing in contrast to the subject of mentation, or the percepts and concepts formed by this subject itself, and so forth. In my opinion, the term should be used only to refer to things thrown before the mind, implying the subject's representations in general. Thus, in my references to the "object" spoken about in the psychoanalytic and philosophical literature, the reader should bear the quotation marks in mind.

[4]The terms "historicity" and "historicized" connote the way in which a discourse changes progressively, building upon itself and transforming itself. In distinction, the terms "historical" and "historicality" denote a discourse that refers to the conditions of a time past, giving an account of these conditions. Although this choice may not be loyal to recent usage in contemporary hermeneutics, it is convenient for the clarity of my thesis.

about the progressive or teleological nisus of human thought, which are better discussed by Fichte and Hegel, or even Jean Piaget, Heinz Werner, and George Kelly, than within the synchronic stasis of the Kantian edifice.

Another possible proposition about the mind as a system of representations is that *the mind may return to prior experiences and understandings*. In distinction to the creation of new representations out of the fabric of prior representations, this statement implies the re-creation of the past within the fabric of the present and the future. In psychology, only Freudian psychoanalysis emphasizes this recursive or reserializing aspect of mental processes. Such directionalities of thought emanate from the vivifying power of desire in mental life, and Freud's psychology, more than others, attends to this desire of the subject within the formation and transformation of the representational world. It gives credence to this repetitious, historicized quality of the representational process, leading to questions about the regressive or archaeological nisus of human thought.

The propositions mentioned here provide a means of critical scrutiny of any theory of mental life. With any psychological formulation, we need to ask about the totality of internal relations in a system of representations, about the dynamic between individual and collective processes, about the rationalities and irrationalities of psychic reality, about the progressive movement of experience and understanding as well as its regressive movement under the impetus of desire—in short, about reality, subject, and the historicity of transformation. Much contemporary research that passes under the rubric of "psychology" indeed inquires upon aspects of the representational process. But the epistemological and ontological grounds of such inquiry must be submitted to further scrutiny.

If epistemological reflection commands that the representational character of mentation be taken seriously, than a serious psychology must also reflect upon this necessarily constructive and significational quality. In this respect, it must be said that some twentieth-century psychologies, notably those derived from classical behaviorism, have never been worth taking seriously. For they have presumptively precluded the activity and creativity of mental life as conatively, affectively, and cognitively expressive. Moreover, if epistemological reflection requires that the mind be understood as a representational system, then psychology should equally reflect upon the representational character of *its own* epistemological process, by which mental life is made known. In this respect, it must be said that most twentieth-century psychologies, because they are founded upon a logical empiricist platform (e.g., the cognitivist models currently dominant in social, developmental, and experimental research), are unreflectively positivistic, naively realist, even tacitly pre-Kantian.[5] As we shall see, psychoanalysis diverges sharply from this dominant mode of psychological research; its epistemology is not that of logical empiricism.

Psychoanalysis as the Study of
Representational Worlds

Why, in developing an argument relevant to all knowledge of mental processes, should we return to Freudian epistemology and ontology? And specifically, why should we emphasize the problem of unconscious mental contents?

The reason for focusing on unconscious processes is twofold. Unconscious mentation, by definition, raises fundamental questions concerning the way in which the life of the mind may be known to us. If we bypass the several claims of philosophical mysticism, we find that our very notion of knowledge is necessarily grounded on some personal or collective faculties of consciousness and communication. As philosophy has dimly recognized since Descartes, "unconscious" ideation, affect, or motive raises the most awkward and hence some of the most educative questions about the subject who seeks to know. As will be elaborated in Chapter 2, Freud discovered the psychic unconscious in a very special *dynamic* sense. Although this radical discovery continues to be a matter of dispute, no one in psychology currently doubts the existence of nonconscious mentation, that is, psychic processes that are "unconscious" in a weaker, descriptive sense. Indeed, the dominant psychology—by which I mean psychology that is not psychoanalytic and is conducted with the experimentalism of the logical empiricist mode—perennially redocuments the poverty of immediately conscious self-understandings. Contemporary "findings" in cognitive psychology, psycholinguistics, developmental research, and elsewhere arrive repeatedly at an "unconscious" of this sort. A focus

---

[5]The term "logical empiricism" is used here in a manner roughly equivalent to the German generic label *analytische Wissenschaftstheorie*, to cover "analytic" philosophies such as that of Karl Popper, as well as positivism, realism, and pragmatism. The common thread of this grouping is their acceptance of some principle of empiricism and their close allegiance to the methodology and epistemology of the natural sciences. Thus, loosely, a logical empiricist psychology is one which attempts to emulate the procedures of contemporary natural sciences.

on the unconscious dimensions of mental life therefore illuminates the entire question of psychological inquiry. And discussion of Freud's discipline in particular, because of the especially strong and controversial notion of the unconscious it advances, serves to call into question in the most acute and hence potentially heuristic manner issues that are ubiquitous.

Freudian psychoanalysis is an abundantly rich psychology, but a profoundly controversial one with respect to its scientificity. In using psychoanalysis to develop a thesis about the conditions of psychological inquiry, I shall treat psychoanalysis as a *method*, as a changeful inquiry. I am less concerned with psychoanalysis as a system of beliefs about the world, an enterprise of theorizing, or an institutionalized profession of acculturation and "adaptation."

To reiterate, psychoanalysis is, first and foremost, a disciplined study of the vicissitudes of personal meaning, a transformative inquiry upon psychic reality. Indeed, it could be shown that Freud, from the start of his psychoanalytic career, was cognizant of the issues concerning the representational world raised here. Despite the positivist influence of the unified science movement, in his early quasi-neurological sketches of 1895, he is adamant that things do not impress themselves upon the subject of experience so much as the subject seeks things in representation by way of desire and memory. "Discovery" of the world is always, in a certain sense, an act of psychic rediscovery. Freud thus advances a particular formulation concerning the dialectic of progression and regression within the psychic reality of human mentation. This formulation, as we shall see, embraces a speculative mythology of the prerogatives of desire over the sense of "reality"—a speculation which, under a more naturalistic mode of description, concerns the primacy of pleasure-unpleasure over the representational vicissitudes of "reality testing" (see Freud, 1895a, 1911a, 1925a).

Apart from such speculation, which is external to anything that could become known in the course of psychoanalytic interrogation, Freud judiciously avoids the problem of "first philosophy"—the problem of the primordium of experience and understanding. Indeed, psychoanalysis successfully counters the claims of first philosophies in the Cartesian and Kantian tradition (see Chapter 3). The decisive priority of psychic reality is evident in Freud's writings, despite lapses into naturalistic assumptions and occasional excursions into an ideology of adaptation. Although Freud never directly addresses the question of the totality of systems of representation, he contributes the radical notion of the splitting of the subject of psychic life, with disjunction between the subject of desire and the subject of semiosis (see

Chapter 2). This discovery does imply a particular thesis about the dynamic between individual and collective processes. Moreover, in pursuing this discovery, Freud follows his philosophical mentor, Franz Brentano, in asserting that the quality of psychic life is *directed toward* things, that it is meaningful and intentional. Psychic reality is, for Freud, always constructive, significational, and split by the vicissitudes of desire in the representational world.

Obviously, I am adopting a particular "reading" of Freud's psychology. It may be helpful at this stage to enumerate the main features of my way of approaching psychoanalysis, as a chart to which the reader can return periodically as the argument becomes more complex.

In my view, psychoanalysis, starting with Freud's work, contributes six uniquely original and paradigmatically revolutionary tenets, which constitute the science of mental life:

—Psychic reality is decisive and must be given priority epistemologically and ontologically.

—This personal reality should be understood as a semiotic system of representations, variously formed and deformed by the vicissitudes of desire. (These vicissitudes could be designated in terms of the erogeneity and aggressivity of mental life.)

—The subject of this representational system is split, due, in a certain sense, to ideological contradictions between individuality and sociality. (This splitting of the human subject could be designated in terms of the dynamic rupture of mental life into conscious, preconscious or foreconscious, nonconscious, and repressed unconscious dimensions.)

—The splitting of the subject—evident in the vicissitudes of the repressed (understood generically), the "return" of the repressed in compromise formations, and the "therapeutic" reappropriation of the repressed—accounts for the historicity and opacity of mental life.

—Mental life may thus be constituted as the locus of the split or contradictory subject in a movement of repeating, recollecting, and reappropriating—a movement that may be frozen for ideological reasons, and that may be reinstated and reinvested in the reflection and interrogation of the psychoanalytic process.

—There is a method of knowing and being, a transformative and truthful praxis of intersubjective discourse, by which Freud's psychology establishes itself as the science of this psychic reality, thereby challenging the prevalent view of science itself.

These points should become clear as my argument unfolds. Psychoanalysis, for the epistemological and ontological questions it raises, needs to be examined and discussed entirely anew. The reading

I propose provides the avenue toward this end. It allows not only psychoanalysis to be philosophically articulated, but the philosophical issues in which all psychological inquiry is ineluctably entangled to be reconfronted and reworked.

Terminology and Classification in the Study of Representations

Let us return to some more general considerations. In referring to psychic reality as a system of representations, the term "representation" has thus far been employed in its broadest sense, to align it with the general semiotic notion of signs, and to include impressions, traces, categories, symbols, and so forth. The problem of terminology, however, is extant.

If the proper study of psychology concerns the mind as a system of representations, how are we to talk about this psychic reality? Perhaps regrettably, there are many ways of talking about the constituents of our mental life. Kantian philosophy offers us the terminology of categories; Ludwig Wittgenstein the jargon of "language games"; Charles Peirce the classification of "signs" into ten trichotomies, of which icon, index, and symbol are the best known. In contemporary psychology, Jerome Bruner has written about iconic, enactive, and symbolic processes; Jean Piaget about schemata and their logical operational structures. George Miller, Eugene Galanter, and Karl Pribram propose a theory of "TOTE units"; and contemporary social and developmental researchers variously employ cognitive and motivational terms such as "memory trace," "schema," "image," "prototype," "attitude," and "action-hierarchy." Other fields of scholarship, such as traditional linguistics and aesthetics, have, rather different lexicons by which representational forms may be designated. In contemporary clinical writing, terms such as "instinctual derivative," "self-representation," "object-representation," "self object," "word presentation," "thing presentation," "introject," and "body image" abound. This is neither the time nor the place to review the plethora of vocabularies in an integrative fashion. It might be simply hoped that the emergence of *semiotics* as a science in its own right will eventually alleviate the exigency of such a work of integration.

The rise of semiotics, or "semiology, in the past decade is, in my opinion, tremendously auspicious for the science of psychology, and for its future confrontation with fundamental epistemological and ontological questions. This recent development makes it possible, indeed enlightening, to view psychology and anthropology, *les sciences humaines*, as semiotic disciplines. In this sense, the intellectual heritage of Marx, Durkheim, and Freud—who in various ways assert the sociocultural constitution of all human experience mediated by the "symbolic" order—provides the context within which all anthropological and psychological phenomena must be analyzed as significational practices. Such phenomena are necessarily meaningful, as significational systems and as loci of discourse between and upon subjects. Therefore, "language," generically conceived, is both model and medium for the understanding of all human events (see Chapter 4).

The rise of semiotics, as a potentially integrative discipline aimed at this sort of understanding, represents the confluence of many trends in modern thought, including this century's philosophical turn toward language as world-founding. This shift can be seen in the work of Martin Heidegger, Ludwig Wittgenstein, and others. Ernst Cassirer, Alfred North Whitehead, and Susanne Langer, for example, all emphasize the privilege of the "symbolic" dimension of human experience. Of course, the most immediate influences on the rise of semiotics are Ferdinand de Saussure and Charles Peirce. Peirce presents a painstaking and exhaustive taxonomy, which treats everything as a sign. And Saussure establishes structural linguistics, providing a synchronic analysis of both paradigmatic relations (contrasts or oppositions between signs) and syntagmatic relations (combinations of signs creating larger units). Whereas Saussure is rather restrictive in his use of this method, Claude Lévi–Strauss' research stands as a prominent example of the application of Saussurean analysis to a range of cultural events. And the post-structuralist critique of Saussurean method, in the provocative work of such writers as Roland Barthes and Jacques Derrida, argues for the reintegration of diachronic analysis in the study of this range of signifying practices. Although the impact of semiotic studies on Anglo-American human sciences is still limited, except perhaps in the fields of literature and aesthetics, the future of psychological science without semiotics is in some ways inconceivable. Semiotics provides a means of inquiry upon mental life that not only establishes a terminology for the analysis of representational systems, but also forces upon us the necessity of confronting questions of epistemology and ontology.

If the proper task of any psychology is the semiotic study of psychic reality as a system of representations, how might such representations be regarded investigatively? There are several dimensions along which a psychology could delineate the subject's representational world of thoughts, images, fantasies, and the like. To begin with, as far as a group of subjects—a culture—is concerned, a representation may be *shared* or *not shared*. As far as a particular subject is concerned, a representation may be *referential* or *figurative, invested with desire to greater* or *lesser degree, conscious* or *not conscious, about the person's self* or *about some "other,"* and so on. Systemically, representations may also be *ordered* or *disordered*. Of course, this aprioristic set of dimensions is by no means exhaustive, and it is quite obviously rudimentary, given the sophisticated categories with which many psychologies, including clinical psychoanalysis, discuss mental life. Moreover, it runs the risk of sounding as if representations could be isolated, understood outside a context, and studied externalistically or objectivistically rather than reflectively and interrogatively. Nevertheless, these dimensions, which have been variously emphasized in different psychological formulations, may prove useful for a preliminary discussion.

By introducing the notion of psychic reality, the interiority of experiences and understandings, we have already broached questions concerning the shared or unshared and the referential or figurative aspects of mental representation. To reiterate, whatever its anchorage in the material conditions of human existence, the reality we know and in which we live is the reality of our representations. For the individual, the real is delimited by the horizon of intrapsychic representations of self and others. Yet this is a shared reality inasmuch as individual human existence finds meaningful articulation only within sociality, and only insofar as this sociality may be comprehended as the operation of a communal system of representations. Such a communal system is a culture, by which the horizons of nature, history, and our own selves are construed. Experience and understanding of this "reality" are given, in that the culture embodies a semiotic system that defines and delimits the possibilities of representational construction. This semiotic system, as the plane of intersubjectivity, is like a "sum" of knowledge that makes it possible for any particular text, communication, or personal experience to have meaning. In other words, the individual's construction of reality is always made within the sociocultural system of signification, by which the totality of the "real" is organized and articulated. My contention is, that the individual's psychic reality, the life historical passage of experience and understanding, is both potentiality and positionality within the totality of a society or culture's semiotic practices: both "project" and "product." As potentiality, the individual's psychic reality may be said variously to distort, transgress, or negate the nomothetic normativity of the sociocultural system of discourse. In this way it *acts as subject within* the totality. To be precise, there is no individuality "outside" of the general semiotic system, no premental mentation, no precultural personhood. Hence, as positionality, it may be said that whatever the idiographic "distortions" of the person's world, it is constructed from and by the general sociocultural system of discourse, which antedates the subject's particular psychic reality, and of which the latter is a part. In this sense, psychic reality *is subjected to* the general semiotic practices of a society or culture.

Intersubjectivity, the field of semiotic practices—not some specious "objectivity" or the persuasive "givenness" of natural things in sensation or perception—is the ground for the formation of the subject, psychic reality, and hence the human world itself. The individual's construction of reality, a horizon of representations of self and other, does not emerge *de novo* from the infant's "blooming, buzzing" collision with the raw existence of things-in-themselves. This common-sensical Jamesian myth—to which, in the guise of a variety of realist and empiricist formulations, the dominant psychology tenaciously clings—is subverted not only by epistemological reflection since Kant, but also by post-behaviorist evidence indicating that all experience at all phases of development is bounded and regulated by the structures and functions of psychic organization. With regard to the infant's entry into the world of representational collectivity, it now seems that the world is significantly organized and articulated before the individual's ontogenetic odyssey—predefined, not naturalistically, but by an entire semiotic system, a sociocultural formation that "presents," or represents, to the child, the totality, or boundaries and rules of meaningfulness, of the real. Yet the totality of semiotic practices is such that its representations appear "essential," acultural or ahistorical, and the universality of its thought is readily assumed—hence, the seductive, ideological power of the naturalistic fallacy, despite the insights of epistemological reflection.

For the moment, the point to be considered is that what we commonly call "objectivity" and "rationality" in exercising judgment about the external world is a matter of signification, determined by the totality of semiotic practices—a matter of the conventions of general agreement about the way the world actually is. Simply put, our judgments concerning actuality, veridicality, and existence depend on the shared quality of representation. Moreover, the notion of judging "the way the world is" introduces us to another dimension—the *referentiality* of mental representation. This dimension bears on our sense of "independent" or "outer" reality. Certain representations are taken to be about something that exists or existed outside the representational system; the mental event has a quality of givenness that is apprehended as an experience of concrete or extra-mental things. Other representations are taken to be the products of the fictive, figmentive activity of mental life; the mental event has a quality of creativity that is apprehended as figurative. Of course, how the individual subject apprehends the particular representation—as referential, figurative, or as some admixture—intersects with the dimension of sharedness, although what the culture holds as imaginative, the individual may hold as veridical, and vice versa. Moreover, the person may or may not recognize the degree of "deviance" of his or her percepts and concepts from the culture's practices. Under a different mode of description, the whole question of reality, illusion, and delusion is transported along these dimensions.

As far as psychic reality is concerned, that is, within the frame of the particular person's mental life, the dimension of referentiality and figurativity concerns the manner in which one appropriates one's mental life. The individual's particular world is an inner medley of percepts, concepts, memories, wishes, fantasies, and ratiocinations—to some of which the subject ascribes existence or rationality, and to others not. The dimension of referentiality and figurativity leads from considerations of personal epistemology to *ontology* and the *ontic*, to the person's account of being and to the way of dealing with being.[6] It raises questions about conviction, faith, and decision in mental life, as well as questions about what might be called the metaphysics of imagination. One might, for instance, discuss veridicality versus imagination, rule-bound versus playful thought, concreteness versus abstraction, or discourse versus metadiscourse. One might also compare judgments of existence, of inner or outer space, with judgments of attribution, of goodness or badness, pleasure or unpleasure; and one might consider the temporality or historicality of a mental representation, whether the subject apprehends it as signifying time past, present, or future. Obviously, the range of issues raised by this dimension is quite broad, and many of these questions have a bearing on therapeutic discourse. My interest in this book, however, is in their relation to the fundamental questions of epistemology and ontology— in particular, in the way in which imagination and veridicality are infused in the production and reproduction of memory and the

---

[6]Throughout, the term "ontology" refers to an account of being, and the term "ontic" refers to a way of dealing with being. Somewhat similarly, "epistemology" denotes an account of knowing, and "epistemic" or "episteme" denotes a way of dealing with knowing.

significance of this "infusion" for the formation and transformation of the representational world.

Consideration of the shared or unshared and the referential or figurative dimensions of psychic life leads to the question of the subject's investment in the representational world. Not all of the representational world has equal significance for the subject. Freud is one of the few psychologists to take seriously the insight that the composition of the representational world implies something more than variation in the *form* of representations; he suggests that the subject makes various or differential *investments* in representations he or she "owns." Descriptively, Freud's proposal is similar to suggesting that the woman I love means more to me than some other women, even though my representations of her may be no more or less differentiated or detailed than those of other women I know. It intimates that the "special something" about being in love, or about hating, or whatever, exists, in some sense, apart from the representation itself—as an intentionality, a type of directionality, of the subject toward the subject's representation of the person or thing. One might say that the vicissitudes of this "investment" affect psychic life without being inherent to the *form* of the representation thus affected.

Presented in this rudimentary fashion, the question of the subject's investment in the representational world is highly problematic. On the one hand, it bespeaks the subject's disposition to the world as it is represented, and is thereby entirely experiential, an aspect of the subject's being with which only the subject can be acquainted and which only the subject can "know" upon reflection. On the other hand, as a way of speaking about psychic life, it is inevitably speculative, for it is a dimension of the representational world found only *in* representational forms; it is not *of* these forms. Nevertheless, the notion is utterly necessary, as clinical work makes evident. The great theorists of psychoanalytic psychology have never successfully relinquished the notion of investment, even though, as we shall see, it has embroiled them in all sorts of chaotic controversies and ill-defined terminologies, including neurophysiological models of energy, instinct, and the like. Except within the model of attentional processes, the dominant psychology, with its penchant for cognitivist models in social and developmental research, usually omits this notion—as it is impossible to study objectivistically and externalistically. The result is a rationalistic model of the structures and functions of the human mind, which ultimately rids psychic reality of individuality and subjectivity.

In the course of his career, Freud tried out several vocabularies to designate his discovery of vicissitudes in the subject's investment in the representational world. Invariably, he depended on physicalistic similes, off-setting the naturalistic implications of their physicalism by employing everyday terms such as "intensity," "investment," and "impetus." Early in his work, Freud wrote of "psychic intensities," or *psychischer Intensitäten* (1895b), and introduced the important notion of *besetzen* and *Besetzung* (1895a; Breuer & Freud, 1893–1895). This idea of course, is central to Freud's originality in emphasizing the animative significance of *wishes* in mental life (e.g., 1898a, 1899, 1900, 1901a, 1907). Later, as is well known, he developed these ideas into a speculative metapsychological account of the "energy economics" of psychic functioning and the vicissitudes in the source, pressure, aim, and object of *Trieb* (e.g., 1905c, 1915a). *Trieb* translates as impetus, urge, impulse, propensity, inclination, instinct, or desire, and it is always apportioned dualistically, in accordance with the conflictual or dynamic character of the psyche. Between 1894 and 1911, Freud wrote of sexual and self-preservative impulses; between 1911 and 1914, of sexual urges and *Ichtriebe*, (the motive powers, *interests*, or narcissistic inclinations of conscious and preconscious mental organization). Then, between 1915 and 1920, Freud offered the influential distinction between *erogeneity* and *aggressivity*, to which he added the dualism of life and death forces in 1920. It should be noted that Freud was, more or less, always aware of the speculative basis of these formulations. He suggested that they are, in a certain sense, extrapsychoanalytic (see 1915c, and my second chapter). And he referred to them as a mythology—for example, insisting that *"Triebe* are mythical creatures, splendid in their indefiniteness" (1933, p. 101).

For the moment, it is important only that we recognize the purpose of such theorizing in pointing to a process of investment that adheres to the forms of the representational world without being of the forms themselves. Freud conveys this notion principally through his use of the verb *besetzen* and the noun *Besetzung*, employing these terms as a way of writing about the interplay of "qualitative" and "quantitative" aspects of psychic life. Regrettably, James Strachey, in the *Standard Edition*, translates these terms with the Greek *cathexis*, and its derivatives "hypercathexis," "cathectic withdrawal," and "anticathexis." In Freud's own language, *besetzen* can mean to occupy territory, to fill a vacancy, to cast a play, to man a garrison, to nominate for an office, to engage a place, or to put or lay on something. For an English-language psychology, the concept of *investment* conveys the notion most felicitously, as was the opinion of Freud's French translators when they decided on the term *investissement*. The key idea here is that representations may be invested to a greater or lesser degree, and that with which they may be invested by the subject can—at least for our purposes at the moment—be conceived as *desire*, a generic notion that embraces ideas about "psychic energy" and *Trieb*, with all the connotations of erogeneity and aggressivity that it typically holds for psychoanalytic psychology.

This discussion of investment in representations ushers in the dimensions of consciousness and of the self or other content of the representational system, as well as introducing the question of the subject. The idea that all representations are conscious, preconscious, or in some sense unconscious leads into the opacity and historicity of human thought. First, however, the issue of content needs further clarification.

Mental representations—whether shared or unshared, referential or figurative, conscious or not—necessarily have content. One dimension along which psychology may delineate psychic content concerns whether it pertains to the person's self, that is, the individual's own being, body, and personhood, or to something other than the self, such as some other person, thing, event, or concept. Indeed, in this regard, the mind may be depicted as a system of self- and other-representations. It is by such a representational system that the various horizons of nature, society, history, relationships, and our own selves are construed.

Representations of the *other* (defined here to denote all that is "not me") are diverse and complex. This subsystem of the representational world includes all experiences and understandings of the world of physical events—the focus of research by experimentalists interested in the traditional areas of perception, cognition, and the like. It also includes all experiences and understandings of the cultural or social world—the focus of research by linguists, anthropologists, ethnomethodologists, clinicians, and social psychologists. As is well known, clinical psychoanalysis, with its focus on the level of interpersonal attributions, refers to the subsystem of other-representations as the intrapsychic repertoire of "object relations."

Self-representations also comprise a diverse and complex subsystem of the person's psychic reality. In the sense used here, "self-representation" denotes all that is "me" as opposed to "not me." Clinical psychoanalysis often refers to this subsystem under the rubric of "narcissistic relations," and suggests that the body with the images it evokes is germinal in the ontogenetic formation of self-representations, just as psychosexuality is germinal in the development of object relations. Obviously, under these headings, we can subsume a wide variety of clinically important issues—for example, what is referred to as object finding and the vicissitudes of narcissism; attachment, separation, and loss; internalization and identification; and structuralization. What is important for us to note here, however, is that self-representations are constituted in the manner of other-representations. That is, a self-representation (of something that is "me") has the same ontic and ontological status as an other-representation (of something that is "not me"). This is a major tenet of developmental research, and one that is elegantly mythologized in the notion of mirroring, about which Jacques Lacan (1936) speculates in his theory of the presymbolic constitution of the imaginary. In Lacan's "mirror phase," the infant experiences an archaic promise of the self as a unified whole, prior to fragmentation of the body and the self (prior to the narcissistic threat of castration and so on). The infant discovers the "self" as distinct from all others by identifying with an image perceived as if in a mirror: this perceived other, which is grasped joyously as a unit, turns out to be "self." In this way, the formation of the self depends on experiences and understandings of the body and all other aspects of the "self" in the manner of an "other."[7]

With the classification of psychic contents as about the person's self or about some other, we come to the systemic character of the representational world as a constructive and significational totality—to the question of the *subject* of psychic reality. It is a question which, on one side, the dominant psychology with its logical empiricist precepts is entirely unable to apprehend, and to which, on the other side, psychoanalysis makes an extraordinary yet enigmatic contribution.

---

[7]The term "objectification" refers to this dialectical process of development in which the self, as a subsystem of representation, is formed by a movement in which it makes itself "other" and then later reapprehends this "other" as self. The term "objectivation" means something different; it refers to an epistemological position in which the there-being of a thing is taken to be represented as "object" of knowledge, which stands as an ontologically impassable externality with respect to the subject's knowing activity. Thus, objectivistic knowledge is that pursued by logical empiricist epistemology. Although the use of these two terms may not be loyal to Hegel's use of similar terms, it is convenient for the clarity of my thesis.

THE QUESTION OF THE SUBJECT

A system of representations, a way of world-making, must have a subject. It cannot be otherwise. And indeed, we owe to first philosophy, to the tradition of Cartesian and Kantian epistemological reflection, the realization that for every experience or understanding, there must be a subject having that experience or understanding. To put it very simply, there must be a subject to whom the mentation belongs. For any thought, there has to be a subject who thinks it, just as for any wish, there has to be a subject who wishes it. All mental contents must, in this sense, be contained within or owned by some conatively, affectively, and cognitively expressive subjectivity.

This notion of the subject is not some picayune proposition. It is not some ethereal piece of philosophizing irrelevant to the scientific investigation of psychological functioning. It is of fundamental importance to the understanding of mental life, and its neglect is key to the contemporary malaise of Anglo-American sciences. For, whereas philosophers have written extensively about the question of the subject, and psychoanalysis broaches this question distinctively and radically, the dominant psychology methodically occludes the issue in the name of a more or less spurious objectivity.

In philosophical writings, this issue is discussed under headings such as "identity," "self," and "ego." These discussions typically embark from the Cartesian insight that it must be possible to know that any knowledge I have is mine. Leibniz, for example, tries to explain this identity of the cognizing subject in terms of the persistence of substance. On the other hand, Hume, for whom the subject is necessary to account for the organized character of thought processes, confesses his inability to explain an issue so basic to his theorizing. Philosophically, the cognizing subject need not be a substantive entity and need not be personal. Indeed, the subject of a system of representations may be extrapersonal. For Descartes, the *ego cogito* is equivalent to the individual mind, whereas Kant's transcendental ego is universal rather than individual (see Chapter 3). The general tendency of twentieth-century philosophy as Foucault (1966) has provocatively discussed, is to endorse anti-humanistically, a kind of subjectless subjectivity—the extrapersonal "subject" of the episteme, paradigm, or sociocultural totality. For example, in his later writings, Wittgenstein (1945–1949), who is sometimes hyperbolically charged with ending the Cartesian era, argues that shared practices, "language games," are the means and medium of self-knowledge. The elderly Husserl (1935) upholds the epistemological priority of intersubjectivity over the Cartesian subject, and proposes that the sociality of the *Lebenswelt* is the grounds of all experience and understanding (see Chapter 3). And in Heidegger's (1950, 1951, 1954) and Gadamer's (1960–1972) romantic totalization of "language," it is "language" as a subjectless totality that thinks the thinker (see Chapter 4).

An examination of Immanuel Kant's (1770, 1781, 1788) notion of the transcendental ego aids the nonphilosopher in grasping some of the significance of this question.[8] The "identity" of the "self" or transcendental ego is basic to Kant's epistemology; it is implied by the supposed unity of mental organization as well as the systemic character of all true knowledge. Kant uses the term "self" philosophically, to imply the subject of mental organization (whatever the content of such organization), just as the Hegelian or quasi-Hegelian notion of "self-consciousness" covers everything psychic. Thus, Kant's "self" should not be confused with the "self" introduced in the preceding section, which was used to denote only representations about the person's own being, body, and individuality, as distinct from those about some "other." As the subject of mentation, Kant's "self" or transcendental ego includes what clinical psychoanalysis calls object representations; it is like an "I think" conjoined to all mental contents, noumenal and phenomenal.

The subject of mental life, this "I-ness" attached to all mental contents, has three qualities: it is unitary, active, and empty.

It is a *unity* in that the subject must, according to Kant, be the same for all mentation—or at least for all knowable mentation. The "I" that is thinking about *this* topic, must be one and the same as the "I" thinking about *that* topic. And the "I" that *is* thinking must be one and the same as the "I" that *was* thinking or that *will be* thinking. In the Kantian scheme, this "I" remains identical for all possible ideas, wishes, fantasies, and so on that I may have. The "I think" of a particu-

---

[8]The following discussion owes much to my notes from lectures given by Professor Dieter Henrich at Harvard University in the early 1970s. Henrich's brilliant exegesis of the Kantian subject drew from Kant's unpublished notes and manuscripts. He succeeded in rendering explicit an aspect of Kant's theorizing which Kant himself left more or less implicit in his published works, for he demonstrated that Kant could have embarked on his epistemology from the apex of the "transcendental self," but chose instead a more concrete way of arguing, because of the need to convince his metaphysically oriented readership. In his publications, Kant persistently avoided discussing the foundation of his system, and expressed disinterest in the procedure of reflection by which he himself arrived at the architectonic structure of noumenal and phenomenal mentation vis-à-vis the thing-in-itself.

lar thought does not define the subject who thinks, nor is this "I" defined by having a particular thought, for it remains the same while having other, quite different thoughts. It can readily be seen that this notion of the subject is necessary to account for any temporal or historical continuity in thinking. And although Kantian epistemology is notorious for its neglect of this diachronic aspect or historicity of human thought, the idea that mentation occurs in time rather than space is one of Kant's better-known dictums. The notion of the subject as a unity is also necessary to account for the systemic character of thinking. And this synchronic aspect of human thought is given full due in the architectonic nisus of Kantian epistemology, in the impetus to establish a fixed and final structure for the conditions of all possible knowledge. Finally, the unitary quality of the subject indicates the nature of mental representation as a totality, an issue to which we shall return.

With the *activity* of the subject, Kant implies that the "I-ness" of representations has to be apprehended as a processive relationship. Any experience or understanding is, in a certain sense, contingent upon the subject and must be actively included in the subject's unity. It is this notion that led Descartes, for instance, to write as though the subject's thinking were always transparent to itself. Together with the unitary quality of the subject, the quality of activity implicates the constructive or significational character of mentation: ideas, wishes, and fantasies do not merely appear in the representational system; their conditions are actively constituted within its subjectivity. Here we might consider the particular thinking involved in reflection, for to say "I think about thinking" intimates the activity of the "I think" that must be conjoined to all mental events. Although reflectivity may never arrive at the subject in itself, since this subject is contentless, but only arrive at further thoughts, it does demonstrate the activity of the subject. For the particular thought that the subject thinks when thinking "I think" convinces us of the active relationship between the subject and the particular thought. Reflection is thus apodictically constructive and significational. (It may also demonstrate the subject's deconstructive potential, but that is a matter to be discussed later.) If this quality of activity is indicated by the particular thinking involved in reflection, it has to hold for all mentation, given the unitary quality of the subject, that the "I think" of particular thought is the same for all possible mental contents. From the Kantian tradition, we therefore learn that the constructive and significational character of mental representation is both necessary and fundamental, that the subject is, in a certain sense, a locus of activity.

The *emptiness* of the Kantian subject follows from the qualities of unity and activity. The "I-ness" of a representation does not indicate its content, since this "I-ness" actively conjoins all representations. No particular content defines the subject of mentation, nor does the subject impute content. Even in reflectivity, the "I-ness" of the representation does not entail its content. Nothing is implied by the "I think" when I think about thinking; what is arrived at is the thought of the "I-ness" of all possible ideas, wishes, and fantasies. In such reflection, the subject may, so to speak, take up a different relationship to its thinking. Yet the subject thinking "I think" does not determine a particular contentful thought; it determines only that there are always further thoughts when thinking about thinking. At the same time one cannot contemplate the subject apart from the subject's representations. Mental contents are thus of a different order from the locus of the subject but contingent upon it, and the subject is itself, according to this argument, necessarily unitary and active but empty.

In Kantian philosophy, the subject's transcendental unity can be seen as a limiting notion, a necessary outcome or a residue. It is the *sine qua non* of the entire epistemological structure, which specifies a two-tier construction of noumenal and phenomenal mentation. The transcendental unity of mind supposedly interprets the unity of nature. Several lines of criticism emerge from this tradition. For our purposes, the most noteworthy is Hegel's trenchant attack on Kantian philosophy for its failure to justify its own procedure of theorizing, that is, its inability to account for its own foundation. Kant's attempt to establish, in fixed and final form, an epistemological structure which is critical of both metaphysics and empiricism, and which comprises an internally consistent account of mental activity and the unity of the subject, requires the presupposition of the "identity" and reflectivity of the "self." Yet Kant does not directly address these metaphysical presuppositions or their connection with the subject's qualities of unity, activity, and emptiness. Both Fichte and Hegel discuss these grounds of the subject's mentation, against the injunctions of the Kantian program. And throughout this book, the question of the subject, and of the reflective potential of human thought, will be a central concern.

For our purposes, the term "subject" is used precisely to refer to the "I-ness" of a system of representations, although some qualifications will be added in the next chapter, when, in discussing Freud's discovery of the contradictoriness or splitting of subjectivity, I shall have occasion to refer to the subject of desire. The philosophical usage of terms such as "identity" and "self" will be dropped. Except when it is used in combination with another word to denote reflectivity, as in a term such as "self-justifying," the term "self" refers only to the *content* of a representation, to an idea, wish, or fantasy that is about "me" as distinct from something "not me." The subject is, of course, not to be confused with a mode of self-representation. Both self- and other-representations must belong to the subject of the representational system. The philosophical term "ego" to denote this subject of mentation will also be dropped, although the psychoanalytic use of the term "ego" will be confronted in Chapters 2 and 3.

Psychoanalysis is an inquiry upon the subject of psychic reality. The changeful character of this inquiry concerns the locus of the human subject within the representational world. The notion of this "subject" presented here implies the realization that all psychic life—all experiences and understandings—entails a subject. In psychic reality, representations, whether they be of ideas, wishes, fantasies, or whatever, must belong to a subject—as a system or totality, the representational world requires a subject who is representing. Similarly, desires entail a subject who his desiring. In psychoanalysis, as has already been intimated, we find that the locus of the subject is split. Throughout this book, we shall address the question of the subject in psychoanalytic discourse, asking in what sense it may be considered unitary, active, or empty, and in what sense its potential for reflectivity may be comprehended. Such matters are fundamental not only to the notion of psychic reality but also to the questions surrounding a scientific study of this reality.

THE QUESTION OF SCIENCE

William James' propositions about reality, with which we began this chapter, point to the dilemma underlying all psychological science: what is it that is studied, and from whence and how does such a study proceed? To inquire upon the human mind requires working between the competing claims of realist and idealist philosophies; we must adopt, at least proleptically, an attitude concerning the reality upon which we are inquiring, *and* the reality upon which the process of inquiry is grounded.

For this reason, I began by discussing the notion of psychic reality, as a way of proposing that any *scientific* psychology must confront the most significant question of the human subject who knows and the "reality" from which that knowing proceeds. This double question is, under a different description, that of ideology and truth. But what

distinguishes a scientific way of knowing from one that is not? A preliminary answer might be that science differs from other belief systems in its readiness to call every belief into question and, most
important, its willingness to call its own beliefs to account. A scientific
system of belief espouses, in some sense, its own corrective function,
and is thus characterized by its refusal to protect any aspect of reality
from inquisition or interrogation. A science cannot be a science if it
gives privilege to some aspects of the world in which it functions, that
is, if it treats some beliefs as articles of faith exempt from scientific
questioning. Thus, not only must a human science adopt some corrective function with respect to its own beliefs, but it must also examine
itself and its own processes of knowing as dimensions of the reality
upon which it is inquiring. In other words, a science that inquires upon
the life of the mind, upon the interiority of representation and desire,
must also be able and willing to inquire upon its own purposes, procedures of representation, and self-tranformations—to inquire back
upon the inquiring subject. I therefore insist that a psychology cannot
be scientific unless it is self-interrogative and reflective. On the other
hand, as we shall see, psychoanalysis shows us that a purely epistemological reflection upon the subject, which does not question the
ontology of its method, becomes entrapped in a false consciousness.
More must be said, therefore, about the scientific character of
psychoanalytic reflection. Indeed, as we pursue this line of argument,
we may find that psychoanalysis is "scientific" in a certain sense,
whereas the dominant psychology, with its base in logical empiricism,
is not.

The richness and eccentricity of psychoanalytic insights have pro-
voked and bemused psychologists trained in a tradition that prides
itself on the interchangeability, reproducibility, quantifiability, and
manipulability of its "data-based" findings. Despite zealous efforts to
do so, this dominant tradition has not succeeded in thoroughly exorciz-
ing the allure of psychoanalytic thinking. And the atmosphere of
cohabitation has rarely been genial, for, as I shall demonstrate,
psychoanalysis stands as an indictment of the operationalist and instrumentalist canons of the dominant mode of investigation.

From a marginal academic pursuit of the nineteenth century, this a
powerful, distinctively Anglo-American discipline, wielding an extensive influence over many aspects of contemporary culture. This psychology has expanded and divided into increasingly compartmental-
ized subdisciplines which investigate, within the paradigm of logical
empiricism, some particular naturalistic or quasi-naturalistic "object"
or "phenomenon": limbic arousal, attention span, verbal skills, attitu-

dinal change, attributional reasoning, and the like. The *summum bonum* of this "psychology" is undoubtedly *technological*. It has aimed for the prediction and control of phenomena, most especially behavioral phenomena. It has burgeoned in the service of monopoly capitalism, with the organizational and administrative imperatives of the state bureaucracy, the military, the schools, and the corporations. However, as will be seen, its impressive technical successes must be distinguished from the question of its scientificity. Nonsense is nonsense even if it is efficacious nonsense. That is, efficacy may have more to do with ideology than truth. I am not, of course, suggesting that the dominant psychology has produced "nonsense," for there is much in contemporary research that is exciting and admirable. Nevertheless, we must consider the possibility that this dominant psychology, by the very nature of its methodological and epistemological attitude, produces a systematically distorted view of the world and of ourselves. That it produces rhetoric rather than dialectic.

Questions about the ideological functions of the dominant psychology, about the potential falsity of its proven "truths," and about its epistemological and ontological presumptions must be taken seriously. Is it really so unfair to ask what this "psychology" has delivered as *psychology?* Indeed, it hardly seems unfair or naive to ask why it is that we learn more about ourselves from Johann Goethe, Marcel Proust, or Georges Bataille than from Hans Eysenck, Leon Festinger, or Robert Zajonc. But, then, what does it mean to "learn more about ourselves"? Surely, this is *the* question—the question of our reality and of our subjectivity—that a psychology cannot and should not avoid. Perusing the score of journals currently published by the American Psychological Association, readers may be struck by the sheer quantity and triviality of so many of the "findings." This preponderance of "data" over wisdom is no trifling matter. It is not that the doubting reader is somehow miseducated, lacking proper appreciation for the enormous effort and expenditure that goes into these research studies. Nor is it a matter of the youthfulness of a "science" that has not yet fulfilled the promise of its inception. Rather, it is the result of the methodological and epistemological approach adopted by a psychology caught up in the task of providing a behavioral technology for the maintenance of social order. Too easily, social scientists become those thinkers of the "ruling class" who "make the formation of the illusions of the class about itself their chief source of livelihood" (Marx & Engels, 1845–1846, p. 60). And we now have a "psychology" that *necessarily* loses sight of larger critical and scientific questions in the interests of providing research that can be used within a specific cultural and historical context. Exchange value and the endorsement of powerful socioeconomic interests readily foreclose the pursuit of a potentially critical and fully reflective science.

This is not the proper place to explore further the sociology of psychological investigation, although a thoroughgoing exploration of this sort would be valuable. For the purposes of my critique, these matters must be comprehended at the more basic philosophical level of their epistemological and ontological discourse. And here the dominant psychology presents us with a most serious paradox: cheerily successful from a technological point of view, it seems imminently and inherently flawed from a scientific point of view. This paradox must be discussed in terms of the attitude toward knowing and being in psychological inquiry and change, leading us toward our focus on psychoanalysis.

It can be argued that during the past century the advances of the dominant psychology have depended on the neglect, obfuscation, and forgetting of such radical questions as those concerning the human subject who knows and the "reality" from which such knowing proceeds. In this context, it is precisely an insistence on "objectivity" that has corrupted the dominant mode of investigation, leading to a technological, "data-oriented," and quantificationally or mathematically idealized discipline that *scientistically* obscures the question of subject and of psychic reality upon which, *nolens volens*, a psychology that inquires *scientifically* must be founded.[9]

In the dominant mode of investigation, the principle of objectivity is taken to be, in the words of Jacques Monod (1972), "the indispensable foundation for knowing." Often it is even equated with rationality (e.g., Scheffler, 1967). Supposedly, objectivity is what ensures knowledge against pure assertion or unscrutinized belief, and the practices of the community of biologists, physicists, chemists, and astronomers are what articulate and epitomize the demands of objectivity. Indeed,

---

[9] "Scientism" here refers pejoratively to a discipline's dogmatic belief in itself, not as a particular way of knowing, but as the source of correct knowledge. Scientistic disciplines typically proclaim scientificity on the grounds of the systematic and methodical appearance of their procedures and techniques, although epistemologically they are flawed by their partiality and by the fixity of their unscrutinized assumptions about knowing and being. In this respect, scientism is characterized by its willingness to protect certain dimensions of its own reality, its experiences and understandings, from reflection, interrogation, and inquisition. The hallmark of a scientistic methodology and epistemology, as opposed to a scientific one, is its failure to call its own fundamental postulates to account.

their procedural rules are allegedly the hallmark of science. According to such procedural rules, scientific investigation *"takes its starting-point outside the mind in nature,* and winnows observations of events which it gathers under concepts, to be expressed mathematically if possible and tested experimentally by their success in predicting new events and suggesting new concepts" (Gillispie, 1960, p. 10, my italics). In this rudimentary definition of what might be called "objectivism," the investigative procedure depends on the "natural attitude" and on an "analytic" theory of knowledge (the denominator of logical empiricist epistemologies). This definition permits us to raise some critical questions about an attitude of objectivity—initially, *in relation to its own precepts;* later, *in the context of its application to the investigation of mental life.*

The familiar "scientific" epistemology of naturalistic objectivism, circumscribed by Charles Gillispie's definition, stands upon the metaphysical presupposition of an ontically impassable dichotomy between knower and known, mind and nature, which is "outside" of mental activity (see also Chapter 3). In the naturalistic scheme, knowledge about the world obtains as the coherence and correspondence of the subject's representational activity with the actual nature of things objectivated. These things are not themselves given in the mind, but are supposedly apprehended indirectly by observation and by conceptualization or inference. What can be known about are not things-in-themselves but things-as-they-appear, "given" to the mind in experience, represented in observation as "objects." Assumed in this epistemological scheme is not only the absolute duality of mind and nature, wherein a unified and self-certain subject interprets the unity of external things through the formation of representations, but also the absolute dichotomy of "facts" or "data" and "theory," "concept," or "inference." From Gillispie's definition, it can be seen that the entire epistemological enterprise pivots upon joint canons of observational fidelity and theoretical coherence, implying the positivistic purity of observation with respect to theory. It thus presumes a two-tier construction of knowledge in which there is the theoretical understanding of conceptualization or rational inference, and "below" it pure observational experience, contingent upon the natural world of things. This world of things is somehow given to experience yet remains "outside" of it; its "external reality" is a matter of metaphysical presupposition. For all objectivistic ways of knowing, this immutable, two-tier construction may be criticized in terms of the anti-realist argument that "external reality" does not constrain "scientific thought"; the contemporary collapse of the bipartite structure of "data" and "theory"; the lack of firm criteria to evaluate disparate modes of theorizing; and the embarrassing evidence that objectivistic "sciences" do not progress in a historically continuous and homogeneous fashion. Each criticism will be briefly considered.

Naturalistic objectivism requires an external reality of things that are not given *in* experience but are somehow given *to* it. For the Kantian tradition of metascience, the mental activity of the investigating subject is unalterably separated from the domain of the things investigated via "object" representation. The independent, outer reality or irrevocable otherness and there-being of the thing-in-itself might be considered a metaphysical projection, as well as the primary ontic presupposition of such epistemologies. Along these lines, the anti-realist argument is that this "reality" does not determine "scientific thought" but is merely its projection. And, ultimately, this criticism is unanswerable. Friedrich Jacobi (1787), for example, was quick to attack Kant's architectonic epistemology for the inconsistency of the thing-in-itself within this formulation. The immutable externality of the thing-in-itself, outside the noumenal and phenomenal activity of mentation, is crucial to the cogency of the entire Kantian edifice. Yet, as Jacobi argued, Kant cannot, on his own grounds, state the distinction and relationship between the thing-in-itself and the contents of "sense intuition," nor can he defend the presumed connection between the nature of the thing-in-itself and the categories of noumenal judgment. Jacobi's solution, which follows certain aspects of Humean thought, is to claim that *belief* in the there-being of things in the world is the basis of all knowing. It is not my present purpose to discuss this solution, except to point to its connection with a line of philosophizing that includes such writers as Schleiermacher, Novalis, Schlegel, Schopenhauer, and Nietzsche, as well as its relation to Freud's assertion of the prerogatives of desire over the sense of "reality" (1895a, 1911a, 1925b).

The anti-realist argument implies that naturalistic epistemology depends on a metaphysical faith, the "intuition of rationality in nature," and that every scientist's commitment is to a vision of reality that is not entailed by any possible "objective criteria of verifiability"—a matter about which Michael Polanyi (1958) writes provocatively. It also implies that "observation" has a *priori* conditions that determine the possibilities of experience and understanding. It is these issues that the epistemology of naturalistic objectivism can neither reflect upon nor justify.

The metaphysical presupposition of an external reality, autonomous from yet somehow given to the mind that knows about it, ushers in the methodological tenet of observational fidelity. The "data" of observation or experience are considered to be pure, contingent upon external reality, unaltered by their articulation, and independent of the mental activity involved in conceptualization, inference, and understanding. With this positivistic aspect of logical empiricist epistemology, we come to the myths of facticity. In the positivistic "sciences," specification and regulation of the conditions of observation or data collection are supposed to give the "facts" privilege and authority—as if quantification and instrumentation of methodology could possibly shore up epistemological presuppositions about the there-being of external reality and the nature of our access to it in experience. Quantification and instrumentation do not secure the requirement of pure facticity and the autonomy of data, although they may spuriously appear to do so. They do result in data-collecting methods that appear interchangeable, reproducible, and manipulable, and here tacit presumptions about the asocial and ahistorical nature of "facts" become evident. The interchangeability, reproducibility, and manipulability of "facts" lend credibility to a particular view of the world, one that may actually be distorted and misleading. Indeed, if such presumptions were called into question, it might be argued that a "reproducible fact" is false precisely because of its reproducibility. This argument bears on the historicized character of reality, which will be discussed further as we proceed.

Through methodological rules, such as the quantification and instrumentation of controlled observation, the community of natural scientists sets standards of discourse, and hence of "reality," that are concordant with the suppositions of their epistemology. But in no way do these procedures verify the suppositions. They merely enact them. Again, behind these methodological canons lurk unexamined and, from the standpoint of naturalistic objectivism, *unexaminable* presumptions about the ontological relations and independence of subject, "object," and things (as represented). Moreover, against these presumptions, it has often been shown that the activity of observation and experience, even when controlled, quantified, and instrumentalized, is by no means "pure." Observation is affected by conceptualization, and in turn influences the "object" being observed. Here we encounter basic questions about the purity and putative responsiveness of sensory experience in general, whether "scientific" or everyday perception (see Ronchi, 1963). As Max Horkheimer (1968) and others have shown, the perceived "fact" is always determined by human ideas, categories, and wishes, even before its conscious theoretical elaboration on the level of conceptualization, inference, or understanding; the factual is thus mediated within a totality of discourse, a culture or sociality.

This consideration brings into focus the question of the two-tier construction of knowledge required by naturalistic objectivism. The requirement, variously phrased, is that raw experience be independent of understanding and provide understanding with its corrective function that "facts" be independent of theorizing yet serve to correct it, that observation or sensation have an autonomous yet determinant relationship with conceptualization or inference. In Kant's formulation, as we have seen, this bipartite structure of mentation is epistemologically fundamental: the noumental, the realm of categories and judgment, and of understanding and reason, represents a further synthesizing of phenomenal appearances, the realm of empirical experience. The distinction between these two realms is necessary to the cogency of the entire Kantian system. Yet Hegel (1807) was quick to criticize this formulation for Kant's failure to maintain or define, and hence to justify, the duality of the two realms. According to Hegel, no such static and anti-dialectical distinction is viable; experience and understanding have a more complex, historicized and interpenetrative relationship. Yet logical empiricist epistemology since Kant continues to assume that experience is autonomous from understanding, yet constrains it. Admittedly, philosophers of logical empiricism have labored for a workable resolution to the problem posed by this assumed duality of formal or aprioristic and experiential or empirical-synthetic components in the construction of knowledge about the world. In one framework, the problem is rather benignly referred to as the "paradox of categorization": either categories determine what is observed and thus observational experience cannot provide independent control over thought, *or* categories do not determine what is observed and thus this experience is uncategorized and cannot provide adjudicative criteria for categorical thought. Yet the question raised by this "paradox" strikes critically at the whole program of naturalistic objectivism, casting doubt upon the supposition of duality. Indeed, as already noted, several advances in the natural sciences themselves have produced awkward and subversive evidence concerning the presumed independence and corrective function of data with respect to theorizing.

In positivistic "sciences," propositional adjudication rests with the prediction of putatively independent data events. In this manner, the scientist's conceptual understanding of the world is put to test. Philosophers from the Vienna circle—Otto Neurath, Moritz Schlick, and others—have even debated the virtues of confirmation versus disconfirmation when theoretical propositions are verified against "data." In logical empiricist methodology, specification and regulation of the conduct of theorizing supposedly secure the testability of a conceptual model in relation to an independent data base. Thus, to use Percy Bridgman's celebrated term, "operationalized theories"—theories purged of empirically undefinable concepts—are given privilege and authority. The result is not only the progressive formalization and mathematicization of "model-building, but also an increasing institutionalization of the knower's conduct. Yet the formalization and mathematicization of theorizing, stipulating a logic of explanation and placing a premium on the testability of propositions, do not shore up the requirement of the autonomy and determinacy of observable data with respect to conceptualization, although they may spuriously appear to do so. Operationalism lends credibility to a view of the world in which the realms of evidence and inference are safely distinct. But operationalist tenets cannot possible *secure* such an epistemological presupposition about "reality," so this view of the world may indeed be distorted and misleading.

It can now be argued that the alleged data are generated by theorizing, as much as theorizing is corrected by the data. That "the most important thing to grasp," as Goethe once suggested, "is that everything factual is already theoretical." Observation is found to be conditioned by conceptualization, experience conditioned by understanding. It can be shown that in the objectivistic mode of investigation, whatever its proclaimed objectivity, theorizing covertly constitutes its own data base. Implicitly, then, the structure of thinking establishes conditions of possibility for the realm of the "factual." From a hermeneutic point of view, this is what Martin Heidegger refers to as preunderstanding, or the "forestructures" of comprehension. In this way, "data" are given *in* the framework of conceptualization rather than given *to* it. "Facts" only *appear* to be independent of thought because of the concealed hegemony of the paradigm or episteme within which thought operates. Indeed the "facts" belonging to a particular paradigm do not prove commensurate with the "facts" belonging to another. A trite but well-known example of this is the incomparability of the "data base" of Newtonian physics to that of the Einsteinian paradigm. Even with respect to the most fundamental notions such as those of mass, space, and time, the physical referents of these Einsteinian concepts prove not to be identical with Newtonian concepts that bear the same name (Kuhn, 1962). It is impossible to derive one from the other. As one eminent contemporary physicist has noted with dismay: theory determines what is seen.

Long after Hegel's speculatively based criticisms of Kant's two-tier system, then, the natural sciences have vindicated this critique. The development of non-Euclidean geometries, the theory of relativity, the beginnings of microphysics, and the so-called revolution in optics, all indicate the complicity of fact and theory, of observation and conceptualization. The two-tier construction of "science" has been indicted.[10] And with it, Hans Reichenbach's famous distinction, between the context of discovery and the context of justification, becomes vacuous. Yet, as Ernest Nagel (1961) so vehemently expounds, the bipartition of observation and conceptualization is foundationally necessary to the cogency of the entire logical empiricist program: it is supposedly what guarantees its "objectivity." This cogency is now subverted. Data can scarcely be the judge of theory if they are in some sense its accomplices.

In positivistic "sciences," the brutal autochthony of "raw data" is supposed to provide theorizing with its corrective function. Yet neither the philosophy of logical empiricism nor the contemporary advances of naturalistic research can maintain the required distinction between observational and theoretical discourse. Simply put, there are no neutral facts by which theoretical controversies may be arbitrated, nor are there any theoretical formulations that succeed in meeting the logical empiricist standard of being intelligible within their own frame as well as testable within the community of some common but independent observational or experiential practices. With this collapse of the two tiers of objectivistic epistemology, how are disparate modes of theorizing to be adjudicated?

It can now be argued that the logical empiricist tradition finds itself in a situation in which rival propositions cannot be evaluated rationally. "Ways of world-making," to use Nelson Goodman's (1978) phrase, are no longer open to assessment by some firmly founded set of metatheoretical criteria, because no such criteria are fixedly and finally established. As we hve seen, Kant's provisional solution to this problem involves the transcendental deduction of noumenal categories of judgment. Kant's line of exit from the impasse created by his predecessors—on the one side by the untenable empiricism of John Locke and David Hume, and on the other by the "dogmatic" rationalism of

---

[10] It is in the wake of this indictment that diverse philosophical works, such as Gaston Bachelard's brilliant exegesis of epistemological history (1928, 1934, 1938, 1940), Michel Foucault's *archaeology* (1969), Paul Feyerabend's salubriously anarchic impulses (1970), and even Nelson Goodman's soul-searching thesis (1978), have flourished.

G. W. von Leibniz and Christian von Wolff—is a "critical" transcendental epistemology, which aims to define, in fixed and final form,
the scope and limitations of *a priori* conditions of knowledge about the
world. Kant adopts a quasi-metaphysical stance against empiricism by
demonstrating that there has to be some valid *a priori* understanding
of things—such as that contained in the principle of causality or in
mathematical propositions—and that certainty cannot be obtained via
exclusive dependence on the content of sensory experience. In this
fashion, the content of experience is necessary but not sufficient for
natural understanding. On the other hand, employing a trascendental
argument against speculative metaphysics, Kant rejects the rationalistic doctrine of pure ideas by demonstrating that valid *a priori* understanding is restricted to knowledge of the conditions of the possibility
of experience. Although *a priori* judgments are not derived from the
contents of sensation, their certainty, in Kant's formulation, requires
the occasion of empirical experience. That is, such judgments must be
ampliative or synthetic—not containing their own predicate—as well
as aprioristic. Kant presents a transcendental deduction of a dozen
such synthetic, *a priori* categories of judgment, including plurality,
causality, necessity, and limitation. The noumenal realm of categories
is supposedly universal and absolute.

The problem here is that Kant's heirs, even while accepting his basic
method and his two-tier framework within which the question of
knowledge is posed, have nonetheless repeatedly disagreed about the
inventory of judgmental categories. To give one example, neo-Kantian
hermeneuts of the late nineteenth century, the so-called *verstehen*
philosophers, wished to add categories specifically for the understanding of historical and social phenomena. We find this tendency in both
major neo-Kantian schools: the Marburg group of Hermann Cohen and
Paul Natorp, and the Baden group of Heinrich Rickert and Wilhelm
Windelband. In a rather different fashion, we also find this in certain
aspects of Wilhelm Dilthey's philosophy, in which the hermeneutic
method is regarded as the sociohistorical complement to a Kantian
epistemology of the natural world. From yet another perspective, the
logico-analytic movement, including G. E. Moore, Bertrand Russell,
and the early Wittgenstein, has attempted to elucidate the boundaries
and characteristics of validity and verification in terms of a uniform
logico-linguistic structure by which the world may be known, and
hence to specify the *a priori*, necessary truths, or "elementary propositions," constituting this structure. Yet these efforts have invariably
been controversial. Increasingly, it seems that no transcendental vantage point of universal and absolute judgment is attainable—that to

understand any framework of conceptualization, one must, in some sense, already have entered it.

In objectivistic "sciences," justification of a theoretical formulation implies not only that discrepant conceptualizations may be arbitrated by the specious autonomy of brute "facts," but also that representational construction is constrained by a logic of explanation, a universal and absolute rationality, as well as certain rule-bound procedures or conventions of theorizing. These suppositions are embraced aprioristically. Yet the logic and the regulation of theorizing are neither open to reflection within the frame of logical empiricism, nor founded independently of this frame.

With respect to the regulation of theorizing, positivistic "sciences" adopt criteria such as parsimony, convenience, and applicability in their procedures of theoretical model-building. Such criteria are, of course, secondary to the capacity of theoretical propositions to predict data events, and it is important to note that in no sense are such conventions to be taken as standards of truth. That is, the canons for the regulation of model-building do not establish a corrective function for conceptualization.

With respect to the rationality of theorizing, logical empiricist epistemology assumes, but cannot establish, criteria by which to adjudicate "ways of world-making." Within a particular system of thinking, propositions may be judged, for the system furnishes its own criteria for this. Between systems of thinking, however, logical empiricism has no means of judgment. Again, that Newtonian and Einsteinian propositions are not intertranslatable exemplifies this profound problem. The very notion of a paradigm, in Thomas Kuhn's (1962) sense, as an episteme within which thought operates, expresses this dilemma. The discourse of an episteme is not translatable into that of another, for the episteme is itself, in a certain sense, constitutive of the conditions of possibility for all thinking. There is no ultimate, fixed and final vantage point, no supraparadigmatic mode of universal and absolute reasoning, from which disparate systems of thinking can be coherently assessed. This is something we should have learned by now from Hegel, who demonstrates that divergent thought positions cannot be judged absolutely, but can only be engaged dialectically and historically. Yet logical empiricism, the philosophy of objectivistic "sciences," depends upon the assumption of a universal and absolute rationality for the coherence of its theoretical discourse. Without data that serve to correct conceptualization, these sciences now face a breakdown in their community of meaning, a crisis in the hegemony and commonality of their theoretical discourse. And this strikes critically and fundamentally at the coherence of their epistemological program.

A closely related critique of the epistemology of naturalistic objectivism draws on the embarrassing evidence of discontinuity and heterogeneity in the history of such sciences. The epistemology rudimentarily defined by Gillispie's view of "objective" research entails an evolutionist depiction of science as a venture of successive approximation. Here conceptualization or theorizing, constrained by aprioristic but supposedly absolute and universal rules of representation, and revised through the corrective function of accumulated "data" experience, comes to know about the external nature, the there-being, of things with ever-increasing accuracy. Logical empiricism thus commands a Peircean notion of reality as progressively revealed. "Science" is supposed to make more or less linear and incremental progress. A well-known example of this point of view is Karl Popper's (1935) explicitly evolutionary formulation of logical empiricist epistemology. "Evolutionism," as Dominique Lecourt (1969, p. 125) remarks, is indeed "the obligatory complement in the history of the sciences to positivism in epistemology." But science has *not* progressed in a steadily evolutionary manner, as Thomas Kuhn's (1962) thesis on scientific revolutions reveals, despite its egregious idealism. This lack of evolutionary progress is also strongly documented in a brilliant series of exegetical writings by Gaston Bachelard (1928, 1934, 1938, 1940), Georges Canguilhem (1952, 1968), and even Michel Foucault (1966, 1969). Their vigorous attack on the alleged historical continuity and homogeneity of knowledge, both scientific and everyday, devastates the evolutionary requirement of logical empiricism and thereby subverts its epistemological program. As will be seen, the issue of discontinuity also raises, critically and most pertinently, the question of the subject who knows, pointing to the occlusion of this subject within the epistemological presumptions of naturalistic objectivism.

We have now briefly considered four significant lines of criticism concerning the objectivity of naturalistic objectivism: the problem of the there-being of things in "external reality"; the indefensible bipartition of observation and conceptualization; the lack of any fixed and final way of comparing systems of thinking; and the nonevolutionary history of logical empiricist investigation. These four points comprise a preliminary critique of the scientistic dimensions of those "sciences" that endorse the world-view and emulate the research practices of the community of biologists, physicists, chemists, and astronomers. In-

deed, these lines of criticism have nowhere been answered satisfactorily (cf. Scheffler, 1967). Each of the currently extant philosophies of
logical empiricism can be faulted severely. Realism, for example, with
its seductive appeal to the brutal firmness of things evident to consciousness, falters because it has to admit mediative processes of ideation and cannot account for error and illusion, where the evident
particularity is not truth but falsity. Pragmatism discusses these
mediative processes in terms of the "biography of action and experience," but inexorably loses sight of the there-being of the things objectivated. Logical positivism, with its hullabaloo over the "unified
science movement," stresses the function of logic and language in
mediating judgment about things observed, but fails to establish adequate criteria for meaning, for the distinction and regulation between
empirical and theoretical discourse.

We have been discussing naturalistic objectivism, as the dominant
mode of "scientific" investigation, in terms of knowing about the "external reality" of things, viewed as physical phenomena. Certain critical questions concerning the objectivity of logical empiricist
epistemology have thus been raised *in the context of its own precepts.*
And adequate answers have been found wanting, for the epistemology
of naturalistic objectivism is by no means as certainly established as is
commonly imagined, even for the investigation of physical events.
Now, however, we should turn towards a preliminary discussion of
objectivity in relation to the question of the subject who knows and the
reality from which knowing proceeds. In short, we must raise critical
questions about logical empiricist epistemology, upon which the dominant psychology is founded, *in the context of its application to the
investigation of mental life,* to our knowledge of the inner reality of
ideas, wishes, fantasies, and the like.

In introducing the notion of the mind as a system of representations,
we might have paused to ask: How can such a system be studied by a
community of investigators who are themselves engaged in representational activity? Can the dimensions that were mentioned—for
instance, the shared and unshared, or the referential and figurative—
in any sense be treated as "objects" of investigation? At first glance, it
might seem that whereas some aspects of the content, form, function,
and structure of mental life could plausibly be studied externalistically
and naturalistically as "objects," other aspects demand an inquiry that
proceeds from within what Carl Rogers and Eugene Gendlin have
called the subject's "inner frame of reference."

Logical empiricism, however, can *never* accord psychic reality its proper prerogative. The dominant program of naturalistic objectivism cannot know the processes of its own knowing without transgressing its own ordinances. The program can only proceed if the priority of psychic reality for *all* experience and understanding of the world and of ourselves is obscured scientistically and ideologically. The dominant psychology therefore proceeds unreflectively and positivistically, typically on the basis of the naivest of realisms. This epistemology and methodology for psychological investigation demurely believes in an *as if*—as if it could take its stand apodictically on the bedrock of "external reality," and could therefore embark upon experimentation with psychic contents and functions, treating them externalistically and naturalistically as things objectivated. Of course, it can do nothing of the kind and thus inextricably blinkers itself to its immersion in its own reality and to the implications of its presumptions. Here we need to open debate around two questions. What aspects of psychic life appear to succumb to investigation within the scientism of naturalistic objectivism, and in what sense is the knowledge thus generated of necessity distorted and degraded ideologically? What happens to the subject of psychic reality, and for that matter the subject of the objectivistic investigation, that seems to be eclipsed by this epistemology?

In rendering mental life an "object" of investigation under the aegis of logical empiricist methodology, psychology makes itself vulnerable to the epistemological critique we have just reviewed. And it immures itself in even further difficulties due to the nature of psychic reality as subjectivity. In this respect, G. W. F. Hegel's *Phenomenology of Spirit* (1807) provides an illuminating polemic. Indeed, I would argue that Hegel's opus is one of the few books that *must* be read and reread by any genuine psychologist. Hegel begins his critical discourse with a discussion of sensation, perception, and understanding. Having refuted the pure primacy of phenomenal experience, he advances, in the section on understanding, three points that are especially germane to the naturalistic conduct of human sciences. In disclosing the fallacy of seeking universal laws about nature in relation to the real being of things, he contends that "understanding imagines that in this unification it has found a universal law which expresses universal reality *as such*; but in fact it has only found the *notion of law itself*, although in such a way that what it is saying is that *all* reality is, *in its own self*, conformable to law" (1807, p. 150). The argument here is twofold. First, general laws become emptier as they become more general, and second, things themselves remain entirely indifferent to these so-called laws of understanding. Hegel then adds a third point—

that the pursuit of generality inevitably partitions the unity of things in order to impute an explanation to them.

These criticisms are, of course, directed at the understanding of nature. But they acquire even greater force if considered in relation to the naturalistic understanding of psychological contents and functions. Objectivistic psychology never arrives at the truth of psychic reality itself; all it can be said to arrive at are generalities concerning the psychologist's own thinking—the community of psychologists' systematization of conceptualization about the world of "other minds." Such generalities, however, *purport* to be about the objectivated things themselves. The dominant psychology thus imagines that it stands on a bedrock of objectivity, that it conducts research on psychological events (on someone else's subjectivity), as things objectivated "out there." What happens is that it remains immersed in its own subjectivity, its own representational world, but neither recognizes nor admits this because it cannot be reflective without breaking the bounds of its own epistemological and methodological canons. It thus ends up researching, without knowing it, events that are projections and prejudices of its own epistemological and methodological discourse, the systematization of its own conceptualization. At best, such research can arrive at a revelation of its own preunderstandings, the "forestructures" of its own comprehension. Yet it will never know that this is where it has arrived. The dominant psychology will inexorably produce "findings" of increasing generality, but also increasingly lacking in specificity, concreteness, and real content. The *psychic reality* of thoughts, wishes, and fantasies will necessarily remain immune from this investigation. Just as, to offer a crude analogy, an efficacious program of behavior modification does not touch the prisoner's inner resentment, so psychic reality elides naturalistic objectivation.

A related criticism—Hegel's third point—is that objectivistic psychology must partition in order to "explain." Here, too, we encounter a projection of the psychologist's epistemology and methodology rather than a truth of the psychic reality that is thereby "explained." As a system of representations, psychic reality must in some sense be a totality, a unity of the subject's mentation. Yet this interrelatedness of thoughts, wishes, fantasies, and the like is foreclosed by the psychologist's rendition of subjectivity as thing objectivated. Again, we should remember that the activity of the dominant psychology is itself representational and part of a totality within which it researches. From this perspective, the naturalistic "explanation" of psychological events seems tautologically and unreflectively immersed in its own representational activity. It is, in Hegel's words, a "verbal recital": objectivation rather than interrogation, a stasis of rhetoric rather than a movement of dialectic. The dominant mode of psychological investigation does not *engage* psychic reality. It takes this totality of thoughts, wishes, and fantasies and renders them as a farrago of things objectivated. With the dominant psychology, psychic reality *as such*, as an interiority and a subjectivity of representation, remains indifferent to the representational activity that takes place within the psychologist's epistemology and methodology.

When mental life is treated objectivistically and externalistically, psychic reality *as such* eludes inquiry. Nonetheless, logical empiricist psychology can be said to *work*—in the sense that its operationalist and instrumentalist canons result in certain technological accomplishments. This dominant psychology "works" best when its "object" is physiological or behavioral. That is, when it is not strictly psychological at all. Technological success in this respect does not imply a science of psychic reality; rather, the reverse. The science *psychology*, defined as the study of an interiority of personal meaning, entirely resists the epistemological and methodological program to which the dominant "psychology" is wedded. This distinction brings us to some further considerations regarding the current vogue of cognitivist approaches in social, developmental, and personality research conducted under the aegis of naturalistic objectivism.

At a later point in his *Phenomenology of Spirit*, following his discussion of the "self-consciousness" of the inquiring mind, Hegel explores three types of "observational and rational inquiry." The first of these concerns the investigation of the natural world, and need not detain us further. But the second and third offer some inchoate yet electrifying insights into the apocryphal development of the dominant psychology. For they concern the self-investigative attempts of this self-consciousness—the fallacies and shortcomings of an "observational and rational inquiry" upon logical and psychological mentation. According to Hegel, in such an investigation, "rational self-consciousness"— under the same objectivistic and externalistic mode as a naturalistic epistemology—tries, with only the smallest success, to know its own functions as if they were inanimate nature, without subjectivity.

In the second of Hegel's types of investigation, observation and conceptualization attempt to know about general "laws" of thought. In arriving at such "laws," Hegel argues, the mind hypostatizes its own being, converting itself into static forms, products rather than processes, and grasping knowledge only as universal categories of judgment and the like. Against the architectonic attempts of logical empiricist philosophies, Hegel suggests that fixed and final "truths" of this sort are a falsity. Mentation comes to be depicted as an assemblage of mute, disconnected forms, at best static and concatenated—as so many "things in a bag." Hegel demonstrates that this depiction systematically precludes consideration of thinking as essentially a *movement*, most especially as a reflective movement en route to the generation of such "laws." In cognitivist psychology, for example, the jargon of schemata, prototypes, operational structures, etc., issues from a methodology that ends up treating such mental functions and contents as "things in a bag." This methodology not only partitions phenomena; it necessarily immobilizes them—at best, capturing the progressive and regressive vicissitudes of mentation as snapshots in an album. Such a methodology, Hegel suggests, may well succeed in offering a catalog of mental functions and contents, but whatever the appeal of such a nosological enterprise, its systematization will be imposed from elsewhere. Its listings will not serve to grasp the true quality of mentation. Indeed, logical empiricist psychology, whatever its cognitivist orientation, *systematically forecloses* a full appreciation of the interrelatedness, historicity, and reflectivity of mental life.

In the third type of investigation that Hegel examines, observation and conceptualization attempt to know about the particular thought of the individual. Here, by proceeding externalistically and objectivistically, the epistemology inevitably judges the inner by the criteria of the "outer"—for example, imputing thought, wish, or fantasy from the accumulation of behavioral "evidence." It thus produces what Jean-Paul Sartre (1948) calls a "peripheric" depiction of mental activity. And it is here that Hegel marshals his devastating critique of physiognomy and phrenology—a critique apposite to the models of "cognitive behaviorism" so preeminent today. In these disciplines, the "schemas," "traits," "dispositions," and other variables, by which the particular thought of individual minds is to be explained, are treated as fixed and determinate, as entities. Against this view, Hegel argues that human actions, behavior by another name, could not possibly result from the operation of fixed, determinate entities, nor even from the conjunctive effects of such static, allegedly causative forms. For their fixity and determinacy are undermined by the very capacity of self-consciousness to discover them—by the transformative impetus of an inquiry that is not instrumental. Action results, Hegel proposes, from a *dynamic*—from a dialectical confrontation within the representational system between "what I am" and "what I am not." The meaning of a situation to an individual is essential not epiphenomenal, even when the situation *appears* to be determinative of behavior. This meaning is not a matter of the operation of static forms, but of a dialectical engagement (cf. Sartre, 1948, 1960). The individual is inquisitive, reflective, and agential in a particular manner that is methodically missed by the conceptual apparatus of a naturalistic investigation. In this respect, cognitive behaviorism necessarily produces a systematically distorted view of human functioning. However significant the move from physiognomy and phrenology to experimentation with "behavioral responses" and "situational determinants" may seem, cognitive behaviorism is still locked into a depiction of human functioning on the level of masks and skulls.

Recall the four "phases" of the notion of individuality discussed at the beginning of this chapter. The logical empiricist investigation of mentation adheres irrevocably to the third "phase": mental activity is methodologically defined, not in terms of the particular individual's own frame of experiences and understandings, but in terms of extrinsic agreement by a community of psychologists about the person's observably distinctive qualities. To reiterate, such a methodology renders the inner thematic as an assemblage of ostensible and fixed categories, framed from without, by operationalist and instrumentalist procedures. It renders the inner movement of experience and understanding as a sequence of partitioned and hypostatized forms. Moreover, it reduces life history to an accidental concatenation of events. With such a methodology, the conative, affective, and cognitive forms, which are imputed via operationalist and instrumentalist treatment of behavioral "evidence," will always tend to appear decontextualized. This is because the methodology itself, by rendering these forms as entities apart from the investigator's discourse, tends systematically to exclude careful consideration of the mediations between individual representation and the sociocultural totality of representational discourse. Logical empiricism is never able to grasp the dialectical interpenetration of the particular and the totality; it can only subsume one to the other. To attempt investigation of psychic reality under the canons of naturalistic objectivism is to admit neither the truly psychic nor the truly real, constitutive character of psychic reality as such. The logical empiricist canons, as Hegel unwaveringly demonstrates, occlude questions about the personalization of all reality, as fundamentally an inner reality of representations of the world and of ourselves that are constitutively meaningful. Questions of the formative and transformative locus of subjectivity are systematically averted in favor of the fragmenting hypostatization of an externalized frame of reference. The movement and interrelatedness of mentation, the formativity, reflective potential, and dialectical character of psychic reality, are thereby entirely precluded. To study ourselves—our reality, sociality, historicity, and individuality—objectivistically preempts reflection, and condemns our science to the investigation of mute, externalized "things," frozen and falsified moments of what is a richly contradictory subjectivity.

The question of the locus of the subject is, of course, central here—not only as the subject of psychic reality, but also as the subject of logical empiricist psychology itself. The arguments I have presented do *not* comprise a call for research on "actor interpretations" and other matters of agential self-representation.[11] Such research typically remains imprisoned within the epistemology of naturalistic objectivism, even when touting a "phenomenological" label and advocating a methodology of sensitive description. If done well, such research on the actor's perspective can usefully serve to bring into focus the whole issue of perspectivism and thus may highlight what is missed. (Indeed, in a similar fashion, even an objectivistic psychology focused on the activity of psychologists, and a sociology of their investigations, might prove valuable in pointing to the shortcomings of the dominant mode of research). But what is called for here is not renewed and redirected research within the hegemony of the epistemological mode. We need an altogether different approach to psychological inquiry. For an inquiry upon psychic reality, and hence upon the reality from which inquiry proceeds, necessitates an epistemological discourse that avows the reflectivity of human thought and thus can grasp the subjectivity or intersubjectivity by which our experiences and understandings of the world and of ourselves are constituted. Only a psychology that can reflect upon its subjectivity can proceed to interrogate psychic reality scientifically.

In logical empiricism, knowledge is *about* things objectivated, and it depends on metaphysical presuppositions about the there-being of things unalloyed by the constitutive processes of human mentation (the dogma of things-in-themselves) and about the bipartition of empirical observation and higher conceptualization. Although this knowledge is indeed a representational activity, its subject rapidly

---

[11] Here one might refer to the tradition of social psychology that runs from George Herbert Mead and Charles Cooley to Erving Goffman's ethnomethodology, to sociological writings by such theorists as Max Weber, Peter Winch, and Alfred Schütz, to the Duquesne school of "phenomenological" psychology, and to a diverse collection of other investigators variously influenced by Wilhelm Dilthey's *Geisteswissenschaften* and the application of *verstehen* philosophy.

disappears from consideration. As already noted, William James (1890) is one of the few thinkers in Anglo-American psychology to give this matter any serious scrutiny. As a pragmatist, he recognizes that knowledge depends on the "biography of action and experience"; thus he tries to discuss the subject's knowing of its own knowledge. However, the result of this attempt—a common distinction between the self-knowledge "of acquaintance" and "knowledge about"—is a transparently weak concession to the reflectivity of mentation. Philosophy in the logical empiricist mode has itself variously discussed the requirements of the primacy, unity, and certainty of the knowing subject. The Cartesian ego is well known in this respect, for it is explicitly articulated and concretely individual. The Kantian ego, as we have seen, is less explicitly articulated, more a presumption within Kant's epistemological system; and it is universalized. In logical empiricist philosophy since Kant, the question of the subject is less and less articulated, more and more taken for granted. Philosophers of logical empiricism are, of course, engaged in an obviously reflective task, a task that bears the insignia of the subject. Yet reflective thinking itself transgresses the bounds of their architectonic epistemology.

In the positivist "sciences" themselves, theorizing has become increasingly formalized and mathematicized, with the knower consequently institutionalized as the meter, technique, and style of the "scientific establishment." This establishment becomes absolute and unalterable in its functioning, an ultimate reference point for the adjudication of all the dilemmas of reality. Here I am not only referring to the superrogatory power of "science" over the particular scientist, a matter emphasized by Kuhn, Bachelard, and many others. I am also pointing to the occlusion of the concretely subjective and intersubjective grounds of all knowing (see Paci, 1963). Even Lenin (1908) intimates that this mode of epistemology and methodology necessarily obfuscates the question of human agency, in maneuvers of fetishism and reification that disguise interpersonal processes as a relation between entities (consider the so-called economic laws of supply and demand). Moreover, beyond the humanity of the "object," naturalistic objectivism obscures the subjectivity of the subject. As György Lukács (1923) and others have succinctly argued, the theorizing subject becomes eclipsed and reified through formalization. The knower is depicted as a purely abstracted subject, a mathematical and projective organization bearing an epistemological ideal of the "object" of knowledge as necessary, natural and systematic "laws," functioning in "objective" reality without the intervention of the real subject. Representational activity is seemingly split from a notion of concrete human praxis and reflectivity.

It must be emphasized again and again: naturalistic objectivism cannot know its own knowing within the context of its own precepts. Logical empiricism offers an epistemology of objectivity that can tell us nothing about the subject of its architectonic construction. Kant, as Hegel shows, could not comprehend his own reflections by which an allegedly complete theory of knowledge had been produced. Kant's knowledge of his own epistemological formulation, despite all its claims of necessity, fixity, finality, and absoluteness, could not be justified within its own terms. Just as Hume stood mute before the subject of mentation, unable to explain how conation, affectivity, and cognition come to be *organized*, and thus held within the unity of an "I-ness," the positivist "sciences" necessarily deny reflection (see Habermas, 1968). They also disavow the notion of mentation as a dialectical movement and cannot adequately apprehend the interrelatedness, sociality, and historicity of our experiences and understandings. The dominant psychology, advancing on the precepts of naturalistic objectivism, may peremptorily and rapaciously treat its own "objects" by operationalist and instrumentalist procedures, but it will not be able to reflect upon the question of the subject, and thus it will scientistically dismiss the prerogatives of psychic reality. Only a psychology that can reflect upon its own representational activity, its constitutive subjectivity, can proceed toward a *scientific* inquiry upon psychic reality. But such a psychology cannot be objectivistic and externalistic; it must be reflectively and interrogatively dialectical.

There are, of course, several different approaches to the question of knowledge, but all transgress the familiar coordinates of logical empiricist philosophy, both classical and contemporary, and subvert its architectonic construction. They advance an altogether different attitude toward the question of the there-being of things objectivated, and they offer an epistemology in which the corrective function of conceptualization is found not in the mythical domain of "pure data," but from within the totalizing movement of conceptualization itself. To entertain such ways of thinking means to take seriously Hegel's dialectic as a recurrent challenge to the epistemological tradition and to consider the significance of semiosis proposed by contemporary hermeneutics, as we shall do in Chapter 4.

Psychology, not as a behavioral technology but as the science of psychic reality, must command an epistemological and ontological discourse that can know the reality upon which we inquire *and* the reality from which the process of inquiry proceeds—a way of knowing that can call beliefs into question without exemption. To pursue the possibility of a science of psychic reality requires that we reopen the question of what science is itself. And this is an unsettling mandate. For we live in an era in which the very notion of knowledge is defined by the achievements of positivistic disciplines—despite the circularity inherent in scientistically defending its technological accomplishments as the sole source of proven knowledge by defining this provenness in terms of these accomplishments. As Marx once pointed out, empiricism and mysticism are twin facets of the bourgeois world-view, posed as the only alternatives. And our thinking all too readily endorses this absurdly binary ideology: what is not positivistically acquired "knowledge," founded by the canons of operationalism and instrumentalism, is not valid knowledge at all. It is at best arbitrary belief, or mere whimsy; at worst, hocus-pocus. This book is not the place to explore the several varieties of mystical philosophy with respect to their proffered ways of knowing. But it is the time and place to rid ourselves of the absurd ideological dogma that poses "science" versus "mysticism" as the only choices of epistemology. For, as we have seen, even in its explorations of the natural world, the "science" of naturalistic objectivism is by no means securely unassailable. And as an epistemology for the exploration of psychic reality, it nowhere approaches adequacy.

We must take the problematic of psychological discourse into the deepest concerns of epistemology and ontology. And psychoanalysis, as we shall see, provides a uniquely heuristic focus on the questions of psychic reality, subject, and science. The stage is now set for a discussion of these fundamentals in relation to the splitting of subjectivity, which is the authentic discovery of psychoanalytic knowing and psychoanalytic transformation.

2 Psychoanalytic Disputation and Psychoanalytic Misapprehension

In the first of his two articles for Max Marcuse's sexological dictionary, Freud (1923b) insists that psychoanalysis is first and foremost a *method*. Only secondarily, Freud informs us, is psychoanalysis to be regarded as a treatment for disorders of acculturation, or as a set of theoretical propositions depicting the functioning of our representational worlds in finalized, systematic form. In the same article, Freud defines the particular activity of psychoanalysis *"als Wissenschaft vom seelisch Unbewussten,"* "as the scientific pursuit of the psychic unconscious" (p. 227). It is a definition worth contemplating for all its implications. Psychoanalysis concerns *psychic* reality, the discourse of meaning and multiple meaning, and its discovery of the psychic *unconscious* comprises a distinctly *scientific* pursuit. And here again we encounter questions about the nature of "science." Each component of this definition deserves renewed scrutiny and discussion. For even today, behind the pervasive rhetoric and despite repeated efforts to assimilate psychoanalytic praxis to familiar concepts and modes of investigation, the implications of this scientific pursuit for a theory of knowledge and an ontology of the human condition remain thoroughly enigmatic.

WHY IS FREUD'S PSYCHOLOGY SO CONTROVERSIAL?

A return to Freud's psychology, to a dialectically critical rereading of his work and to a reconsideration of the character of psychoanalytic discourse, is exigent. For psychoanalysis still has much to teach us about psychic reality, about the human subject, and about the question of scientific pursuits.

In 1915, Freud proclaimed that psychoanalytic inquiry upon unconscious mental processes open us to *"eine entscheidende Neuorientierung in Welt und Wissenschaft,"* "a critical new direction in the world and in science" (1916–1917, p. 15). How are we to comprehend this dramatic proclamation? As a disciplined venture that ascribes to itself the status of science, psychoanalysis has evoked persistent and acrimonious dispute ever since its inception almost ninety years ago. Although it has wielded an extensive—but usually spurious—influence over contemporary life, its opponents' virulence has not abated. Indeed, almost every facet of Freud's life and work—from his biographical particulars to his teachings and techniques—has provided occasion for altercation. His impact has spawned a voluminous literature—perhaps seeming to leave little excuse for another book on psychoanalysis. Yet there is reason enough. For, leaving aside matters of Freud's biography, psychoanalysis' institutional history, its clinical treatment technique, and its "metapsychological" model-building, we find that on the level of *method*, and hence in relation to questions of epistemology and ontology, psychoanalysis has not only been disputed, but it has also been multiply misapprehended, often quite fundamentally so, by its own practitioners. The constitution of psychoanalytic discourse, the unique engagement of patient and psychoanalyst, "as the scientific pursuit of the psychic unconscious," has never been properly comprehended.

The miscomprehension of Freud's psychology is seen clearly in the protracted, noiseful, and generally sterile "debate"—particularly among Anglo-American academics—about whether this psychology is disproven or disprovable. Characteristic of this dispute is that neither side can agree among themselves, let alone between themselves, on the grounds—one might say, the criteria of adjudication—for a resolution. The critics' demands take several forms. One requirement is that the work of patient and psychoanalyst should conform to the procedural rules of the dominant mode of "normal science," in which propositional statements, such as hypotheses, predictions, or conjectures, are tested against shared experience or replicable observation. A weaker variant of this demand is that, even if controlled testing of this kind is impossible within the specifically human, discursive context of the psychoanalytic situation, the dyadic work should at least generate falsifiable propositions for extrapsychoanalytic experimentation, and should then be guided by the results of this research. (From this perspective comes the recurrent appeal for explicit canons of psychoanalytic conduct.) A rather different and seemingly liberal demand made by some critics is that the psychoanalytic process be justified pragmatically. Their argument is that, even if the work of patient and psychoanalyst is too arbitrary and private to meet the precepts of empirical investigation, it should at least withstand external evaluation in terms of its clinical practice—that is, it should be seen to "cure" its participants according to certain cultural standards of "social adjustment" and the like.

In the face of these stringencies, psychoanalysts have variously dodged, feinted, become truculent, and retreated into secluded lamentation. But if the character of psychoanalytic discourse has nowhere been adequately articulated, surely the relevance of such indictments cannot be presupposed? Although this strange scenario may account for certain ludicrous aspects of the backfired dialogue between Freudians and their critics, behind it lies something more startling and serious—namely that, despite their passionate conviction, the protagonists scarcely know the tongue in which they speak.

I have mentioned the vehement opposition to psychoanalysis from the dominant tradition of operationalist and objectivistic "psychology." Yet there is also a certain sense in which Freud's psychology has been accepted too quickly, too widely, and on the basis of significant misunderstandings as well as suppressive modifications. Indeed, on several levels, Freud's extraordinary innovations have been obfuscated by his successors. That Freud himself might, in some measure, have welcomed this domestication of what he called his "revolutionary and inconvenient advances" does not lessen its seriousness. The history of post-Freudian theorizing comprises manifold attempts, implicit and explicit, to relocate a seminally innovational psychology within existing conceptual frameworks to which it is foreign, to make its practice conform to epistemological paradigms it transgresses. Such restructurings, which are usually presented as the right-minded expurgation of a deplorably contumacious doctrine, invariably erode the dissentient power of Freud's distinctive method. These efforts could foreshadow a situation in which the reality of psychoanalysis is peremptorily relegated to history, without the philosophical and anthropological implications of its discourse ever being properly understood. No less chilling is the prospect of a situation in which "psychoanalysis" thrives as a fetishized commodity, as a grab-bag of techniques for cultural adaptation, from which the epistemological and ontological significance of Freud's revolutionary advances, the far-reaching implications of his *entscheidende Neuorientierung in Welt und Wissenschaft*, have long since disappeared. Unfortunately, this scenario is close at hand, for today multiple "revivals" of the language-analytic Freud, the cybernetic Freud, the structuralist Freud, and the like coexist with the much-heralded convergence of "psychoanalysis" and objectivistic disciplines. And all these endeavors, in a certain sense and to no small degree, bear the stamp of misapprehension, cooptation, and loss.

When we regard psychoanalysis as a changeful method of inquiry upon psychic reality, and *not* primarily as a clinical treatment or theoretical statement, we find that this psychology now stands at a strange juncture in its history. On the one hand, psychoanalytic method, the peculiar discourse of patient and psychoanalyst, diverges dramatically from the dominant mode of "psychological" investigation conducted within the precepts of logical empiricism. Accordingly, the contributions of psychoanalysis to mental science have often been a matter for heated dispute. On the other hand, as already intimated, it may well be that psychoanalytic psychology has not yet been controversial enough. It is as method that psychoanalysis still has much to teach us about psychic reality, the human subject, and the question of science. Yet it is as method that psychoanalytic psychology has been most badly misconstrued, even by its own practitioners. Notwithstanding all the rhetoric about psychoanalysis, just how revolutionary and inconvenient Freudian discourse is, has never been fully realized. Indeed, in this specifically methodological sense, the discipline that Freud inaugurates—the emancipatory science of personal meaning—even now resides in the limbo of imminent erasure. Through a history of attempts at ideological assimilation, the radical kernel of Freud's contribution and the intrinsically subversive movement of psychoanalytic praxis may yet be lost.

In beginning by emphasizing the misunderstandings of psychoanalysts themselves, the ideological disjunction between praxis and the public enunciation of praxis, my aim is not to refuel the current wrangling, nor to place myself in the opposition's camp. Rather, my purpose is to draw attention to the implications of this disjunction—the present, highly disconcerting situation in which psychoanalytic practitioners are confident that through their methodology something unique, true, and transformative occurs, even though this sanguine conviction is not anchored in any satisfactorily cogent exposition of what the methodology entails *epistemologically and ontologically.* Psychoanalytic self-misunderstanding actually occurs on several levels: metascientific, metalinguistic, and metatheoretical or "metapsychological." Whereas the latter will be given short shrift in this chapter, the metascientific misapprehension of psychoanalysis comprises a central theme. It is relatively easy to define Freud's psychology as the particular engagement of patient and psychoanalyst wherein the truth of unconscious psychic reality progressively emerges, yet this epithet is still pregnant with unapprehended significance. And it is in this context that the question of knowing and being in psychoanalysis should be reopened.

Psychoanalytic discourse should not be discarded merely because of the confusion and controversy in which it is embroiled. After all, if the reputedly revolutionary character of its method is valid, is it so surprising that its originality is neither readily nor adequately proclaimed in the languages of its prehistory? Consider, for a moment, the quality of "extraordinary science"—those occasional proceedings that change the very mode of human comprehension. We need not review the literature on the structural foundations of scientific theorizing, on the communal establishment of cognitive rules and categorization, or on the circumstances of Kuhnian "paradigm shifts." For our purposes, it need only be noted that at various dramatic stages of human history, there have indeed been certain challenging changes that rendered extant conceptual organizations obsolete, delineating the boundaries of their truthfulness, dislodging entire *Weltanschauungen*, and even dispossessing the episteme upon which cognition had previously been founded. As already indicated, the work of Bachelard, Canguilhem, and Foucault draws attention to the significance of these discontinuities and heterogeneities in the knowing process. Should psychoanalytic method imply a transformation of such far-reaching consequences, it would account for the confusion and controversy, the allure and antagonism, surrounding the discipline. For this imbroglio would emanate from a paradox in which Freud's psychology is now suspended. On one side, something unique, true, and transformative does occur in psychoanalysis, in that what has been repressed in mental life is progressively rediscovered in the course of each psychoanalytic interrogation. On the other side, there is no current notional nexus, no "metalanguage" or "metascience," no available cultural coordinates, within which the discovery may be publicly and satisfactorily articulated, or its scientificity established. If this is the case, then, in a certain sense, the scientific pursuit of the repressed unconscious is still ahead of its time.

   The response to the enigmatic is predictable: attempts to assess the unknown in terms of the familiar are paralleled by efforts to convert any puzzling novelty into conformity with preexisting paradigms. Thus, it was entirely to be expected that those onlookers who were skeptical or antagonistic, who lacked the conviction that psychoanalytic participation seems to create with striking regularity, would evaluate the discipline according to the directives of logical empiricist investigation, or by some other, similarly accepted criteria. As often as not, they arrived at an unfavorable verdict—thus coming to reject an enigmatic and extraordinary venture on the grounds of its failure to meet the hegemonical standards of "normal science." Yet if the originality of Freud's method is not counterfeit but revolutionary, as I am suggesting, then it is the response of the advocates to the paradox in which they find themselves that portends the place of the endeavor in human history. Imprecisely, one might say that this is the paradox of being party to an innovation that is, as yet, publicly unannounced and perhaps unannounceable within the current context. Here, it would seem, the self-misunderstandings of Freudians acquire an ominous dimension. In the absence of a cogent epistemological and ontological exposition of Freud's psychology, they, too, have succumbed to a transmogrification of their discipline—with the disquieting possibility that self-misunderstanding invokes apostasy unawares.

In theorizing about their discourse, Freudians often portray the discipline in a metalanguage not its own and thus allow the extraordinary problematic posed by psychoanalysis to be obscured, the critical tensions to be relaxed, and the enigma to be foreclosed. This happens on two levels. First, there are explicit efforts to speak *about* the discourse in a vocabulary and grammar imported from elsewhere. Indeed, Freud's own "metapsychologial speculations" provide an example of this tendency. There have also been numerous subsequent efforts to integrate Freud's psychology within another discipline's conceptual framework, such as orthogenetic theory, ethology, Piagetian cognitive theory, neurophysiological models, information theory, semantic or pragmatic analysis, and transformational linguistics. Coinciding with some of these efforts, one may discern, particularly within the recent history of the American psychoanalytic establishment, a succession of vogues for "building bridges" between Freud's psychology and other lines of research, notably, general developmental psychology, comparative biology, psychophysiology, and most recently— a "bridge" that at least appears singularly appropriate—general linguistics and communication theory. Perhaps to alleviate certain crises of confidence evident in sectors of this psychoanalytic establishment, such "interdisciplinary exchanges," which are *not* germane to the conduct of psychoanalysis itself, are promoted as if the discipline were on a par with branches of "normal" investigation.

Note that it is not suggested that such enterprises do not occasionally generate interesting *extrapsychoanalytic* research, but merely that they do not, and cannot, answer the most fundamental questions concerning the discourse of patient and psychoanalyst. Indeed, their effect is to evade this problematic, concealing the fact that the character of psychoanalytic discourse has never been, and cannot be, articulated in terms of such "normal" conceptualizations. The essential questions are unanswered; thus, it is a grievous lapse to preempt them by attempts to "translate" the gross features of this distinctive discourse into a metalanguage that can only caricature the psychoanalytic process by expunging its revolutionary character.

The second level on which Freudians have transmogrified their own discipline is implicit, deeper, and hence more serious. It is the almost unavoidable tendency for the approach to Freud's psychology to be structured by the presuppositions of predominant, paradigmatic modes of knowing and being. One example of this is psychoanalytic interpretation predicated on a philosophical stance that assumes semiosis as the ontological and epistemological totality. (The implications of this romantic totalization are submitted to critical scrutiny in Chapter 4, in the light of contemporary hermeneutic and structuralist approaches to Freud's psychology.) A different, readily identifiable example, which I will now dismiss, is provided by the small but constant minority who have embraced mystical interpretations of the psychoanalytic process—a tradition stemming in part from the vitalism of *Lebensphilosophie*. Now, it is not hard for most Anglo-American psychoanalysts to consider the argument that, in this mysticism, Freud's psychology has been approached with certain preconceptions detrimental to its proper exegesis. Yet it is usually more difficult to entertain a similar argument with regard to the thoroughly familiar, but also metaphysical, attitude they themselves have aprioristically espoused. So familiar a mode of thinking as to be scarcely recognizable, here is the paramount "paradigm" by which apprehension of psychoanalysis has been constrained—the one that presumptively posits the naive objectivism of the natural attitude, the stationary dualism of knower and known. For Freud's epigoni, the assumption of this attitude has been virtually automatic. And this attitude may be detrimental to the correct understanding of Freudian method—although, admittedly, Freud himself unwittingly subscribed to it to some extent. This innocent but insidious prejudice underpins an entire tradition of psychoanalytic interpretation, and it instigates the covert yet inapposite impulse to domesticate the discipline within the metascientific coordinates of "normal" investigation.

Much of my thesis is devoted to critical examination of these tacit cooptations. At this point, we should merely take note that in adopting such accepted approaches, psychoanalysts may not only contribute to an erasure of the essential, inconvenient originality of their discipline, but also effectively exclude the possibility that psychoanalysis is genuinely revolutionary, as a discourse *sui generis*. Such a possibility would explain why, beyond the misconstrued attempts to speak *about* this discourse within the confines of some preexisting metalanguage, Freud's psychology remains enigmatic and extraordinary.

THE PROBLEM OF "METAPSYCHOLOGY"

To comprehend the import of Freud's psychology, we must grant primacy to method, rather than focusing on clinical treatment issues or on some finalized, systematic theoretical form allegedly devised on the basis of psychoanalytic particpation. In this, we have, as has been said, the authority of Freud himself (1923a, 1923b, 1926c). The question of knowing and being in psychoanalysis concerns its own discourse as process or project, and not the status of retrospective theoretical products. Indeed, the perturbing uncertainties and controversies surrounding this discipline have often been exacerbated by commentators who persist in identifying psychoanalysis with Freud's "metapsychological speculations" or with some other extrapsychoanalytic enterprise. Because the role of "metapsychology" in Freud's psychology is complicated and such errors are common, it seems advisable to confront them now, at the outset of our philosophically inclined discussion.

What is the function of Freud's "metapsychological speculations," and what is their relation to psychoanalytic discourse? In Freud's texts, the term "metapsychology" has two connotations. In the first instance, Freud (1887–1902) uses the word, in his correspondence with Wilhelm Fliess, to refer to a "depth" psychology that leads beyond consciousness. Elsewhere, he hints at his aspiration to replace metaphysics with such a psychology of the unconscious (1901a, p. 288)—an aspiration that is not so far-fetched, as we shall see. The term's second, more major usage dates from 1915 and refers to a body of naturalistic theorizing. Although it is previewed in Freud's aborted *Entwurf einer Psychologie* (1895a) and in the complex seventh chapter of *Die Traumdeutung* (1900), it is elaborated only later, in the so-called metapsychological papers (1915a, 1915b, 1915c, 1917a, 1917c), reaching its apotheosis in *Das Ich und das Es* (1923a). In its final form, this edifice is composed of the first topography of conscious, preconscious, and unconscious "regions"; the structures or second topography of "ego," "id," and "superego"; and the drive energetics of "cathexis," "decathexis," and so forth. Moreover, as David Rapaport (1960b) indicates in his systematization of metapsychological propositions, its construction deploys a combination of dynamic, economic, structural, genetic, and adaptational principles.

At the time of writing the *Entwurf*, Freud explicitly viewed such propositions as relating to the neurological substrate. He attempted a syncretic enterprise, based on his prepsychoanalytic training under the influence of such investigators as Hermann Helmholtz, Theodor Meynert, Sigmund Exner, Ewald Hering, and Ernst Brücke, as well as his protopsychoanalytic observations from interviewing hysterics and other patients at J. M. Charcot's hospital and in private practice with Josef Breuer. This strongly reductionist ambition, however, was quickly rescinded and publication of these early drafts was never authorized. By 1900, Freud came to see the metapsychological enterprise as a mix of quasi-biological and psychological "generalizations." Later, acknowledging the "hiatus" between biological and psychological statements (1915b, p. 273), he insisted that metapsychology has no direct neural referent, even though he continued to phrase such propositions physicalistically and to found them on unscrutinized assumptions about natural-science explanation. Given its dubious relevance to empirical research on brain processes, and given what is, as we shall see, its oblique connection with the discourse of patient and psychoanalyst, we may legitimately ask why Freud indulged in this, admittedly speculative, enterprise. The most plausible answer is along the following lines.

For Freud, and perhaps also for his successors, the effort to transmute insights acquired in an intersubjective context that is semiological and dialectical, into theoretical models that are substantialistic and objectivistic, had a triple impetus. First, it was a misconceived ploy to gain for psychoanalysis the honorific respectability accorded to the natural sciences. That Freud retained an unquestioning reverence for these sciences' empirical exactitude, such that he was unable to direct his own critical methods toward the ideological implications of the natural attitude, is not surprising, given the emphasis of his schooling and his positivistic milieu. Second, Freud's neuroscientifically oriented speculations were no doubt motivated by the wish that psychoanalytic experiences might be employed to generate hypotheses about brain processes, which could be subjected to experimental test elsewhere. Of course, if this is the purpose of the metapsychological enterprise, it suggests a gravely mistaken view of reductionism. As Margaret Boden (1972) has so elegantly argued, psychological and physiological accounts are not intertranslatable, and this explains why, in the realization of such a purpose, Freud's metapsychological models have not been notably successful.

The third, and ultimately most interesting, possible function of the metapsychology is "metahermeneutic," to use Jürgen Habermas' (1968) terminology. It is the result of Freud's unresolved struggle to communicate publicly something of the character of psychoanalytic innovation, and especially to express extrapsychoanalytically the fragmentation of conscious and repressed mental contents that the discourse of patient and psychoanalyst divulges. To understand the peculiar dilemma that thus precipitates the metapsychological enterprise, we must further discuss the source of these metapsychological propositions and whether their formulation in turn affects the conduct of the dyadic discourse.

Supposedly, the metapsychological edifice is an "abstraction," constructed on the basis of psychoanalytic methodology, a product of the discursive process, formulated *as if* the gross features of this discourse had merely been represented hypostatically as a model of the "mental apparatus." In his autobiographical study, for example, Freud refers to his topographies as spatial "representations belonging to a speculative superstructure—any part of which may be sacrificed or exchanged, without grief or disadvantage, as soon as its inadequacy is demonstrated" (1925a, p. 58). Yet a critical examination of this "superstructure" shows that in no sense are its constituent propositions pure abstractions or generalizations from the psychoanalytic situation, for its construction is thoroughly dependent on the importation of natural-science concepts and premises about "mental" energy, field, and structure. For instance, the engagement of patient and psychoanalyst never evinces "drive mobility" or the "bindability of libido"; such conjectures are imposed from outside the discourse itself. Indeed, it may even be misleading to refer to such materialistic and mechanistic jargon as allegorical, because there is, so to speak, no *thing* within the discourse of patient and psychoanalyst that is being allegorized. Such naturalistic propositions are not simply inferred from the discursive process; thus, they hardly qualify the metapsychology as a theoretical "superstructure" anchored in psychoanalytic methodology.

Moreover, materialistic and mechanistic propositions of this kind do not, according to Freud, determine the course of the psychoanalytic process. Because such metapsychological propositions are, for the most part, naturalistic importations, they might point toward neuroscientific predictions for extrapsychoanalytic experimentation, as Freud occasionally anticipated (1914, 1938/1940). What is significant here, however, is Freud's emphasis that natural-science findings about brain processes do not, and cannot, furnish rules for the conduct of psychoanalysis. In referring to the "hiatus" between biological and psychological statements, Freud concludes that psychoanalytic work is "independent, in this respect, and may advance according to its own necessity" (1915b, p. 274). In other words, psychoanalytic methodology justifiably proceeds without reference to neural events. Although Freud's natural-science speculations may point toward extrapsychoanalytic research, such metapsychology cannot legitimately be employed obversely to direct or restrict the discourse of patient and psychoanalyst.

Recently, the American psychoanalytic establishment has become embroiled in a debate over the usefulness of Freud's metapsychological conceptualizations (e.g., Gill & Holzman, 1976). Although I have elsewhere demonstrated the incogitant elements in Roy Schafer's formulation of an "alternative" to metapsychology (see Barratt, 1978), my comments here might appear to support an unqualified rejection of metapsychological theorizing. So far I have argued that metapsychological speculations are not authentically predicated on psychoanalytic methodology, that the discourse of patient and psychoanalyst is not constrained by such speculations, and that the success or failure of such propositions as natural-science hypotheses for extrapsychoanalytic experimentation is not germane to the conduct of psychoanalytic discourse. But this is not the end of the matter. To the extent that its intention was originally metahermeneutic, more must be said about Freudian metapsychology.

As the foredoomed outcome of a struggle to express extra-psychoanalytically something of the extraordinary character of psychoanalytic discourse, even when publicly available metalanguages precluded its enunciation, metapsychological theorizing might be described as a desperate attempt at "giving good similes," to borrow Wittgenstein's comment on the role of aesthetic theory. Freud recognized the enterprise as one of constructing a *mythology*, and he explicitly acknowledged its proximity to "fantasizing" (1937a, p. 69). In this regard, metapsychology seems an example of what Hegel might call *pictorial thought*, with all its concomitant disadvantages—for, in a scientific pursuit, as in the discourse of patient and psychoanalyst, knowledge does not rest with the biases of such hypostatized depiction. Following this assessment, one would caution against confounding the scientificity of the pursuit with the inadequacies of its depiction; the "simile" should not be mistaken for the reality of the psychological odyssey it analogizes. At best, that is, to the extent one might suppose it to be a metahermeneutic purely abstracted from the concrete workings of the discursive process, the relationship of metapsychology to psychoanalysis might be compared to the relationship of Hegel's *Science of Logic* (1812) to his *Phenomenology of Spirit* (1807)—the former's categorizations and recommendations necessarily concede priority to the itinerary by which they were reached. The concrete discourse of patient and psychoanalyst is privileged, and the status of metapsychological theorizing is, at best, that of a derivative

and retrospective enterprise. There is the scientific pursuit, and lat-
terly a mythology about that pursuit. Having pursued the itinerary of
discourse, Freud formulated extrapsychoanalytically a set of "similes"
for the purposes of public dissemination. It follows that, whereas such
similes might, in a certain sense, be predicated on psychoanalytic participation, the conduct of psychoanalytic discourse cannot be guided by
them.

There is an apparent exception to this dictum, one which has confused many commentators, and which will be expounded later. The
notion of the repressed unconscious—that "first shibboleth" of Freud's
psychology (1923a, p. 239)—does operate proleptically within the engagement of patient and psychoanalyst, ensuring that this engagement is psychoanalytic rather than ordinarily conversational. It is *as if*
patient and psychoanalyst embraced this notion—akin to the aphorism
"that which is cannot be true"—as the means by which to embark upon
the discourse of unmasking, the discourse of the repressed unconscious. Yet this prolepsis hardly comprises metapsychology's entrance
into the operation of the dyadic discourse. Indeed, even if metapsychology were purely hermeneutic, it would still be wrong to suggest that metapsychological propositions organize or propel the
discourse of patient and psychoanalyst, as it would be upside-down to
argue that a scientific pursuit should be guided by the mythology about
such pursuits. In the strictest sense, metapsychology is *not*
psychoanalysis, nor does it prescribe the concrete workings of the
psychoanalytic process.

Freud constructs a naturalistic mythology, an extrapsychoanalytic
schematization, to advertise his innovational psychology. However,
when no existing metalanguage can readily or adequately articulate
the character of its discourse, or of the unconscious it discloses, such
an enterprise necessarily misadvertises, because of the very mode and
medium in which it is formulated. Indeed, it must be said that the
metapsychological enterprise has had a doubly unfortunate effect. In
the first place, the schematization is hegemonic. The objectivistic
similes employed to speak about the discourse of patient and
psychoanalyst constitute a scientistically prejudiced account that
comes to structure the way in which the discourse is apprehended. As
we shall see in the next chapter, the mythological enterprise came to
dominate even Freud's own thinking about his discipline, transforming
his viewpoint and driving him toward significant misrepresentations of
its problematic metascientific character. On the part of his successors,
the various controversies over the "correctness" and "utility" of
specific metapsychological propositions have created the bizarre

spectre of a debate that has long since lost sight of the mythical nature of its subject matter.

Thus, in the second place, metapsychology has repeatedly been equated with Freud's psychology, and metapsychological rhetoric has been substituted for the quintessential questions concerning the engagement of patient and psychoanalyst. Yet, whether viewed as a set of natural-science hypotheses or regarded as metahermeneutic, the metapsychological enterprise is, as I have indicated, *extrapsychoanalytic*, so such a mistaken substitution only obfuscates the more significant issues. This substitution comprises the most common and elementary misapprehension of psychoanalytic discourse. It leaves us at a historical juncture where the metapsychology, however marvelous, must be held in abeyance as much as possible in order that the discourse may be understood. An effort to reappraise psychoanalysis without metapsychological preconceptions is now required.

EGO PSYCHOLOGY AS CUL-DE-SAC

Without overly anticipating my later arguments, a few comments must be made about the particular tradition of metapsychological theorizing known as "ego psychology," which currently comprises the most prestigious, mainstream school of Anglo-American "psychoanalysis." So-called ego psychology virtually identifies "psychoanalysis" with the structural-functional model of "id," "superego," and "the ego organization."[1] This model was formulated by Freud in the 1920s, although he himself remained markedly dissatisfied with it and ambivalent about its usefulness. Nevertheless, a great many of his successors have treated this model as the apogee of Freud's labors. They have even argued that it renders obsolete the distinctive discoveries enunciated in his pre-1914 writings, and they have extensively elaborated this structural-functional formulation into an allegedly finalized and systematic framework for the conceptualization of mental life. This framework gives privilege to the objectivistic investigation of behavioral "adaptation" to a supposedly pregiven "external reality," and it emphasizes the "autonomous functions" or "conflict-free sphere of the ego" as a substantive set of "psychic structures" (see Chapter 3).

In certain respects, ego psychology may be the most flagrantly apos-

---

[1] Hereafter I shall use this school's terminology in the course of my critique, even though it will become clear that "ego," "id," and the accompanying jargon are reified concepts which should be abolished.

tate revision of psychoanalysis, as will become clear as we proceed. At this point it need only be noted that the formulation of ego psychology rescinds all that is extraordinary about psychoanalytic discourse as it concerns psychic reality, the question of the subject, and the process of scientific inquiry. Thus, in the context of my approach to psychoanalysis, the structural-functional formulation is decidedly anti-psychoanalytic.

For example, the notion of psychoanalytic discourse as the intersubjective engagement of patient and psychoanalyst, which gives epistemological and ontological priority to the interiority of *psychic reality*, is wholly contravened by ego psychology's emphasis on adaptation to "external reality," and the epistemological presumptions of "objectivity" this entails. Concomitantly, ego psychology has nothing whatever to say about the *subject* of human mentation. Its formulation entirely loses sight of psychoanalysis as the discourse that articulates and rearticulates the locus of the human subject. Freud's psychology, especially as enunciated before the "metapsychological" papers, is, above all else, an inquiry upon the subject within the representations and desires of the psychic world—a subject that, as we shall see, is split within the dynamic and contradictory discourse of psychic reality. Ego psychology, however, renders itself dumb with respect to these essential issues. Freud's pre-1914 denotation of *Ich*, as refering to the "I-ness" of mentation that is not repressed, is entirely ablated by ego psychology's emphasis on an ego *organization*, which is objectivistically and externalistically defined as a substantive or physicalistic set of psychic structures and functions. It is as if subject were eclipsed by substance. In line with the positivistic tradition (a tradition that in this respect extends back to Hume's confessed inability to account for the necessary subjectivity of mental process), ego psychology, by means of objectivistic and substantialistic concepts such as organization, structure, and bound or unbound energy, entirely obfuscates the question of the subject within the knowing and being of psychological inquiry and change.

Caught in a framework of unexamined naturalistic assumptions, ego psychology is, of course, at a loss to apprehend psychoanalysis as a *discourse*—as an intersubjectivity of interrogation that inquires upon the interiority of personal meaning, and as a discipline that takes full account of the constructivity and reflectivity of human mentation. Consequently, the ego psychology school has no way to apprehend the epistemological and ontological processes of psychoanalytic formation and transformation. Having lost sight of the priority of psychic reality and the question of the subject, and having become aprioristically immured in an objectivistic notion of "science," ego psychology cannot grasp the conjunction of knowing and being, of truth and transformation, in a movement of interrogative and reflective discourse. That is, ego psychology has no means to speak of the necessary conjunction of an *epistemic* dimension—processes of interpretation and insight by which the patient's psychic being is revealed—and its *ontic* significance—the metamorphic movement, transformations of the patient's experience and understanding, in which interpretation and insight are implicated. To put it more simply, ego psychology preempts the possibility of grasping the central and most profound issue of psychoanalytic discourse, namely, that of the enigmatic connection between an exchange of words and silences, the elucidation of some alleged truth concerning the patient's being, and the vicissitudes of psychic experience and understanding. All this will become clearer in the detailed critique of "ego objectivity" presented in Chapter 3. For despite all its trappings of naturalistic scientism, ego psychology incorrigibly forecloses our apprehension of psychoanalytic discourse as *science* itself.

There are, of course, many reasons why ego psychology has attained its preeminence within the establishment. There is, for example, an explicit rationale given by many contemporary metapsychological theorists for their preference for the structural-functional model over so-called topographic and dynamic formulations—and this rationale will be criticized later. Most evidently, the general enterprise of ego psychology represents a misconceived effort to align psychoanalysis with the dominant "psychology" of logical empiricism. Indeed, the ego psychologist's charade of objectivity, and the ego-psychological orientation toward behavioral functions and adaptation to external reality, may well succeed in this enterprise of cooptation. It is quite possible that ego psychology can provide operationalist and instrumentalist propositions for controlled observation and predictive experimentation. It may even be that ego psychology can provide a treatment technology that is effective with respect to goals of sociocultural adjustment. But none of this is psychoanalysis, nor does it bear on the scientificity of psychoanalytic discourse. Successes of this sort are invariably extrapsychoanalytic.

Behind the jargon of metapsychology, the formulations of ego psychology, and other intricate but inapt mythologies, Freud's psychology as the discourse of patient and psychoanalyst must be reconsidered as such. As should be clear, we must avoid the error of identifying psychoanalysis with metapsychology, with the structural-functional model, or with any other extrapsychoanalytic enterprise. Thus, we shall not further discuss that which can be gleaned from psychoanalysis by the practitioners of nonpsychoanalytic methods. In this respect, to take but one example, the feverish debate over the empirical "credibility" of Freud's psychology entirely misses the point. It may well be that the psychoanalytically experienced are able, in circumstances *external* to psychoanalytic discourse, to generate successful hypotheses for observation and experiment according to the formalized procedures of naturalistic investigation. But such successes do not provide evidence relevant to the study of Freudian discourse, nor can they be informative about the actual processes of the psychoanalytic context. As the products of certain presuppositions encoded in a particular unreflective epistemology, these successes cannot answer the claim that psychoanalytic discourse itself comprises a mode of knowing and being *sui generis*. And that, to my mind, is the "test" of credibility—that, in its own right, the discourse of patient and psychoanalyst constitutes a scientific venture that is both valid and mutative.

"EINE PSYCHOLOGIE DER VERDRÄNGUNG"— "A PSYCHOLOGY OF REPRESSION"

To conduct a study such as this requires that we proceed *as if* Freud's psychology could be apprehended from without—*as if* one could write about the engagement of patient and psychoanalyst or about the manner of its external misconstruction in a discourse that is not itself psychoanalytic—when the very character of this psychology might be that it defies such an expository procedure. This difficulty, which may seem utterly absurd from the standpoint of familiar epistemology, is far from trivial. It may well be an inescapable consequence of "the revolutionary and inconvenient advances" made by psychoanalytic science. For, if the possibility that psychoanalytic praxis is constituted as an extraordinary mode of discourse *sui generis* is seriously entertained, then enigmatic incomprehensibility of the praxis, in terms of the metascientific modes of its prehistory, may be the implication of its far-reaching originality. Revolutionary modes of discourse defy prolegomenous exposition within the prevailing metalanguage of clarity and common sense. Thus, although further epistemological and ontological inquiry upon Freud's psychology is long overdue, the demand that this inquiry represent psychoanalytic discourse within the field of the familiar is neither appropriate nor possible.

Freud seems to have been aware of the limitations, if not the impossibility, of presenting his psychology in a manner itself nonpsychoanalytic. Although countering the impression that psychoanalytic practitioners wish to create a secret society immune from the challenges of intellectual exchange, he argues on several occasions that his psychology is truly known only to its participants (e.g., 1933). For example, in his introductory lecture series, Freud forewarns the assembled gathering that "the discourse of which psychoanalytic treatment consists brooks no audience and cannot be demonstrated" (1916–1917, p. 10). Psychoanalytic method, he insists, must be discovered for oneself; it is knowable only through participation. To discuss psychoanalysis outside the privileged context of its discourse is to operate by "hearsay," which is ultimately untenable.

The seriousness of this expository problem accounts for the peculiar form of this book—explaining why my initial emphasis is on what Freud's psychology is *not*. This negative strategy, in which reappraisal emerges only from critique of misapprehensions, betokens the multiple paradox within which this inquiry necessarily unfolds. This paradox should be made plain. On one side, not only will our inquiry approach the question of psychoanalytic discourse through critical examination of the ways in which it has been misapprehended epistemologically and ontologically, but it will proceed *as if* we might write about psychoanalysis without being able, for the moment, to state extrapsychoanalytically what psychoanalysis is. To anticipate one conclusion of this study, we may find that Freudian science cannot conform to the coordinates of normal epistemology, and thus cannot satisfactorily be spoken *about* in the metalanguages of familiar metascience. Yet, on the other side, to embark on any nonpsychoanalytic treatise concerning Freud's psychology requires that *something* be said about psychoanalysis, even though our conclusion may be that no such extrapsychoanalytic exposition can be either entirely cogent or entirely legitimate. Thus, we shall attempt a tentatively denominative "account" of the psychoanalytic context and of the claims about its process that Freud struggles to enunciate. Given the paradoxical position of such an account, we must start from the very beginning, with minimal recourse to cumbersome "technical" terminology, and, as far as possible, without rigid, constricting metascientific or metalinguistic preconceptions.

A psychoanalysis is formed as a discourse engaging the patient and the already-analyzed psychoanalyst. The patient lies comfortably, with minimal external distraction, and is enjoined to speak whatever, in common parlance, "comes to mind." The psychoanalyst attends relaxedly, remaining silent except for infrequent, nonstandardized comments on how or what the patient does or does not say.

Characteristically, the patient develops ideas and feelings about the rather opaque, silent figure of the psychoanalyst, and usually, the discourse turns toward memories of past events. Thus, typically, the discourse may be both historicized, as a present repetition of prior experiences and understandings, and historical, in that it refers explicitly to memories of such past experiences and understandings. As the discourse of patient and psychoanalyst continues for an extended period of time, there are qualitative changes in the patient's utterances and in the psychoanalyst's comments. For the moment, however, we need not mention the specific content of these changes. To keep this account simple, let us hold in abeyance any detailed description of "technique," or of the issues of "transference," "countertransference," "resistance," "therapeutic regression," and "working through." Let us even leave aside for the moment the question of psychoanalysis as a content-laden movement of repetition, recollection, and reappropriation. Indeed, whatever else may occur, the central point here is that *the patient's words and being are transformed* in the course of this lopsided dialogue. The patient's immediate and familiar experiences and understandings come to be seen as partial or false. Concomitantly, alien thoughts or wishes, which previously were disruptively active in the patient's life even though exiled from consciousness or admissible memory, become reaccessible for renewed personality development.

Here, unarguably, is the problematic kernel of the question of knowing and being in psychoanalytic discourse. It is signified by the claim to have discovered a discursive method in which the dispelled or "repressed" contents of the mind are progressively revealed and reintegrated in a way that is mutative and truthful. This discovery of the repressed unconscious is the *sine qua non* of psychoanalysis. For, leaving aside Freud's reaffirmation that our sensuality precedes genital maturation (1898b, 1905b, 1906), the psychoanalytic endeavor must be regarded as developing from Freud's germinal discovery of an interrogation that may liberate the repressed, of a "scientific pursuit" that confronts the tragic yet ubiquitously human estrangement or alienation *"zwischen den zusammenhängenden Ich und dem von ihm abgespaltenen Verdrängten,"* between the cohesive "I"—or as we might interpolate, the conscious and socially designated "I-ness" of mentation—and the repressed, which is split off from it (1923a, p. 244; cf. 1920a, p. 18).

Admittedly, this confrontation between subjectively possessed mental activity and that which it excludes is not all that happens in psychoanalysis. What occurs between patient and psychoanalyst in clinical practice is multiple and complex. Yet it is this special dimension of the process that is profoundly problematic from the standpoint of familiar philosophies and normal metascientific assumptions. Thus, it becomes the focus of our study. The discussion of all that is extraordinary and enigmatic about the knowing and being of psychoanalytic discourse necessarily centers on the question: What is the repressed unconscious, and what happens to it during a psychoanalysis? At this point, we might do well to consult Freud himself.

How is the student to begin reading Freud? Secondary sources are, without exception, thoroughly misleading. Indeed, I might voice the opinion that certain particularly popular "introductory textbooks" do great damage to the student and to the science of psychoanalysis. Freud's texts have to be read anew, and there are strong reasons for commencing at the beginning, with the birth of psychoanalysis in 1896, and by way of an especially meticulous study of *Die Traumdeutung* (1900). To begin with Freud's later works, for example, at the zenith of his metapsychological theorizing as represented by *Das Ich und das Es* (1923a), or Lecture 31 of the *Neue Folge der Vorlesungen* (1933), is to commit a grievous error. For, in these later works, extrapsychoanalytic influences, in two enmeshed forms, come to dominate Freud's own perspective and presentation of his discipline.

In the first place, Freud's mythology, his naturalistic metapsychology, constrains his mature writing, precluding an adequate articulation of the radical originality of psychoanalytic discourse as such. It is as if this schematization—ill-advisedly created for the convenience of public dissemination—had gained a conceptual momentum of its own that overpowered even the critical faculties of its creator. As argued earlier, we must contest the edict that the fuller formulation of this mythology permits an improved image of what psychoanalysis is. On the contrary, metapsychological speculations tend to misrepresent the discipline, occluding the question of its essential character.

In the second place, Freud's mature writings are imbued with the suppositions of a scientistic "ego epistemology," which partially obscures for the reader the highly problematic character and seminal uniqueness of the discursive confrontation between "I" and the repressed. The psychoanalytic discovery of the split-off unconscious is, in some sense, veiled. Between the earlier and the later texts, Freud seems to shift somewhat from his revolutionary vision of the manifest and immediate "I" as a false totality to be unmasked by the demystifying discourse of patient and psychoanalyst, toward an almost positivistic panegyric for the autonomous power of the contemplative "ego" as a Humean organization of mental structures and functions. Ego psychology, of course, completes this shift. The grave complications of such a shift and the incogitant ideology of the later "ego" formulation will be thoroughly discussed in the next chapter, for this shift exemplifies the mistakes incurred by attempts to integrate psychoanalytic process with familiar conceptual structures and metascientific schemes.

Given the inconsistencies in Freud's published thought, as well as the predominant miscomprehension of his psychology, a "neutral" reading of the literature taken as a whole is not possible. The manner of approach to Freud's texts and the reader's preconceptions become issues of paramount importance. Although I do not wish to promote the view that Freud's development is biphasic, the hegemony of the metapsychological myth and "ego epistemology" in Freud's later works makes it absolutely necessary to reemphasize his early psychoanalytic writing, say from 1896 to approximately 1914. To draw an exaggerated contrast, it might be said that Freud's earlier works are the product of a relatively pure and persistent struggle to announce the notion of the repressed unconscious, untrammeled by the later ascendancy of extrapsychoanalytic influences. In my view, then, a reading of Freud's texts must begin with these early works, preferably entering the literature through *Die Traumdeutung* (1900) and the case histories (1905a, 1909a, 1909b, 1918), for it is in such writings that Freud first struggles to enunciate the profound and far-reaching originality of his discipline. It is mainly on the basis of these texts that I shall now briefly suggest a particular way of reading Freud's psychology—a way that has perhaps been eclipsed by the subsequent history of extrapsychoanalytic conceptualization.

Reading through *Die Traumdeutung* is a vertiginous undertaking from which one cannot return undisturbed, for here the third great blow to human narcissism is delivered (cf. Freud, 1916–1917, 1917b, 1925c). Copernicus declared that our earth is not the center of the universe. Darwin declared that our creation was animal not divine. Freud now proclaims that we are not even masters of our own minds. In the perplexing seventh chapter of this 1900 text, the ostensibly sober report of psychoanalytic discoveries contains several abrupt statements, which are both jarring and entirely extraordinary, and by which our attention should be riveted. Freud refers, for example, to the psychic unconscious as *"der Kern unseres Wesens,"* the essence of our being (p. 609). Yet it is elsewhere, a different "scene" from that of consciousness (p. 541), with contents *"nach Ausdruck ringenden, vom Bewusstsein abgeschnitten,"* striving for expression yet severed from consciousness (p. 551). It is in this regard that Freud speaks of *"der*

Zwiespalt zwischen dem Unbewussten und dem Bewussten, dem Verdrängten und dem Ich"—the schism between unconscious and conscious, between the repressed and the "I" (p. 562). The repressed is *the true psychic reality*—*"das Unbewusste ist das eigentlich reale Psychische"* (p. 617). Yet it is *inaccessible to consciousness*— *"bewusstseinunfähig"* (p. 619). We must acknowledge here that it is nothing other than the process of psychoanalytic interrogation and reflection that compels Freud to make daring, eccentric, and seemingly far-fetched pronouncements of this sort.

These pronouncements, which animate Freud's early writings, seem to advance five critical claims about the psychoanalytic venture:

First, Freud unequivocally presents his discipline as concerned with *psychic existence*, and distinctively it is *meaning* or multiple meaning that inheres to the very mode of this existence. Personal meaning or "significance," conscious or unconscious, is the fabric of the discourse of patient and psychoanalyst. In this respect, Freud seems to follow Franz Brentano's (1874) notion of intentionality, and indeed he adopts Brentano's distinction between the physical and the psychological. Throughout these texts, Freud speaks of *mind*, and is careful to treat circumspectly any question about the material substrate or the physicochemical explanation of brain processes. Although Freud does make excursions into neurophysiological speculation, the intrinsically meaningless nature of brain process is not germane to the work of patient and psychoanalyst. Despite such extrapsychoanalytic excursions, "we remain," Freud insists, "on psychological ground" (1900, p. 541). Even in his later writings, at the height of metapsychological theorizing, with all the physicalistic similes, Freud remains clear about the specifically psychological character of his discipline. In his essay in support of "lay" practice, for example, he refers to the question of the material substrate as "of no psychological interest; psychology can be as indifferent to it as optics is to the question whether the walls of the telescope are made of metal or pasteboard" (1926a, p. 221). Indubitably, it is the "question of the significance of dreams" that is of foremost psychoanalytic interest (1901b, p. 646), and this question of significance applies not only to dreams but to all else that psychoanalysis, as the scientific pursuit of personal meaning, confronts.

Second, there is a *psychic unconscious*, upon which Freud's psychology discourses, and it is not only said to be "more extensive and more significant than the familiar activity connected with consciousness" (1913, p. 397), but is also *the source of wishes*, for it "knows no activity other than wish fulfillment and has no power other than the agitation of the wish" (1900, p. 574). Psychoanalysis moves beyond the consciousness of meaning. The manifest text of the dream, for example, is somehow revealed to be a "disguised fulfillment of a repressed wish" (1901b, p. 687, italics omitted), and this discovery of idiographic unconscious meanings stimulates Freud extrapsychoanalytically to tender general historical conjectures about the character of the oldest and most powerful human longings (e.g., 1912–1913). Psychoanalytic discourse leads Freud to write unambiguously of the essence of our being "existing as the movement of unconscious wishes," and to insist that "everything conscious has an unconscious precondition [*Vorstufe*]" (1900, pp. 609, 617). Thus, at least in these early texts, the psychoanalytic unconscious is regarded as the intentional center of psychic reality; in a certain sense, the notion implies the "original" subject of human desire. Freud's adherence to this extreme and seemingly involuted view is indicated by several publications written between 1900 and 1912 (1900, 1901a, 1901b, 1905e, 1907, 1910b, 1912).

Third, although this unconscious is so active, so extensive, and of such general significance, its contents are exiled, dispelled, or *alienated* from consciousness by *repression*. Throughout his work, Freud repeatedly stresses that it is necessary to conceive of this personal alienation in the strongest sense. What psychoanalysis pursues is neither the manifest nor the readily retrievable, but the recondite. Almost tirelessly, Freud reiterates the distinction between this repressed unconscious psyche and the prepsychoanalytic foreconscious or nonconscious. Within his metapsychological enterprise, for example, he justifies his move from pure description to dynamic imagery as necessary to communicate extrapsychoanalytically the severity of this psychic rupture. "Repression," the term for that which determines the cleavage between conscious and unconscious contents, is depicted as a powerful force (1900, 1910b), analogous to the burying of Pompeii (1907, 1909b). As Freud emphasizes in his English note on the psychoanalytic unconscious, repressed activity is "cut off from consciousness," an "unconscious idea is excluded from consciousness by living forces which oppose themselves to its reception," as if there were "a barrier which keeps them asunder" (1912, pp. 263–264). Hence, although the unconscious is mental, it is quite unlike a foreconscious or preconscious content that might, upon a certain reflection, enter into immediate awareness. This notion of repression is of seminal significance in the conduct of psychoanalytic discourse.

Freud claims that the unconscious he has discovered is a *psychic* unconscious, wishful and repressed. And here we should pause to disclaim certain misnomers and indicate most emphatically what this unconscious is not. In both historical views of the discovery of the unconscious and contemporary understandings of Freud's innovation, there is frequently a failure to grasp the significance of these particular claims. From a historiographic perspective, for example, several commentators have insisted on "precursors" to Freud's work in European philosophy; they have thereby obfuscated the break with all prior conceptions of unconsciousness that Freud's method signifies. The "unconscious" of which diverse philosophers, such as Friedrich von Schelling, Carl Carus, Arthur Schopenhauer, and Eduard von Hartmann, wrote is entirely different from the psychoanalytic notion, either because it is purely organic (a nonconscious state of meaningless nature rather than the meaningfulness of mind) or because, if held to be mental, it is not regarded as repressed from consciousness, but merely has the character of an unaware occurrence, such as a "leap of inference," or represents the store of foreconscious memories retrievable to consciousness.

The error of this insistence on spurious historical connections between the repressed unconscious and pre-Freudian conceptions is regrettably replicated by many modern theorists, several of whom are supposedly sympathetic to psychoanalysis. In the contemporary literature, one finds various assertions implying that the Freudian distinction of the unconscious may profitably be compared to some other type of statement about consciousness and that which is not conscious. It has been suggested, for instance, that this psychoanalytic unconscious is somehow equivalent to the "deep syntactical rules" of linguistic competence, to "organismic" processes of neurophysiology, or to the "automatization" or apparent reflective ignorance of successfully employed cognitive strategies. Many other examples could be given. All would illustrate the fundamental errors that are made when the notion of the repressed unconscious is not brought into a discussion of the subject of psychic reality. All effectively reduce the Freudian notion to the mechanisms or meanings of nonconsciousness or foreconsciousness respectively. They thus fail, in one way or another, to take adequate cognizance of the distinctive and unprecedented claims made for the psychoanalytic discovery of a *psychic* unconscious that is wishful and repressed.

Now we come to Freud's *fourth* claim, which concerns the revelatory power of the psychoanalytic process itself. Despite his notion of repression as sustaining a severe alienation from consciousness, Freud contends that the psychoanalytic interrogation *discloses the repressed* (1904, 1905c, 1905c, 1910a, 1910b, 1913). Through this process, repressed unconscious contents are made known, even though knowledge adheres to consciousness and communication. Freud's method effects an "uncovering of the concealed, forgotten, and repressed," serving "to bring that which is repressed in the psyche to conscious recognition" (1910a, pp. 38–39), or to "translate into consciousness what is already known in the unconscious" (1905a, p. 209). Apparently purposeless actions may "prove to be fully intended and determined by motives unknown to consciousness" (1901a, p. 267, italics omitted), for unconscious wishes can somehow be revealed in the course of the debate between patient and psychoanalyst. There is indeed a discovering of the unconscious.

At the same time, with his *fifth* claim, Freud points to what is perhaps the most philosophically and anthropologically radical feature of psychoanalytic discipline: despite the severity of the disjunction between conscious and unconscious, psychoanalytic reflection and interrogation not only reveal but somehow *reappropriate the repressed*. The knowing is transformative as, in some sense, repressed wishes are restored to the "I-ness" of self-consciousness. In his brief essay on psychoanalytic method, Freud defines its aim: "to abolish amnesias . . . to put an end to all repressions . . . to make the unconscious accessible to consciousness" (1904, p. 8). Elsewhere, he writes of "bringing the repressed back into conscious mental activity" (1910a, p. 25), of "redressing the repressions" and "reinstating the genuine psychic contents [*Objektes*]" (1898a, p. 525). Freud is not, of course, advocating total licentious indulgence of our innermost desires, for he makes it clear that the repressed content, having been made conscious, may well be inhibited or *condemned* even while repossessed in awareness (1909a, p. 375; 1910a, p. 57). But the "involuntary" is rendered "voluntary"; the unconscious is procured within the domain of consciousness (1900). Through psychoanalysis, the repressed is now a wish or thought owned by the "I-ness" of conscious and foreconscious mentation. "It" is no longer alien; thing-being becomes "I."

Thus, the knowing of psychoanalysis is neither "purely contemplative" nor ontically inconsequential, for there is a dialectical reciprocity whereby such a reappropriation of the repressed necessarily changes not only the unconscious but also the locus of consciousness and hence of the subject. Moreover, since Freud writes of the "I" as "guardian of entrance" into awareness, one may say that the knowing and being of this "I-ness" of psychic reality are transformed through psychoanalytic discourse. This recuperative aspect of an interrogation that is "analytic" or critical would seem to entail a metamorphic movement of the human subject ontologically. As we shall see, this reappropriative movement of the subject is, from the standpoint of familiar philosophies and normal metasciences, quite perplexing and probably wholly incomprehensible. Here is the question that will become the recurrent theme of our study, for the entire problematic or psychoanalytic discourse may appropriately be posed around it. What does Freud mean when, six years before his death yet in a phraseology that echoes the radical pronouncements of earlier writings, he succinctly summarizes this reappropriative directionality of psychoanalytic discourse? *"Wo Es war, soll Ich werden"*—"Where It was, should I become" (1933, p. 86).

The Freudian unconscious as repressed and the directionality of psychoanalytic discourse as reappropriating the repressed are highlighted in a reading of Freud's early texts. We must now look at a closely related concept, which is of critical importance to my thesis, and which I have renamed *the condition of polysemous contradiction*. I am referring to Freud's concept of the "return of the repressed," so designated in his early essay on "defenses" in neurosis (1896), to indicate how, in the psychodynamics of so-called pathology, repressed contents may disrupt the continuity and coherence of consciousness and foreconsciousness. This pathogenic "return" refers to "representations that are a compromise between the repressed and the repressing images" or ideas (1896, p. 387, italics omitted). It thus entails the distortion and deformation of mentation by a disguised obtrusion of wishes and thoughts that are alien to the "I," and it imputes a thoroughly symbolic—that is, condensed and displaced—character to all the manifestations of consciousness.

Parapraxes, amnesias, dreams, and the general plurivocality or "overdeterminacy" of symptoms all exemplify such compromises between meanings that are conscious and unconscious in their "origin." As Freud states in a footnote appended to *Die Traumdeutung* in 1914, "one constituent of the symptom corresponds to the unconscious wish fulfillment and another to the reaction against this wish" (1900, p. 547n). To the prepsychoanalyzed "I," such disguised obtrusions or compromises appear only as inconsistencies, lapses, or opacities in the familiar "text" of self-consciousness. They are, so to speak, *in* consciousness but not *of* consciousness. The alienation between consciousness, broadly conceived, and the psychoanalytic unconscious— between the "I" and the repressed—is such that immediate reflective consciousness cannot apprehend the concealed wishful purpose of the symptom, experiencing such disguised intrusions only as senseless, disruptive aberrations.

Character style must also be apprehended as a form of polysemous contradiction, as a compromise between meanings conscious and unconscious. Character is, in this sense, like a fused and well-coordinated set of symptoms. There are, of course, some important clinical distinctions between characterological and symptomatological formations, particularly with respect to how readily they appear dystonic to the reflectivity of consciousness. For the purposes of our epistemological and ontological inquiry, however, it is important to acknowledge that *all* manifestations of self-consciousness are to be treated in psychoanalytic discourse for their potential as polysemous contradictions—as compromises that conceal as well as reveal, compromises formed by the disguised obtrusion of unconscious contents upon the conscious and foreconscious mind.

Prepsychoanalytically, the contradictions in self-consciousness may or may not be manifest. Indeed, one might suggest that with symptoms, conscious reflection knows that there is something operative not its own, whereas with character, the contradictions may not be so readily recognizable as such. But, whichever way, the meaningful unconscious constituent of their polysemy remains incomprehensible to the reflectivity of consciousness. It is only after psychoanalytic interrogation of such polysemous contradictions that these compromised mental representations are found to be expressive of a disguised unconscious wish or thought and of a culturally designated prohibition against it. Thus, much of our inquiry upon knowing and being in psychoanalytic discourse must focus on three interrelated notions: that a wishful unconscious psyche is repressed from the conscious and foreconscious domain; that the "I-ness" of reflective consciousness is distorted and deformed by the disguised "return" of the repressed; and that psychoanalytic discourse is an authentic reappropriation of the repressed.

In his introductory "brochure" on dreaming, Freud (1901b) makes one of his many efforts to articulate and emphasize the distinctiveness of psychoanalytic discourse and discovery. He contrasts his discipline with all earlier "philosophies of consciousness," and, by implication, contrasts it with earlier conceptions of the nonconscious or the foreconscious. In doing so, he refers to psychoanalysis as *"eine Psychologie der Verdrängung,"* "a psychology of repression" (p. 689). At this time of writing, he uses the term *Verdrängung* generically, to denote an active excluding from reflective consciousness, the condition under which unconscious purposes are disowned by the "I" of conscious recognition. Admittedly, the manner in which Freud employs this notion, its technicality and specificity, does change somewhat with the burgeoning of metapsychological speculation and the elaboration of new terminological distinctions in the jargon of "defensive processes." But, despite these vicissitudes, there is a certain consistency throughout

Freud's thinking about his discipline—a persistent centrality of the notion of repression as the condition of the split-off unconscious, that wishful "essence" of our being. Twenty-two years after his brochure on dreaming, the repressed is still named *"das Vorbild des Unbewussten,"* "the prototype of the unconscious" (1923a, p. 241). "One can," Freud writes in his autobiographical study, "take repression as the center and bring all the elements of psychoanalytic doctrine into relation with it" (1925a, p. 56). It is in this context that a reappraisal of psychoanalytic discourse, as "the scientific pursuit of the psychic unconscious," must be undertaken. And in this context it is proposed that, above all else, psychoanalysis must be apprehended as *Psychologie der Verdrängung*, as the psychology of repression and the discursive praxis of anti-repression—the emancipatory science of meaning.

PSYCHOANALYSIS AND THE SUBJECT

In mental life, there is much that is, one way or another, not conscious. The term "unconscious," however, has been employed diversely, resulting in endless confusion in the psychological and psychoanalytic literature. Most generally, it has been used descriptively to denote any mental content or function that is not presently in awareness. This usage is unfortunate. For, in my opinion, *ontologically* it conflates three "levels" that are utterly distinct: the dynamic unconscious announced by Freud's *Psychologie der Verdrängung;* preconscious or foreconscious contents, which are retrievable to awareness with sufficient effort of attention; and the numerous functions that are neither repressed nor available to reflective consciousness, which are here called "nonconscious."

The conflation of these "levels" has precipitated perplexity. In large measure, the reason for this confusion is the extraordinary and enigmatic quality of the psychoanalytic notion of the repressed: that the repressed can only be designated as such when its "return" is encountered as polysemous contradictions *in* the text of consciousness but not *of* this text, and that the repressed can eventually be recollected and reappropriated by the subject of self-consciousness, *not* by any mere effort of attention, however well-sustained, but specifically through the rigors of psychoanalytic reflection and interrogation.

The distinction between the nonconscious and the repressed unconscious may be partly clarified by specification of the difference between function and content. Repression seems to apply to the content of ideas, wishes, fantasies, and the like, rather than to function as such. Just as the neurophysiological interactions biologically necessary to sustain psychological processes are not available to reflective consciousness, so, too, many functions of the representational system, such as the operation of certain rules and principles by which representations are formed, may not themselves be open to reflection. Yet they are neither repressed, nor, as we shall see, "suppressed."

The appearance of a grammatical sentence in consciousness, for example, depends on certain generative rules of syntax, semantics, and pragmatics—rules employed in the productions of consciousness yet not necessarily specifiable upon immediate conscious reflection. A linguist, such as Noam Chomsky, using a particular procedure of reflection, induction and deduction, may be able to tell us about some of these rules of "deep structure," but most of us evidently employ them without being able to say what they are—and Chomsky's knowledge *about* such rules always remains akin to knowledge about an exteriority. Similarly, a behavioral researcher or "psychophysicist" may be able to inform us about certain principles of sensorimotor coordination, which again are used without awareness. There is no need to believe those operative rules and principles of conative, affective, and cognitive functioning that we cannot articulate or specify consciously have been, in any sense, ousted from awareness. They are simply nonconscious. This distinction has been a source of confusion for many commentators, especially ego psychologists. In particular—much like the generative rules of syntax, semantics, and pragmatics—the "defensive functions" of consciousness, by which certain mental contents are kept from reflective awareness, may not be articulable or specifiable by conscious reflection. Conscious representational processes may employ such functions without awareness. If such functions cease to be employed, then, of course, there is some awareness on the part of consciousness of new mental contents entering its purview. The point here, however, is that this does not imply that "defenses" are repressed or suppressed, merely that they are nonconscious.

Failure to distinguish the preconscious or foreconscious from the repressed unconscious is probably facilitated by the resistance of many preconscious contents to conscious recognition, despite their potential for entrance into awareness. Indeed, Freud differentiates "suppression" *(Unterdrückung)* from repression in order to indicate gradations in the retrievability of preconscious contents to consciousness (1900, pp. 611–612n). Some preconscious contents are not at all easy for consciousness to bring into its purview, despite sustained effort of attention. This obscurity, together with the potential for reappropriation of repressed contents through psychoanalytic work, has also been a source of confusion for many commentators.

Given these difficulties in conceptualization, how are the conscious, nonconscious, preconscious, and unconscious dimensions of mental life to be properly distinguished? Again, we must turn to Freud's early writings, where the answer to this question is evident, although left implicit. The conscious, nonconscious, preconscious, or unconscious status of representational contents and functions cannot be properly apprehended except in relation to the subject of psychic reality.

Dating from his earliest psychoanalytic publications, Freud stresses, as the key to his discipline, the schism between the repressed and the "I" (1900). He thus poses *the contradiction between the cohesive "I-ness" of mentation and the repressed, split-off from this "I."* In Chapter 1, we broached this question of the subject of a representational system without reference to Freud's discovery of the unconscious. It was argued, following the insights of "first philosophy," that for every experience and understanding, there must be a subject who experiences and understands. This subject (for example, in the Kantian tradition) is like an "I think" conjoined to every mental representation—active and empty but bestowing on mentation a unity, continuity, and coherence of "belonging." In this manner, all mental contents and functions must be contained within, or owned by, some conatively, affectively, and cognitively expressive "I-ness."

Along these lines, we can redefine the conscious, nonconscious, and preconscious dimensions of psychic reality. Nonconscious and preconscious functions "belong" to the very same subject as consciousness, despite their variable availability to the reflections of consciousness. Nonconscious operative rules and principles of representation may never become reflectively available to consciousness. Nevertheless, these functions are deployed by the same subject as consciousness. Some preconscious ideas, wishes, and fantasies may readily enter consciousness. Other preconscious mentation may be virtually impossible for consciousness to bring within its purview. Nevertheless, all such contents, whatever their degree of suppression from consciousness, are possessed by the same subject as consciousness as contents that are "I." Indeed, examples of relatively inaccessible preconscious contents are commonplace in clinical work. A patient may struggle, by means of prodigious and sustained efforts of attention, to arrive at some misplaced ideation, whereupon the psychoanalyst intervenes with a speculative interpretation concerning the missing content. The patient's reflective response may then be something like: "Yes, I did think that . . ." Preconscious contents, however "deeply" suppressed, are embraced within the same "I-ness" as that of conscious reflection.

Conscious mentation, nonconscious functions, and preconscious contents, belonging to the same subject, thus form a more or less cohesive domain of ideas, wishes, fantasies, and so on—a semiotic system, in short. But "cohesive" does not necessarily mean harmonious. The domain of conscious, nonconscious, and preconscious mentation may contain conflicts, incongruities, and disparities of a certain sort within the representations embraced by its subject. Nevertheless, all mentation contained within this domain is, so to speak, possessed by the "I" upon which consciousness can reflect. In this respect, the representational functions and contents of conscious, nonconscious, and preconscious mentation are a system, forming a unity, with a continuity and coherence of mentation, due to their common "I-ness." Whatever their degree of availability to reflective awareness, these representational functions and contents are all of the very same "I" that is known to reflective consciousness, to "self-consciousness," as this term is used in philosophy.

What, then, of mental contents that are repressed? Recall the five critical claims of psychoanalytic discourse enumerated in the previous section. With these in mind, we can see that the profound philosophical difficulty in grasping Freud's notion of the unconscious is due to its complex implications for the *locus* of subjectivity. First philosophy, in the tradition of Descartes and Kant, shows that every experience and understanding must belong to a subject who experiences and understands, and this accounts for the unity of mental activity systemically. In this frame, *the notion of the subject imposes a limit on the possible conditions of experience and understanding*, rendering the systemic cohesiveness of the representational world. Freud's revolution subverts the Cartesian subject with *a discourse that discovers and recovers mental activity beyond the limit*. Repressed ideas, wishes, and fantasies are, in themselves, beyond the bounds of ordinary representational activity, beyond conscious, nonconscious, and preconscious activity. Repressed contents may persist and insist themselves upon the cohesive domain of ordinary mentation in the formation of polysemous contradictions. Yet the repressed as such remains "out of bounds"; it is not possessed by the "I-ness" of ordinary mentation.

In his early writings, Freud makes very plain his belief in the "I-less-ness" of the repressed vis-à-vis the domain of conscious, nonconscious, and preconscious representational activity. He introduces and then adheres to the common, yet philosophically and semiotically evocative, German word *Ich* or "I," arguing that his discourse involves the dynamic of contradiction between the "I-ness" of mentation and that which is repressed. In this context, we can now advance in more explicit detail the epistemological and ontological distinctions Freud offers concerning the vicissitudes of mentation in relation to the "I think" of reflective consciousness, especially with respect to so-called defensive processes.[2] As mentioned, there are nonconscious functions, not available epistemically to conscious reflection, but nonetheless belonging ontically to the same "I" as consciousness. Then there are mental contents that are under "condemnation" *(Verurteilung or Urteilsverwerfung)*, possessed in reflective consciousness as an idea, wish, fantasy, or whatever, but not put into action, or otherwise indulged. In addition, there are mental contents that are under "suppression" *(Unterdrücking)*, potentially available epistemically to conscious reflection, and belonging ontically to the same "I" as consciousness. Finally, there are mental contents that are under "repression" *(Verdrängung)*, not available epistemically to conscious reflection, except after transformation in the particular recollective work of psychoanalytic interrogation, and not belonging ontically to the "I" of conscious, nonconscious, and preconscious mentation, except after transformation in the particular reappropriative work of psychoanalytic interrogation.

What Freud proposes is that, whereas there are "gradations" between consciousness and preconsciousness, there is a "schism" between this domain of mental contents and that of the repressed unconscious. This is not just an epistemological distinction involving the knowability of mental contents upon reflection. It is an *ontological* distinction, involving the being of mental life—the locus and boundary of the "I-ness" of ordinary mentation.

Clinically, we find that *within* this boundary—within the "I-ness" of the domain of conscious, nonconscious, and preconscious activity—there are a number of "defensive" processes serving to distort and deform what is brought into the purview of reflective awareness. Broadly speaking, all such maneuvers involve condensations and displacements of representations and of their investment with desire. Let us recall the various dimensions of representational systems that we discussed in the first chapter: a representation may be shared or not shared, referential or figurative, invested with desire to a greater or lesser degree, about the person's "self" or about some "other," and so

---

[2]The problem with the terminology of "defenses" is, of course, not only its mechanistic quality, but also that it conflates conflicts within the domain of the "I-ness" of ordinary mentation and the disjunction between this realm and the "I-less-ness" of the repressed.

on. With these dimensions in mind, we can envisage various permutations and combinations by which a mental content may be altered in the service of this so-called defense. The clinician's catalog of defensive processes, such as internalization, identification, isolation, and reaction formation, could usefully be redefined and redescribed according to these dimensions. To give just one example, "projection" evidently involves a representation about "me," that is, a self-representation, being reattributed to someone or something "not me" or "other." But let us proceed to the pertinent point for our purposes here: the relation of mental contents thus transmogrified to the notion of the subject. For the most part, this battery of defenses, distorting and deforming conscious reflection, occurs within the domain of the subject of nonconscious and preconscious mentation—an "I-ness" which is that of consciousness. In this sense, these defensive processes are epistemologically and ontologically equivalent to suppression, whatever their important clinical differences. In projection, for example, both the projected "not-me" content and the preprojected "me" representation belong to the "I-ness" of ordinary mentation. However clinically obstinate such defenses may be, they are, for the most part, transpositions of representation and desire occurring *within* the ontological bounds of a subject who is the very same as that of consciousness.

It is known, clinically, that these defenses never occur singly. Indeed, in most, if not all, so-called defensive maneuvers of the conscious, nonconscious, and preconscious domain, repression is also implicated. Yet repression involves a transformation of mental contents such that they are, so to speak, exiled *without* the boundary of "I-ness" that circumscribes and renders more or less cohesive the domain of ordinary mentation. And the repressed is only knowable via the ontically transmutative interrogation of its "return" in polysemous contradictions constituted by condensations and displacements. That is, defensive processes may result in all manner of conflicts, incongruities, and disparities within the subjectivity of conscious, nonconscious, and preconscious mentation, but repression *ipso facto* entails a *contradiction* between this "I-ness" and the repressed, which is of another order.

In this respect, the notion of compromise formation, of the dynamics of symptomatology and characterology, may be reconfronted in relation to the question of the subject. As we shall discuss later, the representational compromise of a symptomatic or characterological formation can be comprehended as an arrested interlocution of "I" and the repressed—which psychoanalytic interrogation may be able to release. That is, as a polysemous contradiction, such a formation manifests itself as a frozen and falsified moment of subjectivity. It is an interruption in the historicity and continuity of the "I-ness" of experience and understanding, as well as a curtailment of the reflective movement of consciousness. Hence, it appears as an opacity in the belongingness of ideas, wishes, fantasies, and reflections. It belies the constructivity of the subject of ordinary mentation, indicating that the formation of the representational world is never the exclusive prerogative of this subject. The praxis of psychoanalysis, as we shall see, works against this arrest or interruption in the formation of mental activity; it empowers consciousness by restarting the full reflectivity of its "I-ness" with respect to the "return" of the repressed that is in its midst. In this way, psychoanalytic discourse has an emancipatory potential for the subject vis-à-vis the repressed unconscious.

The point here is that we must acknowledge the implications of Freud's discovery of the repressed unconscious for the subjectivity of psychic reality. Psychoanalytic discourse may reinstate the interlocution of "I" and that which is "without," but *prior to* psychoanalytic inquiry, this "interlocution" only appears as polysemous contradiction in the hypostatized form of frozen and falsified experiences and understandings. The notion of repression imputes mental content beyond the limit of "I-ness," but the repressed as such is never manifest. It is known only because of its persistence and insistence, because it presumes upon the domain of ordinary mentation in the form of the return of the repressed. This "return" as compromise formations, as polysemous contradictions, is "in the midst" of consciousness and preconsciousness, yet not belonging to this domain. These formations thus inform reflective consciousness of its prepsychoanalytic limit and intimate mentation beyond its "I-ness." Schematically, we might say that, to this reflective consciousness, the return of the repressed is a disruptive and apparently senseless obtrusion of "I-less-ness" within the bounds of its subjectivity, even though this "I-less-ness" of mental contents never appears in itself. As far as this subject is concerned, the return of the repressed is mentation formed from without. This extraordinary ontological proposition is, of course, made difficult to grasp by its enigmatic epistemological status.

Through its particular transformative interrogation of the return of the repressed, psychoanalytic discourse demonstrates the *split subject* of psychic reality. As we have seen, the repressed involves ideas, wishes, fantasies, and the like, exiled from the subjectivity of the conscious, nonconscious, and preconscious domain. Yet the repressed, too, being mental, must entail a "subject" to whom these ideas, wishes, fantasies belong. Thus, against an entire tradition of philosophical reasoning, Freud's discourse reveals the interlocution—prepsychoanalytically arrested but psychoanalytically released—of the ruptured subjectivity of psychic reality. Very schematically—and we must remember the dangers of any schematization—we might envision the splitting of subjectivity in the following manner.

On one side, the subject of conscious, nonconscious, and preconscious mentation is like that described by the tradition of first philosophy. This mentation may be individual, yet it is part and parcel of the sociocultural totality of representational processes. Its subject is formed in the sociality of discourse—formed ideologically, as we shall see. This mental activity is thus semiotically rule-governed and necessarily ideological in its functioning. The systemic character of this domain, its cohesiveness, continuity, and coherence, is due to a subject that is, in a certain sense, unitary, active, and empty. This subject's domain is also self-totalizing. However, although this subject is the locus of reflection, the potential of its reflectivity is constrained. Although it is active and constructive with respect to its representational functioning, the potential of its constructivity is curtailed. The constraint and curtailment are due to this subject's passive relationship to an extrinsic "subjectivity" beyond its bounds: the obstrusion, persistence, and insistence of the repressed in relation to this "I-ness" of ordinary mentation.

On the other side, the repressed involves a "subject" that would seem to be quite unlike the subject described by first philosophy. It invokes meaning, yet it is scarcely unitary, having no cohesiveness or coherence, and continuity only with respect to its persistence. Its mentation is neither intrinsically rule-governed nor ideologically constituted in the sociality of discourse. Here we may recall Freud's arguments about the absence of logic, time, or space "in" the unconscious mind. The repressed "subject" seems to abuse dimensions such as those of referentiality or figurativity. The repressed "subject" is not active, except in a peculiar sense. It may be constructive—or rather, destructive—but in this respect it acts upon representation, without, so to speak, supplying the fabric of representation. It is not reflective, and in this respect it is quite unlike the affirmative image of an "I think" conjoined to all representations, incurred in the movement from thought to metathought. The activity of the repressed "subject" punctures the systemic character of ordinary mentation, and yet ordinary mentation owes its existence to the animative character of the repressed unconscious, as Freud intimates. Thus, the repressed "subject" is, in a particular sense, not empty. It is desirous, and desire has a relentless and inexorable nature. And here we may recall Freud's arguments about the wishful or pleasure-seeking impetus of the unconscious mind, as well as the recurrent clinical impression that erogeneity and aggressivity are what is "in" the unconscious.

Unlike nature itself, the unconscious is not mute. It is as desire that the repressed "subject" is significational, or intentional in Brentano's sense: it is necessarily and determinately directed toward representation. In Freud's words, it "strives for expression." And, in this sense, the mental activity of the repressed "subject" comprises, again in Freud's words, "the essence of our being." Essence negates appearance here: the repressed is cast beyond the bounds of ordinary mentation, yet acts obtrusively, disruptively, and desirously upon it. What stands out is the enigmatic character of this "subject." We cannot readily discuss the qualities of the repressed "subject" as such, because, as has been said, it is known only as it appears in the return of the repressed. The knowability of the repressed unconscious and the preeminent nature of its being are essentially negative: *the repressed "subject" stands as the negation of the "I-ness of ordinary mentation.*

What I am trying to articulate here is the dialectical locus of the subject of psychic reality vis-à-vis the ideological dislocation of boundary, the arrest and fixation of the horizons of reflectivity and constructivity in ordinary mentation. In this context, it may be thoroughly misleading to write about two "sides." Such a depiction is an abstraction implying independent existence, and this belies the inherent interpenetration of the repressed "subject" and the "I-ness of ordinary mentation. We can perhaps mitigate the dangers of our schematization of the two "sides" by suggesting a yet more vertiginous depiction in which each "subject" exists only as the interstices of the other. The superordinate issue that must be reemphasized here is that all we can know is the return of the repressed. This is the crux of all that is enigmatic and extraordinary in psychoanalytic discourse. What subverts an entire tradition of philosophizing is the discovery that the subject of psychic reality is semiotically split as a locus of contradiction.

Freud specifically contrasts psychoanalysis, as *Psychologie der Verdrängung*, with the "philosophies of consciousness" that preceded his work. It is his notion of the repressed vis-à-vis the subject of ordinary mentation that is at the heart of his seminal break both with all "surface psychologies" and with all psychotherapies that merely chart the boundaries of the conscious-preconscious domain, "working over" the contents within *(Psychische Verarbeitung;* see Freud, 1895b, 1926b). Admittedly, Freud has contributed enormously to our ability to give an account of those conflicts, incongruities, and disparities occurring within the limits of subjectivity or ordinary mentation, and the clinical significance of this is not to be underestimated. The day-to-day workings of psychoanalysis are, in this sense, thoroughly psychotherapeutic. But the psychoanalytic process is much more than a therapy of clarification, interpersonal relearning, and "working over." The unique innovation of Freud's psychology goes awesomely beyond this, by disclosing the negativity of mental being in the contradictory locus of the subject. The notions of repression, the return of the repressed, and the psychoanalytic reappropriation of the repressed render this discourse a changeful inquiry upon the very boundaries of the subject itself. As a study of psychic reality, Freud's psychology moves against the inevitable tendency of realist and objectivistic thought to eclipse the question of the subject. But, as we shall see, psychoanalytic discourse also moves against the inevitable tendency of idealist and subjectivistic thought to treat the subject affirmatively or to regard it as transcending scientific interrogation. Psychoanalysis as a discipline *sui generis* cannot be apprehended except as a dialectical semiology of the contradictory locus of the subject. And this has profound significance for our notion of science itself.

PSYCHOANALYSIS AS SCIENCE

Our preliminary discussion of subjectivity in psychoanalysis intimates the philosophical complexity of the questions raised by this revolutionary discipline. And even in this rudimentary discussion, we have perhaps overly anticipated issues that need further elaboration and argumentation. For the moment, the point is that the unmasking of the human subject as a locus of contradiction shatters the framework of suppositions about knowing and being to which we are ordinarily accustomed. If we return to Freud's vision of psychoanalysis "as the scientific pursuit of the psychic unconscious," it becomes evident that his *Psychologie der Verdrängung* raises serious questions about the character of such a "scientific pursuit," the *method*, and hence the epistemology and ontology by which it might be conducted. In sum, psychoanalytic discourse demands that we take seriously Freud's claim that this changeful inquiry upon the repressed unconscious entails *eine entscheidende Neuorientierung in Welt und Wissenschaft.*

Pointing to the disputation and misapprehension that surround psychoanalysis, I have argued that to approach Freud's psychology anew, we must relinquish metapsychological, ego-psychological, and all other extrapsychoanalytic preconceptions of what this psychology comprises. Psychoanalysis must be considered as the constitution of the discourse of patient and psychoanalyst. To reapproach the discipline in this way also requires that we relinquish metalinguistic or metatheoretical preconceptions of what this psychology comprises. Indeed, the requirement of psychoanalytic discourse is yet more radical, for we must be prepared to relinquish, or better to reexamine, our preconceptions of science itself.

A threefold misapprehension of psychoanalysis has been described: metapsychological, metalinguistic or metatheoretical, and metascientific. The most mundane mistake is that of identifying psychoanalytic discourse with the inapposite mythology in which Freud strove to depict it publicly. The second, metalinguistic misapprehension subsumes the metapsychological. It is the explicit, preemptive tendency to speak *about* psychoanalytic discourse in a preexisting vocabulary and grammar to which it is foreign. (Of course, strictly speaking, because of the character of its discourse, there are unique difficulties to any inquiry upon psychoanalysis that is not itself psychoanalytic, and my thesis is not immune to these.) Here, however, we need to consider a third, more serious but related misapprehension—the metascientific one. This is the implicit transmogrifying tendency for comprehension of psychoanalytic discourse to be determined by preconceptions about the possible conditions of epistemology and ontology—preconceptions that are perhaps transgressed by the very character of knowing and being in psychoanalysis. Indeed, if psychoanalysis is science, and I believe it is, then it is not "normal science." It is "extraordinary science." Again, to pose the question of the scientific conduct of Freud's psychology requires that we are prepared to pose the question of scientific conduct itself.

Freud repeatedly insists that psychoanalytic discourse is *scientific*, yet it is worth noting an ambiguity in this insistence, especially because it has caused certain confusions among his successors. Freud seems sure that his discourse is scientific, *wissenschaftlich*, but, despite his personal enthusiasm for the neo-positivism of the "unified science" movement, he admits doubt about whether the discipline of psychoanalysis is natural-scientific, *naturwissenschaftlich*. In his posthumously published *Abriss der Psychoanalyse*, for example, Freud writes of his psychology as "a natural science like any other" (1938–1940, p. 80). Yet a few years earlier, he refers, with somewhat neo-Kantian undertones, to the existence of "two sciences, psychology . . . and natural science" (1933, p. 194). For Freud's commentators who do not read the German original, this ambiguity is exacerbated in part by James Strachey's routine translation of *Wissenschaft* as "science." Whereas in English "science" commonly implies objectivistic investigations of the natural world within the framework of logical empiricism, the German *Wissenschaft* has a broader connotation that includes any disciplined, scholarly pursuit.

Although Freud's pronouncements on this issue need not be documented further here, it might be proposed that, although psychoanalytic discourse may not be, or indeed cannot be, naturalistic or objectivistic, Freud's insistence on its scientific status is a correct assertion of its rigorous, disciplined, and necessary character. To enter Freud's psychology, the neo-positivist dogma that restricts "science" to the enterprise of controlled observation, instrumentalist experimentation, and mathematicized inference must be abandoned. For the "problem" of psychoanalysis is not that of a specific, paradigmatically marginal doctrine, but the comprehensively human problem of knowledge itself. Thus, what is and what is not *scientific* cannot be decided beforehand if Freud's seminally innovational psychology is to be reapprehended. Indeed, as we shall discover, this is a question that psychoanalytic discourse itself revolutionizes most inconveniently.

In the present context of debate over psychoanalysis, not only does the constitution of its discourse remain enigmatic and extraordinary, but misconstructions threaten to erase the putatively unique, true, and transformative quality of psychoanalytic praxis. A reappraisal of psychoanalysis is thus compelled to proceed by way of a thorough discussion of what the discipline is not and cannot be. Along these lines, the next two chapters will largely be devoted to critique of the two major metascientific misconstructions of psychoanalysis: the epistemologically "analytic" and the ontologically hermeneutic. Only when the field is thus cleared of metascientific misapprehensions will we be able to move toward a discussion of the philosophical and anthropological implications of psychoanalytic discourse—as a semiotics of the split subject and as a hermeneutic odyssey that is deconstructively dialectical.

The misapprehension of psychoanalytic psychology has entailed an almost complete failure, on the part of its practitioners, to pose the question of psychoanalytic discourse in a most fundamental fashion, one which would demand a critical deconstruction and "working through" of preconceptions about science and human life. Yet the question of the discourse between patient and psychoanalyst has to be posed in this most radical, complex and allusive fashion, if we are ever to apprehend how this distinctive discourse obeys or overthrows that of familiar modes and media of knowing and being. And hence, if we are ever to grasp fully the contribution of psychoanalysis to the notions of psychic reality, subject, and science—indeed, to the whole problematic of inquiry and change.

3

"Analytic" Epistemology

In considering the processes of knowing, there is a familiar scheme that seems so commonsensical it is virtually unquestioned outside of the sophisticated reflections of certain philosophies. This scheme posits the stationary dualism of knower and known, establishing static specifications of the subject who investigates, observes, or infers; the distinctly separate domain of the thing studied, which the subject renders as object; and the supposedly dissociate "relations" between them. The there-being of things-in-themselves, rendered as objects of investigation, is metaphysically presumed. In this scheme, subject and objectivated thing are ontically apart and different, and necessarily remain so throughout the knowing process. Knowledge about the world obtains as the correspondence of the subject's representational activities with the nature of things. Yet, despite this correlation, neither knower nor known is altered, with respect to each other, by the knower's accretion of knowledge about the known. The object may appear manipulated in the process of being known about—for example, by instrumentalist control in experimentation—but its essential nature, as something apart and different from the subject, remains unaltered. The subject may undergo changes in its inferential constructs or manner of observation through its investigation of the object domain, but its essential position as subject, apart and different from the objectivated thing, remains unaltered. To say that the subject may acquire knowledge about things is definitely not to imply that the existence of such things thereby becomes part of the subject.

In this scheme, the presupposed rift between knower and known entails the impassable externality of the objectivated domain to the epistemological activity of the subject. Although a subject may be engaged in knowing about this objectivated domain—for example, in constructing thing representations as objects—the thing does not, in and of itself, enter into the subject's activity. Indeed, following the assumption of this naturalistic attitude, it would be an absurdity to suggest that, in the course of knowing, the thing might, so to speak, become subject, or the subject convert iself into something that is subjectless, for the separateness between the ontological loci of knower and known is posited as a constant, irrespective of epistemological processes. The immutability of this stationary dualism, in which the inviolate distinction of mentality and materiality generally accords with that of knower and known, is held as metaphysically given; it is fundamental to the naturalistic scheme.

To pose the problem of epistemology in this bipartite fashion—as the question of the subject's activity with respect to the nature of an irrevocably external domain of objectivated things—entails, in a certain sense, two types of knowing. In the first place, there is the subject's supposedly immediate and direct "knowledge" of itself—the unity or self-certainty of the subject that allows it to "know" its activity as its own. Indeed, the naturalistic scheme just described entirely depends on the inherent capacity of the epistemological subject, whether human individual, scientific collective, or some formalized system, to possess and, so to speak, take responsibility for its own observational, inferential, and representation-generating processes. In the second place, there is the knowledge that the subject may acquire about the object by means of its own observational and inferential activity. This refers to the correspondence and secondarily to the coherence of the subject's information-gathering or representational processes with respect to the nature of the thing objectivated. How this coherent correspondence, or natural experience and understanding, is attained is the classical problem addressed by epistemology. It is the question, for example, of how the mind may achieve experience and understanding about the natural or external world—how the sensory and organizational structure of the knowing subject may secure truth or certainty about an investigated domain of things "out there," rendered as objects.

This sketch crudely delineates the "natural" attitude, in relation to which the claims of psychoanalytic discourse must be reconfronted. Such an attitude epitomizes the general epistemological framework traditionally tied to philosophy of natural science, and it girds a diverse group of "analytic" theories of knowledge, all of which fall under the admittedly polemical and generic rubric of *analytische Wissenschaftstheorie* or "logical empiricism." For our purposes, the group comprises all philosophies that operate upon this set of philosophically "analytic" presuppositions about subject and object in the experience and understanding of the there-being of things. It includes, for example, formalism, pragmatism, Popperian philosophy, and all positivist doctrines. Indeed, the only "Anglo-Saxon" epistemological theorizing that might be exempted from this rubric is a certain mode of language-analytic philosophy which does not presume the natural attitude (see the discussion of hermeneutics in Chapter 4).

The question here is: Can psychoanalytic discourse possibly be comprehended within any epistemological framework that presupposes this natural attitude? More precisely, we need to ask: Can the discovery of the repressed unconscious be comprehended within the fixedly bipartite structure of subject and thing objectivated, prescribed by this attitude? In line with the two types of knowing defined by this scheme, there are two possible, but mutually exclusive, answers to such a question: If one is to speak of knowledge within the psychoanalytic situation, of a "scientific pursuit of the psychic unconscious," then the contents of the repressed unconscious that are known must be either on the side of the epistemological subject or on the side of the epistemological object. The first answer means that these contents are somehow an integral but hitherto neglected aspect or phase of the self-consciousness or "I-ness" of the knowing subject. Under the second answer, such contents feature as a knowable domain of things rendered as objects to be investigated by an external subject. Taking up each of these answers in turn, we are led into a critique of attempts to reform Freud's psychology in accordance with either subjectivistic or objectivistic precepts.

PSYCHOANALYTIC KNOWING IS NOT SUBJECTIVISTIC

Cartesian and Kantian theories of knowledge are the fountainhead of modern "analytic" epistemology. As we saw in Chapter 1, Descartes' (1637) method of doubt and quest for mental procedures by which certainty might be secured inaugurates the break with medieval interests. This transition from medieval to modern philosophy culminated in Kant's (1781) systematic and syncretic formulation. Such theorizing became the frame of reference for most nineteenth-century theories of knowledge. Nor is the significance of Descartes and Kant merely historical; their influence is unarguably contemporary, in that, directly or indirectly, current epistemology hinges on their work. Although current logical empiricist formulations may not share Descartes' starting point, diverging from his characterization of the knower as individual, these formulations nonetheless adhere to certain Cartesian assumptions about the locus and certainty of the epistemological subject. Descartes' specification of the knowing process can therefore be used to ascertain whether Freud's discovery could be knowledge in the subjectivistic sense of Cartesian epistemology.

Standing at the very beginning of modern philosophy, René Descartes advances the rejection of medievalist submission to authority in favor of the Enlightenment spirit of free inquiry. His work emerges in opposition to the revival of skepticism in Renaissance thought. Indeed, his quest for certainty is profoundly influenced by the advances of Renaissance science, particularly the introduction of the mathematical ideal as the model of "objective" reasoning. As is well known, Descartes' philosophy attempts to resolve the Galilean problem of mechanistic explanation of the human soul by positing a sharp dualism of mind and body. Mentality, subject to freedom and teleology, is viewed as if a soul, partly transcending the mechanistic causality of material substance (which Descartes, influenced by Euclidean method, equates with geometrical extension). This dualism is part of Descartes' ambition toward a comprehensive scientific philosophy—a "first philosophy" that breaks with the dogma of scholastic logic to found an entirely new and allegedly unassailable epistemological procedure. And it is with this seminal *method* that we are concerned.

Descartes' epistemological enterprise commences with methodical doubt—a determination to submit all that he once presumed to the test of skeptical scrutiny; indeed, to proceed as if there were some *malin génie* systematically deceiving him. The aim of this procedure is to arrive, via doubt, at some truth that is indubitable, thus calling a halt to doubt and constituting a secure starting point for the intuition and deduction of all other truths. Descartes asserts that he has found such an indubitable starting point in the primary existential proposition *cogito ergo sum* (cf. 1637, 1641). Although there are several interpretations of this dictum—for example, in the controversy over its status as premise, proof, or self-confirmatory profession—its distinguished role as the existentially self-verifiable datum, employed as the axiom of an entire epistemological program, is not in dispute.

Cogito, as the seemingly evident quality of certain acts of consciousness, is taken by Descartes as a secure truth, the certainty of which is absolutely assured by every immediate instance of reflective inspection. Effectively presuming the identity of the mind and that which is available to consciousness, the dictum refers to all of which the individual's mind may be immediately aware as operating within itself, including feeling and willing as well as understanding. Thus, Descartes, seeking an immutable state of mind, safely anchored in certain indubitables, arrives at the reflective certitude of subjectivity in the finite individual mind. Yet this *cogito* is more than a formula by which the existence of one's own thoughts may be ascertained. Descartes employs it inferentially, proceeding from this manifest certainty of the personal subject to knowledge of other, extra-mental existences. Not resting with subjectivism, Descartes aspires to use this first certainty as the foundation for objective, impersonal truth, which is, in his opinion, exemplified by the power of mathematical logic. Although initially only the existence of the self-conscious experient is asserted and affirmed by the *cogito*, it is on the basis of this "truth" that, according to Descartes, all other knowledge is possible.

Descartes argues that no knowledge is possible until the mind has come to know the author of its own being. He thus regards the establishment of the *cogito* as securing the necessary subjective foundation for the study of objects—first, metaphysical (in which a proof of God's existence is predicated on the primary truth of self-consciousness), and later, naturalistic (in which all knowledge about the world depends on this privileged self-referent). Although we need not be concerned with the sequence and detail of these proofs, the role of the *cogito* as the epistemological starting point must be made clear. From this certainty, Descartes postulates general criteria of truth and certainty— that is, from the allegedly rudimentary, secure, and unmediated character of reflective consciousness, he imputes the general validity of direct acquaintance by consciousness. Deciding that clarity and distinctiveness are what assure the truth of the *cogito*, he assumes that whatever appears to consciousness with such clarity and distinctiveness must also be true (and here we see the tie to the quality of a mathematical principle, which is such that the mind is compelled to assent to it).

This move from the clear and distinct perception or conception to the proclamation of its truth is wedded to Descartes' general supposition of the truthfulness of the mind's intuitions and deductions. He does not question the fallibility of the unhindered operations of this self-consciousness. Instead, he implies that the secure reflective recognition of consciousness is part of the subject's virtually innate capacity to recognize the nature of existence and certainty—truth is somehow intrinsic to self-consciousness. What must be underlined here is that, although epistemological rules are propounded, especially in the pre-*cogito* texts, Descartes' method is not merely a set of canons functioning without reference to the particular human mind. His epistemology is anchored in the ability of the individual mind to understand and employ its own fundamental and naturally perfect operations. It is from the first certitude of self-consciousness that the foundation of all other knowledge is posited. This "ego" is taken as the epistemological starting point of any first philosophy.

Post-Cartesian naturalistic theories of knowledge frequently diverge from Descartes' specific designation of the subject as the individual's finite, empirical "ego." But all such epistemology assumes the apodicticity of the knower's stationary certainty of itself as knower. Despite the divergences, it is this common character that needs to be stressed. For instance, in Kantian philosophy, as has been discussed, the possibility of a permanent judgment or truth about the there-being of things has only one necessary condition—the unity and universality of mental activity. The immutable identity of the epistemological subject is the most fundamental supposition of the Kantian scheme. Like the Cartesian certainty of the "I-ness" of the individual's own operations, Kant's transcendental ego, as the overarching unity of self-consciousness, resolves the requirement that, for the subject to attain experience or knowledge about the world, this subject has to be aware of such experience or knowledge as its own. According to Kant, an "I think" is conjoined to all mental representations—and this "I" of consciousness, as we have seen, is unitary, active, and empty. Yet Kant rarely addresses or elaborates his assumptions about the "I think" in the way that Descartes explicates his formulation of the substantival ego. It is left to Fichte (1794, *et alia*) to develop a theory of knowledge on the basis of an explicit philosophy of the self-positing subject.

In subsequent epistemological formulations, formal structures increasingly substitute for the "ego" as the locus of the knower. Kant's attempt to determine a fixed and final epistemological scheme issues into increasingly codified logical empiricist formulations, rendering the contemplative "subject" more abstract. With the growing influence of the mathematical ideal, in which nature is to be revealed by superimposition of a system of logical rules and categories, the system itself begins to eclipse the subjectivity of the human subject. As György Lukács (1923) argues in his critique of formalism:

> The ideal of knowledge represented by the purely distilled formal conception of the object of knowledge, the mathematical organization and the ideal of necessary natural laws all transform knowledge more and more into the systematic and conscious contemplation of those purely formal conceptions, those 'laws' which function in—objective—reality *without the intervention of the subject*. . . . [This contemplative tendency serves] to drive a wedge between the subject of knowledge and 'man,' and to transform the knower into a pure and purely formal subject. [p. 128]

In contemporary epistemology, less is said about the knower as the humanity of psychic reality, and more about the supra-individual system of naturalistic science—the conventions of methodology, the corporate establishment of research activities, the mathematical model of explanation and certitude, the determinative quality of "paradigms," and the pregiven structure of rational theorizing. Whether the epistemological subject is characterized as empirical ego, transcendental ego, or formalized system of rationality, the point is that all such formulations assume that the subject of knowledge is directly and immediately known to itself and hence can be taken as an absolutely secure methodological starting point, as an agent of objective knowledge itself, immune from doubt. Crudely, one could rephrase the assumption as the unassailability of the agent's recognition of its activity as its own, for this is, in brief, the legacy of the Cartesian *cogito*.

We may now ask whether, in the framework of such naturalistic epistemologies, the Freudian discovery of the repressed unconscious could be the discovery of an aspect or phase of the self-consciousness of the Cartesian knowing subject. If I seem to be reiterating this issue, it is because so many post-Freudian psychologists, ignoring the import of repression, have tried to view psychoanalysis from within the tradition of the *ego cogito*. They have thus slid into a prepsychoanalytic doctrine of the noncontradictory subject of personal mentation. Yet, if one takes Freud's quintessential notion of repression seriously, it is not hard to detect the flaw in the attempt to locate the Freudian unconscious within the unity of a Cartesian self-consciousness. Again, following Descartes, subjectivistic and objectivistic doctrines take the necessary first condition of any experience or understanding as some subject's capacity to recognize this experience or understanding as part of its own activity, and this belongingness of mentation is taken as self-evident. For Freud, however, it is precisely the character of unconscious mental contents that the reflective "I" of conscious and preconscious mentation exiles these repressed ideas, wishes, and fantasies beyond its bounds. Whatever their status after psychoanalytic interrogation, repressed contents as such, even when "returning" to consciousness in the disguised, disruptive form of polysemous contradiction, are not recognized by this domain as part of its own activity.

Indeed, Freud adopts the dynamic imagery of force and space precisely in order to emphasize that these contents keep "apart from consciousness in spite of their intensity" (1912, p. 262), that the repressed unconscious is not the realm of "latent" contents proprietarily retrievable by the "I" of reflective awareness (cf. 1915b, 1915c, 1916–1917). He writes of "a foreconscious activity passing into consciousness with no difficulty, and an unconscious activity which remains so and seems to be cut off from consciousness" (1912, p. 263, italics omitted), and he attacks Pierre Janet's use of the term "unconscious" for merely unnoticed or foreconscious psychic activity as a vacuous *manière de parler* (1923b, 1925a). Freud never ceases to emphasize the distinction between the repressed unconscious and those contents that are recognized by the "I" as its own. Even in his major metapsychological text, *Das Ich und das Es* (1923a), he argues that "the psychic distinction between conscious and unconscious is the fundamental psychoanalytic postulate . . . psychoanalysis cannot locate psychic reality within consciousness but has to regard consciousness as a quality of the psychic which may be present, as with other qualities, or may be absent" (p. 239). Insisting that unconscious mental processes may have effects like conscious ones without ever becoming conscious, he differentiates this unconscious activity from the latency of "that which is able to become conscious at any time"((p. 240, italics omitted), for "we acquire our notion of the unconscious from the doctrine of repression" (p. 241).

Freud adamantly dismisses the idea that repressed activity may be equated with a mere "shading in the clarity of consciousness" (p. 242n). Refuting "such an assimilation of the unnoticed and the unconscious," he points out "firstly that it is very hard and requires a great struggle to bring enough concentration to bear upon such an unnoticed content, and secondly, even if this were to be achieved, the previously unnoticed content is not recognized by consciousness, but frequently seems entirely alien, and, appearing antithetical [*gegensätzlich*], it is abruptly disavowed by consciousness" (p. 243n). Here we might note that customarily an unconscious content can only become conscious on the condition of its negation, denial, or contradiction (see Freud, 1925b). What Freud calls "foreconscious activity"—the latent, potentially retrievable preconscious—could be said to fall within the reflectivity of the Cartesian mind, for its contents are owned by the conscious "I," as are, for instance, mnemonic representations. In contrast, the repressed unconscious, although psychic, is disavowed. And here we might note that, in a certain sense, Freud's psychology is concerned not so much with apparent pellucidity as with the opaque contradictions constituted by repressive processes.

In sum, we see that Freud's distinctive notion of repression—as the expulsion of certain psychic contents from the domain of conscious, nonconscious, and preconscious mentation—implies that the ideas, wishes, and fantasies of the unconscious are alien to the "I-ness" of this domain; are not admitted as part of its own activity; and hence do not fall within the unity of a Cartesian self-consciousness. Even the disruptive return of the repressed contents, as memory gaps, slips, symptoms, and characterological formations, does not fall within the

Cartesian scheme. For these polysemous contradictions are not possessed by the conscious "I," nor are they recognized by this "I-ness" as such. Rather, they are regarded, so to speak, as aberrations within itself, the concealed wishful purpose of which is entirely opaque. The return of the repressed is alien to self-consciousness, and is, to be schematic, experienced by the "I" not as its own activity but as something being done to itself while not part of itself. Freud's discovery of the return of the repressed, which proceeds by a reflective interrogation, thus *dis*confirms Descartes' fundamental belief in the automatic veracity and pellucidity of reflection in consciousness. There is no sense in which the repressed unconscious can be construed as an aspect or phase of the Cartesian mind, of an apodictic and adequate subjectivity immediately, directly, and validly known to itself.

Beyond this demonstration that Freud's discovery of the unconscious cannot be construed as conforming to the definition of Cartesian self-consciousness lies a more radical proposition—that psychoanalytic discourse actually subverts the presuppositional foundation of the entire Cartesian tradition. The present task is merely to demonstrate what Freud's psychology is not, and only later will this iconoclastic theme be elaborated. Nevertheless, one or two points should be mentioned now. For, in a certain sense, the discovery of repressed psychic activity implies the falsity of prepsychoanalytic self-consciousness, and hence impugns the self-certainty of subjectivity in the finite "ego"— perhaps vindicating that *malin génie* who leaves nothing immune from doubt. Descartes founds his epistemology on the allegedly unmediated and hence adequate datum of reflective consciousness, employing the *cogito* not just as a procedure for ascertaining the existence of one's own thoughts, but as an assertion of the validity of direct and immediate acquaintance by consciousness. He thus proceeds inferentially from the assumed security of the subject's recognition of its own activity as transparent to itself. In opposition, Freud argues that conscious experience and understanding are *not* unmediated, univocal, or self-subsistent, but depend on a more extensive, "essential" and "original" psychic reality that is unconscious (see 1900, 1901a). Psychoanalysis determines that the knowledge achieved by the "I" of consciousness is at best partial and tenuous (1923a, 1925b), and that the veracity of the subject's prepsychoanalytic reflections is ubiquitously distorted and deformed by the opacities and fixities of polysemous contradiction (1896, 1916–1917).

In sum, whereas the Cartesian tradition requires the immutable assurance of a subject, employing the assumed certainty of its acquaintance of itself affirmatively as the secure foundation for all objective knowledge, psychoanalysis treats this subject with suspicion and thus opposes both the transcendental unity of self-consciousness and the apodictic givenness of the *ego cogito*. The very "truth" that is the starting point for Descartes—the truth of self-consciousness as it attains immediately and directly to itself—is shown to be partial, negated and sublated in the movement of psychoanalytic discourse. For the moment, however, we need proceed no further than the conclusion that the repressed unconscious, if it is as Freud claims, cannot be located within the self-consciousness of the knowing subject as prescribed by "analytic" epistemology. Indeed, as will be shown, to try to apprehend the notion of the psychoanalytic unconscious in this way unavoidably erases the repressed in favor of the merely unnoticed, making for a metatheoretical and metascientific regression to a pre-Freudian philosophy of consciousness.

NOTES ON PSYCHOANALYSIS AND TRANSCENDENTAL SUBJECTIVISM ("PHENOMENOLOGY")

As just indicated, psychoanalytic interrogation calls into question the pellucidity and veracity that are affirmatively claimed for the reflectivity of the conscious subject by the Cartesian tradition. Against Cartesian meditations, psychoanalysis bears upon the opacity, partiality, and falsity of experience and understanding in the conscious-preconscious domain, treating its subject negatively in order to reveal and reinstate what this domain conceals in its distortions and deformations. In this sense, psychoanalysis is a changeful inquiry upon the repressed unconscious, which is not discoverable by the affirmative reflections of Cartesian method.

Here we must go further into the whole issue of subjectivistic methodology, and its subversion by psychoanalytic interrogation. Having introduced an argument concerning Freud's break with the Cartesian view of the subject, we can now open up the more far-reaching question of "phenomenology" in relation to the discourse of patient and psychoanalyst.

As the term crossed the Atlantic, "phenomenology" acquired a vitiated usage, in which it has come to connote any procedure that is subjectively or intersubjectively descriptive. My use of the term here, however, is in the rigorous sense intended by Freud's contemporary, Edmund Husserl. His "phenomenological science" may be regarded as transcendental subjectivism: a methodology purporting to deepen and extend Cartesian reflection upon the subject of experience and understanding. A brief review of the Husserlian endeavor will thus lead us into a more powerful and precise comprehension of the transgressions and indiscretions of psychoanalytic methodology.

Husserl's philosophy—particularly as expressed in his later works, written as prolegomena to "phenomenological science"—is a response to the "crisis" imputed to natural-science objectivism. Husserl attributes this "crisis" to the legacy of the scientific ideal associated with the Renaissance: the twin triumphs of the Galilean mathematicization of nature and the generalization of Euclidean geometry into a formal and universally applicable mathematics. As we saw in Chapter 1, the advances of naturalistic knowledge that follow from these historic triumphs depend on the "naive" positing of the world of objects—on unarticulated suppositions about the pregiveness of experience in observed facticity and on an implicit assumption of the preconstitution of abstract forms as the criteria of "reality." Husserl, however, neither denies nor diminishes the significance and impressive achievements of the natural-science discipline. For him, the "crisis" of this naive objectivism is not a failure to produce an understanding of the natural world, but a failure to recognize the one-sidedness of this understanding, insofar as its objectivistic achievements obscure the character of this object world as a work of the subjective. In this way, according to Husserl, the naturalistic discipline comes to lose its meaning for humanity, promoting a kind of pseudo-rationality which can say nothing about the creative subject.

For Husserl, then, there is a "crisis" of objectivism because the mathematicized categorization that is the mainspring of post-Renaissance science eclipses the concrete experience of the constitution of the categorized object. That is, it eclipses the subjective, precategorical foundation of the pregiveness that is naively experienced within the natural attitude, and in this manner the meaningfulness of the objectivated world is lost. Truth cannot remain with objectivism but must move beyond and behind this attitude. To Husserl, this implies the need for a method that surpasses naturalism to arrive at the subjectivity that constitutes the pregivenness of objective experience. His aim, therefore, is to promulgate a rigorous, scientific inquiry by which the meaning beneath the natural experience of things objectivated may be revealed. And, in Husserl's opinion, the method that represents these ideas in opposition to objectivism is the prerogative of transcendental philosophy (cf. Husserl, 1929, 1935).

Unlike certain of his followers, notably the phenomenological existentialists, Husserl never suggests that the problem of objectivistic knowledge is insolubly grounded in the very nature of existence. Rather, he argues that the one-sidedness of the natural attitude can be resolved through a deepening of the reflective maneuvers of transcendental method. Husserl places himself in the tradition of Descartes and Kant, proposing that their programmatic turn toward the subjective conditions of objective knowledge must be extended.

Descartes—the "originator of the transcendental motif," who represents the initial philosophical response to the objectivism of Renaissance science—exercises a particular fascination for Husserl, because Cartesian method "begins anew" by reflecting upon the priority of the subjective in establishing certainty of knowledge about objects. Phenomenology is conceived as a radicalization of this project. Descartes' method of doubt did not allow him naively to assume the validity of the objective world as given in experience, and thus he sought, in the subject, a self-certain starting point upon which all knowledge of objects could be predicated. Husserl, however, argues that Descartes failed to realize the full implications of this transcendental turn toward the subjective foundation of objective experience, for the Cartesian doubt that arrives at the *cogito* as transcendental subject should thereby have put an end to all objective externality (see 1935, pp. 73–84). Instead of proceeding in the direction of interiority, Descartes took the apodicticity of this immediate subject as the starting point for a series of deductions and intuitions which, with the aid of divine veracity, move from the *res cogitans* to an affirmation of the preconstituted existence of objective nature. Thus, Descartes announced transcendental method but failed to use it to the full. As Husserl points out, in this sense, Descartes relinquished the significance of transcendental subjectivism, remaining imprisoned in the naive presumptions of Renaissance science.

Somewhat similarly, Kantian epistemology prefigures Husserl's project, for it contains an implicit phenomenology, even though Kant's formulation curtails the Husserlian inquiry. Unlike Husserl's endeavor, Kant's reflection upon the subjective conditions of natural understanding is not an unrestrained return to the *ego cogito* so much as a determination of forms and categories that are, so to speak, the "objective moment of subjectivity." In his *Critique* (1787), Kant aimed to specify the validity of objective consciousness by an epistemology of phenomenality, in which the ontological intentions were evident in the manner Kant envisaged limits to the possible conditions of phenomena. Husserl, however, foregoes this ontological aspect of phenomena, aspiring to an "egology"—that is, to a full description of subjectivity that seeks the origin of the world of objects insofar as it is constituted by the "ego." He is looking for a method in which the subject may be freed from the natural attitude to discover the way in which it is itself the foundation of its experiences and understandings of the world. Thus, from Husserl's viewpoint, the full significance of Kant's disclosure of the transcendental constitution of the world of objects is prevented by his positing the metaphysical thing-in-itself. In this sense, Husserl contends that the Kantian inquiry remains immured in an objectivistic rationalism, one that precludes a more complete realization of the transcendental aim to reveal the subjectivity behind the constitution of naturalistic experience. Husserl's project therefore attempts to extend the Cartesain program into that interiority which Descartes foreclosed and which Kant never sufficiently recovered—the interiority of the constitutive subject.

Throughout his early works, Husserl tries to break with the naive objectivism of the natural attitude, but remains, in many respects, bound by the neo-Kantanian philosophy of the late nineteenth century. It is the designation of the subject as an intentional pole—regarding phenomena as objects of intentional acts with subjective consciousness as their origin and medium—that guides Husserl toward his particular methodological innovation. This approach, which is advanced in several essays and lectures leading up to the *Cartesian Meditations* (1929), is somewhat influenced by Brentano's doctrine of intentionality. It points to the originative *Lebenswelt* of the subject as the bearer of meanings that are anterior to the givenness of the natural world. Phenomena are hence to be considered "essences," that is, aspects of objects-as-intended by the subject.

To circumvent naturalism and surmount the "crisis" of objectivistic epistemology, Husserl seeks a method both transcendental and reflective: a method for the inspection or intuition of these essences in a "purified consciousness," arriving at the essential structure of a subjectivity released from the suppositions of the natural attitude. Now, in writing of this subjectivity as constitutive, Husserl does not, of course, suggest that the subject comprises or creates the being of those things rendered as objects in any metaphysical sense, but that it is the originative ground of the knowability of these objects. Indeed, the Husserlian project deals with "real" as well as "possible" essences, treating the "factual" as an exemplification of some essential structure. That is, the proposed method must hold in abeyance the fact world as such, requiring no assertions about real existences. The apophantic and factual existent is relinquished in the turn toward the sphere of precategorical or prepredicative experience. Husserl identifies his project as an *egology without ontology*, for he aspires to a "universal

science of the how," a discipline that is able to investigate the "ultimate foundations" or "original meaning structure" of the subject's experience of the world.

The method sought is to be without presuppositions, setting aside
belief in the world with the goal of attaining some ultimate and original
"evidence," in line with the ambition of first philosophies. Of course,
Husserl would not be interested in seeking such a method were it not
for the anticipation that the subject investigated would prove to be the
true ground of all knowledge, but this anticipation is not equivalent to
a presupposition upon which the method depends. If Husserl's project
is the exposition of a first method, it must also comprise a perennial
and universally applicable method, for the return to origins has to be
undertaken again by each particular subject. The discipline it involves
is, by the very character of its intent, always obliged to reconsider its
project, never achieving a fixed and final formulation. In other words,
Husserl's project is a method rather than a doctrine.

The initial and principal feature of phenomenological method is its
effort to suspend the beliefs of the natural attitude and thus move
toward the sphere of constitutive subjectivity. A novel and rigorous
"science" of knowing is to be established gradually by means of successive steps that appear as suspensions of judgment. The first of these
must suspend the preconstituted suppositions of objectivism,
"bracketing" the general thesis of the world posited by the natural
attitude. This maneuver, in which natural beliefs about the givenness
of the world of objects are held in abeyance, is named the technique of
phenomenological "reduction" or *epoché*. Indeed, it is frequently, although controversially, claimed that the major achievement of
phenomenological method is that, by means of this reductive technique, it elevates the investigation of things as they appear in consciousness to the status of a philosophical science. Reputedly, the
successive steps of suspension institute a new nonnaturalistic method
for the inspection or intuition of the scope and structure of the knowing
consciousness. For the injunction that directs these steps is progressively to bracket or set aside all assertions that cannot be ascertained
by direct appeal to immanent consciousness.

Several types of reduction can be found in Husserl's work, and here
we should note two general levels: the eidetic and the transcendental.
The eidetic reduction is a more or less explicitly psychological technique, employing the subject's capacity for free variation in imagination. By such variation, facticity is irrealized, that is, the perceived
existent is deliberately divested of its actuality (e.g., its spatial and
temporal determinations) so that consciousness may turn from the

ordinary fact of perception to the essential structure of the perceiving consciousness. This irreality, resulting from a preliminary suspension of the pregiven, discloses the subjective dimension of mundane experience, through the reflective inspection or intuition of essences. In its application, then, the eidetic technique discriminates an essentialist from a merely empirical psychology of consciousness, because, or so it is claimed, in relinquishing the immediately given, consciousness begins to "grasp" the essential character of its cognitions. In this sense, the eidetic technique is a move from mere description to inquiry. From this beginning, the transcendental reduction treats this essence as an exemplar of transcendental subjectivity. Here the technique approaches the *Lebenswelt* as the "realm of original self-evidences," in which consciousness "grasps" its originative intentionality, implying the further reflective inspection or intuition of what Husserl (1923, 1929) now calls "pure consciousness in its own absolute being."

According to Husserl, absolute consciousness is what remains after the progressive nullification of the world by the phenomenological method. The *epoché* supposedly arrives at the "residual" subjectivity of "original self-experience," which represents the genesis of "being for meaning." In this sense, the method attempts the recursion of consciousness on its own being. Reputedly, the techniques of reduction effect a movement from the naive to the apodictic—that is, from the beliefs of the natural attitude to self-revelation of the constitutive intentionality of self-consciousness, from the natural thesis positing the world to the "purified consciousness" of "original self-experience."

The phenomenological sphere thus attained cannot be understood in naturalistic terms, nor apprehended by a mundane logic, nor even "communicated" in ordinary or any other language. Of course, such claims about the attainments of phenomenological method raise problems and paradoxes, prohibiting any attempt to apprehend the method externally. Nevertheless, the reduction does not enter a previously unconceived sphere, for it is not itself a construction—nor a deconstruction—but an intuition or inspection of the meaningful interiority of the *Lebenswelt* that is anterior to the mundane, factual experience of the natural world. The phenomenological method is said to be "genetic" in the sense that the suspension of the natural thesis of the world represents an inversion of this world's transcendental constitution in consciousness. According to Husserl (1929), it is a "regressive inquiry" back to the last conceivable ground in the transcendental ego. This statement does not imply that phenomenology is a procedure of ontogenetic psychology, tracing ideation back to its actual historical origination in the mind of a particular individual within the spatial and temporal framework of the natural world. Rather, it stipulates the Husserlian method's claim to investigate recursively the constitution of "given" mentation, intuiting or inspecting its essential origin. This technique may be regarded as purely philosophical insofar as, for Husserl at least, it involves the abstraction of idealized meanings disengaged from the actual historical conditions of the individual and from the concrete historicity of psychic reality.

Yet the *eidos ego*, at which Husserl's very first steps of reduction arrive, is not a category. Nor is it a Platonic form or the purely formal subject of a Kantian scheme. Rather, it is a personal "I," somewhat similar to the Cartesian *ego cogito*. Its concreteness lies in its ontological status as a "communally grounded reality." At the same time the "I" that carries out the bracketing of the pregiven world, in order to return to "things themselves" in some essential form, is itself excluded from the procedure. Thus, according to Husserl, it approaches its own apodicticity and, indeed, itself as transcendentally constitutive. In this way, even the initial steps of reduction presage the sphere of transcendental subjectivity—the domain of certain and first being—within which all objectivity is constituted.

As Husserl proceeds—and this progression is most evident in his *Cartesian Meditations* (1929), which provide a bridge between his earlier work and the radical reworking in the lectures given during his last years of life—the method that claims to lose the world via reduction, in order to refind it later in the sphere of a universal "self-consciousness," is elaborated. Against the Kantian construction, Husserl's phenomena have no noumena; there is nothing, so to speak, "behind" them. Yet, despite the tension between idealism and realism that is maintained throughout the Husserlian enterprise—and despite the consistent decision in favor of idealism, to the point where Husserl must pass through the deepest solipsism—phenomenology does not purport a denial of the there-being of "external reality." Rather, it offers a methodological procedure that effectively disontologizes this reality.

With the *Cartesian Meditations*, phenomenology is explicitly identified as an egology without ontology. Phenomena are treated as essences, and ontology is concomitantly renounced as, through the reduction, the "for the I" becomes "from the I"—through the successive steps of bracketing, the world no longer appears as "for the I" but is seen as drawing all its knowable status "from the I." The sphere of a constitutive transcendental subjectivity is allegedly approached. In this sense, the movement of reflection from natural to phenomenological attitudes, along with the deepening of phenomenological procedure toward pure egology, entails, if not so much a shift in the subject's position within its reality, then certainly an alteration in that subject's stance toward its reality. This methodological alteration of attitude relinquishes the world as given, taking it instead as the subject's transcendental correlate. Yet, as we shall later see, Husserl continues to assert an isomorphism between findings in the sphere of the transcendentally reduced and those in the world of the natural attitude. It is not that the thematized concern of phenomenology should be regarded as with the world on one side and with transcendental subjectivity on the other. Rather, its concern is with "the world's becoming in the constitution of transcendental subjectivity." With the *Cartesian Meditations*, then, Husserl's enterprise becomes unconstrainedly egological, aiming sequentially and comprehensively at "the explication of the self and of its self-constitution, of the Other, of the objective world, and of communities of persons."

It can be seen that initially Husserl retraces, through the procedure of reduction, Descartes' path, proceeding toward that transcendental subjectivity within which objective experience is precategorically constituted—the subjective source of objectivity. Yet, it is also evident that the Cartesian program is extended in phenomenology. Against Descartes, what follows from the *ego cogito* is, for Husserl, still within it. Whereas Descartes introduces divinity to found the natural world and validate the subject's experiences and understandings of it, Husserl radicalizes the Cartesian position by proceeding further with a methodology that claims to reveal the transcendental subject. Indeed, a shift in Husserl's writing from Cartesian to Leibnizian terminology marks the "triumph" of interiority over exteriority in his philosophical development.

The phenomenological method claims to arrive at the pure consciousness of an "ego" that is fundamental, an original *Ur-Ich* comprising the transcendental subjectivity upon which the objectivity of world experience is founded. As has already been suggested, this claim depends critically on the notion of the intentionality of the subjective. Husserlian intentionality implies that designating or bestowing meaning is the first act of "consciousness." Consciousness is necessarily consciousness of something, and hence its primordial function lies in the "constitutive ego's" empty act of signifying. Although Husserl employs the word "consciousness" with several connotations—as the immanent phenomenological unity of the "empirical ego's" experiences and understandings, and as an inner becoming aware of one's own psychic experiences and understandings—it may generally be taken as a comprehensive term for all kinds of psychic acts or intentional experiences. When spoken of as transcendental, however, it stands for that pure egological sphere wherein objective experience is constituted through the inherent intentionality of the subject's consciousness. The phenomenological reduction of world experience to the constitutive egological sphere, to a pure, autonomous, anonymously functioning, and universal subjectivity, or self-consciousness, inevitably raises serious philosophical problems with regard to temporality or historicity, and to the existence of the "Other." It is these questions that instigate a final shift in Husserl's writings, notably between his *Cartesian Meditations* (1929) and his lectures on *The Crisis of European Sciences* (1935).

In his methodological radicalization of the Cartesian program, Husserl undertakes to enter and emerge from the depths of transcendental solipsism. This struggle to pass methodically through solipsism is manifested by the introduction of intersubjectivity to the *cogito* philosophy of his earlier writings. Having proceeded beyond Descartes through a Leibnizian reduction to the monadic life of the "ego," Husserl encounters two major problems. First is the difficulty created by the actuality of history in view of the assertion of the ego as fundamental and original in the constitution of the knowable world. If one arrives at transcendental subjectivity as founding all being, how can one adequately account for the historicity of experience and understanding? A second, parallel difficulty issues from the Leibnizian shift, which is that of the Other. When Husserl commits himself to following the reduction to the end—to an arrival at some ultimate ground of the world experience of self-consciousness—the originality and specificity of the experience of the Other must still be reconciled. If the ambition toward a science of the *Lebenswelt*, as the ground of all precategorical experience, is to be realized, then the structures of the "ego pole" must be investigated within the context of intermonadic and intersubjective life.

To resolve these difficulties, Husserl seems to distinguish the unique transcendental ego of self-consciousness from the ego as one and many in the foundation of precategorical life experience. He broaches intermonadology by initially asserting—perhaps under the influence of Dilthey, but in opposition to Heidegger and, for that matter, to the later work of Lacan—empathy as a primordial function. Husserl (1929) introduces the notion of the *Paarung* of the *Ur-Ich* as "self-evident ego" and as the more obscure but also fundamental structure of the "alter ego." The latter is then used by Husserl as a way out of the solipsism of the *ego cogito*, in much the same manner that Descartes uses the assumption of divinity. Thus, Husserlian phenomenology moves toward the revelation of an intersubjective foundation for objectivity. Husserl proceeds to explicate the constitution of the Other by way of three stages of "analogical" apprehension: grasping the Other as other through the primordial function of empathy and through a disquisition on the relations between *Lieb* and *Korper*, the "interlacing" of the owned and the physical body (see 1923); grasping the constitution of the objective world as shared by all subjects; and grasping thence the constitution of communities and histories. In this way, a methodical progression from solipsism to community is articulated. Husserl's final thesis—expounded in the *Crisis* (1935)—then advances *sociality* as the ground of all experience and understanding—a sociality that has been apprehended by way of the methodology of egological reduction.

We have now outlined Husserl's phenomenological enterprise. Briefly, leaving aside his earliest explorations in the descriptive phenomenology of empirical consciousness, Husserl initially attempts to inaugurate a transcendental phenomenology of "pure consciousness"—the investigation of a supposedly universal subjectivity comprising invariant structures of consciousness held to be the ground of all world experience. Through the reductive procedure, the individual's own experiences and understandings are deployed to arrive at a transcendental ego, at an "anonymously functioning subjectivity" that constitutes the object of experience and understanding as from itself. By the later sections of the *Cartesian Meditations*, however, Husserl relinquishes this reduction to the monadic life of the ego, recognizing that his procedures cannot refer solely to the experiencing subject. By an analysis of the experience of the Other, intersubjectivity becomes the ground of all meaning. Then, because intersubjectivity manifests itself historically, sociality becomes the foundation of world experience. The *Lebenswelt* to be investigated is shared, and thus the subject seems to be relocated within the constitutive context of its historical and sociocultural determinations. Yet, whatever the shifts in Husserl's philosophy, his method of *reduction* is underlying. It is this rigorous suspension of the naiveté that accepts the givenness of things, in order for the foundation of human consciousness eventually to be investigated and ascertained anew, that animates the Husserlian enterprise.

Before we bring this enterprise into confrontation with the claims of psychoanalytic discourse, certain difficulties in the reading of Husserl's work may be useful to note. Even if the shifts in his philosophy could generously be interpreted as comprising a cogent and uniform trajectory, certain serious, unresolved problems in his methodological thesis remain. These problems present themselves as internal inconsistencies—or, more charitably, as paradoxes without evident means of resolution—and they are symptomatized in Husserl's presentation of his writings as a series of prolegomena.

One problem concerns the findings of objectivistic investigation and their status following phenomenological procedure. On one side, Husserl, the trenchant critic of naive objectivism and of the crisis of contemporary naturalistic sciences, develops phenomenology as the fundamental science of knowing, seeming to undermine the hegemony of scientistic objectivity by investigating the scaffolding of the natural attitude. The point of his endeavor is "not to secure objectivity but to understand it" (1935, p. 189), and this is neither objectivistic nor mundane, for it indicts the "transcendental naiveté" of philosophies that uphold such objectivistic or mundane experience. Indeed, arriving at the "pregivenness of the world as such," Husserl informs us, can be accomplished "only through a *total change* of the natural attitude" (p. 148).

Yet, on the other side, Husserl (1935) suggests that—because "knowledge of the objective-scientific world is 'grounded' in the self-evidence of the life-world" (p. 130)—there will be an isomorphism or correlation between findings in the world of the natural attitude and those in the sphere of the transcendentally reduced. He indicates that, after the procedure of bracketing, although the "old naiveté" can never be regained, some sort of nonnaive but reaffirmative return to naturalism may be possible. Implied is a certain direct and harmonious "parallelism" between the outcome of phenomenological inquiries and the understanding held by the prephenomenological consciousness experiencing objects within the naiveté of the natural attitude—as well as a concordance of intentional subjectivity and the preconstitutively given sphere of world experience. Husserl thus argues that, through phenomenology, the objectivated world is revealed as the "logical substructure" of the *Lebenswelt*. Accordingly, he can aspire to establish logic transcendentally, upon this categorically unmediated sphere of all experience. Husserl's, adherence to this sort of isomorphic argument invariably puts a stop to the potential for dynamic contradiction between the subjectivity and objectivity of experience and understanding. Nevertheless, it is important to recognize that the alleged correlative cross-reference, between the objectivity of the natural attitude and the revelations of phenomenology, remains, for Husserl, an admitted and considerable "enigma."

A further problem in Husserl's work, already briefly mentioned, is that of historicity. Paul Ricoeur (1967) has called attention to the inevi-

table opposition of transcendental philosophy to historical considerations. As indicated, a methodology that aims to arrive at some ultimate
transcendental foundation of all experience and understanding has insuperable difficulties accounting for the historical determinations and
development of such experience and understanding. And this difficulty
is not overcome by Husserl's later emphasis on the *Lebenswelt*, as the
constitutive sociality of experience and understanding, for this emphasis does not suggest how phenomenology could apprehend the historical dimension of this constitutive sphere. Moreover, as we must
particularly note, a methodology such as Husserl's has even greater
difficulty embracing the historicity of its own mode of inquiry. The
possibility that phenomenological procedure engages itself, with its
subject, in a historicized movement of investigation with metamorphic
implications, is myopically denied by the asserted disontologization of
the investigation. Husserlian methodology is left seeming to claim—
spuriously, as we shall eventually show—that it could reflect upon the
foundations of knowing while leaving them untouched.

The question we need to examine now is: Do phenomenological
methods have a transformative impact for their subject? Transcendental subjectivity, as the constitutive source of world experience
or the *Lebenswelt*, is not regarded as a philosophical construction, but
as intuitable in principle. It is revealed by phenomenological investigation, which supposedly shows not only that it is the ground of objectivity, but also that objective experience is somehow its isomorphic
substructure. To repeat our question: Does this investigative methodology itself have any significant metamorphic effect on its subject,
either in the sense that the procedure transforms the character of its
subject, or in the sense that it empowers the subject to act transformatively upon the world? Because the reduction reputedly makes the
world freely available for us, it has been suggested that
phenomenological methodology must imply possibilities for praxis: a
procedure from which a reconstructing of the world through a return
to the subject, and a remaking of ourselves refound as the creative
source of experience and understanding of the world, might at least
embark. Herein lies the appeal of Husserl's later writings, in particular for more recent work by "phenomenological Marxists." Yet, in this
respect, one again encounters certain problems in Husserl's pronouncements about his doctrine; the proposed implication of
phenomenology for praxis seems at best a tenuous and equivocal extension of his thought.

Despite Husserl's self-proclaimed "radicalism" and his attack on the
naiveté of objectivism, it can be argued that the project of "beginning

anew" remains thematically and concretely undeveloped in his work. The *epoché*, for instance, is billed as a "complete personal trans-formation" for the subject, altering its stance toward reality, with the "for the subject" becoming "from the subject." Phenomenological in-sights, according to Husserl (1935), entail a "radical reshaping of our whole way of looking at the world." Yet the results of the *epoché* are not an interpretation of the world or an action upon it, but a "standing *above*" the world. Husserl insists that his procedure places the phenomenologist above participation in concrete interests and, indeed, above theoretically or practically oriented knowledge about the being or nonbeing of the world (see 1935, pp. 174–178). Thus, for example, the "validities" suspended by the *epoché* remain unchanged such that the methodological procedure can be "actualized again and again, at different times, in this identical sense." Although Husserl argues that this does not amount to "a meaningless, habitual absention," it is an absention nonetheless.

Moreover, it can be said that, necessarily, a transcendental return to a universal and anonymously functioning subjectivity that is con-stitutive of world experience—a return that brackets the world to investigate the supposedly invariant structures of a "pure conscious-ness"—provides as little concession to the concrete individual subject's capacity to act within and upon its world, as it does to the historicity of the bracketed experience of objects. Even Husserl's analysis of inter-subjectivity as the level upon which objectivity is constituted, with his eventual arrival at sociality as the ground of meaning, provides little or no scope for the particular subject to reinterpret or otherwise act upon this sociality by and within which it is constituted. Disavowing ontology, Husserl's phenomenology supposes the subject could investi-gate itself, or its foundation of world experience, contemplatively, without the investigation entailing a historicized praxis of formation and transformation. In other words, Husserl's methodology assumes that it is possible to arrive at a ground of experience and understand-ing without disabusing the privileges that false self-consciousness claims for itself. This supposition, as we shall see, is thoroughly dis-credited by the discourse of the repressed unconscious.

The question of transformation leads us to a final major problem in Husserl's writings—namely, the "paradox," as Husserl guilelessly calls it, between intentionality and intersubjectivity. As indicated, the earlier writings proclaim the phenomenological return to tran-scendental origins, referred to as the constitutive and intentional "ego pole," whereas the later writings, following the development of an analysis of the experience of the Other, emphasize the function of the

Lebenswelt in the constitution of meaning. Still, throughout the Husserlian project, the accomplishment of subjectivity is taken to be concordant or even identical with the communalization of experience and understanding. Phenomenology deploys, so to speak, the individual's subjectivity in order to arrive at some general and allegedly invariant structure, such as that designated by the notions of the *Lebenswelt* or the "pure consciousness" of a transcendental ego. Thus, the methodology requires the universality of the mental life of the particular subject.

In Husserl's earlier writings, it seems to be simply presumed that, whereas the methodology of reduction leads to the apodicticity of the absolutely single ego, this apodicticity must necessarily hold universally. In his later work, however, the presumption takes on greater weight, for Husserl comes to speak of the bracketing of subjectivity as leading to "transcendental intersubjectivity" or "transcendental communalization" as the universal foundation of all world experience and understanding. Here Husserl is obliged to discuss what he terms "the paradox of human subjectivity"—namely, that of "being a subject for the world and simultaneously an object in the world," of arriving at the single, individual "ego pole" as well as the communalized unity of multiple subjectivities as the constitutive ground of objective experience (1935, pp. 103–189). Husserl admits that "everything becomes complicated as soon as we consider that *subjectivity is what it is . . .* an ego functioning constitutively . . . *only within intersubjectivity*" (p. 172, my italics). But it can be argued that he fails to confront the gravity of these "complications." To my mind, his very manner of posing the question of subject and sociality predefines a simplistic, anti-dialectical, and thoroughly false "resolution" to the "paradox." From the viewpoint of Freudian discourse, his methodological procedure forecloses what psychoanalysis reveals—the alienation precipitated dynamically in mental life of an intentional or desirous, repressed subjectivity and a preconstituted intersubjectivity given in the sociocultural system of representations.

Husserl's "resolution" to this "paradox of human subjectivity" asserts that "as primal ego, I constitute my horizon of transcendental others as cosubjects within the transcendental intersubjectivity which constitutes the world" (1935, p. 184). In other words, the "total intentional accomplishment" of phenomenological investigation attains a subjectivity that is the subjectivity not only of the isolated subject, but also of an entire intersubjectivity that constitutes "what is." Hereafter the "individual ego pole," since its "subjectivity is what it is . . . only within intersubjectivity," is not of so much interest, except as the unavoidable entry point by which phenomenology can "methodically exhibit transcendental intersubjectivity and its transcendental communalization" (see pp. 178–186). The coherence of the entire methodological enterprise comes to rest on this presumption—conveniently but spuriously dressed as an investigative discovery—that the intentionality of the individual "ego pole" is essentially and necessarily concordant with the constitutive function of the intersubjective nexus. As we shall see, this presumption represents an ideology of identitarianism.

Husserl's thesis is that the objective world is somehow founded as syntheses, which are the overlapping intentionalities of multiple subjects forming a transcendental communalized unity. On a psychological level, the individual soul "stands in community with others which are intentionally interrelated, that is in a purely intentional, internally and essentially closed nexus, that of intersubjectivity" (1935, p. 238). Thus "all souls make up a single unity of intentionality . . . a unity that can be unfolded systematically through phenomenology" (p. 257). In other words, the "polar unity" of individual subjectivity is supposedly integrated within the unity of an intentional nexus comprising the "simultaneity of ego poles"—a transcendental synthesis of "I" and Other in the constitutive communalization that transcendentally founds world experiences and understandings (see 1935, pp. 235–257). But isn't this "solution" legerdemain—a false discovery brought about by procedures of inquiry that presume what they then "discover," prohibiting all other possibilities? Husserlian methodology cannot entertain the notion of a discrepancy between the subject's intentionality and the constitution of experience and understanding within the nexus of sociality. The possibility of such a discrepancy—let alone, a dynamic of contradictoriness—is methodologically ignored by phenomenological "science"; its existence is denied or resisted on the presumption that it can be no more than a meaningless and insignificant remainder. Indeed, phenomenology moves systematically to suppress any negativity of the subject—in its disavowal of ontology, its affirmative stance toward the pregiven experience (which it sanctifies in the act of investigating its ground by bracketing its validity), and its impulse toward the reified unity of a supposedly transcendent identity. Husserl can admit no contradiction within the epistemological locus of contemplation. Faced with the alienation of mental life, his enterprise, its glib appearance notwithstanding, falters and fails, disingenuously unaware of the myopia it promotes and of its epistemological stasis. To confront this doctrine with Freudian claims is telling.

At the outset, bringing phenomenology into direct confrontation with the methodological claims of psychoanalytic discourse encounters a difficulty in Husserl's own vicissitudes and equivocations with regard to the psychological import of his inquiry. On the one hand, Husserl rejects psychological interests, that is, interests in the content of the particular mind. On the other hand, he views his methodology as having essential psychological implications, such that an "indissoluble inner alliance obtains between psychology and transcendental philosophy," with the former designated as "the decisive field" presaging the latter's investigations (1935, pp. 206, 203). In part, of course, these discrepant statements revolve around two different usages: "psychology" as naturalistic, and the continued use of this term, after relinquishing the objectivism of the natural attitude, in an attempt to delineate nonnaturalistic modes of inquiry upon mental processes. Yet, whereas Husserl shares with Freud a critique of the objectivisitic study of mental processes, his remarks concerning the potential of nonnaturalistic psychological discourse reveal the contrast with psychoanalytic methodology.

Renouncing his youthful interest in a psychological approach to epistemological questions, which he shared with his neo-Kantian contemporaries, Husserl developed, early in his career, a critique of such "psychologism." In this respect, the phenomenological enterprise is predicated upon the tenet that questions of conceptual understanding are not to be studied as psychological events, but as general issues about representation, independent of their particular expressions. In thus rejecting psychological interests, however, Husserl presumes the meaningfulness of an investigation of mental representations by methodology divorced from concrete content—an ideal that accommodates Husserl's allegation that mental contents could be left untransformed by reflection, but is indicted as chimerical by psychoanalysis. As Husserl moves from descriptive to transcendental phenomenological procedures, he slowly rehabilitates nonnaturalistic psychology, by which he means a purely descriptive account of mental contents, and gives it a role as a precursory mode of inquiry that issues into transcendental investigation. A major portion of the *Crisis* (1935), for example, is devoted to a discussion of the "way into phenomenological transcendental philosophy" by inquiry back from the pregivenness of the *Lebenswelt*, specifically by psychological inquiry.

According to Husserl, psychological reflection—in which he includes thematic self-reflection, recollection, empathic use of another's self-apperceptions, and thematic inquiry upon society's history—remains within transcendental naiveté while at the same time its practice constitutes a thematic phase on the way toward transcendental inquiry.

Such reflection furnishes a "psychology based upon inner experiences," which is incompatible with an objectivistic "psychology" conducted within the physicalistic framework of the natural sciences. It comprises a concretely executed, descriptive discipline, viewed by Husserl as a particularly phenomenological form of empirical investigation. He argues that "in order to attain the pure and actual subject matter of the required 'descriptive psychology,' a fully consciously practiced method is required [namely] the *phenomenological-psychological reduction*" (1935, p. 236). In other words, this psychology involves not only the description of mental contents, but a stance of "disinterested spectator," acquired through an *epoché* that reveals the intentional relatedness of consciousness.

Husserl clearly suggests that such a phenomenological-psychological investigation of internal representations somehow mirrors anticipatorily the accomplishment of the transcendental attitude. He writes that "as a human being and a human soul, I first become a theme for psychophysics and psychology; but then in a new and higher dimension I become a transcendental theme" (1935, p. 205). Study of the particular mind "as an ego already made part of the world, objectified with a particular real meaning" is thus supposed to pass into Husserlian transcendental inquiry upon the meaning conferring accomplishment (p. 206). Yet it must be noted that Husserl sedulously evades specification of the relationship between the results of the phenomenological-psychological reduction and those of the transcendental reduction. Similarly, he leaves his distinction between "empirical subjectivity" and "transcendental subjectivity"—between "I" as a human "ego" in the world and "I" as a "transcendental ego" that "constitutes" the world—rather vague. It is a problematic that is, even for him, both incomprehensible and unavoidable (see 1935, pp. 198–203).

Unable to specify the methodological itinerary by which the psychological might issue into the "transcendental," Husserl jettisons the concrete content of the former. He thus precludes the possibility that a more rigorous, or better yet, a more suspicious, inquiry upon the particulars of concrete individual subjectivity might reveal the constitution of mental processes. In a sense that must now be defined, it is Husserl's transcendentalist presuppositions and preoccupations that lead him astray. The errors of his methodological claims—for example, concerning the purity of conscious subjectivity—are revealed in the demystifying methodological stringencies of psychoanalytic suspicion.

The convergence between phenomenology and psychoanalysis cannot be altogether denied—although, in my judgment, it has been grossly and misleadingly exaggerated in Maurice Merleau-Ponty's qualified claim that the two aim "towards the same latency," or in Paul Ricoeur's preamble about phenomenology as a "true approximation" of Freudian methodology. This celebrated convergence is seen in an allegedly common methodological displacement of the epistemological adequacy of immediate consciousness, that is, consciousness immured in the natural attitude. Ricoeur (1970), whose discussion of the phenomenological "approach" to the psychoanalytic field is, in certain respects, the most lucid available, enumerates four "steps" toward the Freudian unconscious adumbrated by phenomenology. He points to: phenomenology's attitude of reduction, its theme of intentionality, its concern with language, and its consideration of intersubjectivity. The latter two "steps," however, seem questionable. An explicit emphasis on the constitutive function of language and an extended theory of intersubjectivity are far more characteristic of post-Husserlian developments than of Husserl's own methodological writings. One might say that when Heidegger and later Sartre place "phenomenology" in the service of ontological theorizing, when Ricoeur promotes his so-called hermeneutic phenomenology, or when numerous twentieth-century writers turn toward language as the ground for their philosophizing, then new possibilities for a *rapprochement* with Freud's psychology are opened (see Chapter 4). But a rapprochement is not an approach, and even here the debt to Husserlian methodology is debatable. Thus, for our present purpose—an examination of Husserl's phenomenological project in relation to the claims of psychoanalytic discourse—we shall turn only to the first two of the reputed steps, namely, those concerning the phenomenological attitude and theme.

As we have seen, meaning or intentionality is the all-embracing medium of phenomenological description, and subjectivity, toward which the Husserlian enterprise turns, is understood as the bearer or progenitor of intentionality. The philosophical or psychological method of reduction is designed as the reflective technique that purportedly reveals this "being for meaning." Here we glimpse an alluring but deceptive similarity, for intentionality is equally the *sine qua non* of the psychoanalytic endeavor, and "being for meaning" seems equally the subject of psychic reality that psychoanalysis interrogates. For Husserl, however, both the theme and attitude of the proposed reflective investigation of subjectivity are predicated on a certain presumption that the constitutive intentionality or subjectivity to be revealed is primordially and essentially indigenous to the experience of consciousness. And it can be argued that this is a determinative presumption, preventing the psychoanalytic discovery that, to borrow a phrase from Theodor Adorno's (1966) critique of Husserl, the "essence" is alien to the consciousness that grasps it. This distinction between phenomenology and psychoanalytic discourse is crucial to our comprehension of the latter. The touted "convergence" of these methodologies, which highlights their reflective displacement of the immediacy of consciousness, beclouds an initial and critical divergence, for this subjective immediacy is "displaced" by these methodologies in an entirely different fashion.

Husserlian methodology has been aptly described as a repetitious movement to a presumptive starting point. The *epoché* sets aside belief in the world, and in this sense—indeed, in this sense alone—it "displaces" the immediacy of meaning in natural consciousness, proceeding reflectively, through the description of consciousness, to the supposed revelation of a pure and essential subjectivity as exemplar of the transcendental constitution of consciousness' world experience. Intentionality is elucidated, not within the immediate givenness of natural experience, but "in" the subject's consciousness that is allegedly constitutive of this experience. Thus, as Ricoeur (1970, 1974) has amply discussed, phenomenology dissociates its actual beginning in the particular immediate consciousness from its putatively true beginning in the universal consciousness of the *cogito* that is reputedly constitutive and transcendental. Husserlian phenomenology only exists upon the presupposition of this sort of "nucleus of primordial experience," that is, the ideal Cartesian starting point of the subjectivity of an originative and immutable consciousness, and it is to this sort of starting point that this methodical, reflective program continually aspires to return.

As we have seen, Husserl, in pursuing his methodological program, avoids making the mistake of confusing the apparent apodicticity of immediate consciousness with the adequacy of its knowledge, trying to take quite seriously the possibility that one is deceived, in every ontic statement that one pronounces about oneself. In this sense, Husserl's methodology does proceed beyond the naiveté of immediacy—displacing it, after a fashion—and can legitimately claim to extend the program of Cartesian meditations. In thus expatiating the philosophical tradition that upholds the prerogatives of the reflective subject of consciousness, Husserl promulgates the notion of the "passive genesis" of meaning in consciousness, a way of referring to the transcendental constitution of the activity that yields the givenness of objective experience in consciousness. Yet, whatever the diminution in the status of consciousness implied by such a notion, consciousness itself, as the means of access to the transcendental and universal from the particular and content-laden, continues to be regarded affirmatively. From its actual starting point in immediate consciousness to its supposedly true starting point in the originative subjectivity of the transcendental, phenomenology's itinerary is, so to speak, presumptively direct and concordant. The unity of the subject is preserved; its identity affirmed. Hence the potential of contradictoriness is not admitted.

However much it concedes that the self-understanding of immediate consciousness may initially be naive, the phenomenological program is grounded upon the presumption that the particular and the transcendental, the immediate and the essential, are harmoniously aligned. It thus necessarily respects the subject of immediate consciousness as its authentic point of departure, extrapolating positively but reflectively from it. Whatever phenomenology's claim to extend the philosophical program that follows from Cartesian doubt, and whatever the gravity of Husserl's notion of the "passive genesis" of meaning in consciousness, phenomenological methodology continues to share the philosophical tradition's assumption that intentionality is integral to reflective consciousness, that in consciousness, meaning and consciousness of meaning coincide. Thus, in seeking to reveal the intentionality of transcendental constitution, the first requirement, Husserl consistently argues, "is to take the conscious life, completely without prejudice, just as what it quite immediately gives itself, as itself, to be" (1935, p. 233).

Developing as a reflection upon the subject of consciousness and assuming the indigenousness of intentionality and its subject to consciousness—although purporting to reveal a "latency" beyond the mundane immediacy of the natural attitude—phenomenological procedure inevitably engages the subjectivity of consciousness in a manner that is respectful and preservative. It assumes throughout the identity of self-consciousness and its meanings. Thus, the self-evidence of direct insight, within and through consciousness' affirmative extension of itself, remains the measure of phenomenological success. Whatever the much-advertised progression beyond the immediacy of natural consciousness, this methodological procedure presumes to leave the subject of consciousness, and indeed the factuality of its knowledge, intact. Similarly, whatever depreciation of immediate consciousness is implied by the notion of "passive genesis," the phenomenologist continues to take consciousness as meaning just whatever, as consciousness, it proposes itself to mean. The underlying transcendentalist supposition—the presumed concordance or identity of the particular consciousness and its transcendental constitution—makes for a methodological stance that presumes the ontological neutrality of descriptive or reflective, "egological" procedures and that proclaims the univocality of consciousness. By committing itself to the assumption of consciousness' capacity for affirmative self-totalization, this stance forecloses the potential of polysemous contradictions that are *in* self-consciousness but not *of* its subjectivity.

If we follow the claims of psychoanalytic discovery concerning repression, the return of the repressed, and its reappropriation, then we see that phenomenological methodology remains within the bounds of that which is owned by the subject of conscious and preconscious mental contents. The phenomenological enterprise is indicted by the psychoanalytic discovery of the dynamic of repression between consciousness and the unconscious, the splitting or contradictoriness of subjectivity. This indictment may be comprehended in three ways, all of which center on the profound difference between an affirmative disquisition within the bounds of the subject of self-consciousness, a disquisition that assumes its identity as subject, and the negativity of a radical dispossession of self-consciousness that transgresses these bounds by pursuing the nonidentity of its subjectivity.

First, whereas phenomenological description and reflection affirmatively develop conscious and preconscious mentation on the supposition of concordance between its immediacy or particularity and its "essence" or transcendental source, psychoanalytic interrogation impugns such mentation as the disguise of formative desire.

Second, whereas the phenomenological treatment of consciousness and preconsciousness is an "egological" procedure that preserves the status of self-consciousness as intentional subject of the reflection, thus claiming ontological neutrality, the movement of psychoanalysis implicates both the knowing and the being of subjectivity as an "archaeology," in which it is found that self-consciousness must be disabused of the privilege it assumes for itself in order for the being of the repressed "subject" to be retrieved and rehabilitated in its desirous authenticity.

Third, and similarly, whereas phenomenology respects the appearance of apodicticity and univocality in self-consciousness, psychoanalysis apprehends self-consciousness as the condition of polysemous contradiction. It is this condition of alienation that phenomenological procedure, by ignoring the contradictoriness of self-consciousness, unwittingly endorses.

In line with the Cartesian philosophical tradition, phenomenology upholds the sanctity of the subject of reflective awareness as the authentic, unitary, and identitarian source of mental life. Its methodological reduction aims to reveal the subject's "free disposition" of itself as self-consciousness. What its premises and procedures decisively preclude is the possibility that the subject's disposition and freedom could be other than integral and identical to the consciousness that reflects upon itself. There is no possibility of an intentionality that lies, not within the sphere owned by the subject of self-consciousness, but against it. The "passive genesis" of meaning in consciousness and preconsciousness is not a notion that admits the potential of contradiction between a repressed constitutive meaning and the consciousness that describes and reflects itself. Proceeding affirmatively by "pure" description and reflection within the bounds of that which the subject of self-consciousness can possess as its own mentation, phenomenology does not and cannot move against self-consciousness in such a way as to disclose a "subject" that self-consciousness has ousted from itself. Whatever is "held in abeyance," "suspended," or "displaced" in this ontically inconsequential manner is not cast into question, rendered suspect, or transformatively dispossessed. In this respect, it is precisely wrong to suggest, as Ricoeur (1970) has done, the "homology" between the subject of phenomenological reflection and the "subject" that is mutatively reinstated in the course of psychoanalytic work—the latter is entirely antithetical to the former.

Baldly stated, Husserl's phenomenology merely extends the purview of the initial subject of natural consciousness. In contrast, Freud's psychology proclaims that, in a certain radical and dialectical sense, consciousness must be dispossessed in order for the subject to be found. That is, the polysemous contradictions of self-consciousness must be interrogated to restore a subjectivity that the subject of immediately reflective self-consciousness conceals. Phenomenology's egological investigation affirms the identical, unitary, and univocal "I-ness" of consciousness and preconsciousness, but leaves the unconscious repressed. Rather than representing a step toward the archaeology of psychoanalytic interrogation, the phenomenological enterprise simply stops short the psychoanalytic work. The shared starting point is deceptive, for phenomenological methodology ratifies a subject that, in a fundamentally metamorphic movement, psychoanalysis dispossesses. Phenomenological investigation can never even begin to apprehend the polysemy that signifies contradiction between the apparently unitary and univocal subject of egological self-consciousness and the repressed "subject," the alienated anteriority of the desirous constitution of psychic reality.

Husserl's program for "phenomenological science" has been presented and criticized in some detail here precisely because his writings, prolegomenal though they often are, comprise the most explicit and vigorous effort to extend and deepen Cartesian meditations into a thoroughgoing discipline of subjectivistic investigation. Given an interest in psychological inquiry and change, reading Husserl's philosophy proves heuristic. His phenomenology offers an immensely useful perspective from which to discuss the whole question of subjectivism, and indeed to clarify what psychoanalytic discourse is not.

Taking for granted the ontological stationariness of the dichotomy of the subject's mental activity versus the there-being of things objectivated, Husserl sets aside the pursuit of objectivistic knowledge in order to inquire upon the subjectivistic grounds of all knowing. Hence, he arrives at a disontologized egological discipline: subjectivism is a recursion of the subject of conscious and preconscious mentation upon its own being. Subjectivistic reflection, whatever its allegedly transcendental import, necessarily assumes the identity of the subject as the unitary "I-ness" of self-consciousness, and thus remains within the boundaries of its own being. From a psychoanalytic perspective, such subjectivistic methodology, "for all its backing and forthing"—to borrow Hegel's (1807, p. 29) phrase—"never moves beyond its own boundaries, but does not realize it."

Against this, psychoanalytic discourse breaks the bounds of subjectivistic knowing and being. Psychoanalysts may seem to begin their investigations with a similar procedure of "irrealization"—forsaking the apparent givenness of things in the objectivistic mode. But psychoanalytic suspicion differs radically from phenomenological suspension. The nullification of a "reduction," by which phenomenological reflection sets aside the world of objectivism, is not the negativity by which patient and psychoanalyst traverse the limit of "I-ness" via the interrogation of polysemous contradictions. Psychoanalystic inquiry moves against the subjectivistic alternative offered by the presumption of the naturalistic dichotomy. It opposes the Husserlian program of transcendental subjectivism posed as the complemental alternative to the objectivism of the dominant logical empiricist program. In sum, psychoanalytic discourse is anti-phenomenological.

Phenomenological method may issue into a palliative therapy for the insufficiencies of immediate consciousness—although in this respect the ontology of contemporary hermeneutic philosophies has more to offer (see Chapter 4). What phenomenological reflectivity utterly fails to apprehend, however, is the guile of conscious, nonconscious, and preconscious mentation—its distortions and deformations in the repression of unconscious ideas, wishes, fantasies, and the like. A phenomenological approach cannot address the contradictory locus of the subject of psychic reality; it thus forecloses the possibility of polysemous formations. That is, by affirming the identity of self-consciousness, phenomenology necessarily endorses the ideological functioning of a false identitarianism. Psychoanalytic method, by contrast, would seem to follow Hegel in demonstrating that consciousness, and its reflective subjectivity, cannot totalize itself affirmatively. The limitation of pure affirmative reflection by the "I" of conscious and preconscious mentation is that it can only grasp what already belongs to it.

As we shall see the movement of psychoanalysis indicts subjectivistic procedures as a naive attempt to transcend an alleged naiveté which is, so to speak, far from innocent. Against phenomenology's transcendental confirmation of an "I-ness" that, because of polysemous contradiction, should be sublated as false, we shall find that Freud's psychology deconstructs this inauthenticity of self-consciousness. Through an anti-phenomenological movement of negativity, it reappropriates an alienated yet intrinsically constitutive or meaningful "subject," one the phenomenologist can never come to know. Psychoanalytic discourse may well provide the answer to the phenomenological problematic of the givenness of objectivism, but it is not phenomenology, for it is neither subjectivistic nor a disontologized, ahistorical inquiry.

PSYCHOANALYTIC KNOWING
IS NOT OBJECTIVISTIC

Within the frame of "analytic" epistemology, knowedge must either be subjectivistic, grounded in the knower's own consciousness, or objectivistic, deriving from a correspondence of the knower's representational activity with the there-being of things. But where would one fit the contents of the dynamic unconscious within this frame? According to *analytische Wissenschaftheorie*, if they are not an integral but unnoticed aspect or phase of the unitary self-consciousness of the knowing subject, then they must be on the side of the "object." That is, if the repressed "subject" is not ultimately identical with the subject of consciousness, then it can only be known as a thing-in-itself rendered as an object in the subject's representational system, to which, ontically, it is irrevocably eternal. From this perspective, we must ask whether, in the discourse of patient and psychoanalyst, repressed contents are objects of knowledge in a manner concordant with the dominant "analytic" epistemology. With this question, of course, we are asking whether psychoanalytic discourse complies in any sense with logical empiricist precepts about subject, object, being, and method in the process of knowing about some externally existent thing—whether the knowledge of psychoanalysis is even remotely in conformity with the canons of normal, naturalistic "science."

Kant's architectonic specification of the epistemological structure by which things objectivated are knowable to self-consciousness could advantageously be employed here to determine whether psychoanalytic inquiry upon unconscious contents is similarly objectivistic. Logical empiricist formulations since Kant's may differ in their specific solutions to epistemological issues, but they pose the problem of knowledge, of being and consciousness, in the same general manner: mind or self-consciousness, as a contemplative unity of representational activity, must be able to interpret validly the material unity of nature as a world of things whose existence is unalterably external to the knowing subject of mentation. There must be an epistemological procedure or structure by which self-consciousness comes to know something about the there-being of things other than its own being. And this procedure must involve the subject's formation of "object" representations about this "other" thing—representations that, to be valid, must somehow be coherent and correspondent with the actual nature of this other.

Kant's solution to this epistemological problem is so well known that it need only be sketched in here. For him, nature—the thing-in-itself—is incontrovertably nonmental. That is, the there-being of the thing known about is always ontologically outside of the "being-with" of the mind's experiential and organizational activity, which is articulated as the unity of self-consciousness. This ontological dichotomy between mind and thing-in-itself is insurpassable. As we have seen, Kant defines the mind as having an indissolubly bipartite structure such that both experiential or empirical-synthetic and formal, a priori or higher synthetic functions are admitted. These faculties of phenomenal and noumenal mentation, of sensory experience and the conceptual understanding of higher cognitive organization, are entirely irreducible, yet operate cooperatively or correlatively within the unity of the knowing subject. The phenomenal can represent things as they appear in time and space, whereas the noumenal can approximate a representation of things as they are by logical rules and the deduction of categories of a priori judgment such as plurality, causality, substance, necessity, and limitation. Thus, conceptual understanding is distinct from yet a further synthesis of sensory experience. Beyond this, Kant has to assume and affirm the existence of a metaphysical thing-in-itself that is outside of this bipartite structure, yet somehow "given to" sensory experience, and somehow conforming to the rules and categories of conceptual understanding. Kantian metascience, like all logical empiricist and naturalistic epistemologies, requires that, beyond the experience and understandings of the epistemological subject and its objectivations in representational activity, the ontological existence of the ultimate epistemological there-being of the thing that is objectivated must remain motionless and mute.

Along these lines, if we assume that psychoanalytic knowledge is objectivistic, then the contents of the dynamic unconscious must occupy the position of the thing-in-itself, albeit perhaps a particular and peculiar thing-in-itself. In other words, knowledge of repressed contents is acquired and utilized in the psychoanalytic situation in a way that more or less parallels "natural-science" and technological procedures in investigating physical things. The dynamic process may be more tender and humane, but its epistemology is the same. Indeed, with this epistemological attitude, it makes little or no difference that the unconscious is distinguished from physical things, such as fossils or furniture, by being an independent existence within the individual's personhood rather than without. For the crucial assumption is that it can only be known about when rendered an "object"; its there-being can only be comprehended vicariously through the coordinated representational activity of observation and inference on the part of the knowing subject, whether patient or psychoanalyst.

Regarding psychoanalytic knowledge as objectivistic, and the repressed unconscious as a kind of thing-in-itself, is a seductive line of argument—one that has done immense damage to our comprehension of the knowing and being of psychoanalytic inquiry and change. The argument is seemingly so commonsensical. After all, if psychoanalysis is not subjectivistic, because the repressed unconscious does not belong to the "I-ness" of self-consciousness, then what can it be but an objectivistic discipline, with unconscious mental life as its object? To continue the argument: if some truth of personal being emerges in psychoanalytic discourse, then surely there must be someone who knows. There must also be some rules that this someone employs, and ultimately there must be something "other" that is known about. All this is a mistake. As we shall see, the very manner in which the question of knowledge is posed within the familiar "analytic" framework is condemned by the scientificity of psychoanalytic discourse. Psychoanalysis does not fit within the presuppositional coordinates of naturalistic epistemology: it thereby challenges the scientistic claims of objectivism, in which the ontic status of subject and the there-being of things objectivated are deemed mutually inconvertible.

For convenience and clarity in refuting the objectivistic argument, let us schematize the form psychoanalytic investigation would take if the unconscious were cast in the role of thing-in-itself for the patient's self-consciousness. We might imagine, for example, the ego organization of Freud's later metapsychology as corresponding to the Cartesian unity of self-consciousness, with the world (including the contents of the unconscious) as its epistemological thing-in-itself, whose there-being is necessarily severed from this ego organization and cannot be directly apprehended. Then again, borrowing from topographic vocabulary, we might imagine the domain of preconscious and conscious mentation as embracing the Kantian realm of phenomenal and noumenal cognition, of appearances or sensory impressions and of secondary synthetic processes of higher reasoning. Thus, the formation in preconsciousness of a phenomenal representation might, as indicated by the higher processes of conscious and preconscious conceptualization, be held to bear upon either the independent existence of things "outside" of the conscious-preconscious domain in the physical world, or the ontically independent existence of things such as unconscious contents which are also "outside" of this domain but within the individual's personhood—or some admixture of this. In these terms, an image of an item of furniture involves phenomenal and noumenal synthesis and is taken to bear upon the being-there of things in the physical world, whereas a dream image involves phenomenal and noumenal synthesis and is taken to bear upon the being-there of things in the unconscious world. The key point in this scheme is that knowledge about the unconscious is attained as in the Kantian formulation of knowledge about the physical world.

What are the implications of this Kantian scheme? To begin with, in this scheme Freud's originality appears as simply an innovation, however extraordinary, within a normal, "natural-science" discipline. Loosely speaking, it might be argued that his investigations led him to "discover" previously unemployed categories of the noumenon or, rather, a previously unemployed conceptual application of such categories. (Concepts pertaining to oedipal conflict or to the auguries of parapraxis might be taken as examples of such novelties.) The use of these investigative "insights" then permitted the "discovery" of a previously neglected aspect of certain phenomena and thus of a particular thing-in-itself.

On another level, this scheme implies that the goal of psychoanalytic interchange is for the patient to be educated in the use of Freud's "new" skills of higher cognition for the indirect investigation and control of the quasi-private object domain of unconscious contents. The parallel here is to way that apprenticeship in a "natural-science" discipline enables the novitiate to master procedures for the inferential and instrumental investigation of the world in general. Induction of the patient into this method and mode of personal conduct, then, effectively comprises the learning of categories and techniques. As will be discussed later in this chapter, it seems that these would have to be obtained didactically, either through the psychoanalyst's explicit tutorial activity or through the patient's identification and emulation of the psychoanalyst's "ego strengths."

For our present purposes, however, the most salient implication of such a Kantian scheme is that, whatever the individual character of the unconscious as "internal to personhood," it is cast in the epistemological role of an ontically independent thing-in-itself, which must remain "object" to the subject. In *analytische Wissenschaftstheorie*, subject and thing objectivated are a static antinomy—mind and nature are stationarily and irreducibly dichotomous. Even in the instance of one mind's attempt to know another mind, the ontic insurpassability of the naturalistic dichotomy still pertains to the epistemological structure. Thus, cast in the epistemological role of thing-in-itself, the unconscious is necessarily and immutably external to the knowing self-consciousness. It must always have been ontically other than "I," distinct and separate in its existence, and it will always remain so. Further, because direct apprehension of the thing-in-itself is impossible, the unconscious can only be known about or manipulatively controlled by the indirect observational, inferential, and instrumental activity of the subject's representational self-consciousness.

The error of mapping Freud's psychology onto the framework of naturalistic epistemology now begins to become evident. Although psychoanalysis confronts the rupture of split-off mentation and is not to be reduced to a psychology of subjectivism, the alienation of the "I-ness" of reflective consciousness and the psychic contents of the unconscious is quite unlike that of the Kantian dichotomy between the representational activity of self-consciousness and the natural ontology of the thing-in-itself, or the changeless disjuncture between subject and object specified by *analytische Wissenschaftstheorie*. The difference is sharpened if we once again consider the critical and distinctively Freudian notions of repression, the return of the repressed, and the psychoanalytic reappropriation of the repressed. As we shall see, the familiar metascientific framework requires an ontically static antinomy between knower and known, whereas the psychoanalytic self-consciousness and repressed unconscious are in *dynamic* contradiction. The epistemological subject and thing objectivated in this metascience remain, in their status as being-with and there-being respectively, unalterably separate and distinct, whereas the alienation of the prepsychoanalyzed "I" from the repressed may be surpassed.

The essential psychoanalytic notion of repression indicates that unconscious contents are exiled from self-consciousness, for, as Freud describes, it is a process of "sending away and keeping at a distance from consciousness" (1915b, p. 250). Yet, within the "analytic" epistemological framework, it is nonsense to suggest that an investigating agent might somehow be actively engaged in ousting the domain to be investigated from itself. From the Kantian viewpoint, for example, it would be utterly absurd to suggest that the subject of self-consciousness expels the thing-in-itself from its own subjectivity, that the representational activity of sensory experience and conceptual understanding somehow ejects the existence of the natural thing that it represents as "object."

Conversely, there is the Freudian notion of the return of the repressed—those polysemous contradictions in self-consciousness but not of self-consciousness, formed as compromise between the obtrusion of a repressed idea, wish, or fantasy and the organized prohibition of the conscious, nonconscious, and preconscious domain against such contents. This notion of a "return" connotes the distortion and deformation of the "I-ness" of reflective consciousness by an eruption of the repressed, wherein the aberrant opacity of the concealed unconscious purpose signifies its dispossession by the subject's belongingness. The intentional character of the unconscious as "striving for expression yet severed from consciousness" is thus indicated. In psychoanalysis, there is an intentionality—to borrow Brentano's use of the term—that inheres within "things" unconscious toward the manifest "subject" and that is found to be meaningful, for the "return" of the repressed implies the disguised emergence of ideas, wishes, and fantasies from the locus of that which is *other than* the subject of self-consciousness, yet is also subject in a certain sense.

Yet again, within the epistemology of *analytische Wissenschaftstheorie*, it would be unmitigated nonsense to suggest that natural things could be dynamic and desirous in relation to the contemplative epistemological subject: that they could themselves be subject. Consider, for a moment, the Kantian example. The thing-in-itself, although somehow "given to" the representations of the knowing subject, is essentially passive. Natural objects supposedly conform to the "two-stock" structure of mental activity within the unity of the transcendental ego, and it is solely the representational constructions of this activity that bestow meaning upon the world. "Meaning" in this scheme only results, for the subject, from the methodical activity of its own sensible and categorical constructions. It cannot be said to inhere within the there-being of the things objectivated, for, in and of itself, the natural realm, the thing-in-itself, is passively meaningless. Thus, in the Kantian epistemological scheme, if the unconscious were such an ultimate thing-in-itself, it could not conceivably be said to "return," engendering meaning or obtruding disruptively upon the activity of the "I-ness" of self-consciousness. Yet, for Freud, this is exactly what the unconscious does.

From the psychoanalytic perspective, unconscious meaning underlies or imposes itself upon the representational activity of conscious, nonconscious, and preconscious mentation, implying that the "knowledge" of this domain—the representational contents owned by its "I-ness"—is a one-sided apprehension and even, in a certain sense, a state of false consciousness. The intentionality and repression of unconscious mental life, proclaimed in Freud's earliest writings (1887–1902), entail the active, purposive, and formative qualities of the unconscious with respect to the conscious-preconscious domain. These qualities are not those of the mute and motionless thing-in-itself of Kantian epistemology. Subject and object in familiar logical empiricist metascience, self-consciousness and the there-being of things, are unalterably dissociated—always distinct and separate. Yet the antithetical correlativity of repression and the return of the repressed means that, quite unlike knowing self-consciousness and the thing objectivated, reflective awareness and the repressed unconscious—that is, "I-ness" and the subject beyond its bounds—impinge within the contradictions of an alienated psychic reality.

The expulsion of unconscious mental contents from the subjectivity of ordinary mentation in the process of repression and the obtrusion of these contents upon the latter domain in the form of the return of the repressed indicate that the contradiction between the subject of reflective awareness and the striving of unconscious signification is not the naturalistic disjunction between an epistemological subject and the passive thing objectivated. This conclusion is reinforced by a consideration of the reappropriative claim of Freud's psychology. Here, again, the implication is that consciousness and the unconscious, "I" and that which is repressed, are somehow transformatively related and ontically interpenetrating. Although the unconscious is repressively disappropriated by the "I" of reflective consciousness, even in its "return" as polysemous contradictions, the psychoanalytic interrogation of these contradictions claims not just to reveal the repressed contents to self-consciousness, but also to effect their reappropriation by its "I-ness." Note that, unlike the symptomatic and characterological return of the repressed, the psychoanalytic *transduction* of these previously unconscious contents implies that the "I" of self-consciousness comes to repossess them ontically as its own. The boundaries of the subject are thereby transformed dialectically.

Freud repeatedly insists that "we can come to know the unconscious only by making it conscious" (1932a, p. 246), for all knowledge adheres to consciousness and communication. But the psychoanalytic process of "making conscious" is definitely not a contemplative acquisition of knowledge about an object domain, as specified by "analytic" epistemology. According to "analytic" metascience, a representation is constructed, and the conscious subject knows the construction to be its own activity, but believes it to be correspondingly *about* the existence of something ontically "other." In the Kantian scheme, this "other" existence is the mute and motionless thing-in-itself. Psychoanalytic knowledge is entirely different. Even if we adopt Kantian phraseology, we must say that not only have unconscious "things" been repressed from the subject's self-consciousness, but they themselves are constitutively meaningful or intentional. Moreover, upon psychoanalytic interrogation, they become ontically reintegrated with the conscious "I," that is, taken into its own existence.

Thus, Freud's psychology evidences an interrelationship between knowing and being wholly unlike that of naturalistic objectivism. Naturalistic metascience presupposes that things are ontically passive with respect to the epistemological process, and that knowledge lies in the structuring of the subject's activity as a coherent and corresponding object representation of the there-being of things. From this standpoint, it is utterly incomprehensible to claim that there is a thing objectivated for investigation which should be allowed to speak for itself. Yet it might be said that allowing the unconscious to speak is precisely the direction of the discourse of patient and psychoanalyst, in which the intentionality of the thing objectivated is discovered and restored to subjectivity through the destructuring of the manifest subject's repressive activity or state of ontically hypostatized, false consciousness. To reiterate, such a reciprocally transformative dialogue is unthinkable within the natural attitude, with its assumption of the stationary ontological duality of knower and known. The epistemological subject may be said to observe the object, to make formal logical inferences about it, or even to control it instrumentally, by codified procedures of prediction and manipulation. But none of these investigative contingencies alters the mutual externality of the subject's being and the thing objectivated. For the epistemological subject, whether we speak of the Kantian "transcendental ego" or the collective agent implicit in contemporary "natural science," there are no ontic consequences to acquiring representational knowledge about the object domain. The construction of these representations is, after all, solely the subject's activity. Moreover, the there-being of the domain of things objectivated does not change as a result of the subject's investigation. Throughout such an objectivistic investigation, subject and thing objectivated remain apart and different.

We should note that this separateness holds for all logical empiricist investigation, even when the epistemological object is another person's mental activity. Although it might be argued that the "problem of other minds" is a special case, differing from knowledge about the materiality of nature and hence requiring specific rules and categories, it would still be maintained that the knowing mind and the other that is known about are ontically apart and different, their mutual externality unaffected by the investigation. That is, the investigation would still be an objectivistic inquiry upon something treated as inexorably exterior to the knower's self-consciousness. Within the framework of the natural attitude, the ontological separateness of subject and thing objectivated is constant, regardless of epistemological activity. Quite simply, in the process of knowing, the thing objectivated cannot become subjective, nor can the subject alter its proclamation of self-pellucidity, adequacy, and apodicticity.

In contrast, the psychoanalytic reappropriation of unconscious contents does have such ontological consequences; it is not contemplative knowledge but a knowing that transforms the there-being of the known. Unlike the immutable dichotomy of subject and thing objectivated in the logical empiricist scheme, the alienation of self-consciousness and the repressed may be overcome. To use objectivistic terminology, in the movement of psychoanalytic discourse, the "thing objectivated for investigation" is repossessed by the "investigating self-consciousness." This claim is illustrated in the psychoanalytic interrogation of a dream image. Initially, a dream image appears as purporting a reality entirely alien to the patient's self-consciousness, but the "other subject" of this reality eventually comes within its own belongingness—"thing" becomes "I" (see Freud, 1900). Somehow, through the interrogation of such polysemous contradictions in consciousness but not of consciousness, the limits of the "I-ness" of ordinary mentation are changed, the fixity and definiteness of this subject are dislodged, and the intentionality of what, as repressed unconscious, is initially opaque and alien, is regained. Such a reciprocal transmutation, in which the thing objectivated becomes reinstated as subjective, with a concomitant metamorphic movement of the "I" of self-consciousness, entirely transgresses the epistemology of the natural attitude.

In sum, psychoanalytic discourse is neither subjectivistic nor objectivistic. Psychoanalysis becomes aligned with critiques of "natural consciousness" or "natural understanding" (Hegel, 1807, 1817) and of "instrumental reason" (Adorno, 1966; Horkheimer, 1968). The naturalistic epistemology has delivered innumerable technical successes in our understanding and control of the physical world, and these are not to be discounted. Nevertheless, as Husserl and many others have incisively argued, such technical successes do not ensure the ultimate universality and truth of knowledge. As should now be clear, these successes are built upon a presuppositional attitude that psychoanalysis as *Psychologie der Verdrängung* transgresses. The psychoanalytic discourse of the repressed unconscious cannot be assimilated to the natural attitude, which maintains an unmediated dichotomy between the ontic loci of knower and known. For the unconscious is, so to speak, neither on the side of the epistemological "subject" nor on the side of the thing epistemologically objectivated.

The structure of logical empiricist metascience has two further ramifications which should be briefly expounded. The first is an adherence to an empirical principle, that is, a validation of inferences by appeal to observable facts. The second is an orientation of inferential constructions to a mathematicized ideal, that is, a procedural reference to formal logic as the model of certitude. Note that here we are not concerned, as we were in Chapter 1, with the question of whether the two-tier scheme of fact and theory is a possible account of the epistemology of "natural sciences" and the dominant "psychology," but simply with the discordance of psychoanalysis with such a scheme.

Unlike the disciplines of *analytische Wissenschaftstheorie*, Freud's psychology does not accept the empirical principle of observational investigation, for it cannot assume the pregiven construction of immediate facticity. Thus, in a peculiar and specific manner, it rejects the doctrine that knowledge is necessarily limited to that which is experientially *given*. The psychoanalytic claims concerning the contradiction between the reflectivity of consciousness and the alienated "subject" of the unconscious point to this divergence. The personal alienation, which psychoanalysis interrogates, implies the discrepancy of appearance and reality. Through psychoanalytic interrogation of polysemous contradictions, the "falsity" or partiality of that which appeared certain and univocal to prepsychoanalytic consciousness is revealed, and a reality of contents previously repressed by the immediacy of this false consciousness emerges. In this sense, Freud's psychology comprises knowledge grounded upon an unmasking of the immediate "facts" or appearances, rather than an epistemology that builds affirmatively upon such "facts."

A convenient illustration is, again, the psychoanalytic interrogation of dreams. As Freud often insists, the discourse of patient and psychoanalyst does not rest with the manifest content of the dream image, accepting the immediate phenomenon as a pure fact to which meanings may be directly imputed. Rather, the image is interrogated—treated with suspicion as a tendentious content, which does not offer the truth about the subject's being so much as the polysemous potential for such truth. The outcome of this interrogation is the uncovering of the "latent," hidden, disguised and unobservable content of repressed mentation. Given that the connection between the belongingness of the manifest and of the repressed is symbolically constituted, such that one may well stand for the other's opposite, it is evident that immediate appearance cannot be accepted as a valid and reliable epistemological starting point. Rather, the seeming certainty and transparency of the immediate must be dislodged for the reality to be revealed. The "fact" of the dream image is not in itself the content of the unconscious reality; it is taken as a "road" to that content (Freud, 1900).

Against psychoanalytic discourse, positivistic doctrines assume a pregiven world of self-subsistent facticity, proceeding as if the immediate appearance of facts were concordant or even coterminus with the essential reality. Freud's method directly challenges this epistemological stance by demonstrating the possibility of a discourse that recovers the formative conditions that underlie the partiality or falsity of appearances. Psychoanalytic discourse arraigns the certainty of things as they immediately appear objectivated in conscious and preconscious representations, taking them as instances of polysemous contradiction, and thereby going beyond these "facts" to disclose the intentional reality, a dispossessed subjectivity, from which they are constituted. Thus, hidden meanings are exposed behind "phenomena." It could be said that, whereas naturalistic epistemologies view "facts" as given, taking them for what they seem to be, psychoanalysis apprehends "facts" for what they exclude. It treats them negatively. How this is accomplished must be postponed for later discussion, but we should note here that psychoanalytic inquiry is not, like logical empiricist investigation, a deduction from the appearances of facticity, so much as a displacement of these facts in a manner that challenges their domination, in the interest of restoring the personal meaning behind them. It does not assume the identity of the subject, nor the ontic externality of things objectivated. Rather, it interrogates the subject beyond its limits.

Also unlike the disciplines of *analytische Wissenschaftstheorie*, Freud's psychology does not subscribe to the architectonic effort toward the construction of a fixed and final theory of knowledge. Specifically, psychoanalytic discourse rejects the ideal of formal or mathematicized epistemology. It may be recalled that, in part at least, the thrust of Kantian criticism was to indicate the untenability of a strong empiricist position, in that empirical experience has to be organized by the structure of the knowing subject's activity. Along these lines, to the extent that the epistemological program of logical empiricism has attempted to remedy the dogma of pure facticity, it has expounded structures of cognition by which the object may be represented and to which things must conform if they are to be known about objectively.

Kant, for example, argues that space and time are the *a priori* conditions by which phenomenal appearances are possible, and that the synthetic *a priori* categories of the noumenon are the inferential and deductive conditions of higher representation. Following the advances of Galileo and others, the epistemological procedures governing "scientific" investigations became increasingly codified and formalized, and mathematical logic, as the model of certainty and exactitude, came to furnish the rules of higher inferential and deductive representation. In line with Galilean principles, Kant insists that a science can only be such to the extent that it is mathematical, and this insistence continues in contemporary epistemological formulations. By thus attempting a detailed specification of the permanent structures of knowledge, the disciplines of logical empiricism espouse a fundamental assumption, propagated by Descartes, but more notably by Kant—that the ultimate thing objectivated conforms to these *a priori* structures. The Galilean principle, for example, implies that nature is mathematical in character; thus, mathematics is the language by which it may be comprehended. The conditions may vary—with time and space as the condition of the experience of objects, noumenal categories as the condition of natural understanding, or mathematical logic as the condition of inference and explanation—but the common metaphysical presupposition is that things must somehow conform to these conditions if they are to be knowable.

The Freudian unconscious, however, does not conform. Although intentionally meaningful, repressed ideas, wishes, and fantasies elude the architectonic conditions of possible knowledge that logical empiricist metascience requires. For example, the unconscious is not spatial, despite the topographic similes of naturalistic metapsychology. Moreover, Freud frequently argues that unconscious contents may not even obey the normal conditions of temporality—a disobedience that seems to contradict Kant's belief that all mentation must be temporally organized. Psychoanalytic interrogation confronts intricate psychic relations between personal meanings, but these are not the causality and lawful invariance attributed to material events. The discourse of patient and psychoanalyst does not, for instance, pretend independence of human intentionality, and hence cannot prognosticate from the meanings it discovers, as with the predictions about the physical world demanded by Baconian method. On this point, Freud (1920b) seems unequivocal. Furthermore, repressed contents may be illogical yet have meaning—for example, they may disregard the basic logic of formal negation, the proposition that a thing cannot both be and not be, or they may abuse the rules of syllogistic form (Freud, 1900, 1901b, 1925b). Thus, the unconscious, like the polysemous contradiction of the dream image, departs bewilderingly from "what we recognize as rational thought processes" (Freud, 1900, p. 597). And yet it is claimed that unconscious meanings may be recovered through psychoanalytic interrogation. Obviously, such an interrogation cannot be contained within the formal, logical and mathematicized model of theoretical inference, categorization, and explanation embraced by logical empiricism.

Freud's psychology claims to make sense of arcane mental contents that a formalized epistemology necessarily condemns to senselessness. Its method must involve the suspension of the formal structures of "rationality," upon which the "analytic" epistemology of logical empiricism operates, so that the split-off meaning of "irrational" repressed contents may be recouped. As has been mentioned, psychoanalysis deliberately sharpens contradictions by focusing on "phenomena" that are polysemous and opaque to self-consciousness. In contrast, logical empiricist investigation, through its ideological commitment to univocality, parsimony, coherence, and correspondence,precludes inquiry upon these arcane intricacies of personal meaning.

A radical implication of these arguments is that psychoanalytic method actually subverts the presuppositional foundations of both subjectivistic and objectivistic epistemologies. We have, of course, still to discuss the conditions of psychoanalytic discourse. Even now, however, we can discern that if psychoanalytic inquiry and change indeed fulfill the claims of revelation and repossession of the repressed unconscious, if indeed psychoanalysis is an interrogation of a contradictory or nonidentical subjectivity, then its method jeopardizes the edifice of familiar naturalistic metascience. Later, we shall look more closely at the discourse in which patient and psychoanalyst, through subversion of the investigative rules of *analytische Wissenschaftstheorie*, enter, with rigor and sensibility, into a realm of "madness," "irrationality," and "unknowability" to retrieve a split-off "subject." For the moment, we need only remark how the movement of psychoanalytic method pursues that which necessarily eludes the objectivism of familiar metascience, with its hypostatized dichotomy between knower and known.

FREUD'S PSYCHOLOGY AND "ANALYTIC" COOPTATIONS

In showing, on a more or less philosophical plane, how psychoanalytic discourse must transgress the epistemological framework of subjectivism and objectivism, we have begun the move toward an overt critique of ideology. As intimated, psychoanalytic conduct implies the prejudicial limitations or ideological partiality of methods of "psychological investigation" based on the presupposition of an immutable dichotomy between the knower and known. That is, if the genuinely scientific quality of the discourse of patient and psychoanalyst—the necessity and truth of its movement—can be apprehended, then the egregious scientism of logical empiricist presuppositions will be demonstrated. To develop this argument, however, we need first to examine, on a less philosophical plane, various implicit and explicit attempts to assimilate Freud's psychology to the metascientific framework of "analytic" epistemology. In looking at these apostatic efforts to induce conformity, we shall find ourselves inevitably entering into an ideological critique. For the contention here is that theoretical reformulations by certain of Freud's "successors" effectively suppress the innovative and extraordinary *science*, which Freud strove to enunciate, in the expedient interests of a scientistic ideology—they "normalize" Freud's "scientific pursuit of the psychic unconscious." Although this thesis will only be vindicated when we eventually approach a discussion of what psychoanalysis is, rather than what it is not—when we demonstrate the scientificity of Freud's discipline—at this point we can at least underline how certain post-Freudian attempts at assimilation eradicate the essentially original and extraordinary quality of psychoanalysis, proclaimed in its notions of a psychology of repression and a discursive praxis of anti-repression.

With the debatable exception of certain Kleinian formulations, most Anglo-American theorizing since Freud may be characterized, not inaptly, in terms of this pervasive effort to domesticate psychoanalysis under the mandates of logical empiricist epistemology. Of course, it is not that these theorists are "conscious" ideologues, deliberately conspiring to sabotage the seminal uniqueness of the psychoanalytic venture. Such is the influential power of the logical empiricist framework that the apostasy, however serious, is "innocently" undertaken. The modifications and renovations are frequently impelled, not by deviationist ambition, but by seemingly benign and loyal concerns to iron out the apparent ambiguities and inconsistencies in Freud's pronouncements, or to bring Freudian psychology into alignment with the honorific institution of "science" (i.e., the precepts of naturalistic investigation). Indeed, these theoretical reforms often seem of minor significance, given the scope of Freud's work, and usually appear innocuous—particularly because Freud's own opinion, especially in his later writings, may sometimes be adduced as inviting this sort of amendment. Nevertheless, as will be seen, even these seemingly right-minded alterations and expurgations have insidious consequences—not only for the appraisal of the philosophical and anthropological implications of psychoanalytic discourse, but also for the revolutionary possibility of a psychoanalytic critique of the character of science.

As we have seen, there are two directions in which the apostatic attempt to assimilate Freud's psychology to the metascientific framework of "analytic" epistemology may proceed. First, the unconscious may be subordinated to a theory of unitary (albeit multifaceted) self-consciousness; the term itself is either abandoned entirely or disappears into the concept of that which is neglected, unnoticed, or otherwise ill-attended in mental life. Here one might think of the so-called neo-Freudian schools with their "culturalist" emphasis. Second, the unconscious may be rendered as the naturalistic thing of an objective investigation; its contents are regarded as a thing-in-itself within the individual's personhood and an autonomous self-consciousness is posited as the identitarian epistemological subject. To the extent that it has retained a concept of the "unconscious," one might think here of the tradition of ego psychology, which is often noted for its "biologistic" emphasis. Both directions are anti-psychoanalytic inasmuch as they expunge essential and original claims about the character of

Freud's discourse. Before we discuss the particulars of these efforts further, however, we should pause to consider Freud's own role in "encouraging" the ideology of such metatheoretical reformulations.

Although in his own mind Freud may have been entirely clear about the character of his discursive methodology, his writings contain certain ambiguities and inconsistencies, making a "neutral" reading of his work impossible. As discussed in Chapter 2, his very struggle in publicly articulating his innovations may be taken as an indication of their extraordinary and enigmatic quality. Freud's writings, especially those penned before the five "metapsychological papers" of 1915 to 1917, do offer abundant evidence of his recognition of the revolutionary quality of his discipline; it was on the basis of these that we delineated the critical claims germane to psychoanalytic discourse. There is, however, also evidence of Freud's hope that his seminal discoveries would augment the content of "normal science," fitting in rather than changing the very form of science itself. Freud is known not only for his distrust of religious or mystical doctrines, but also for his fervent admiration of the positivist milieu in which his career developed. It could be argued that the powerful influence of this logical empiricist ideology is reflected in his inability to recognize the scientistic fundaments of naturalistic epistemology revealed by his own anti-ideological discourse. Whatever his ambivalence and misgivings, Freud succumbed, at least in part, to the pressure to present his work as if it did conform to the dictates of naturalistic metascience.

Freud never made the first mistake—that of viewing the unconscious as an aspect or phase of unitary and univocal self-consciousness—for, as indicated, he strenuously insists on the alienation of conscious and unconscious, and hence on the distinction between the unconscious and the realm of retrievable foreconscious contents that belong to the very same "I" as conscious mentation. It seems, however, that occasionally in his texts Freud does lapse into the second error of treating the unconscious as an object of naturalistic investigation. These lapses occur more frequently in the later writings, where metapsychological myth comes to dominate Freud's meditations on his own psychology. As was argued in Chapter 2, it is as if the schematization of topography, energy, and structure acquired a conceptual momentum of its own that constrained and peverted Freud's perspective on psychoanalytic discourse as such. The physicalistic metapsychology augments hypostatized and substantialistic preconceptions about the character of psychoanalytic knowledge—ushering in a depiction of its method wherein "the ego agency," aided by the psychoanalyst's skills, is engaged in the contemplative and manipulative investigation or control of the objectivated domain of "id" contents. This depiction implies that knowledge of the unconscious is obtained in the manner of Kantian knowledge about the independent existence of physical things, even though the unconscious is somehow a private and personal thing. Thus, we may find Freud equating the problem of cognizing "external reality" with that of cognizing the "internal" domain (1938/1940), and even suggesting directly, on one occasion, that psychoanalysis may take its place as the complement to Kant's theory of "external" perception and conception (1915b, p. 270).

Ludwig Binswanger (1957) indicates that Freud toyed with the equivalence of the unconscious and the thing-in-itself, and Lou Andreas-Salomé (1912–1913) documents his preference for dualistic philosophy. Yet more salient are Freud's own assertions of the objectivism of his method, reinforced by his numerous references to observational and inferential processes in psychoanalysis. Earlier, it was proposed that Freud's emphasis on the *scientific* status of psychoanalysis can, more often than not, be taken as a correct insistence upon the rigorous, necessary, and truthful character of the discourse, rather than a mistaken belief in its naturalistic or objectivistic properties. Nevertheless, Freud does sometimes write of his method in an unequivocally naturalistic and objectivistic fashion. At one point, for example, he argues that the mind can be the object of investigation in the same manner as the physical world (1933, p. 171); at another point he proposes that his psychology, like chemistry or physics, aims to arrive "at what is termed an 'understanding' of the field of natural phenomena in question" (1938/1940, pp. 80–81). He suggests that, unlike "direct proofs" of conscious acquaintance, the unconscious content is only known by "indirect proofs of the most cogent kind" (1912, p. 262). And he describes his methodology as one in which the psychoanalyst observes, infers, and informs, while the patient "processes" the information (1910b, p. 105), or even as one in which this transmission of information occurs as if the patient were the object of procedures of modification as in a physicist's experiment (1938/1940). Here, alongside a view of the unconscious as the epistemological thing objectivated in a naturalistic scheme, and of the method as correspondingly objectivistic, we find a view of the transformations occurring in psychoanalysis as equivalent to technical procedures for the prediction, manipulation, and control of the physical world. Talk of the psychoanalytic goal as "conquest" of the unconscious (1923a) or as the "taming" of essentially biological drives (1937a) hints at such an instrumentalist conception of the discourse.

In my opinion, to the extent that Freud may have held to a naturalistic, objectivistic, and even instrumentalist view of the psychoanalytic process, he woefully misapprehended his own discipline. But I do not believe that Freud did embrace such a viewpoint, despite his inclinations and the influence of his positivistic milieu. Indeed, looking at his earlier writings, I think we may be assured of this judgment. In other words, the scattered evidence for such scientistic self-misunderstanding is to be understood as a lapse, made in the course of Freud's arduous and perhaps foredoomed struggle to express extrapsychoanalytically the seminal originality of his discourse. Nonetheless, as a lapse, it takes on a grievous contemporary significance, because, to speak candidly even at the risk of discourtesy, it is exactly this misapprehension that lies at the root of an entire history of post-Freudian falsification.

Against Psychologies of "Selfhood" and Subjectivity

Let us now confront the first direction by which the assimilation of psychoanalytic doctrine to the metascientific framework of "analytic" epistemology has been attempted. This effort—the one Freud did not in any way commit or induce—entails a reconceptualization of the unconscious as merely an aspect or phase of psychic contents possessed by the Cartesian subject of self-consciousness. It might seem that such a gross reconceptualization should be given short shrift, yet the reduction of the unconscious to the belongingness of the unnoticed but retrievable—a reduction against which Freud frequently and vehemently cautioned—is a persistent error in the work of "new" theorists after Freud.

Refashioning psychoanalysis to expunge Freud's discovery of a repressed unconscious dates from the earliest defection—illustrated by Alfred Adler's theory, in which the critical notion of repression gives way to concepts bearing on processes within the conscious-preconscious domain. Very often this refashioning is implemented under the banner of doctrinal "liberalization," and accompanied by an emphasis on education, the "wholeness of personality," the requirements of expedient psychotherapy, and—perhaps most tellingly—a new orientation to the manifest, established conditions of society and culture. Owing much to Adler—as well as to a "liberal," pluralistic tradition of Americanized social theory, exemplified by writers as diverse as Charles Cooley, George Herbert Mead, John Dewey, Franz Boas, and Edward Sapir—the "neo-Freudians" have advanced formulations oriented to interpersonal events and underpinned by presuppositions about the unity of personhood. Such formulations are particularly to be found in the writings of Erich Fromm, Karen Horney, Harry Stack Sullivan, and Clara Thompson.

Clearly, presuppositions about a unified, albeit multifaceted, subject stand against the discovery of contradictory subjectivity claimed by psychoanalytic discourse. Whatever its contribution in other respects, the neo-Freudian emphasis on interpersonal or interactional "dynamics" obviates the notion of intrapsychic alienation, by giving priority to an autonomous self-consciousness that is harmoniously adapted to the sociocultural milieu. In promoting an ideology of personhood or "selfhood," neo-Freudian formulations treat the subject of self-consciousness as fundamentally inviolate—but Freud's scientific *Psychologie der Verdrängung* critically and precisely indicates the hollow falsity of this inviolateness. Whereas psychoanalysis sharpens the polysemous contradictions of self-consciousness in the interests of the scientific pursuit of the repressed unconscious, the ideology of a unified subject silences such contradictions. In the interests of an essentially conformist psychology, it eschews the scientific renunciation of common sense that is germane to psychoanalytic method. When the manifestations of personhood are given such privilege, therapy becomes a matter of adjusting to the sociocultural milieu of interpersonal outcomes, or of rearranging self- and other-perceptions and conceptions within the arena of conscious and preconscious mentation. Within the neo-Freudian framework, the domain of awareness may be re-formed as the surfaces of a multifaceted self-consciousness are traversed, but the recondite contents of the repressed unconscious will inevitably be left undisclosed. Thus, the rupture of psychic reality will be perpetuated in the interests of adjustment.

The neo-Freudians are not the only theorists who continue to pledge a certain allegiance to psychoanalytic method yet adhere to a flawed revisionism. Certain versions of British "object relations theory," for example, are not exempt from this line of criticism. Indeed, there are links between the neo-Freudian and the British schools, as Harry Guntrip (1971) and others have documented. The formulations of the British school are particularly to be found in the writings of D. W. Winnicott and W. R. D. Fairbairn.[1] These formulations often offer a rich and sophisticated account of various intrapsychic dimensions and ontogenetic processes, even though they usually employ mistakenly Cartesian concepts. Here it is not so much that intrapsychic conflict is ignored, as that the stability, certainty, and transparency of some

---

[1] In many respects, my comments here also apply to the formulations and controversies generated in America by Otto Kernberg and Heinz Kohut.

"general ego structure" or "self" are asserted and given methodological priority. Personal alienation is thus reduced to problems of the "internalization of objects," and the engagement of patient and psychoanalyst becomes not so much an archaeology of repressed contents, with emancipation of their "subject," as a matter of relearning object relations. Talk of "relations with internal objects" not only implies the static reification of some fixed and definite self, but also obscures the falsity of self-consciousness that is due to the repression of desire. In this manner, a Cartesian conceptual framework and terminology threaten to eclipse Freud's quintessential notion of the repressed unconscious and the contradictory locus of the subject of psychic reality.

Mitigation or eradication of Freud's notion of repression, with the concomitant "rediscovery" and rehabilitation of "selfhood," is the hallmark of an attempt to domesticate psychoanalysis to the familiar, common-sense framework that upholds self-consciousness, treating its contents affirmatively. This tendency characterizes a wide range of contemporary "psychologies," many of which are explicit in their rejection of Freud's doctrine, and thus extend beyond errorful revisionism. From neo-Freudian to post-Freudian psychology is actually no large step. Post-Freudian psychologies of self-consciousness surface in the writings of Gordon Allport, Abraham Maslow, Carl Rogers, and the like—as well as in the plethora of "humanistic" therapies such as encounter, psychodrama, psychosynthesis, transactional analysis, and gestalt. These "new" theories and therapies share an exaltation of the "whole person," accompanied by a proliferation of banalities about "fulfillment," "self-actualization," "awareness," and "adjustment." With psychoanalytic science rescinded, adulation of the harmonious psyche of "personhood" proceeds mindlessly. Baldly stated, from the knowledge of psychoanalytic discipline, this celebrated integrity of mental life is a lie; it is a fractured individuality existing in the polysemous and hypostatized state of false consciousness.

Indeed, it is with this post-Freudian dogma—more than with the scientistic revisionism of the neo-Freudians and British object relations theorists—that the ideological impact of suppressing the critical notion of the repressed unconscious, in favor of a cult of precritical subjectivity, becomes very evident. This cult of subjectivity, with its affirmation of an essentially Cartesian self-consciousness, resonantly accords with the ideology of the individual consumer's autonomy and unitary independence in a "free-market" society, with the bourgeois myth of positive individual effort and self-reliance. It inevitably affirms existing sociocultural discourse, ingenuously promoting the intrinsic harmony of personhood within the wholeness of the sociocultural order and endorsing a conception of psychotherapy as the affirmation of this harmony. The suppression of Freud's discovery of the personal alienation of "I" and the repressed is impelled by the requirement of sociocultural conformity in conceptual organization, which operates at both manifestly political and subtly ideological levels. Indeed, psychoanalytic discourse, as the scientific pursuit of the repressed unconscious, reveals that an acritical psychology of personhood cultivates an ideology that blithely ignores the oppressive and exploitative conditions of existing sociocultural arrangements, while perpetuating the psychic fragmentation of individuality.

The apotheosis of "selfhood," as an integrated, unitary personality to be experienced, understood, and even modified by the procedures of what is characteristically a "surface psychology," implies that all meaningful psychic contents may be recognized and possessed by the "I" of reflective consciousness. It also implies the essential rightness of the sociocultural matrix into which the individual fits. In this manner, the discourse of repressed ideas, wishes, and fantasies is precluded; the psychotherapeutic enterprise is limited to charting and reorganizing the domain of self-consciousness, of conscious and preconscious representations of ourselves and our worlds. The contents may be readjusted and realigned, but the preestablished "I-ness" of this domain is never called into question. In other words, whatever its successes according to criteria of acculturation, this psychotherapeutic enterprise leaves the fixity and limit of the subject unaltered, only modifying contents already belonging to it. The contradictoriness of "I," the repressed "subject," and the sociality of experience and understanding is thus perpetuated. These therapeutic efforts may be very important, and may well be a part of everyday clinical psychoanalysis in some measure, but their efficacy is not to be taken as a mark of their scientificity, nor as an indication of that which is truly extraordinary and enigmatic in psychoanalytic discourse. The theoretical "liberalization" of psychologies of "selfhood" and subjectivity implements an ideological function. By its anti-scientific reduction of Freud's critical notions of the repressed unconscious and the contradictory locus of the subject, this tendency promotes a relapse into a pre-Freudian philosophy of the individual's identity as a unitary and univocal self-consciousness, within a harmonious sociocultural nexus.

Against Psychologies of "Ego Objectivity"

Other attempts to accommodate psychoanalysis within the meta-scientific framework of "analytic" epistemology move toward objectivism. Here the influential but fundamentally mistaken theorizing posits the dynamic unconscious in the role of epistemological object of naturalistic investigation. Again, the erroneous assumption is that, in the dialogue between patient and psychoanalyst, knowledge about repressed mental contents can be acquired and utilized in the manner that the precepts of logical empiricism dictate for the physical world—contemplatively and manipulatively researched by observational, inferential, and instrumental procedures within the dichotomous framework of knower and known. That psychoanalytic discourse necessarily transgresses this objectivistic framework has already been demonstrated. What we need to examine here are the apostatic implications of this cooptive attempt.

The attempt to make the dynamic unconscious the object of naturalistic investigation coincides precisely with the ascendancy of an objectivistic "ego" epistemology in the prestigious tradition of ego psychology. As was indicated in Chapter 2, this tradition is characterized by its proposals about the "autonomous functions" or "conflict-free sphere" of "the ego organization" as a substantive set of "psychic structures." Ego psychology developed more or less concurrently with object relations theory, and, like the latter, its proponents generally conceive their tradition as a "scientific" reaction against early psychoanalytic formulations, which are denounced under the seemingly pejorative rubric of "drive theory" or "id psychology."

Commencing with the influential papers on higher "ego functions" by Hermann Nunberg (1931) and Franz Alexander (1933), and with Anna Freud's *The Ego and the Mechanisms of Defense* (1936), ego psychology purports to represent an extrapolation of Freud's later metapsychological theory of ego, id, and superego structures (1923a, 1926b). It is Heinz Hartmann's work that stands as the authoritative source of this tradition, from his early lectures published in *Ego Psychology and the Problem of Adaptation* (1939), through his *Essays on Ego Psychology* (1924–1959), to his collaboration with Ernst Kris and Rudolph Loewenstein. The tradition issues into the extensive writings of Hartmann's major successor, David Rapaport, and into the contemporary work of a whole group of Rapaport's students and colleagues. In addition, the prominent theoretical efforts of René Spitz, Margaret Mahler, and Edith Jacobson, as well as those of Jacob Arlow, Charles Brenner, and their adherents, should be included in the ego psychology tradition. The critique that follows, however, will focus on the work of Hartmann and Rapaport. Hartmann is selected for his foundational influence on this tradition and Rapaport, for his philosophical sophistication, his honest intellectual acumen, and his ardor for systematic theorizing, which can be conveniently exploited to illustrate some of the grave and far-reaching consequences of ego-psychological revisionism.

There are several reasons why the Hartmann-Rapaport tradition has achieved preeminence within the American establishment, and in particular why the structural-functional metapsychology of id, superego, and ego organization has been endowed with superordinate significance by clinical practitioners. The value of ego-psychological conceptualization is usually argued both on technical and on metalinguistic or metatheoretical grounds. But as we confront each of these, we shall find that, although the proffered arguments may purport to be scientifically instigated, they are typically motivated by an underlying scientistic ideology.

Structural-functional formulations are introduced as affording technical improvement to psychoanalytic therapy in several ways. They serve to guard the clinician against the improprieties of "direct" or "id" interpretations, to alert the practitioner to the multiple functioning of every psychic event, and thus to widen the scope of therapeutic interventions designed to improve, by whatever means, the "fit" between individuality and the demands of sociocultural normativity. To begin with, however, the clinician cannot actually address the id or the repressed unconscious in some "direct" manner; thus, the threat of dangerously direct interpretations seems somewhat exaggerated and mythical. Certainly, there may be interpretations that are "before their time," destructive rather than systemically deconstructive, and we shall discuss these later. Nevertheless, the bugaboo of id psychology, perilous for bourgeois morality, serves only the ideological purpose of committing the clinician to interpretations that foster socioculturally adaptive functioning. Indeed, it is the introduction of principles of adaptation to clinical practice that is a key to the technical accomplishments of ego psychology. Yet it is not a principle indigenous to psychoanalysis. Even more, in a certain sense, it is profoundly antipsychoanalytic.

Adaptation is brought into ego psychology by Hartmann and others as if to effect an alignment of psychoanalytic practice with the honorific "science" of Darwinian biology. Its influence on clinical practice, however, is entirely scientistic. As a guiding concept for ego psychologists, the adaptive viewpoint loses its original connotations and issues into a pseudo-Darwinian ideology of adjustment or acculturation. Clinicians come to endorse functioning that adapts the individual to "objective reality," that is, to the shared representational system that encodes sociocultural normativity. And who is the arbiter of this "objective reality"? The answer, of course, is, all too easily, the ego psychologist as sociocultural technician. Adaptation necessarily comes to imply therapeutic modification of the patient's psychic reality in accordance with the standards set by the therapist's (psychic) reality, which is scientistically purported to be "scientifically objective." Quite frankly, adaptation in psychological therapies is an incorrigibly ideological concept, one that inevitably contravenes scientific inquiry upon psychic reality as an idiographically constructive representational world. To give privilege to adaptive functioning abrogates the priority and primacy of the patient's psychic reality. The scientistic goal of sociocultural adjustment supersedes the scientific pursuit of the psychic unconscious. However efficacious ego psychology may be in using the concept of adaptation to develop therapeutic techniques for acculturation, this emphasis and viewpoint fundamentally rescind the scientific distinctiveness of psychoanalytic inquiry. Once again, ideological efficacy must not be taken as a criterion of scientificity.

Ego psychology also advocates structural-functional formulations as a theoretical improvement in metapsychology. The model of id, superego, and ego organization supposedly generates conceptualizations that are "more clinically accurate" and "more logically consistent," metalinguistically and metatheoretically, than topographic or energy-economic metapsychology. Unfortunately, this advocacy usually depends on some very confused theorizing about consciousness, reflectivity, and the unconscious—with conflation of epistemological and ontological issues. Specifically, ego psychologists tend to argue that the inability of consciousness to reflect upon and recognize much of its own repressive and defensive activity points to insurmountable problems in topographic and energy-economy models, and demonstrates the superiority of structural-functional conceptualizations. This is a mistaken and wretchedly overworked argument. Interestingly enough, it is the same conundrum that Jean-Paul Sartre used in *Being and Nothingness* (1943) as a reason to dismiss psychoanalytic doctrine wholesale: how does the being of consciousness know what it has itself repressed? This sort of criticism persuasively influences philosophical skepticism about psychoanalysis as a mental science, and it resembles a legitimate argument for the ascendancy of structural-functional formulations. Yet the "conundrum" posed here can be refuted without introducing and upgrading the concept of the ego organization, for it is not a conundrum but a mistaken interpretation. It derives from a failure to realize that the knowing and not-knowing discovered by psychoanalysis are also issues of the being of psychic life. That is, it derives from a failure to realize that Freud's

Psychologie der Verdrängung makes *both* epistemological and ontological claims about psychic reality.

It will be recalled that we set out five critical claims about psychoanalytic discourse vis-à-vis the repressed unconscious, and then related these to the question of the subject. Conscious and preconscious contents are variously available to the reflective potential of "I," belonging to its being yet subject to condemnation and suppression. Nonconscious functions, although not available to reflection, nonetheless belong to the subject-being of consciousness. Repressed mentation, however, is neither epistemologically available to the reflective "I" nor ontologically within its bounds. A serious examination of this way of posing psychoanalytic inquiry and change allows us to rebut the Sartrean line of criticism without trying to posit fanciful naturalistic models that are inherently extrapsychoanalytic. The implications of this approach to psychoanalytic discourse are thoroughly dialectical, entailing the ontologization of psychoanalytic method. But this is not the direction in which ego psychology proceeds. Instead, ego psychology responds to the Sartrean line of criticism as if it could be answered by giving psychoanalysis a more naturalistic, quasi-biological garb. The structural-functional model is upgraded, obliterating the question of the subject of psychic reality and rendering psychoanalysis an objectivistic and externalistic doctrine.

To be more precise, there are two main theoretical moves by which ego psychology upgrades the structural-functional model to resolve the alleged problems and limitations of other metapsychological formulations. Because consciousness does not necessarily know its own repressive and defensive activity, and cannot necessarily become aware of it upon reflection, it is suggested: first, that the ego must be partly unconscious, not only in the descriptive sense of foreconsciousness, but also in some systematic sense; and, second, that the repression barrier must be within the ego. Let us examine each of these proposals in turn.

The first suggestion involves nonsequitur, as well as conflation of nonconscious mental activity with that which is repressed and dynamically unconscious. That repressive and defensive activity, by which mental contents are excluded from the conscious-preconscious domain, is not available to reflection by the "I" of consciousness may well imply that such activity is systematically *not* conscious, but it does not imply that it is *unconscious* in the dynamic sense. There are, of course, a great many mental activities that are nonconscious, yet they are entirely different from Freud's discovery of the repressed unconscious—

for although they are not epistemologically available to reflective awareness, they belong ontologically to the same subject as that of conscious and preconscious mentation. The "deep structure" of generative grammar is a good example of a nonconscious "ego" function. Even if the rules of syntax cannot be brought into the knowing of reflective consciousness, they belong to the same subject-being. The repressive and defensive activity of the subject of consciousness seems to be similarly nonconscious. It belongs ontologically, although it may be unavailable epistemologically. In contradistinction, the Freudian unconscious is neither available epistemologically, nor is it possessed ontologically by the subject-being of "I-ness."

The second point of structural-functional theorizing, which locates the repression barrier within the ego organization, increases the confusion of ideas about the unconscious and endlessly muddles the distinctive claims of psychoanalytic discourse. Some rather specious arguments are marshaled in favor of the conceptualization of repression within the ego. For instance, it is suggested that the id contains only instinct, not psychic representations; that the repressed unconscious involves the content of representations; and that repressed representations must therefore be located within the ego. Similar metapsychological sophistry is evident in the suggestion that the contents of the superego, which is formed by identifications and internalizations of the ego organization, may be repressed, and that therefore this repression must occur within the ego-superego system. It can readily be seen that these arguments are scarcely derived from psychoanalytic discourse—they are not extrapolations of the experience and understanding generated in the dialogue of patient and psychoanalyst. Rather, they are internal to the extrapsychoanalytic logic of the naturalistic metapsychology; hence, their quasi-syllogistic form, with two metapsychological propositions followed by the metapsychological apodosis.

An additional irrelevancy is often appended to these ego-psychological arguments—namely, that because there are many forms of resistance and censorship within the ego (for example, between consciousness and preconsciousness), it cannot be theoretically detrimental to view repression as similarly within this organization. Actually, it is theoretically disastrous. For, again, we encounter the effects of a fundamental misapprehension of the epistemological and ontological claims about psychic reality inherent in the scientific pursuit of the repressed unconscious.

We have now challenged ego psychology's reasons for insisting on an unconscious ego and the operation of repression within the ego organization. What are the consequences of these metalinguistic and metatheoretical renovations? It can be seen how easily the notion of repression as the limit of "I-ness" in psychic reality, against which a contradictory "subject" (the there-being of mentation which is "I-less," other, or "it") persists and insists, is ablated by the objectivistic and externalistic rhetoric of "structures," "functions," and "organization." In ego psychology, the notion of repression loses its epistemological and ontological distinctiveness; hence, ultimately, the discovery of the unconscious loses its significance. Concomitantly, the "ego" either loses its denotation as subject of conscious, nonconscious, and preconscious representational activity or is totalized in a manner that portends to bring ego psychology into alignment with subjectivistic psychologies proclaiming the unified, identitarian nature of mental activity.

To place repression with the ego, for example, means not only that little or nothing can be said about the boundary and relations between this ego organization and that which is ontologically other than "ego"— "it" or "id." It also means that repression ceases to have any ontological significance, for the repressed is now within the being of the ego organization. It certainly follows that ego psychology is entirely unable to distinguish repression from suppression. To locate the repression barrier within the being of the ego implies that repression, like suppression, has only epistemological significance. Whatever the jargon of "barrier," in practice, repression become indistinguishable from gradations of suppression. Thus, the discovery of the dynamic unconscious as a locus of contradiction, epistemologically and ontologically, is obscured.

At the same time, the notion of "ego" as subject virtually disappears once repression is located within the ego organization. The splitting of the subject, as a dialectic of "I-ness" and "I-less-ness," gives way to an exclusive emphasis on conflicts, incongruities, and disparities within the conscious-preconscious domain. The boundary of "I" can no longer be interrogated because it is beyond the repression barrier; besides, it cannot intimate anything other than the limits of mentality in nature. Ego psychology thus becomes an objectivistic and externalistic organizational psychology, the discipline of choice for sociocultural technicians making interventions on the individual level. Here the privilege given to "structural" metapsychology may be deceptive, for this emphasis has little or no bearing on "structuralism" as it has developed in contemporary human sciences in Moscow, Prague, and Paris. Rather, it is a functionalist formulation, in which "ego" as a group of ideas belonging to the subject gives way to "*the* ego," biologically analogized as a group of functions containing mental contents. As was discussed in Chapter 2, the subject disappears beneath the Humean or positivist view of an organization of mental functions. The ego organization, objectivistically and externalistically defined as functionally related mentation, abrogates the significance of psychoanalysis as a discourse upon the split subject of psychic reality.

At the risk of repetition, let us now reapproach the tradition of ego psychology for its metascientific implications. It may be heuristic to begin by itemizing the gross revisions necessitated by an attempt to render psychoanalysis as objectivistic, "normal science." These revisions may roughly be divided into four areas:

First, the question of psychoanalytic knowledge has to be reposed in such a manner that distinctly and unalterably separate domains of knower and known can be designated. Clearly, because ego psychologists, unlike most post-Freudians, have not manifestly forgotten the unconscious and still hold that their investigation is somehow about this domain (among other things), the unconscious has to be cast in the role of epistemological thing objectivated.

Second, on the other "side" of this epistemology, the concept of the ego has to be substantially refashioned to fulfill the requirement of a secure and inviolate epistemological subject. It should be obvious that this innovation is the salient feature of ego-psychological revisionism.

Third, any exposition about the unconscious must also be reconceptualized in accordance with the epistemological requirement of the naturalistic object, or thing-in-itself, which is necessarily mute and motionless. As has been noted, this refashioning compels the expurgation of Freud's original notions of repression, the return of the repressed, and the psychoanalytic reappropriation of the repressed.

Fourth, this naturalistic epistemology must entail an objectivistic account of the method involved in the engagement of patient and psychoanalyst. Correspondingly, it must offer a rather specifically instrumentalist conception of the transformative effects of this engagement.

In the interests of clarity and conciseness, I shall organize the remainder of my critique of ego psychology more or less around these four general issues.

The explicit impetus of ego psychology is to adapt psychoanalysis to "general psychology" (meaning the naturalistic disciplines occupied with the investigation of brain and behavior) and to link Freudian psychology with other empirical and pragmatic disciplines. "Psychoanalysis," Rapaport declares, "is meant to be the natural science of the psyche" (1944, p. 186). Yet, again, the naturalistic scheme is founded on the irrevocable ontic externality and static dichotomy of the subject's being-with and the being-there of things objectivated. So, for Rapaport and Hartmann to make good this declaration, the psyche, or at least its unconscious contents, must be rendered as epistemological object. The dynamic and surpassable contradiction of the reflective "I" and the repressed must be converted into an ontologically static and insurpassable antinomy.

This reconceptualization of Freud's psychology entails a double set of epistemological dichotomies. On one side, it supposes that the patient's psychic processes, both conscious and unconscious can somehow be cast as the epistemological object of the psychoanalyst's naturalistic investigation, or, for that matter, of such an investigation by any other external epistemological agent. In ego-psychological theorizing, there is, for instance, much unreflective talk about the "evidential value of verbal productions" or of the patient's other behaviors during psychoanalytic sessions. Yet, given the character of the repressed psyche as Freud strove to enunciate it, such talk about the psychoanalyst's observational and inferential activity is, even in an epistemological sense, entirely spurious (see Chapter 4). At any rate, the psychoanalyst's alleged investigation could never comprise the entire epistemological activity of the psychoanalytic situation. The ego-psychological scheme must also admit the patient's self-knowledge as integral to the process.

On the other side, then, it is supposed that the patient's unconscious can somehow be cast as the epistemological object of a naturalistic investigation by the patient's self-consciousness or ego functioning as epistemological agent. Indeed, we shall find that ego psychology introduces a plethora of tautologies about the "self-observing ego" and the "ego's capacity for insight." In any case, this antinomy of epistemological subject and object is presumptively dissociated and ontologically inconsequential. According to this naturalistic scheme, the "relation" of the subject's epistemological activity to the passive domain of the thing objectivated is ontically external and contemplative.

What are the ramifications of this attempt to locate the naturalistic subject-object dichotomy within the psychoanalytic situation? To begin with, as epistemological subject the ego must be able to know about its object without, so to speak, being moved by it. Thus, ego-psychological revisions are predicated on a principal interest, not in the dynamic contradictions of polysemous contents, but rather in "mental states of equilibrium" (Hartmann, 1939), which supposedly include the "quasi-stationary" or "nonconflictual" functioning of an ego that has "relative autonomy" (Rapaport, 1957). This interest underpins the tradition's emphasis on structure or organization in psychic functioning. In delineating their program, Hartmann and his followers announce a theoretical reorganization that gives privilege to the structural-functional metapsychological myth (e.g., Hartmann, Kris, and Loewenstein, 1946; Rapaport and Gill, 1959). Although this emphasis is usually billed as part of an ambition to explain the dynamic-sounding "encounter between drive and reality," its naturalistic presuppositions require that the "autonomous ego structures" be given priority and be counterposed both to "external reality" and to the "undifferentiated drives of the id." The static depiction of "structure," which signifies the "ego's autonomy," accords with a naturalistic epistemology, in which a stationary, secure subject contemplates or manipulates the irrevocably separate domain of the object. This adherence to the naturalistic framework implies that the question of psychoanalytic knowledge will be reposed in the traditional form of the classic epistemological problem—the problem of the mind's attainment of knowledge about the world.

In Rapaport's writings, psychoanalysis is explicitly subsumed under the problematic of classical epistemology, and Freudian psychology is perversely rearranged to conform to the traditional question of the means by which the mind may form knowledge about things represented as objects (see Rapaport, 1960b). Rapaport insists that Freud is Kant's heir in two respects. First, Rapaport promotes the idea that psychoanalytic psychology supplements the Kantian account of the mind's epistemological structure by explicating the ontogenesis of "the ego's higher perceptual and conceptual activities." He thus tries to connect Freud's psychology with Heinz Werner's orthogenetic theory of structuration and with developmental "Kantianisms" such as the theories of Erik Erikson and Jean Piaget (see Rapaport, 1942b, 1951c). Second, Rapaport argues that psychoanalytic psychology supplements Kant's account of the mind's knowledge about the "external" world by describing the equivalent activity involved in the ego's knowledge about the "internal" world (1947, 1951b). Thus, he writes that, unlike the questions concerning psychic functioning confronted by Bacon, Descartes, Hobbes, Locke, or Hume, Freud's "point of departure" concerns "evaluation [by] the psychic apparatus"—implying "the ego structures"—of "internal stimuli (drives, needs) rather than external stimuli" (1951b, pp. 316–317, n. 6, italics omitted). Rapaport even regrets that Freud was "tardy" in confronting the question of knowledge about the "outer world" or the question of "reality adaptation."[2]

In reorganizing Freud's psychology as primarily a naturalistic theory of reality adaptation, Rapaport comes to pose psychoanalytic epistemology as a modification of Leibniz's rationalistic question. Leibniz asked how reasoning could arrive at conclusions corresponding to the nature of external reality. According to Rapaport, Freud now asks how an "apparatus" stimulated by "drives" could also be "adapted to reality" (1951b, pp. 316–317, n. 6). Given this interest in guaranteeing the ego's epistemological correspondence with, or adaptation to, "reality," the unconscious must be reconceptualized as merely the "energetics" of acategorical primary processes, somehow subjacent to the autonomy of the neutral "informational activity" of the ego agent's categorical and controlling secondary processes. For Rapaport, it is as if Freud's psychology represented a Schopenhauerian conception of will or energy merely tacked onto a Kantian theory of the mental activity involved in knowing about the world. Following Paul Schilder, Rapaport (1951b) treats Freud's discovery of "internal drive forces" simply as a metaphysical addition to the self-enclosed epistemological structure of a Kantian "pure mind."

The mistake here should be obvious by now. As indicated earlier, Freud's unconscious is not simply an appendix to the naturalistic scheme, leaving untouched the premise of a static and self-certain consciousness that contemplates the world of things objectivated. Rather, Freud's discovery jeopardizes the presuppositions of the natural attitude, inasmuch as the existence of repressed contents subverts Kantian assumptions about the "pure mind," about the autonomy of the structures of "rational" cognitive activity. As we have seen, Freud's critical notions about repression imply that the knowing of psychoanalysis is ontologized, and thus indict the architectonic impetus to determine a fixed and final form for epistemological activity. Indeed, if psychoanalytic discourse, as the scientific pursuit of the

---

[2]This regret, incidently, is in line with Rapaport's persistent tendency to denigrate Freud's early work. He sees *Die Traumdeutung*, for example, as merely an anticipatory contribution toward the metapsychology of the structural–functional model, and he pictures the discovery of "internal drive forces" as dangerously close to "solipsism." Thus, he ultimately misunderstands, in the most gross and serious fashion, the originality of Freud's discovery of the repressed unconscious (see Rapaport, 1957, 1958, 1960b).

repressed unconscious, is apprehended, then the logical empiricist myth of an epistemological agent, immune from the sociality and historicity of human desire, collapses.

The Hartmann-Rapaport tradition thus inaugurates an egregious misapprehension of the extraordinary quality of psychoanalytic discourse. It ineludibly expunges Freud's quintessential dialectical discovery, which characterizes the subject of the conscious "I" as the agent mediating the repression of certain ideas, wishes, fantasies, and so forth, and which thereby exposes the falsity of prepsychoanalyzed self-consciousness. The hegemony of a naturalistic metascience leads to an ideological rehabilitation of the classical epistemological view of the mind's knowledge about or adjustment to a pregiven world. With little exaggeration, we can conclude that, whereas the kernel of psychoanalytic discourse is the question of *personal alienation* between "I" and the repressed content of unconsciousness, in the Hartmann-Rapaport tradition of ego psychology this question is entirely displaced by a pre-Freudian preoccupation with processes of *personal adaptation* to some supposedly pregiven external reality.

In attempting to make psychoanalytic psychology conform to the framework of naturalistic epistemology, the concept of the ego is, of course, the very first to be substantially refashioned. The move toward a hypostatized "ego structure"—a stationary and secure subject contemplating or manipulating the incontrovertably separate ontic domain of the id, the unconscious, or the outer world—accords with the naturalistic scheme. As Rapaport states, "the ego's relative autonomy from the id [is] the guarantee of our relatively even and solid relationship to the outside world" (1957, p. 724). The ego, then, is conceived as an entity, a general structure, existing for the most part independently of any unconscious contents and engaged in knowing about or adjusting to the presumably predetermined world of things objectivated. Proceeding from Freud's (1933) injunction that relating to the "external world" is decisive in the development of the "I," ego psychology enlarges the functions of the ego to include not only a range of defensive mechanisms against "instinctual danger" (A. Freud, 1936), but also the control of a set of allegedly nonconflictual operations, such as attention, motility, synthesis or drive integration, higher conceptualization or categorical inference, and the perception of self, others, and the world in general (see Hartmann, 1939, 1950). The ego thus established is autonomous with respect to the drive forces or the id, and it operates as a quasi-unified and noncontradictory structure of rational and organizational secondary processes (Hartmann, 1939; Rapaport, 1951b, 1951c, 1957).

What are some of the specific dangers of this reconceptualization? First of all, the enlargement of the scope of ego functions to embrace those that are supposedly nonconflictual—that is, those that do not exist as the false consciousness of polysemous contradiction—entails a reformed account of the ontogenesis of "psychic structure." This account connects the concept of the ego to a naturalistic psychology of individual development. The "structure" is now conceived as constitutionally or congenitally based, and hence the putative autonomy of the ego is assured (Rapaport, 1957, 1960a). Freud's notion of the unconscious as the "original" and intentional "essence" of psychic reality, from which the reflective "I" of awareness emerges as a contradiction, is rejected. Against Freud's early discoveries, the Hartmann-Rapaport tradition returns to consciousness, of which the ego is the guardian, its pre-Freudian status as the independent and essential psychic reality. The concept of the ego has been expanded to encompass a set of epistemological, organizational, or adaptational functions, which operate as a "pure mind"—autonomous and neutral with respect to the intentionality of unconscious desire, to the "subjectivity" of the repressed.

It is noteworthy that many of the early psychoanalysts, endorsing the orientation of Freud's premetapsychological writings, viewed the investigation of "ego structure" as nonpsychoanalytic or anti-psychoanalytic. They saw it as counter to the essential originality and interests of psychoanalytic work. Anna Freud (1936) was the first to break with this view. Yet, in the effort to reorient psychoanalysis as a "general psychology" in the naturalistic mode, Anna Freud and the whole Hartmann-Rapaport tradition have effectively expurgated Freud's characterization of the subject of consciousness as the agent mediating the repression of unconscious contents. To reiterate, the concept of an autonomous ego structure, with its diversified yet harmonious and nonconflictual functions, tends to delete Freud's particular interrogation of the false consciousness of the "I" in the state of polysemous contradiction. The notion of ego defenses becomes a "partial concept," a way of buttressing the allegedly autonomous and neutral functioning of the epistemological, organizational, or adaptational processes of the general ego structure. The personal alienation of which Freud spoke is now necessary and beneficial for the "proper functioning" of this "general ego structure"; it is effectively reduced to a physicalistic and regulative matter of the "mutual influences of ego and id" (Hartmann, 1952). Priority is now given, not to the rupture of prepsychoanalyzed self-consciousness and the repressed unconscious, but to the "strengthening" of the ego as an ontically stationary, structural system. A requisite task of this ego is the manipulative control of the unstructured and unconscious drive forces of the id, in the interests of adaptation to a presupposed given—the objective "external" world.

As the repressive "I" is re-formed into a general ego structure, functioning like a "pure mind" that knows about and adjusts to "external reality," so, too, is the repressed unconscious revised as a "pure object" or thing-in-itself. What is involved here is a fundamental reconceptualization of Freud's realm of repressed mental contents either as part of the ego or as the nonconscious existence of nature. This pre-Freudian lapse begins with Hartmann's (1939) tendency to view the unconscious merely as that which is not the ego, namely, the "biological part" of personality. It is a view based on the physicalism of Freud's later metapsychology. Taking *Das Ich und das Es* (Freud, 1923b) as the *opus magnum*, the ego-psychological tradition juxtaposes the psychic activity of the ego structure with respect to the "outer" world and the biological activity of "inner drive forces." In the same way, Rapaport interprets *Hemmung, Symptom und Angst* (Freud, 1926b) as the thesis in which "the structural concepts are recognized as in part representing external reality referents and the drives are recognized as in part representing biological referents" (1960b, p. 19). This naturalization of the unconscious, in which its psychic or intentional character is ignored, coincides with a conflation of Freud's discovery with nonconscious processes. Rapaport, for instance, argues that the psychoanalytic unconscious is entailed by the assumption of psychic causality. Thus, to give just a single example, he proposes that the occurrence of gaps in memory furnishes logical evidence for the unconscious (1944, 1960b). Even granting the mistaken supposition of causality, we can see this as a lacuna in Rapaport's usually rigorous ratiocination: the mere occurrence of gaps may prove the operation of processes that are not conscious, but by no means does a gap in and of itself testify to the exile of the memory to an unconscious that is repressed. The latter can only be demonstrated by reappropriation of the memory in the course of psychoanalytic interrogation. The point is that in offering this argument, Rapaport seems to forget the repressed and psychic character of the Freudian unconscious.

To maintain their naturalistic presuppositions, Rapaport and his colleagues are obliged to biologize the unconscious into the nonpsychic substrate of the ego structure, or Kantian "pure mind." In his treatise on "Dynamic Psychology and Kantian Epistemology" (1947), one finds Rapaport badly confusing the determinacy of Freudian psychology with an untenable application of a physicalistic assumption about causality to the plane of a specifically mental activity. He thus insists that "unconscious determination implies . . . either unconscious determination without further specification, or instinctual determination, or, driven further, physiological and even hereditary determination of personality make-up as well as individual action and thought—the chain of unconscious, instinctual, physiological, hereditary came about as an attempt at further- and further-reaching causal reduction" (p. 296, italics omitted). In all this, the ostensibly faithful retention of the metapsychological unconscious tends to conceal the extent to which the unconscious as repressed and psychic has been disposed—reconceptualized as merely the biological realm of "mobile drive energy," not bounded in the course of ego development (Hartmann, 1948, 1950; Rapaport, 1951c, 1960b). The alienation of conscious and unconscious is reduced to a distinction between the psychic activity of the epistemological or adaptational agent and the raw material of natural force.

Not only is the physicalistic and mechanistic jargon of metapsychology deployed to implement this reductive reconceptualization, but there is also a literalistic interpretation of this mythology, which results in some remarkably incogitant assertions. For example, Rapaport, having colluded in biologizing the unconscious in antinomy to the secure entity of ego structure, nonetheless derides the dichotomy between the mental and the natural as "one of the beloved hobby-horses of metaphysical psychology" (1951b, p. 525, n. 32). But isn't this his own hobby-horse? He himself assumes such a static antinomy in his Kantian account of the dichotomy between ego and inner drive forces. The reason he is blind to his own inconsistency lies in his belief that the mythical constructs of metapsychology resolve the problematic relationship between mind and matter, the belief that Freud's great discovery was of the structuration of drives in "the encounter with reality," of the biological forces from which the architecture of all psychic activity is composed. Rather than confront the subversive psychic character of the unconscious as repressed ideas, wishes, and fantasies, Rapaport seems to move toward a strictly physicalistic reduction of all mental activity, even the "rationality" of ego structure. For him, it is, so to speak, better to detranscendentalize Kant's subject in the most incogitant manner than to apprehend the significance of Freud's discovery as radically subverting the metaphysical presuppositions of naturalistic metascience.

The central argument here, however, is that ego psychology inevitably comes to view the unconscious either as part of the ego or as a biological substrate of this psychic "apparatus"—the domain of raw nature, or "unbounded energy," not controlled by the regulatory activity of psychic structuration. Not only does this reconceptualization ideologically suppress Freud's discovery of the unconscious as repressed psyche, not belonging to the "I-ness" of ordinary mentation, but it cannot even comprehend why the personal alienation of conscious and unconscious should be problematic. The static ontological duality of mind and matter is totally unlike Freud's notion of dynamic contradiction between "I" and the repressed. A dichotomy of the mental and the natural does not, for example, admit the distinctly Freudian notion of the return of the repressed; thus, those contradictions that are polysemous, and hence may be psychoanalytically interrogated to disclose concealed ideas, wishes, fantasies, and the like, are deprived of meaning, for the natural thing objectivated is not intentional in this manner. Instead, the ego-psychological renovation implies that these contradictions—such as symptomatic and characterological formations—are only indicative of inadequacies in the ego's structuration or regulatory control of its biological substrate. Obviously, this view has consequences for the ego-psychological conduct of psychotherapy, as will be discussed shortly. The relationship between psyche and soma may be dystonic, as in the experience of physical pain, but it cannot be meaningful and contradictory, for the somatic could not be said, in and of itself, to comprise an intentionality striving for conscious expression. Again, the tendency for ego psychology to biologize the unconscious, with the aid of metapsychological myths, precludes the articulation of Freud's quintessential notion of those polysemous contradictions, existing *in* self-consciousness but not *of* self-consciousness, as the disguised obtrusion of unconscious ideas, wishes, fantasies, and the like. There is no place for the insistence of the repressed upon the text of the "I" of reflective awareness. In this sense, ego psychology ultimately does away with Freud's discovery of the unconscious.

Now it should be noted here that even if the proponents of ego psychology were to deny this description of their reformulation as overemphasizing the naturalization of the unconscious, and argued instead that, at least in part, the id is still psychic, or that the repressed is within the ego organization, they would not thereby avert the weight of these criticisms. One response to these comments might be to assert that the id in ego psychology is the place where biological requirements somehow come to be represented in the form of "freely mobile," "drive-related," or "primary-process" ideation—the space beyond the repression barrier, wherein physiological energy somehow becomes psychological thought. But such an assertion does not circumvent the crucial issue. It still represents the dualism of ego and id as a naturalistic dichotomy, in which the id is unalterably the epistemological thing objectivated. It cannot see how psychoanalytic discourse demonstrates the rupture of conscious and unconscious as dynamic contradiction.

This misconceptualization is exposed in ego psychology's outright failure to comprehend the significance of Freud's notions of repression and the return of the repressed. On the one hand, the ego-psychological reconceptualization cannot account for why this mentation is repressed, why it does not belong to the "I-ness" of ordinary, organized mentation. On the other hand, because this reformulation conceives of the ego as unified and relatively nonconflictual or autonomous, it relegates the return of the repressed to an ultimately inexplicable anomaly within a hypostatized theoretical edifice. Rapaport, for example, manages to define the topography of the unconscious without reference to the repression of unconscious contents (1960b, pp. 46–47), and his discussion of repression, couched in metapsychological jargon, manages to obliterate the radical implication of this notion (1942a, pp. 166–168). As already indicated, the reconceptualization of the general ego structure as bounded energy relegates the unconscious to a domain of nonconscious, unstructured energy, and the privileged position given to ego autonomy and to the automatization involved in ego structuration erases the contradiction of unconscious mental contents in the conscious-preconscious domain. "Repression" is redefined as the internal equivalent of a "stimulus barrier," which "scales down the intensity of external stimuli to a degree which the organism can manage" (Rapaport, 1951c, p. 694). This wholly inadequate version of repression dispenses with any mention of the meaningful *content* of what is repressed; it serves only to establish conceptually the supposed *form* of the effectively immobilized dichotomy between ego structure and undifferentiated id. Moreover, by tossing aside Freud's claim about the intentional character of the unconscious as dynamic and desirous with respect to the "I-ness" of self-consciousness, this redefinition implies the meaninglessness of the notion of the return of the repressed. The intentionality of the unconscious is now occluded by metapsychological mythology, in which force and mechanism substitute for any more psychologically germane notion. To give just one example, the "wish-fulfilling" aim of the unconscious psyche is now mystified, or trivialized on the psychological level, as "the unrestrained tendency toward full discharge by the shortest path" (Rapaport, 1951c, p. 694). In line with the assumption of a naturalistic framework, Freud's discovery of the psychological meaningfulness of the disguised obtrusion of unconscious contents must be ablated. Thus, we find, for example, that Rapaport denigrates Brentano's influence upon the young Freud, failing to see "unconscious drive" as "psychic intentionality" in a sense that approximates Brentano's.

Indeed, psychological meaning or purpose—the fabric of psychoanalytic discourse—entirely eludes the theorizing of the Hartmann-Rapaport tradition, disappearing into a concept of the "binding of drive cathexes," which is the prerogative of the regulatory and controlling mechanisms of the ego structure (Rapaport, 1951c, 1960b). The naturalistic presuppositions of ego psychology result in the abrogation of Freud's germinal discovery that the contents of the repressed unconscious bear psychological meaning, yet are not "ego." All this betokens how far from Freud's psychoanalytic science the tradition's scientistic theoretical reformation has regressed. Despite all the dynamic-sounding rhetoric about the "id's unbound drive energy" and despite the tentatively promoted admission that there might be contents and not just "physiological energy" in the unconscious, the reconceptualization of ego psychology excludes the alienated intentionality of the unconscious that is the core of psychoanalytic discovery. Despite its employment of the terminology of repression and the return of the repressed in a vitiated metapsychological form, these critical notions are effectively expurgated, because the contents of the domesticated unconscious are now, in the psychological sense that concerns meaning and significance, as motionless and mute as the naturalistic thing-in-itself. Although the Hartmann-Rapaport tradition makes its theoretical failure to apprehend the originality of Freud's discovery of repressed unconscious meaning somewhat inconspicuous through its prolific use of metapsychological myths, its implications are fundamentally anti-psychoanalytic.

The ego-psychological theoretical rendition is accompanied by an objectivistic reconceptualization of the method of psychoanalytic psychology, as well as of the process involved in the engagement of patient and psychoanalyst. A scheme in which an autonomous ego apparatus adapts to a pregiven external reality, by the contemplative manipulation of the unconscious treated as thing objectivated, entirely abandons the anti-objectivistic notion of psychoanalytic discourse as an interrogation of polysemous contradictions. The critical notion of a reappropriation of the repressed eludes the naturalistic reformulations of ego psychology. In this scheme, the thing contemplated or manipulated remains in itself, *ontologically* opposed to the subject's epistemological, organizational, and adaptational activity. As object or substrate, the unconscious cannot be said to contradict the contents of the ego disruptively, nor can it be restored to subjectivity in the course of psychoanalytic reflection and interrogation. The only "reappropriation" that ego psychology can thematize is the reconjunction of mental contents already within the ego system, that is, already owned by the "I." Therapy focuses on the conflicts, incongruities, and disparities within the conscious-preconscious domain. It may be palliative to integrate diverse "ego functions" by reinforcing "the ego's capacity for higher synthesis" of its own contents. But psychotherapy in the ego-psychological tradition can only mean the strengthening of this "organization," without calling its subject fundamentally into question. Unnoticed activities may be brought into immediate awareness, but the boundaries of its subjectivity cannot be interrogated. The ego itself, after all, is the mediating agent of repression.

The objectivistic attitude of ego psychology disbars the archaeological directionality of Freud's discourse, as a progressive uncovering movement of reflection and interrogation, in the course of which the false consciousness of the "I" of immediate reflective awareness is unmasked to disclose repressed contents and to restore them to a transformed self-consciousness. This recuperative "archaeology" could be said to imply a destructuring of the prepsychoanalyzed "ego system," allowing the unconscious "thing" to speak as subject. Unlike naturalistic investigation, the historicized discourse of psychoanalysis does not terminate while the "object" is alien. But this essential character of psychoanalytic discourse as an interrogative movement is wholly incomprehensible in terms of the naturalistic reconceptualization of ego psychology.

Instead of offering an "archaeology" of the repressed unconscious, the Hartmann-Rapaport tradition objectivistically remodels Freud's psychology in line with an acritical ideology of pedagogy and health, conceived as organismic adaptation to the presumed givenness of "objective reality." Hartmann (1939, 1956), for example, advertises his psychology as the "objectivistic study of subjectivity." A major implication of this naturalistic program is that the discovery of the unconscious is of a previously unknown "object" domain, now made epistemologically available to the ego by the application of new conceptual categories and rules of inference or regulatory control, which the subject imposes upon existing "phenomena." Hence it is further implied that the psychoanalytic process must, in large measure, involve the psychoanalyst's transmitting to the patient either information about the patient's unconscious and its regulatory control, or the conceptual and inferential means for the patient to acquire such information, or both.

Thus, in the interests of rendering a "natural-science" account of psychoanalytic methodology, the Hartmann-Rapaport tradition ushers in a biphasic concept of the psychoanalytic process. Hartmann makes this explicit when he suggests that "in the course of analysis the new insights the patient gains by way of objectivation can be gradually integrated, in a secondary way, also in his immediate experience" (1958, p. 309). He seems to mean that, first, the patient learns (or worse, is taught), about his or her unconscious and its "proper control" in the service of "reality testing" and "adaptation," and second, changes in the patient's person are somehow effected on the basis of this new information. Just how spurious this biphasic depiction is will become clear when we discuss the dialectical character of psychoanalytic discourse in Chapter 4. Indeed, it will be found that, in contrast to naturalistic investigation, nothing is observed, inferred, or manipulated during psychoanalysis. This is not to say that observation and inference, as understood in common parlance, may not occur on the part of the patient or the psychoanalyst, but that, in the sense embodied by logical empiricist epistemology, the ontological consequences of psychological discourse are not contingent upon such activities. For the moment, however, my argument will be confined to a demonstration of the utter inadequacy of ego psychology's attempt to account for the ontically transformative character of psychoanalytic discourse.

Tellingly, Hartmann and Rapaport rarely write about the process of the psychoanalytic situation, yet, when they do so, their theoretical difficulties are striking. In approaching the crucial issue of the way in which the knowing of psychoanalysis is transformative, both customarily take recourse to the rhetoric of metapsychology. But writing about the goal of "binding cathexes" or "changing existing structure" (Rapaport, 1951c, 1960b) ill conceals the lack of cogency in such formulas. The inapposite adoption of a physicalistic lexicon to speak of processes of psychological transformation hardly comprises an account of what is involved in these processes. We would even be justified in concluding that it obfuscates the issue. Moreover, even if a literal reading of metapsychology were acceptable, and even if it could be shown that by observation and inference the psychoanalyst can know about such physicalistic matters as the patient's internal "cathexes" and "structure," it would still have to be explained how interpretation about these matters through *words*—the *communications* and *meanings* that are the fabric of the debate between patient and psychoanalyst—could possibly affect substantive and material forces or entities. Rapaport, for example, argues that "phenomena must be explained in terms of forces and entities immanent in the observable phenomena themselves" (Rapaport & Weber, 1941, p. 84). But how do such "explanations," spoken in the interpretations of the psychoanalyst, who neither prods nor pokes, ever come to change these naturalistic things? To write metapsychologically about the issue of psychoanalytic transformation never resolves this gaping problem. Hartmann (1927, 1951, 1956) brazens the problem by virtually refusing to discuss the question of language in psychoanalysis. And Rapaport (1951a), whose disinterest in language is a notable lacuna in his otherwise raptorial curiosity, simply skirts the difficulty in relating a process of interpersonal communication to the metapsychological mythology. Objectivistic and physicalistic theorizing cannot adequately broach the issue of the transformative power of words in the discourse of patient and psychoanalyst.

Beyond this vacuity of metapsychological speculation in relation to the psychoanalytic process, there are other criticisms of the ego-psychological view of psychoanalytic discourse. Hartmann and Rapaport both assert the objectivism of psychoanalytic knowledge. Hartmann, for instance, proclaims that "in the process of analysis itself, the patient's relations to inner and outer reality are restructured, distortions are undone, and a more 'objective' picture is substituted for them . . . analysis means increased knowledge of reality, inner and outer, in the strict, objective sense" (1956, p. 265). Rapaport (1944) is seemingly more cautious about the psychoanalytic situation, but more enthusiastic for extrapsychoanalytic experimental proof of Freud's notions, including that of the unconscious. He argues that the "clinical-historical" method of psychoanalysis cannot "vouch for the validity of the results it obtains" because "the validity and the limitation of all methods can be obtained only from empirical observation" (p. 186). He even adds that this method "does not imply anything about the laws that operate in the unconscious" (p. 191). Yet Rapaport also insists that the clinical method may be "characterized by asking for information about psychological behavior" (p. 192); it is a matter of "dealing with the subject of experience and the object of investigation by making him the subject of questioning" (p. 184). Such pronouncments contain two propositions about psychoanalysis—both false. The first is the erroneous idea that the truth of unconscious mental contents may be obtained *objectivistically*, and the second is the scientistic belief that such knowledge is *instrumental* in the transformations of psychoanalysis. Both mistakes are part of an ideology of adaptation which, in the theorizing of ego psychology, deposes

Freud's principal interest in unraveling the dynamic contradictions of the "I" and the repressed.

With Hartmann and Rapaport, an immutable, pregiven world is presumed, in line with the naturalistic framework. The task of the psychoanalytic situation is therefore to help the patient's ego structure to acquire "objective" knowledge about the world, both "inner" and "outer." Indeed, because the thing-in-itself is supposed to be ontically mute and motionless, the acquisition of such knowledge in the interests of adaptation is even upheld as an impartial, value-free, and "scientific" enterprise (see Hartmann, 1939). By equating the problem of knowledge about "outer" and "inner" objects, Hartmann (1939) views the psychoanalytic method as a matter of reinforcing the given "rationality" or "intelligence" of the ego—of strengthening "the highest synthetic and differentiating functions of the ego" (p. 69). He argues that "the functioning of intelligence on this level may have two kinds of effects: it may lead to a better mastery of the environment . . . and, what is particularly important, to a better control of one's own person" (p. 70).[3]

Who, it might well be asked, is to acquire this objectivistic knowledge about the patient's mind? According to the Hartmann-Rapaport tradition, the first answer is the psychoanalyst and the second is some special function of the patient's own ego apparatus.

Allegedly, the psychoanalyst must be able, by observation and inference, to contemplate the patient's psychic contents and functioning, both conscious and unconscious. In the interests of adaptive change, the patient must somehow learn to do the same. Here we find that the notion of psychoanalytic discipline as the science of meaning disappears altogether. In order for the psychoanalyst to carry out the role of "empirical psychologist," he or she must have "data" upon which to conduct this naturalistic investigation. Thus, even though Freud warns against the wish for "objective verification" (1916–1917, p. 12) or public scrutiny (1925a, p. 67) of psychoanalytic process, the epigoni proceed to redefine psychoanalysis as the investigation of "behavior" (Rapaport, 1960b, p. 39). This redefinition may appear to be minor, especially given the continued talk about the "psychological determi-

---

[3] This viewpoint leads to some remarkable inconsistencies—for instance, Hartmann's passing reference to amnesia and repression as "self-deception" (1939), his limp and convoluted essay on psychoanalysis as "scientific theory" (1959), and his indecisive disquisition on the errors of self-understanding (1927), with its baffling assertion about the applicability of "causality" to mental activity itself when, for Kant, this is a synthetic *a priori* principle employed by the mind in representation of the natural object.

nants" of behavior. Nevertheless, its purpose is to operationalize the discipline, reducing it to an "empirical psychology" by designating "data" for the psychoanalyst's observation. And its eventual consequence is to erase Freud's discovery of the polyvalence of behavior with respect to the constitutive intentionality of private, nonobservable meaning.

Rapaport (1942b, 1944), for example, promulgates a tortuous and ultimately incoherent thesis, which acknowledges the existence of processes behind appearances, yet at the same time defends an epistemology that treats appearances affirmatively as authentic or "pure data" from which underlying processes may be directly and immediately inferred. This attitude is also illustrated in Hartmann's (1939) idea that the "rational regulations" of the epistemological agent should be able to treat irrational processes merely as facts. Again, in the attempt to affirm the static facticity of what is observed, ego psychology abnegates the transformative movement of Freud's methodology as a progressive, historicized discourse revealing a reality of contents repressed "behind" the manifest appearances of false-consciousness.

Having provided the psychoanalyst with "pure data" for naturalistic observation of the patient, ego psychology is obliged to prescribe a formal logic of inference, by which the psychoanalyst arrives at valid conclusions about the patient's psychological contents. The recurrent appeal for fixed canons or rules of psychoanalytic interpretation—along with the Jacobinist conception of "psychotherapy" it promotes—is indeed tied to this tradition's objectivistic epistemological reformation. Yet here, interestingly enough, we find that Rapaport, having a sophisticated understanding of Kant, equivocates. Unlike Hartmann, he seems to recognize that the method by which the unconscious is comprehended in psychoanalysis might not be an ordinary formalistic procedure, for he admits that the contents of the unconscious are "not necessarily approachable by logic" (1944, p. 181). Rapaport tries to circumvent the problem—which is not unlike the Kantian problem of other minds—by introducing Kant's naturalistic distinction between phenomenal appearance and thing-in-itself. He seems to argue that Kantian principles of the organization of self-consciousness are "applied" to the representations of appearances, making possible the prediction and hence control of future appearances. He then intimates similar principles of the organization of ego structure, permitting the comprehension and control of appearances that somehow emanate, physicalistically, from "inner drive forces" (see 1944, 1947). Although this "solution" represents some of the best theorizing of ego psychology, it continues to miss Freud's innovation.

Once again it evidences the assumption that the unconscious, like the thing-in-itself, is mutely meaningless or ontologically unobtainable in itself—thus, ignoring Freud's claim of reappropriation of the repressed. Moreover, it fails to discern the significance of Freud's methodology as the demystifying revelation that appearances are not always what they seem, that they are not neutral "facts." In this sense, it obliterates the notion of the "return" of the repressed, of polysemous contradictions in the manifest content of experience and understanding.

Despite his equivocation, it is quite evident that Rapaport *does* require synthetic principles for the organization and modification of the observable "facts." In this regard, he subscribes, as unambiguously as all the rest of the Hartmann tradition, to the objectivistic ideal of some, as yet unspecified, inferential logic of psychoanalytic investigation. And here it is telling to note that the requisite elaboration of such a logic has never been fulfilled—not withstanding the misconceived attempts to offer standard interpretations for "fixed symbolism," or the feeble efforts to expound rules of interpretative technique. If we comprehend Freud's notion of the repressed unconscious, such a categorical apprehension of contents precluded from ordinary mentation is simply not possible. Nor can a static formal logic be applied to psychoanalytic interrogation of the intentionality immanent in polysemous contradictions. The knowing of psychoanalytic discourse that reveals and reappropriates the repressed cannot be made to conform to the objectivistic epistemology of observable fact and formal inference.

With the second part of ego psychology's naturalistic account of psychoanalytic process, we encounter even further theoretical difficulties. Here the patient's "ego structure" must also acquire objectivistic knowledge about his or her "inner" and "outer" world—the psychoanalyst's knowledge must come to be shared by the patient in the interests of adaptive change. Allegedly, the patient acquires objectivistic self-knowledge through the operation of a special "self-observing" function of the ego organization, which is a capacity for "insight," conceived "as a turning upon itself and the processes underlying it" on the part of the "rationality" of secondary-process thought (Rapaport, 1942b, p. 112). What such metapsychological legerdemain, which appears to convey the acknowledged reflectivity of supposedly objectivistic knowledge, really signifies, is never adequately explained. Ernst Kris (1956), for example, writes rhetorically about the ego observing "the self," and of "one of the functions of the ego" being "pitted against others." Rapaport (1960b) blandly asserts that the aim of psychoanalytic method is to foster an ontogenetically repetitious relationship between the patient and the psychoanalyst, so that the patient may somehow gain information about and insight into this relationship. Yet behind these vague allusions, serious questions about who acquires this insight and information, or, more saliently, how it is acquired, are left unanswered.

Freud (1915b, 1916–1917) argues that the transmission of information to the patient about his or her psychological contents is ineffective, and he vigorously refutes didacticism in psychoanalysis. Yet the Hartmann-Rapaport tradition—because it holds objective knowledge as the key to psychoanalytic methodology—inevitably ends up endorsing a conception of therapy in which the psychoanalyst deploys tutorial skills to enable the patient to gain objectivistic information about personhood and world. The goal of therapy is now to remodel the patient's ego structure upon the psychoanalyst's in the interests of "mental health." The "objective picture" of inner and outer reality the patient must acquire is that asserted by the psychoanalyst—the "reality" to which the patient must adapt is the one defined by this psychoanalyst.

Moreover, ego psychology never explains the ontological efficacy of the imparted, objectivistic information. The transformative effect of this naturalistic knowing upon the patient's being raises questions that the Hartmann-Rapaport tradition is at a loss to answer. The ritualistic use of metapsychological mythology does not obviate the failure of this tradition to account for what Hartmann assumes is the "secondary" integration of objectivistic insights into immediate experience and understanding. Indeed, it is under the auspices of ego psychology that it seems to have become almost fashionable in Anglo-American circles to regard the essential metamorphic character of Freudian discourse as one of the inscrutable and even unspeakable mysteries of the psychoanalytic situation.

To the extent that the theorizing of the Hartmann-Rapaport tradition does try to specify the transformative effect of psychoanalytic methodology, it adopts the scientistic view that objectivistic knowledge is instrumental to this transformation. The psychotherapy of ego psychology thus becomes equivalent to procedures whereby the world of nature is brought under the technological domination of the epistemological agent—the inner drive forces of the id are to be harnessed instrumentally and manipulatively by the organizational activity of the "ego structure." The anti-psychoanalytic character of this instrumentalism should be evident by now. Whereas psychoanalytic discourse is a reflective and interrogative movement that aims to restore the unconscious content to consciousness, progressively surpassing the alienation of "I" and the repressed, the psychotherapeutic goal of ego psychology is to strengthen the dominance of the ego structure, im-

proving defensive or repressive functions to effect a "sharper differentiation of the ego and the id . . . which on the one hand makes for a
superior, more flexible, relation to the external world, and on the
other increases the alienation of the id from reality" (Hartmann, 1939,
p. 48, italics omitted). Although it is tentatively acknowledged that
repression "constricts" or even distorts the functioning of the ego
(A. Freud, 1936), the ego-psychological tradition nonetheless must
strenuously insist that repression against "instinctual danger" is to be
safeguarded and supported by "psychotherapy" in the service of adaptation to the sociocultural order (Rapaport, 1951b, 1951c).

The anti-scientific and anti-psychoanalytic character of this position
should also be evident. When personal alienation becomes a virtue for
individual adaptation to existing sociocultural conditions (the normativity of "objective reality" by another name), even if it is cautiously
recognized that the repression involved restricts ego functioning, then
the proponents of ego psychology are obliged to specify criteria to
discriminate optimal and less optimal processes of repression or "defense." Such criteria *cannot* be derived from scientific reason, but only
by reference to the socioculturally expedient adaptation of the individual. Indeed, with this instrumentalist and manipulative conception
of psychotherapy, any practice that serves to adapt the patient to the
milieu becomes acceptable on a purely pragmatic basis. Apart from the
benign ethics of its practitioners, nothing in the theorizing of ego psychology prevents the political expediency of the shoddiest and most
inhumane forms of behavioral manipulation. Rapaport (1944), for example, confronts insuperable difficulties in attempting to differentiate
his conception of treatment from the practice of "suppressive
psychotherapy." However much the canonization of ego structure is
couched in an attempt to assimilate psychoanalysis to the objectivism
of logical empiricist epistemology, it is impelled by the ideological
requirement of sociocultural conformity in conceptual organization.
The Hartmann-Rapaport tradition effectively subordinates
psychoanalysis, as the scientific pursuit of the repressed unconscious,
to an ideology that exalts the normativity of the manifest and precludes critique of this sociocultural order, adaptation to which is contingent upon the personal alienation of psychic reality.

PSYCHOANALYSIS AS A
DIFFERENT KIND OF SCIENCE

It now becomes evident that the twin apostasies—the subjectivistic
adulation of "selfhood" and the objectivistic apotheosis of the ego—are

not so significantly different. Both emerge from a common ideology that is anti-scientific and anti-psychoanalytic. In this regard, the heated debate between "culturalistic" and "biologistic" approaches, which has preoccupied the Anglo-American scene for many years, is irrelevant to the scientific conduct of genuinely psychoanalytic discourse. I am not denying the differences. The neo-Freudian approach tends to omit the dynamic unconscious altogether to focus on the sociocultural harmony of integrated self-consciousness, whereas ego psychology tends to reconceptualize the unconscious as the biological side of the dichotomy between mental activity and its "object." The former slides into a "surface psychotherapy" of adaptive "awareness of self and environment," whereas the latter endorses a psychotherapy of instrumentalist domination and self-manipulation in the service of adaptive "reality testing." Yet both take the individual's healthy adaptation to external reality, naively conceived as pregiven and unalterable, as their starting point. Thus, both relapse into a pre-Freudian stance; they relocate psychoanalysis in a framework that can neither recognize nor articulate the extraordinary and enigmatic character of Freudian discourse.

Now, part of the familiar scientistic ideology is the belief that the sole alternative to naturalistic epistemology, in which knower and known are irrevocably distinct and ontically separate, is the arbitrariness of mystical doctrines, wherein subject and object evaporate or are juggled indeterminately. Similarly, it is commonly believed that the sole alternative to "ego epistemology," in which the subject is stationarily self-certain in its ontic location, is some sort of id psychology, in which the unconscious is directly and immediately intuited. Both beliefs are false. An id psychology as such is not possible. But there *is* a scientific pursuit of the repressed unconscious in which the reciprocal interpenetration of the being of the subject and the being of the thing is progressive and determinate. Thus, our elucidation of the scientistic ideology of Anglo-American reformulations does not imply advocacy of some mystical id psychology, nor does it mean that all talk of the subject and object of knowing need be jettisoned. As we shall see in the next chapter, the scientific, anti-ideological quality of psychoanalytic discourse involves a movement in which the supposedly immutable dichotomy of the being of the subject and the being of things is surpassed.

For the moment, we need only reiterate that the primary anti-scientific error of the Anglo-American impulse to coopt psychoanalysis is its ideological assumption of the authenticity of the adapted "ego agent." Conceived as a neutral, objective entity for epistemological and organizational adaptation to an unchangeable, pregiven world, encoded in the normativity of shared discourse, the ego is an ideological starting point rather than a scientific methodological notion. Against this conception, Freud's discourse is scientific precisely because, having relinquished naturalistic presuppositions about external reality and the validity of self-consciousness, it arraigns this "ego," which it finds to be the "guardian" of a false consciousness. Psychoanalysis indicts the ego as a symptom, its repressive or "defensive" functioning constituting a form of falsification (see Freud, 1900, 1915b, 1937a, 1937b). As Lacan (1953b) indicates, the ego is known as "the resistance to the dialectic process" of psychoanalysis (p. 12), which is the "essential resistance to the elusive process of Becoming, to the variations of Desire" (p. 15).

Far from being the *summum bonum* of human personality, the "ego organization" is shown by scientific interrogation to be a false totality—a contradictory or phantasmagoric structure, formed as an arrest of the dialectic of desire, as an accretion of alienating sociocultural relations. Fixated in the alienated condition of polysemous contradiction, it is a false identity of mentation, whose foremost character is, in Lacan's words, *méconnaissance systematique*—the refusal to acknowledge the inner realities of desire. Thus, against *analytische Wissenschaftstheorie*, the science of psychoanalytic reflection and interrogation disabuses the autarchy of self-consciousness. It demonstrates that knowledge is a discursive metamorphosis of the subject, rather than the result of a stationary agent imposing a static and formalistic ideal upon an immutably external domain of things objectivated. Against the conformist ideology, in which the entification of "ego" or "selfhood" legitimates established conditions as the fixed and final form of the world to which the individual must adapt, psychoanalysis sets its discourse as the directionality of emancipation.

What does it mean to write of a scientific pursuit that sets its discourse as the directionality of emancipation? Against the assumptions of "analytic" epistemology, psychoanalytic discourse discovers and recovers the formative intentionality underlying all knowing processes, the workings of contradiction within the representational and desirous constitution of psychic reality. Psychoanalysis implodes the architectonic preoccupation with the myth of an absolutely certain or final, ahistorical, asocial, and universally valid reflective or contemplative knowledge. In so doing, psychoanalytic discourse wrecks all the distinctive dichotomies that are fetishistically cherished by the ideologies of naturalistic investigation—between the contexts of discovery and validation, between knowledge and praxis, between truth and value, and, of course, between the being-with of the knowing subject and the there-being of the thing that comes to be known. Avowing its ontic consequences, the knowing and being of psychoanalytic discourse comprise a critique of the inevitable insufficiency—the ideological partiality and fixation—of the metascience of "analytic" epistemology.

To recapitulate, according to this familiar metascience of "normal" investigation, knowledge requires a knower and a known, whose beings are irrevocably apart and different—self-consciousness with its apparent subjectivity and the there-being of things objectivated. In this framework, knowing must be either subjectivistic or objectivistic.

In subjectivism, knowing its reflective, involving an affirmative recursion of self-consciousness upon its own being. It is an inquiry upon being that already belongs to the subject. And its truth does not alter the being of the subject. Transformation is evident only in the most palliative manner which retains faithfully the locus and boundary of the affirmatively treated subject.

In objectivism, knowing is contemplative, involving investigation by an affirmatively treated self-consciousness of the there-being of things represented as "objects." Truth is a matter of correspondence in contemplation between the subject's representations and the nature of things. It is positivistically acquired in an investigation about a being that has never belonged to the subject and never will. Truth alters neither the being of the subject nor the being of the thing objectivated, with respect to their mutual ontic externality. Transformation is evident only in an instrumental and operational manner, which retains faithfully and affirmatively the ontological dichotomy of the knower's self-consciousness and the domain of the things investigated.

Psychoanalysis is neither subjectivistic nor objectivistic. Its changeful inquiry does not fit the metascientific coordinates of familiar epistemology. Psychoanalytic discourse is neither affirmatively reflective nor contemplative in the "analytic" philosophical sense. Its interrogative movement is neither the disontologized egology of subjectivism, nor the fixatively dichotomous ontology of objectivism. In psychoanalytic discourse, there is an ontologization of method such that truth is inherently transformative. Truth is not a matter of reflective apodicticity, proclamation, coherence, or contemplative correspondence. It is a praxis, a knowing that is intrinsically mutative with respect to being. Indeed, psychoanalysis shows that to treat the being of self-consciousness affirmatively, and to treat the there-being of things objectivated positively, is to preclude an inquiry upon psychic reality and its subject-being as a nonidentity, a locus of contradictoriness. Such an inquiry must involve truth as praxis, and the interweaving of knowing and being as dialectically negative. All this leads to the conclusion that psychoanalysis is a different kind of science. Freud seems to sense this radical implication when he refers to "a conflict with official science" as "the destiny of psychoanalysis" (1913, p. 395).

4 Hermeneutic Ontology and the Dialectics of Deconstruction

What have we achieved thus far? Principally, the first three chapters have offered a *critique*. Less has been said about what psychoanalysis is than about what it is not. Less has been said about the proper conduct of psychology, as the science of psychic reality, than about the pitfalls of dominant modes of investigation. It should be quite clear that Freudian claims concerning repression, the return of the repressed, and the discursive reappropriation of the repressed cannot be accommodated within the Cartesian-Kantian world-view, the underlying metaphysical ground of the traditional epistemology of "natural science." Psychoanalytic discourse transgresses the presumptive coordinates of this episteme. It concords neither with objectivism nor with subjectivism, even when the latter is purified by transcendental reflection. To try to comprehend psychoanalytic inquiry and change from within this frame is ultimately to lose all that is extraordinary and enigmatic about Freud's science of mental activity. In this context, I have endeavored to show how seriously psychologies of subjectivity, as well as psychologies of objectivity, miss the point—even though they may make contributions in other ways and on other levels.

There is another, more general implication of my critique. Not only does logical empiricism fail to apprehend the specific praxis of psychoanalytic discourse, but it is also a badly limited and ideologically partial framework from which to undertake *any* study of mental life. It is not just that psychoanalysis is somehow overlooked by logical empiricist precepts, but that the scientificity of the discourse between patient and psychoanalyst *indicts* the coordinates of subjectivism and objectivism, despite the technological accomplishments they proclaim, and even when their metaphysical suppositions are empowered by the vigor of transcendental technique. In other words, the psychoanalytic question is not merely methodological. It is not simply a problem raised by one method of investigation among many, like a debate between sociologies involving participant observation, controlled experimentation, or large-scale survey techniques, all of which operate within a common framework of assumptions about knower and known. Rather, the psychoanalytic question strikes at the heart of our epistemological and ontological stance, engendering the most fundamental controversy over truth and transformation in any psychological endeavor.

Psychoanalytic discourse cannot be contained within the dominant psychology, but shatters it paradigmatically. As we shall see, against the dominant mode of investigation, psychoanalysis emerges as an authentically scientific psychology. Freudian reflection and interrogation may apprehend the experiences and understandings attained by psychologies of objectivistic and subjectivistic persuasion, but not the reverse. Indeed, the dialectical discourse that psychoanalysis entails may hold these attainments as momentary terms within a progressive movement of sublation. But psychoanalytic psychology goes beyond the dominant modes of investigation, revealing the falsity of their limited and partial achievements. In this sense, it is not just that the knowing and being of psychoanalytic discourse cannot conform to the fundamental attitudes and interests of the dominant psychology and naturalistic epistemology, but that this discourse necessarily and dramatically points to the prejudices of their hegemonical configuration of subject, object, being, and method. Psychoanalysis breaks the epistemic mold.

Wherein does the scientificity of psychoanalysis lie? To answer that Freud's discoveries are hermeneutic rather than logical empiricist is both beguilingly correct and misleadingly oversimple. To be sure, psychoanalytic discourse implies interpretative epistemology, as a continual work of experience and understanding moving within our representational worlds. Yet, in this sense, as was argued earlier, all knowledge is hermeneutic—whether it recognizes it or not—for it is bound and determined by its sociocultural and intersubjective conditions. Whereas the epistemological formulations of logical empiricism characteristically depend on an unreflective appeal to "data," without acknowledging that this corrective function is itself representationally constituted, the traditions of hermeneutic philosophy acknowledge the sociocultural and historical conditions of all experience and understanding, as either the intersubjective contextuality or the ontological ground of knowledge itself. Hermeneutics then presents the knowing process as a trajectory *within* worlds that are, for us, semiotically constituted.

Admittedly, psychoanalysis is a hermeneutic science of a certain sort. Freud himself seems to recognize this when he indicates that to enter psychoanalytic inquiry and change is to acknowledge the marvelous and inescapable power of language (1905c, 1926a), for "nothing takes place in a psychoanalytic treatment but an interchange of words between the patient and the psychoanalyst" (1916–1917, p. 9). And as is well known, he compares his discipline to the study of a rebus or scripture, and its method to that of philology and textual criticism (1900, 1913, 1923b, 1938, 1940). These comparisons are not entirely appropriate, however, as we shall see. Again, "hermeneutics" as an answer to the radical and profound questions raised by psychoanalytic discourse, or as a solution to the malaise of the dominant mode of contemporary psychology, is absurdly facile—even though it seems to have satisfied some recent commentators. Hermeneutic formulations, fashionable as they may be for a certain minority, typically neglect the critical notions of repression, the return of the repressed, and the reappropriation of the repressed, as well as Freud's seminal discovery of psychic reality as the subject's locus of contradiction. In this respect, psychoanalytic discourse challenges hermeneutic philosophies in the most fundamental manner.

If we look at the two distinct traditions of hermeneutic philosophy, we find that psychoanalysis belongs to neither. Its discourse does not accord with nineteenth-century hermeneutics, the world-view of Friedrich Schleiermacher, Wilhelm Dilthey, and some neo-Kantian investigators of mind, history, and culture. Nor does it accord with contemporary ontological and existential hermeneutics, the world-view of Martin Heidegger, Hans-Georg Gadamer, and others. To the first tradition, we shall give short shrift, because for the most part it comprises an epistemological formulation within the framework of subjectivism and objectivism, already discussed in Chapter 3. The second tradition deserves a fuller confrontation, as it brings into focus complex and fundamental questions within the philosophy of science, notably on the nature of totality, truth, and transformation. It is here that discourse of patient and psychoanalyst makes a unique and revolutionary contribution. Psychoanalytic reflection and interrogation call into question the precepts and canons of "normal" hermeneutic doctrines, subverting their intelligibility and giving the lie to their epistemological and ontological horizons. Indeed, psychoanalytic discourse compels hermeneutic epistemology and ontology in an entirely new direction. By setting normal discourse against itself, psychoanalysis pursues a changeful inquiry upon the interiority of psychic reality. It is both scientific and emancipatory.

PSYCHOANALYSIS IS NOT HERMENEUTIC
IN THE TRADITIONAL MENTALIST SENSE

Historically, hermeneutic metascience has had several facets. Traditionally, heremeneutics comprises technical disciplines for the annunciation, explication, and translation of ordinary language communications, notably religious and literary documents. As the practice of exegesis, the field of hermeneutics derives from the classical crafts of grammar and rhetoric and is closely associated with Judeo-Christian teaching of scriptural materials. Systematic hermeneutic methodology burgeoned in the seventeenth century with the erosion of institutionalized religious dogma and the liberalization of bourgeois thought. It continues into the present as a philological adjunct to theology and jurisprudence. As a technical aid, formalized hermeneutics also girds such current specialties as semantics, syntactics, pragmatics, historiography, and literary criticism.

The spirit of hermeneutics, however, has broader and deeper significance. Beginning with the philosophy of Friedrich Schleiermacher at the turn of the nineteenth century, and less explicitly with his predecessors J. G. Fichte and G. W. F. Hegel, hermeneutics becomes the foundation for an entire theory of knowledge, in which interpretation is not merely an auxiliary technique for the therapeutic remedy of impaired communication, but the way of all experience and understanding. During the late nineteenth century, under the influence of so-called *verstehen* philosophy, this program is elaborated as the special methodological platform for human studies or *Geisteswissenschaften*. Although this methodology is designed for the investigation of historical, cultural, and mental processes, it essentially stands as a *complement* to the epistemology of objectivistic investigation in the realm of physical and material events. Subsequent theorizing involves a reversal of the epistemological and neo-idealist implications of the nineteenth-century stance. Hermeneutics now becomes an existential and ontological grounding, from which *all* processes of knowing issue, and which accounts, through the exegesis of linguistic events, for the revealing and concealing of the conditions of human being-in-the-world. It is this program of twentieth-century hermeneutics, that bears significantly on our comprehension of the psychoanalytic venture, but it will not be discussed until the next section, for it is quite distinct from the nineteenth-century tradition, from which it receives its name.

Schleiermacher's romantic theology makes the act of understanding, *verstehen*, the basic principle of epistemology and thus inaugurates the modern era of philosophical hermeneutics. After Schleiermacher, neo-Kantian and neo-Fichtean philosophers of the late nineteenth century, such as the Baden school of Wilhelm Windelband and Heinrich Rickert, advocate the *verstehen* principle as the distinctive feature of human science, complementing the observational and inferential principles of natural science. Drawing on the Cartesian-Kantian heritage of philosophical analysis of the knowing process, the hermeneutic theorists of this era characteristically endorse a "two-worlds" ontology that distinguishes the realm of facts and physical objects from the realm of values and human subjects. They react against the infiltration of positivistic sterility into the sociocultural sciences by elaborating a neo-idealist defense of subjectivity. Natural and sociocultural phenomena are dichotomized, and the understanding of everyday communicative experience is systematized as a methodical discipline for the investigation of history, culture, and mental activity. The Baden school, for example, adheres uncritically to the precepts of logical empiricism for the study of natural phenomena, but proposes a methodological division between the formalistic procedures of naturalistic investigation and the historical, value-related and comparatively idiographic conduct required for understanding sociocultural phenomena. Despite its contribution to technical issues of interpretation in the human sciences, this phase of hermeneutics, with its naive view of objectivistic epistemology, is quickly exhausted by difficulties in specifying the relationship between natural and sociocultural science, and by the indefensible implications of the "two-worlds" framework.

To pursue this matter a little further, let us consider Wilhelm Dilthey's famous maxim: "Nature we explain, psychic life we understand." Freud himself seems to have flirted briefly with this formulation—for example, when he writes that while dream interpretation gives rise to "greater understanding," as a "psychic process, it is not possible to *explain* dreams" (1900, p. 515). Conceding the validity of the objectivistic investigation of nature, Dilthey attempts to specify investigative procedures appropriate to the historical, sociocultural, and psychic worlds.[1]

Reading Dilthey on the conditions of "understanding" illustrates clearly how, *within* the presuppositional coordinates common to the subjectivistic and objectivistic episteme, "differing attitudes of the

---

[1] Through his struggle with such issues, Dilthey has exercised an enormous influence on Continental theories of knowledge. Although, with the notable exception of Emilio Betti's contemporary historical research, there are almost no current adherents to the tradition of hermeneutics expounded by Schleiermacher and Dilthey, this tradition has nonetheless given issue in three major directions: the transcendental subjectivism of Husserlian phenomenology, the ontological and existential hermeneutics of Heideggerian philosophy, and the almost mystical vitalism of the "life philosophies" enunciated by Henri Bergson and Georg Simmel.

subject in the cognitive process [may result] in different configurations of experience and theory in the natural and cultural sciences respectively" (Habermas, 1968, p. 143, italics omitted). Dilthey, as Schleiermacher's successor, takes autobiography as his hermeneutic model, on the premise that autobiographical communication is, at least potentially and immanently, an inherently pellucid and apodictic unity. That is, he assumes, as did Schleiermacher, the identity of valid understanding and the expressed immediacy of lived experience in the individual's self-consciousness. Given such far-reaching assumptions, Dilthey is able to take the everyday communicative experience of understanding oneself as a wholly valid and reliable method for understanding other people. He then makes it into a systematic methodology for the investigation of the sociocultural world. The particular unity of autobiographical speech, writing, and action is, Dilthey assumes, a part of the "community of life unities." Thus, interpretation can supposedly proceed directly from the presumed givenness of immediate self-awareness to knowledge of other lives. The subject's self-knowledge is automatic, according to the assumptions of this tradition; it is the occurrence of misunderstanding within the intersubjective community that raises philosophical problems.

In his early writings, Dilthey appeals for a descriptive and "analytical" psychology as the systematic foundation for all sociocultural science—an appeal that influenced the Wurzburg and Gestalt schools, as well as the psychologies of William McDougall, Karl Jaspers, Eduard Spranger, and probably C. G. Jung. In response to several critics, Dilthey later modifies his early emphasis on the individual psyche and writes about the structural unity of "life" as the foundation of immediate certitude. It can be seen here that Dilthey's notion of "understanding," as distinct from "explanation" of nature, is anchored in a monadological notion of *verstehen* as empathy. In both his earlier and later philosophy of human studies, the particular monad knows itself indubitably by its own expressiveness, and is concordant with the totality of monads in such a way that this knowledge of the particular permits knowledge of all others. In the romantic tradition, Dilthey asserts his belief that the expressive self-knowledge of the freely determinant individual mind is more or less unproblematic, offering valid and reliable access to the minds of others, and thence to an understanding of the sociocultural whole.

For Dilthey, individual understanding of personal life experiences depends on the fusion of expression and interpretation. The life experiences of others may be understood by the activity of empathic "transposition" or "projection of the self into the other." This activity seems to be an admixture of positivistic inference and an occult leap of imagination or intuition. Having taken the apparent factual evidence into account, the transpositive act (which is similar to Schleiermacher's notion of "divination") is a vicarious or "reproductive" experience of "reliving" or "reconstruction." Because of the presumed monadic identity of human minds with the totality, it allows the inner experiences of another person to become as freely available to awareness as one's own supposedly are. Thus, according to Dilthey, individual self-consciousness is a pellucid and apodictic unit of a uniform and universal totality. His hermeneutics assumes the validity of awareness by self-inspection, and proceeds to specify a methodological technique—namely, empathy—by which other minds may be known.

Dilthey dimly recognizes that empathy, or "reexperiencing," as the main method advocated for human studies in general and psychic understanding in particular, must depend on the community of semiotic processes—although, of course, he does not write about the issue in this manner. Indeed, without specification of the intersubjective "medium" through which the intermonadic act of transposition becomes possible, his hermeneutics would rapidly devolve into a variant of mystical intuitionism, as might be said of some of the vitalistic philosophies that follow Dilthey. From the standpoint of psychoanalytic suspicion, we may immediately ask to what extent this transposition is merely a tacit appeal to the conventionality of *sensus communis*. Tellingly, when Dilthey attempts to deal with such problems, he sets aside the subjectivistic and "intersubjectivistic" tendencies of his program, and reverts to a thoroughly objectivistic and neo-Kantian call for systematic categories and rules for application to historical, sociocultural, and psychic "data." It is as if Kant derived a noumenal canon for knowledge about the thing-in-itself of nature, and now hermeneutics will provide a homologous canon for the thing-in-itself of other minds. Hermeneutics becomes simultaneously a commonsensical mode of analysis directed toward a semiotic "object" and a form of subjective and intersubjective experience that is allegedly readily self-understandable. Neither this objectivistic "logic," nor the metaphysical assertions about the intermonadic subjectivism of transposition, withstands the rigors of psychoanalytic scrutiny.

At this point we may appropriately pause to reconsider the comparison between psychoanalysis and the interpretation of texts, for textual hermeneutics is typically viewed as involving both of Dilthey's methods: objectivistic rules for analysis of the textual "object" and the subjectivistic leaps of imagination or intuition, by which means it may even be claimed that the exegete can arrive "empathically" or "reconstructively" at the author's intentions. Assuming the pregiven unity of textual meaning, traditional hermeneutics necessarily proceeds holistically. Its exegeses obey what is known as the "hermeneutic circle," in that the whole text must be apprehended before the meaning of the parts can be adequately understood, and a grasp of the parts, a willingness to accept them as they present themselves, is required for the satisfactory comprehension of the whole unity of meanings. Similarly, it may be said that the understanding of a particular text depends on the contextuality of all such communications. Thus, in practice, interpretative technique must move back and forth across the text or series of texts until, supposedly, a final moment of completed insight is attained.

According to Schleiermacher and Dilthey, the exegete's self-knowledge is to be taken for granted, due to the presumed identity of understanding and expressive experience in the individual's self-consciousness. The exegete's apprehension of the textual object, and even presumedly of the subjectivity of its author, proceeds by "divination," "transposition," or "empathy," as well as by inferences based on canons of interpretation generated by the dominant *sensus communis*. Indeed, according to Schleiermacher and Dilthey, the interpreter, moving more freely from part to whole, may acquire a better understanding of the work than the creator, whose expressive understanding in "lived experience" is assumed. Understanding another is thus axiomatically unproblematic. Concomitantly, the occurrence of misunderstanding merely implies partiality or restriction of hermeneutic purview—a failure to move from the particular to the semiotic totality of all possible experiences and understandings. Imperfections in the text—for example, gaps in the transparency of its entire meaning as apprehended by the exegete—are to be repaired by appeal to the conventionality of ordinary meaning, philological logic, or prevailing common sense, to the everyday self-understandings of communicative experience or some specialist's algorithm thereof.

Traditional hermeneutics may thus have a "therapeutic" function, according to an "ideal" of discourse embodied in the sociocultural system. In this "therapy," however, the textual object is unmoved; its subjectivity, by the very fact of its immobility, cannot develop. The authority, by which interpretation operates, appears to be the presupposed coherence and unity of the text itself, although actually this authority is that of the exegete's representational world as a totality—a totality within which the text is already inscribed, and within which the conditions of exegetic experience and understanding are already constituted. Upon this totality, the exegete need neither reflect nor interrogate. In this respect, the exegetic oscillation, between the particular expression of experience and immutable totality of possible understandings, cannot call into question the ontological locus of the exegetic subject in the work of interpretation. Meaning may be *bestowed upon* the textual object; thus, interpretation becomes an operation in which the exegetic subject, assured of the apodicticity and boundary of its being, imposes a frame of reference upon the there-being of the objectivated text. However, the subject cannot thereby be disrupted or split. In this respect, meaning cannot be *educed from* the textual object because, as an objectivated thing, it has long since ceased to speak as subject. Textual interpretation does not and cannot entail an ontological movement of reflection and interrogation. Believing itself epistemologically pure, through the secure stasis of subject and thing objectivated, this heremeneutic method disavows any dialectical movement by arresting the interlocutory potential of its discourse.

Here we see how unlike the movement of psychoanalytic discourse the traditional mode of textual interpretation is. Traditional hermeneutics preserves the epistemology of the Cartesian-Kantian worldview, adopting a stance wherein knowledge is either subjectivistic or objectivistic. If an analogy between psychology and the conventions of textual interpretation must be drawn, it would underline the repressive ideology of a "therapy" that "closes over." In contrast to the historicized movement of psychoanalytic interlocution, the "text" neither participates in the hermeneutic work transforming the ontic locus of the exegetic subject, nor is it itself progressively transformed. Although Freud (1900) toys with the philological comparison, he insists that psychoanalysis is necessarily an interlocutory discourse, not a simple translative decoding. The clinical notions of resistance, transference, countertransference, and working through point to the demystifying character of dialogue, in which the ontological loci of subject and the there-being of things objectivated are progressively transformed. Such a dialogue eludes the ahistorical and univocal operation of traditional hermeneutics, which functions as a disontologized method within the dominant epistemological configuration of subject and object.

Moreover, traditional hermeneutics must take the appearance of the text as it is given. From this affirmatively treated starting point, it tries to fill in any manifest gaps. Psychoanalysis, in contradistinction, doubts the authenticity of the text even as it is apparently given. This is why Freud makes such a seemingly odd statement about the dream "text"—that it "does not wish to say anything to anyone for it is not a

vehicle for communication; on the contrary it is meant to remain mis-
understood" (1916–1917, p. 238). Freudian reflection upon and interrogation of such a text never aims for the expedient or parsimonious
abridgment of imperfections in conscious experience and understanding. Psychoanalytic methodology never accepts the interpretation that
makes most immediate sense to the patient—nor, indeed, does it ever
accept the interpretation that makes most immediate sense to the
psychoanalyst. It does not take the apparent meanings of the patient's
conscious, nonconscious, and preconscious mind as an authority. Nor
does it appeal to an interpretative logic by which the psychoanalyst
diplomatically imposes meanings on the patient. Nor does it rectify the
patient's text by upbraiding it according to the standards of coherence
embodied in common sense or some similar sociocultural ideal of communication. For all such hermeneutic methods leave untouched the
sociocultural designation of the "I-ness" of the participiant's mentation. And here lies a methodological distinction of utmost importance.

Traditional textual hermeneutics, bound by the dominant episteme,
may result either in an objectivistic, instrumentalist modification of
the textual object, or in a subjectivistic therapy of "clarification," palli-
ation, and "working over," which charts the boundaries of conscious
and preconscious mental content but leaves the locus of the subject
unmoved. Psychoanalytic hermeneutics, in contradistinction, is not
restricted to the amelioration of imperfection in the "text" of consciousness, for the discovery of the repressed unconscious, of the contradictoriness of the subject within psychic reality, indicts the
manifest and apparent text as a falsification of desire. As Freud expresses it, "psychoanalysis is aptly suspicious" (1900, p. 521). Its
changeful inquiry is not confined within the boundaries of ordinary
representation, for Freud's psychology demonstrates that even an innocent, ordinary communication—semantically "transparent," syn-
tactically "correct," and pragmatically "appropriate"—will prove to be
a compromise formation of psychic reality, concealing as much of the
person's being as it reveals. Through the radical dispossession of the
"I" of reflective awareness, psychoanalysis reinstates a split-off subjectivity "behind" the givenness of the "text." Thus, in opposition to
the logicalness and conventionality of the methodology of textual hermeneutics, psychoanalysis confirms Ernst Bloch's aphorism, "that
which is cannot be true."

As far as apprehension of the unique discourse of psychoanalytic
hermeneutics is concerned, we see here how greatly in error the
philological comparison is—methodologically, epistemologically, and
ontologically. Although the current fashion for theorizing about

psychoanalysis as if it were textual interpretation is valuable insofar as it recognizes the character of this discourse as a semiotic process, the comparison between psychoanalytic hermeneutics and the normal study of texts is thoroughly misleading—both as a model for the psychoanalyst's experience and understanding of the patient and as a model of the patient's own "reconstructive" apprehension of the unconscious and the past. To reiterate, the traditional study of texts is locked within the dominant framework of pure epistemology: knowing is either subjectivistic or objectivistic. In contrast to the negativity of Freudian suspicion, it treats the textual object affirmatively as the starting point of its annunciatory, explicative, and translational investigations. In this way, it necessarily credits the ontological authenticity of appearances. Thus, comparing psychoanalysis to textual hermeneutics misses the crucial and critical significance of the dynamic of contradiction, the prepsychoanalytic falsity of the manifest fabric of discourse. The ontological contradiction of the subject of psychic reality is reduced to a matter of textual deception, and going "behind" the text can only imply an epistemology of decoding or reinscription. It cannot entail the ontological consequences of a dispossession and reinstatement of subjectivity. To pursue mental inquiry and change in the manner of traditional interpretative disciplines is, as psychoanalysis demonstrates, to become entrapped in a hermeneutic circle of false consciousness.

Let us return now to Dilthey's program, which may aptly be regarded as an extension of Cartesian-Kantian epistemology, designed to accommodate the problem of knowledge about other minds. Along the lines developed in Chapter 3, we find that psychoanalytic discourse fundamentally discredits Dilthey's suppositional coordinates: his assumptions about the intermonadic identity and unity of human minds within the sociocultural totality, and his romanticist assumptions about this totality as immutably given and harmoniously preconstituted. The psychoanalytic notion of repression, with its disclosure of self-consciousness as compromise formation, radically challenges Dilthey's affirmation of the identity of interpretative understanding and the lived immediacy of expressive experience in the individual's mind or life history. Moreover, even as subjectivism, Dilthey's methods are weak. For he offers no new means for deepening Cartesian reflections; the supposed givenness of the individual's knowledge is merely self-asserted. The adequacy of the monad's descriptive awareness or inspection through lived experience and understanding is assumed, and the problems or procedures of such inspection, let alone a more penetrating reflectivity, are scarcely addressed. Here it

can be noted that Dilthey's subjectivism is markedly pre-Husserlian—
for Husserl does offer a deepening of Cartesian technique, when he
transcendentalizes subjectivistic reflection and attempts to specify
rigorous procedures of phenomenological reduction. As we have
shown, Husserlian subjectivism is indicted by psychoanalytic discourse as an affirmative treatment of a falsely apodictic subject. And,
of course, Dilthey's subjectivism, with its lesser sophistication, is
wholly vulnerable to the same indictment.

Psychoanalysis adduces a similar critique of the intermonadic scaffolding of nineteenth-century mentalism. The notion of psychic reality
as an *idiographic* world of representation and desire, ruptured by the
contradictoriness of its subject, radically challenges Dilthey's assumption that, from the subjectivistic apprehension of one individual, hermeneutics may proceed by transposition, to know another. By the
same token, as was discussed in Chapter 3, psychoanalysis casts doubt
upon the Leibnizian phase of Husserl's philosophy, in which he claims
to have passed through solipsism. Dilthey's fundamental ideas about
empathy and "reexperiencing," so central to his program for understanding all historical, sociocultural, and psychic events, rest on assumptions about the totality of such events as a pregiven, unalterable,
and harmonious uniformity. Such affirmative assumptions about the
sociocultural system—the totality of possible conditions of experience
and understanding, or "life," as Dilthey insists on calling it—are subverted by the negativity and dynamic of psychoanalytic discourse, in
which the notion of contradiction and the praxis of truth and transformation are given privileges. (This issue of "totality," on which all
hermeneutics in some way depends, will be explored further as we
come to our critique of the existential and ontological program of contemporary hermeneutic philosophy.)

Finally, it should be noted that, when the methodology derived from
Dilthey's assumptions about subjectivism, intermonadology, and the
totality of human minds seems to falter, he takes recourse to an objectivistic investigation of historical, sociocultural, and psychic events,
upholding an understanding of these phenomena through special categories, inferential procedures, and positivistic assumptions about the
facticity of the world totality. Here too, as has been shown,
psychoanalysis undermines the configuration of subject, object, and
the total there-being of things, upon which such hermeneutic methods
are founded.

Oscillating between a mentalist or intermonadological subjectivism
and an objectivism employing special concepts intended for knowledge
of those things objectivated that are not of nature itself, the traditional

hermeneutics of the nineteenth century is unremittingly subverted by the dialectical negativity of psychoanalytic reflection and interrogation. Methodologically, nineteenth-century *verstehen* philosophy might claim to have advanced the meditations of the Cartesian-Kantian tradition upon topics of sociocultural interest. But epistemologically, these meditations do not depart from the subjectivist and objectivist world-view; they are therefore entirely vulnerable to the psychoanalytic challenge to this episteme expounded in Chapter 3. Traditional hermeneutics does not help us to apprehend psychoanalysis, nor indeed can it contribute a scientific approach to mental inquiry and change in general, for as far as *verstehen* philosophies are concerned, psychoanalysis shatters the hermeneutic mold.

PSYCHOANALYSIS IS NOT HERMENEUTIC
IN THE CONTEMPORARY ONTOLOGICAL SENSE

Up to now, we have been exploring the question of psychoanalytic inquiry and change vis-à-vis the traditional coordinates of epistemology. Identity thinking is the *sine qua non* of this epistemological tradition. The subject, the "I-ness" of mental life, forms concepts or representations, things objectivated. It is, so to speak, "in charge of" a semiotic system. And these things objectivated are held to be a coherent and correspondent account of there-being, the way the world is "out there," existing in-itself. As we have seen, the methodology, by which such epistemological *knowledge about* the world is accrued, does not have ontic consequences. Supposedly, the knowing subject of mentation remains, in its being, distinct and apart from the there-being of things objectivated, regardless of shifts within the conceptual or representational horizon of objects.

Twentieth-century hermeneutics fundamentally rearranges this picture of knowing and being. It is in relation to this program, exemplified by the writings of Martin Heidegger and Hans-Georg Gadamer, that the question of psychoanalytic inquiry and change must now be posed. Indeed, Heideggerian-Gadamerian philosophizing may be said to put a stop to the Cartesian-Kantian manner of specifying the problem of knowledge. For in this hermeneutic philosophy, the mandate of epistemology is displaced by an existential and ontological exposition. And this alters entirely the manner in which we may raise questions concerning mentation and being, conceptual representation and the materiality of existence, or—the kerygma of psychoanalytic discourse—*semiosis and desire*. As with psychoanalysis, to grasp the contemporary hermeneutic program, we must relinquish the ordinary way of *looking at* the world and *acting upon* it, the epistemic ideology that partitions subjectivistic and objectivistic mentation. Moreover, we must be ready to consider the dual impact of the Heideggerian-Gadamerian position: its radical displacement of the episteme and its ontological thesis on the finite yet absolute accessibility of things within the determinate totality of *language*.[2] Aphoristically, its basic ontological position is that "being is language," and thus that all that can be experienced or understood is language.

It is appropriate to begin by bringing clearly into focus the apparent radicalism of contemporary hermeneutics with regard to the traditional metascientific framework. For example, against the hermeneutic *Geisteswissenschaften* of the nineteenth century, in which an interpreter generates an understanding of historical, cultural, and psychic "phenomena," Heidegger's and Gadamer's position is, so to speak, that tradition constitutes the interpretation and the interpreter. The exegete can never master the text; he or she can only be its servant. Contemporary hermeneutics sides with Husserl against the "two-worlds" epistemological platform of *verstehen* philosophy, in which mind and nature are presumptively distinguished in order to justify the procedures of historical, cultural, and psychic investigation. Instead, natural science is to be brought within the general question of experience and understanding. However, against Husserlian phenomenology, contemporary hermeneutics does not renovate investigation within a subjectivistic epistemological mode, advocating a disontologized transcendental reflection as the remedy for naive objectivism. Rather, Heidegger and Gadamer take hermeneutics as there-being's mode of being. Understanding and experience are thereby thoroughly ontologized. Hermeneutics is now the potentiality for being itself. Rather than adopting an epistemological attitude, contemporary hermeneutics claims to invoke the horizon of possibility for being-in-the-world.

According to Heideggerian-Gadamerian hermeneutics, "thinking thinks the thinker" and "language speaks us." Such aphoristic formula-

---

[2]Obviously, when Heidegger and Gadamer write about language they intend something much more general than such common languages as French, German, or Sanskrit. The term "semiosis," connoting the totality of representational, significational or meaningful practices, would be preferable. (Heidegger and Gadamer often use the term "linguisticality" in a somewhat similar sense.) In any case, "language" should generally be read as the totality of semiotic systems.

tions hint at the fundamental break with epistemological philosophizing, for they suggest at least an inversion of the usual configuration of subject, object, and the being of things. This break is not merely a shift in attitude within the traditional mandate of epistemology; rather, the hermeneutic exposition of an ontological horizon supposedly displaces the epistemological problematic. When Husserl decides to withhold credence from the apparent givenness of the world of objects in order to inquire upon the subject's constitution of this world and its knowability, he offers a shift in epistemological attitude that operates within Cartesian-Kantian metaphysics. Husserl relinquishes objectivistic contemplation to pursue reflections that are subjectivistic and transcendental. In contrast, when Heidegger unfolds his hermeneutic ontology, he turns his back on the bipartite metaphysical structure of the subjectivistic and objectivistic epistemological tradition. Heidegger's exposition of the being of things—and, in his later work, of their accessibility within language—demotes questions about the activity of subject and object in the putative processes of knowing.

In a certain sense, what we encounter here is a break with the aspirations of "first philosophy" and a reversal of epistemological interests. The idea that the ultimate foundation of knowing processes can be specified is subordinated to an exposition of the primordial ground of the being of things. Subject and object are thus no longer issues of primary significance, but, so to speak, mere derivatives or positionings within this ontological ground. To oversimplify, whereas in the Cartesian-Kantian world-view, epistemology is fundamental and ontology may follow, for Heidegger's and Gadamer's hermeneutics, ontology is fundamental and an account of the processes of knowing is secondary.

With Heidegger, ontology displaces mentation, and existence displaces the metaphysics of the there-being of things that are ontically apart from the subject's knowledge about them in objectivistic form. Aside from Hegel's *Logic* (1812), of which Heidegger is severely critical, ontology has not been so addressed since the writings of Aristotle and St. Thomas Aquinas. Indeed, Heidegger views this neglect as the impasse of Western metaphysics from Plato to Hegel and into this century. Specifically, he refers to this impasse as the obliviousness of metaphysical thought to being. His philosophizing is designed as an exit from this impasse and a response to the crisis of its epistemology from Descartes to Husserl via Kant. Fundamental ontology, Heidegger's project, is necessarily hermeneutic, and hermeneutics issues from the question of being itself, in such a way as to end the speculative dogma of the thing-in-itself as well as the primacy of the contemplative subject in the epistemological process. In moving against the

epistemological nisus of philosophy, Heidegger embarks with a pre-
paratory discourse on human *Dasein*, the notion of being-in-the-world,
and maintains a dogged allegiance to "things themselves." To follow
this revival of classical Greek interests in the question of the meaning
of being and its interpretation, we must grasp the denotations and
connotations of Heidegger's "thing" and "being."

At first glance, it may seem that Heidegger shares Husserl's interest in how things become known to us. But Heidegger's philosophizing
rapidly departs from any semblance of its original Husserlian tutelage.
Being and Time (1927) might initially seem like an extension of transcendental reflections. After all, Heidegger himself refers to it as a
"phenomenological" work—a use of the term that came to offend Husserl. Yet, although the work purports to employ phenomenology in the
service of ontological philosophizing, it is much more than an application of Husserlian methods to a new topic. Heidegger breaks with the
Kantian notion of things as objects, and with Husserl's fundamental
emphasis on essence and subject. Like Husserl, he proposes to go
"behind" apophantic mentation, the knowledge provided by fixed categories and logical rules of inference. But unlike Husserl, he proceeds in
a nonepistomological direction. The Heideggerian effort to exhibit the
ground of our being clearly diverges from Husserl's epistemological
effort to establish transcendentally the foundation of our knowing in
reflection upon the constitutive ground of subjectivity and intersubjectivity. Indeed, the notion of "ground" is turned about. Heidegger de-
legitimizes interest in objectivistic knowledge *and* in the
epistemological subject. Instead, he turns to the meaning of being and
thence to the belongingness of "subject" and "object" in this grounding
of human existence.

Despite Heidegger's reference to his discourse on ontology as
"phenomenological," being is not, strictly speaking, ever treated as if
it were or could be a phenomenon. It is at once more elusive, more
present, and more encompassing. Yet, being is, Heidegger asserts,
inherently accessible—and this assertion, as we shall see, is elaborated
in his later writings on language (1950, 1951, 1959), as well as in
Gadamer's essays (1960, 1960–1972). Being is accessible, Heidegger
insists, because human existence *is*, in a certain sense, an understanding of being in its fullness. Thus, the hermeneutic exposition of being is
not only possible, but also, it would seem, automatic and ubiquitous.

Heidegger's philosophizing, as such an exposition, represents the
notion of "being" in several dozen ways—from "being among-one-
another" to "being toward-what-is-talked-about." What is important
for us to realize here is that, from the definitional spectrum designated

by Aristotle, Heidegger asserts the leading sense of being as *presence*, or *presencing*. Being evades the fixity of objectivation. Accordingly, Heidegger's alliance to "things themselves" involves an ontology of the thing as nonconceptual or noncategorical, very different from the epistemological notion of thing rendered as mental object. And Heidegger emphasizes this difference by developing the word *Sache*, as distinct from the Kantian *Ding*. Heidegger's notion is that hermeneutics—the "logos of phenomenology," as he initially wished to announce it—is to "make manifest" the way in which things themselves "show themselves" to be. Here we again see how the fundamental notion of "things that show themselves" reverses the epistemic perspective on subject, object, and being, and abandons the methodological search for coherent and correspondent truth. We can also see how Heidegger's writing is both, somewhat inconspicuously, a critique and, more emphatically, a proclamation.

It is perhaps difficult to recognize Heidegger's work as a critique because he rarely *argues* anything, merely counterposing an entirely different mode of philosophizing to that of his predecessors. Yet as a critique, his writings are quite profound. As has already been suggested, contemporary hermeneutics promulgates the fundamentality of ontological exposition *against* the epistemological abyss of apodictic subjectivism and the metaphysical dogma of the thing-in-itself, necessitating objectivation. On the side of idealism, this abyss arises from the unworkability of self-certainty and the untenability of aprioristic and experiential givenness as the foundation for the systems of understanding propounded by first philosophy. On the side of realism, this abyss is due to the problematic division of mentation and the notion of the world "out there," existing in-itself. Against the apotheosis of cognition (as perception and conception) within Western metaphysics, Heidegger juxtaposes the temporality, finitude, and futurity of human existence. In a certain sense, his exposition is a move against rationality, if rationality is to be equated with an epistemology of predicative logics and the ontic immobility of conceptual categories.

Heidegger has a critique of objectivism. But it is a critique different from Hegel's sublation of the static forms of objectivating cognition, and different from Husserl's call for a reflection upon the subject who supposedly constitutes objective experience.[3] Husserl retains rationality in a program of transcendental subjectivism that remains within the Cartesian-Kantian world-view. Hegel, breaking from Cartesian-

---

[3] It is also, as we shall see, different from Theodor Adorno's demonstration of the negativity of true conceptual labor.

Kantian epistemology, promotes a notion of reason as the dialectical movement of mentation (as we shall discuss later). Heidegger, however, offers neither a method for mentation nor a means by which truth might be *actively* pursued in praxis. He might be said to assert the prerogatives of human existence over the controversies of reason. Bitterly opposed to the technological ideology that holds sway over modern thought, Heidegger indicates that this ideology— "technization," as he calls it—is derived from the traditionl epistemological configuration of subject, object, and thing. Against this dominant ideology, Heidegger's "argument" is that predicative or categorical *knowing about* the world necessarily loses the authentic thingness of things. This contention, of course, comprises a profound indictment of the contemplative and instrumental attitude.

As a proclamation, Heidegger's work expounds the nexus of being, thing, world, existence, and understanding. Ontology depends on the "making manifest" of hermeneutics as an event in which things are allowed to show themselves. Supposedly, things elude captivity in the fixed conceptual form of *object*—that is, as representations that purport to be about something else. Stepping back from conceptualization, Heidegger asserts the notion of being as the presencing of things and the belongingness of things as being-in-the-world. Again, although Heidegger writes of an astoundingly wide variety of "beings," the leading meaning of being is always presence or presencing. Truth thus comes to mean the unconcealedness of being, for being is continually emerging and receding from the grasp of presentness. The formation of subject and object arises within this ontic context of "world"— human being-in-the-world is prior to the dichotomization of the subject of mentation and the things objectivated in mentation. With conceptualization, being is treated as if fixed or hypostatized, whereas the nature of being is as a presencing that is concealed and revealed.

Because a thing is a presencing of being, object representation, according to Heidegger, annihilates the thing. As objects, things are "pointed to" but not connected to the primordial totality of "world." Heidegger's famous illustrations—for example, of the jug as thing, or of the hammer not as instrument but as tool or utensil for an encounter of being-in-the-world—are poetic attempts to demonstrate that apophantic knowing obscures the primacy of hermeneutic being, that conceptualization shatters the original unity and totality of belongingness. As objects, things *qua* things disappear. An object never reaches the thingness of things.

Similarly, the notion of the subject obstructs the primacy and priority of hermeneutic being. Heidegger attempts to demonstrate that the traditional epistemological demand for the subject's reflective self-grounding, from Descartes through Fichte to Husserl, is unfulfilled. Instead, Heidegger's notion of *care*, as human being concerned about its being, is elaborated into a comprehensive ontological statement about human relatedness to the world, and this displaces the notion of the subjectivity of mental life. Heidegger not only attempts to show that self-certainty, which is objectivating, is not a fundamental ontic category, but he proposes the notion of "care" in lieu of the traditional philosophical ideas about "ego." This renders "I," not as subject, but as an ontological presencing, a process, in Heidegger's phraseology, of "letting a world come to stand" (a point we shall take up later in bringing into focus the significance of language).

Confronted as the interpretative process that displaces epistemological accounts of things as objects, the logos of hermeneutics is an event of the disclosing or unconcealing of being. In this view, hermeneutics is not a methodological art, craft, or technique, but the real experience and understanding that knowing and being incur. Hermeneutics is itself ontological, as the fundamental mode of human being-in-the-world. "Understanding" no longer implies conceptualization; rather, it implies the transmission of there-being and being-in-the-world. In this sense, understanding is held to be ontologically fundamental. It is a foundational mode of existing, with a certain priority over existence itself.

From our preliminary discussion of Heidegger's notions of thing, being, and understanding, the significance and complexity of his exposition of human being-in-the-world begins to unfold. Influenced by Parmenides, Heraclitus, and Anaxagoras, Heidegger deploys the term "world" to indicate the totality of being that is "present-at-hand," the multiplicity of entities and events that comprise the worldliness of the lived world of experience and understanding—a usage akin to that of the term "reality" throughout this book. Given his formulation concerning being as understanding or interpretation of itself, there is being only when there is appearing, and entering into unconcealment.

From this position, Heidegger (1927, 1953) discusses several modalities of human being-in-the-world. It has existentiality—that is, it is situated or presented as a "mood." And here Heidegger offers some of his well-known precepts on fear and dread, care, and "being-toward-death," and on authenticity with respect to conscience, guilt, and resolve. (These precepts, which bear some similarity to Georg Simmel's "life philosophy" and Max Scheler's call for a philosophical anthropology, germinally influenced the mid-century European vogue of existentialism.) Human being-in-the-world, Heidegger intimates, also has potentiality. It involves the "thrownness" of there-being, as well as the quality of a project, a directionality toward the future, in the context of its finitude. (One might compare this notion to that of psychic reality as both project and product.) Finally, human being-in-the-world entails understanding, as we have discussed. And, as we have yet to discuss, it entails the proximity of understanding to speech and language, to articulation as a "setting forth" of the world. Here again, according to Heidegger, the very quality of human belongingness to the world, being-in-the-world, is itself hermeneutic. In his phraseology, understanding is the mode of being of there-being itself. Human being-in-the-world, human *Dasein*, poses itself in the manner of a question. It is inherently being that questions being. Following Søren Kierkegaard, the problem of human existence is an existential one.

In the contemporary hermeneutics of Heidegger and Gadamer, temporality and language form the "transcendental horizon"—the ground and limit—of being-in-the-world. Turning about Kant's dictum that mentation itself occurs only in time and not in space, and diverging significantly from Husserl's and Henri Bergson's contemporaneous writings on time, Heidegger shows how the meaning of being is hermeneutically bound to time. The notion of being as continually emerging and receding from the grasp of presentness, and the notion of understanding as always related to future, as a "thrownness" and a project that transmits there-being as being-with, already indicate the significance of temporal relations and of finitude for Heidegger. The relation of being to past, present, and future is integral to the very conditions of possibility of being-in-the-world. Temporality comprises the primordial ground from which the fundamental distinction between there-being *(Dasein)* and being-with *(Mitsein)* emerges. Thus, the belongingness of being-in-the-world to time is the *sine qua non* of all hermeneutic experience and understanding.

Influenced by Dilthey and Nietszche, Heidegger's writing stresses the *historicized* quality of human there-being. Both he and Gadamer advance a thesis on historical interpretation, in opposition to the historicist school of Johann Droysen and Leopold von Ranke. For Heidegger and Gadamer, as we shall see, language, being, and history, are prodigiously infused. The important point to note at this juncture is the historicized character of understanding that this implies. Heidegger and Gadamer promote a characterization of understanding as reiteration, a retracing of pathways within language in order to repeat an original disclosure of being. This characterization—to which the dialectic of psychoanalytic discourse is vigorously opposed, as I shall demonstrate—depends on presumptions about the finitude and totality of being-in-the-world.

In Heidegger's early writings, temporality is discussed as the *horizon* of human being-in-the-world, meaning that it is both ground and limit—a designation of the finitude of being as a totality. If being is presencing, its counterpart is nothingness or death. Indeed, we can scarcely underestimate the importance of the notion of death for Heidegger's philosophy. In his view, the nature of human existence is its relation to the future. Human being-in-the-world is marked by its finitude and futurity. The notion of "being-toward-death" propels the Heideggerian exposition. Heidegger points to death as the innermost, nonrelative or absolute, insurmountable and certain potential of human being-in-the-world, toward which this being-in-the-world is thrown. It is also a temporally indefinite future, a finitude of being. In this sense, being is defined by death: being is propelled toward death, and death marks its finitude.

For the moment, we may bypass any similarity between this Heideggerian notion and the Freudian idea of *Thanatos* (a "similarity" upon which Lacan's theorizing is constructed). What we need to recognize here is that death allegedly vindicates assumptions about the totality of being-in-the-world upon which the entire enterprise of contemporary hermeneutics rests. To reiterate, the temporality of being is finite, the being-in-the-world is thrown toward this finitude. The finitude is the delimitation by death, and in this sense the notion of death entails the boundaries of being-in-the-world. This delimitation, Heidegger takes to mean that care, or being-in-the-world, is a *totality*—a totality in a particular sense, fabricated by language, within which hermeneutic being is articulated. Without this particular sense of totality, the Heideggerian-Gadamerian world-view collapses. Indeed, we shall find that the reflection and interrogation of psychoanalytic discourse bring about such a collapse. Before proceeding to this remarkable finding, however, we need to clarify the role of thinking and speaking, of language, in Heideggerian-Gadamerian philosophy.

Given the contemporary hermeneutic project of fundamental ontology, what sense is now to be made of thinking and the truth of thought? Heidegger's account of thinking follows from his exposition of interpretation and understanding. As was indicated, understanding, from the Heideggerian-Gadamerian position, is an inherent mode of the being of things, a transmission of there-being and being-with, and a foundational mode of existing. It is itself an ontological process, rather than a mental or epistemological one. Thus, hermeneutics now signifies a fundamental being-in-motion of there-being, incurring the historicity, finitude, and futurity of being and implicating the notion of being-in-the-world as a totality. It concerns ontological unconcealment, as a laying open of existence and a disclosure of human being-in-the-world.

In this context, hermeneutics is not a conceptually objectivating discipline (as logical empiricism would demand), nor is it a philological technique. It is not an epistemological method at all, as it was in the nineteenth century. Rather, hermeneutics is the primordium of things bringing themselves from concealment. It is an interpretation of the being of there-being, but it is also an aspect of the very nature of there-being in that the latter unconceals itself in understanding: there-being becomes being-with. In other words, hermeneutics is an announcing process by which there-being makes itself known. Understanding, as the unconcealment of being through hermeneutic enunciation, is ontologically fundamental, "prior" to the activity of existence. Understanding is not a subject's grasp of events in the formation of objects, nor is it in any way spatialized. Rather, it is the temporal unconcealment of concrete potentialities for being within the horizon of belongingness, of being-with, as human existentiality.

Bereft of its former designation as the activity of a subject, understanding is now a basic way of there-being's being-in-the-world. Accordingly, thinking is no longer an epistemic process, but the articulation of understanding, a hermeneutic enunciation (see Heidegger, 1935–1936, 1954). Interpretation is no longer founded in mentation, as categorical understanding or the speculative formation of the perceptual and conceptual object. Rather, interpretation is founded in the manifestness of things encountered as "world." Stepping back from thinking as ideational, instrumental, and explanatory, Heidegger asserts thought as presentational, an enunciation of being wherein human being-in-the-world spans the chasm of concealment and unconcealment, of being and not-being. Thinking is thus neither contemplative nor instrumental, but "creative"—an "intentionality" of being itself rather than an activity of a subject.

In this manner, Heidegger makes clear his opinion that humans never contend with being, but are simply open to it. Thinking is never a struggle, but simply a responsiveness to the address of being. Thus, it is neither a conceptual invention nor a conceptual manipulation of the already disclosed, but a disclosure of the hidden. Thinking is an exegetic openness to being that, by repetition of an original act of disclosure, brings forth further disclosure. It is a response to the evocative and invitational voice of being, transmuting the ontological difference between being and the being of beings. As a response to the original call of being-in-the-world, thinking is a recalling and remembering, a memorializing of being's past disclosures. Interpretation, then, is a repetition or retrieval of prior events of unconcealment. Although it is not a simple return to the past, inasmuch as it brings forth further disclosure, it comes, within the horizon of language, to have the sense of a transmission of tradition. Hermeneutic experience and understanding thus comes to imply the constitutive determinacy of heritage or tradition—"tradition" not as the product of human subjects, nor as an object encountered by such a subjectivity, but "tradition" as identified with the totality of language.

Now, given these coordinates of the contemporary hermeneutic position, what is the truth of thinking? As we have seen, within Cartesian-Kantian epistemology, truth is a matter of conformity between knower and known: a correspondence and a coherence of rationality, permitting the subject's certainty of this conformity. The subject is an ultimate reference point, and being is only comprehended within the mental polarity of the subject and its intentionality toward objects. In contrast, truth in contemporary hermeneutics is not a matter of subjective assertion and speculative objectivation, nor of perception, conception, and judgment in the ordinary sense. Rather, truth is grounded in existence itself, in the manner in which there-being unconceals itself as being-with. Thus, it is not fixed and final as form or content, but a mobile process of ontic revelation in lived experience and understanding. This process is historicized, "thrown" toward the future, and hence determined by the totality of being-in-the-world. In Heidegger's exegesis of the Platonic analogy of the cave, for example, the point is not to comprehend truth as the coherence and correspondence of representations that are about something else, but to grasp truth as the mobility of unconcealment and openness of things without epistemic deliberation—a stepping out of the cave, so to speak.

Parenthetically, we can see here to what extent, from the viewpoint of logical empiricism, Heidegger is vulnerable to charges of mysticism. For he espouses a position in which thinking is not perceptual, conceptual, or judgmentive; in which interpretation is never a matter of correctness or agreement; and in which truth criteria of contemplative veridicality and instrumental efficacy are abandoned. The charge of mysticism—of a doctrine of intuitionism, or of an arbitrariness in the grasp of things—would indeed be unanswerable if contemporary hermeneutics were not able to make good its claim of an ontological displacement of the epistemological problematic. But having made ontology fundamental, contemporary hermeneutics sidesteps the charge of mysticism. Given its promotion of an ontological notion of truth, a different sort of question must be asked of contemporary hermeneutic philosophizing—namely, what *determines* thinking and what guides interpretation, as ontological movements? The answer given by Heidegger and Gadamer points to being itself, to the determinacy of the "structure" of the meaning of being-in-the-world as a totality comprised by the horizons of temporality and semiosis.

For Heidegger and Gadamer, hermeneutics takes up a stance of responsive openness to the play of being-in-the-world. It allows for the address of being, by a movement of discourse on the margin of the concealing and unconcealing of being. There is no *method* for thinking to follow, except in the sense that the mandate of interpretation is to play upon this margin. Interpretation—as a sort of playfulness and as a questioning, in the sense of being's own questioning of its own being—memorializes the fundamental being-in-motion of there-being. Thus, interpretation, as a mode of being-in-the-world, could be said to have threefold determinacy. It is temporally conditioned as a historicized movement, in that it affirmatively brings into play the "prejudices" or dogmas of tradition, rendering preunderstandings manifest as new understandings. It is also temporally conditioned as an anticipatory movement, for, just as being-in-the-world is projected toward its futurity and finitude in death as the delimitation of being-as-a-whole, so, too, understanding is "thrown" toward an anticipated completion in the supposedly immanent unity of all possible meanings of being-in-the-world. Finally, because interpretation comprises a deepening and widening of prior understandings, a renewed presencing of being in a new event of the "making manifest" of "things that show themselves," it is conditioned by the totality of possible meanings of being-in-the-world—a totality again marked by the horizon of temporality and, as we shall see, by the ground of semiosis as being itself.

Interpretation comes to mean a certain "placing in the open" of being. To be "authentic," it requires a questioning or playfulness that in Heidegger's phrase, "lets a world come to stand." This hermeneutics is not arbitrary in its movements, for it is governed by the determinacy of being-in-the-world as a whole over the particularity of hermeneutic events. All understanding thus occurs within a "hermeneutic circle" of a certain sort: the particular can only be understood by understanding the whole; to understand one must already have understood. The notion of further understanding or further unconcealing of being in a particular hermeneutic event is a deepening and widening of hermeneutic movement and a retracing of prior pathways of unconcealment. It is governed by being-in-the-world as a totality of preunderstandings, and is thus historicized. It is also governed by the anticipation of completion, the movement of understanding from the particular event of unconcealment toward revelation of the totality of being-in-the-world. In this sense, hermeneutics is thoroughly determined as the being-in-motion of human there-being, and is always, in August Boeckh's (1877) words, "a knowing of the known" (see Gadamer, 1960–1972, p. 45).

This "circularity" of hermeneutics is not methodological, for it is neither subjective nor objective. It is, according to Heidegger and Gadamer, a benign necessity, an aspect of the very nature of being-in-the-world, rather than an epistemological entrapment. In their philosophy, the hermeneutic circle has positive ontological significance. It designates the ontological interplay of the movement of the interpreter with the movement of tradition, the quality of understanding as a temporal retracing of the pathways of preunderstanding in a manner that allows being disclosure anew, and as the directionality implied by the anticipation of completion as the manifestation of being-as-a-whole. Being-in-the-world is treated as if it were a "structure" of preunderstandings, through which things themselves emerge and recede in hermeneutic movements of "letting a world come to stand." Human there-being is presumed to be a structural whole, a primordial totality defined by its horizons. And here we come to the most basic presumptions of contemporary hermeneutics—namely, the notions of being-in-the-world as language or semiosis, as a harmonious, determinate totality of meaningfulness within which all human experience and understanding takes place.

Contemporary hermeneutics extends the Augustinean aphorism that language "governs the inner workings of the mind itself," offering such formulations as: "reality happens precisely *within* language" (Gadamer, 1960–1972, p. 35), that language is the house of being (see Heidegger, 1959), and that "that which can be understood is language" (Gadamer, 1960, p. 432). Heidegger and Gadamer thus participate in this century's philosophical turn toward language as the key to an account of human knowing and being. (So does psychoanalysis, although in a radically divergent and critical manner.) In contemporary hermeneutics, however, unlike language-analytic philosophies or techniques, language is not merely an epistemological vehicle; it is fundamentally ontological. Language is not the means by which we speak *about* the being of the world; rather, language is the ontological totality of preunderstandings through which being-in-the-world speaks us.

Semiosis is not a set of symbols for pointing at something that is spatially or temporally elsewhere; it is the temporalized transmission of being itself, the ontological horizon, the ground and limit, within which things may show themselves. Thus, for contemporary hermeneutics, just as understanding is an ontological movement of unconcealment, rather than a product of some subject's perception, conception, and judgment, so too does language imply a totality of ontic eventuations, rather than a medium or instrument of epistemological process.

As his hermeneutic exposition of being-in-the-world unfolds, Heidegger turns to the semiotics of ontology—although "semiotics" is not a term that either Heidegger or Gadamer generally employ. As has been indicated, the notion of being disclosing itself as understanding (which is prior to its existence as being-with, insofar as understanding implies "letting a world come to stand") leads Heidegger and Gadamer to identify being-in-the-world with language. For instance, Heidegger (1953) proposes that it is in words and language that things come into being and are. Thus, being presences itself semiotically—language *is* the human way of being. World and language are a common ground, determinately binding, constitutive and delimiting, of human being-in-the-world. They are, so to speak, suprapersonal but not impersonal. Humans are in a world precisely because of language. In this sense, language is not a possession, but possesses us. It is not the activity of a subject, nor an expression of some subject's intentionality by which objects are representationally formed, contemplated and manipulated. Semiosis is not invented, any more than humans may invent existence. Rather, language speaks itself, and speaking is not an expression, formalization, or instrumentalist use of technique, but an appearing or unconcealing. It has an inherently hermeneutic character.

Semiosis is there-being's way of being-in-the-world through interpretation and understanding. Interpretation, as the event of understanding that allows things to show themselves, lets being happen semiotically. As this disclosure of being, it must play along the margin of concealing and unconcealing of being itself. Language is inherently a creative potentiality of this sort, and in this sense, it is speculative.

As their hermeneutics unfolds, Heidegger and Gadamer are increasingly preoccupied with the world-revealing properties of speech and aesthetic creativity. The playfulness of certain modes of thinking—notably conversation, art, and poetry—is hermeneutically privileged. Speaking is privileged because it is manifestly a semiotic way of showing being. Saying preserves and respects what is heard, and is thus

conducive to the hermeneutic event of memorializing the prior disclosures of being. And of course, in the sense in which Heidegger writes,
it is often the case that silence speaks. Art is a manner of speaking, in
that it also bring a world to stand. Because speech and artistic creativity are responsive to the concealing and unconcealing of being, they
entail the calling forth of being-in-the-world. It is in this context that
Heidegger's own writings, under the influence of Friedrich Hölderlin,
turn increasingly to poetic evocation rather than logical argument as
the mode of authentic philosophical insight.

Poetizing, as the artistic exemplification of creative speaking, brings
being into the open. It is a pathway of creativity within language. In
this respect, semiosis is inherently hermeneutic, and hermeneutics is
inherently a trajectory of poetizing, upon the ground of semiosis and
within the horizons it sets (see Heidegger, 1950, 1959). Poetizing incurs the becoming and happening of truth, by clearing an opening for
being, in which a world may come to stand. Language thus allows the
voicing of being-in-the-world, and the pathways of poetical-
hermeneutic eventuation bid the ontological difference between there-
being and being-with. In this ontology, there is no extrasemiotic
contact with the world.

Indeed, one might grasp the Heideggerian-Gadamerian position better if one took it as an assertion of the identity of language and world.
To say this does not, of course, imply the epistemological relativity of
the world with respect to language, for semiosis has affirmative ontological significance. In this sense, the common experience of a world
of objects is specious, for hermeneutically this experience is an event
in which language "lets a world come to stand." The notion of the
originative, productive subject is now also taken as specious, for there
is no extrasemiotic vantage point from which the hermeneutic process
may be perceived, conceived, and judged. Semiosis has no epistemologically contemplative, intentional, or manipulative self-
consciousness standing over it. Rather, hermeneutically, the
experience of "self-consciousness" is again an event in which language
"lets a world come to stand." Both interpretation and interpreter are
thus manifestations of "tradition," as the sociocultural embodiment of
language.

Tradition is itself authoritative. That is, it is not the invention of
human subjects, nor is language invented by intersubjective agreement. In contemporary hermeneutics, the epistemological notion of
the subject is displaced by the ontological fundamentality of language
(which is held to be inherently "I-less") and by a thesis about "care" (as
a metaphysics of everyday life affirming the ubiquity and fundamental-

ity of human belongingness). Shortly, as we come to see how psychoanalytic discourse gives the lie to Heideggerian-Gadamerian ontology, we shall discover the errors of this ontological desubjectivation of discourse. As far as contemporary hermeneutics is concerned, however, we only experience ourselves as "having" a world because language poetically bespeaks both "us" and "other." The world and "I-ness" meet only *within* the ontologically determinate ground or horizon of language, and this ontological ground or horizon is presumptively treated as a harmonious, romantic totality of human being-in-the-world.

Gadamer writes that "language is the fundamental mode of operation of our being-in-the-world and the all-embracing form of our constitution of the world" (1960–1972, p. 3). Yet we have already glimpsed some of the problematic implications of this totalization of language. Just as being is a finitude and futurity bounded by nothingness or death, so too is language taken as an ontological totality equivalent to being-as-a-whole. Moreover, language is readily identified with world, for language is supposedly "I-less" and universal, exposing the emerging and receding of being because it is itself at once self-transparent and self-forgetful. As such a totality, language determines the possibility of all particular hermeneutic events, and it is the ground of all belongingness, reconciling the polarity of there-being and being-with. In sum, this notion of totality is the *sine qua non* of contemporary hermeneutics, placing its project of fundamental ontology in a romantic tradition that fundamentally accepts the world as it is given, blinkers itself to the contradictoriness of human being-in-the-world, and assumes that the truth is the whole and the whole is affirmatively accessible.

From this perspective, Heidegger and Gadamer can scarcely avoid the charge of having replaced the epistemological dogma of thing-in-itself with an ontological dogma of meaning-in-itself, and of having displaced the metaphysics of subjectivism and objectivism by installing a metaphysics of the hermeneutic totality. Their philosophy takes the totality of language, not merely as a methodological guide, but as the most necessary condition of the ontic, their most fundamental precept about the way the world is. Without this presumption, the entire hermeneutic exposition would be unintelligible.

To underline the romantic and traditionalist limitations of this approach, let us review the notion of totality from a slightly different angle. The totality is a structural whole or system of temporalized hermeneutic events that comprise human being-in-the-world. There is no extrasemiotic reality in a meaningful sense, since being-as-a-whole is bounded by nothingness or death. Hence there is nothing external that could act upon the totality of semiosis. The totality is finite, primordial, and absolute. It determines the particular events of which it is composed. Again, the insistence on the priority and predominance of the whole over the parts is fundamental, not merely as a methodological mandate, but as a necessary supposition about the way the world is. The whole—semiosis as a world-forming totality—is a preestablished and transcendent harmony of the parts—the particular hermeneutic events. Determined by the structural whole of language, these events are harmoniously interelated in a manner projected or "thrown toward" the whole, so that interpretation can only proceed affirmatively from the particular event toward an anticipated revelation of being-as-a-whole. This notion of the totality balks the notion of any fundamental contradictoriness in human being-in-the-world. In other words, the totality is immutable, for there is nothing internally that could act upon the totality of semiosis. The particulars may seem to undergo modifications, changes in their ordering, recession in their availability, or widening in their hermeneutic scope, as with the concealing and unconcealing of being, or when tradition appears to evolve. But being-as-a-whole, as absolute and determinate, is never transformed or affected by these lawfully bound, internal fluctuations. Thus, the semiotic system is "closed," without fundamental contradictoriness in its being. This notion of totality is identitarian—unitary, active, and ultimately empty. As psychoanalytic discourse demonstrates, it is thus pseudo-concrete and false.

Contemporary hermeneutics treats the totality of human being-in-the-world rather like an anonymously functioning and temporally transcendent subjectivity. It is not quite this, of course, inasmuch as the hermeneutic exposition is ontological and not epistemic. In the face of such criticism, Gadamer would probably demur, protesting that language, the hermeneutic totality of human existence, is not regarded as some absolute, fixed and finally found anonymous subject. Indeed, he might plead that the idea of the totality need be understood "only relatively." However, this is a febrile and unsubstantiated protest, for there is no notion in contemporary hermeneutics that would mitigate this charge. Gadamer does assert an almost metaphysical belief that "the essential linguisticality of all human experience of the world . . . has as its only way of fulfillment a constantly self-renewing contemporaneousness . . . [and] precisely this contemporaneousness and this linguisticality point to a truth that goes questioningly behind all knowledge and anticipatingly before it" (1960–1972, p. 19). But this belief does not add or alter anything ontologically. Whatever the evident vivacity of human experience and understanding in semiosis, the apparent quality of "self-renewing contemporaneousness," the notion of language as a certain sort of *totality* remains the *sine qua non* of hermeneutic exposition.

As an interpretative calling forth, disclosing being-in-the-world, hermeneutics tracks back and forth along the pathways of preunderstanding. All meanings emerge from such preunderstandings. They are sustained by the nexus of prior meanings, and projected forward by the anticipation of completion in meaning-as-a-whole. All meanings are presumed to be concordantly interwoven as the fabric of being-in-the-world. Again, these pathways of preunderstanding form a structural whole—namely, *tradition* as the embodiment of an ontological notion of totality. Thus, hermeneutics can only treat the "prejudices" of tradition affirmatively.

Tellingly, Heidegger again and again returns to an idolatry of the *Volkgeist*. And repeatedly, Gadamer informs us that hermeneutic experience will return us to commonalities of sociocultural understanding. Even to appear to interpret against tradition is nonetheless to endorse it and to be directed by it. Because preunderstandings always determine understanding, interpretation can neither break from existing pathways of disclosure, nor effect change upon the systemic totality of being-in-the-world. It can only retrace these pathways, extending them forward in response to the enjoining and invitational voice of being. Interpretation is thus historicized as a product of tradition, as well as projected productively toward the futurity of completion in the finitude of tradition. The "self-renewing contemporaneousness" of language amounts to nothing more than this. Beyond all else, Heidegger's and Gadamer's discourse on the hermeneutic disclosure of being is only intelligible if the world is a harmoniously interconnected system of events of concealing and unconcealing, comprising a determinate, absolute, and immutable totality.

As a preestablished and transcendent harmony, the Heideggerian-Gadamerian notion of totality follows a certain romanticism, influenced by Friedrich Schelling's metaphysical assertion that nature is the unity of product and productivity. It is precisely this notion of totality that psychoanalytic discourse on the fundamental contradictoriness of psychic reality abjures and profoundly indicts. As we shall soon see, psychoanalysis implodes the hermeneutic totality, and thus demonstrates the falsity of the Heideggerian-Gadamerian ontological exposition.

Admittedly, there is a certain convergence between contemporary hermeneutics and psychoanalysis, but this convergence has been grossly and misleadingly exaggerated. At one extreme, it has been surreptitiously cultivated into a mystique by the Lacanian school. Still, given the profound problems associated with logical empiricist renditions of psychoanalysis, a reading of contemporary hermeneutics can at least be transiently heuristic. The convergence, simply stated, is that psychoanalytic discourse is indeed hermeneutic in a certain sense—it breaks with the metaphysics of the epistemological tradition; it apprehends reality as a semiotic process; and it succeeds in an ontologization and historicization of the knowing process.

As was indicated in Chapter 3, psychoanalysis represents a devastating critique of Western metaphysics, showing that its fixated and finalized configuration of subject, object, and the there-being of things is untenable. Because psychoanalysis and contemporary hermeneutics are both moves against the metaphysics of this epistemological configuration, they might be said to share a certain moment of critique, even though their moves are very different. Heidegger insists that the thingness of things is lost in their conceptualization as objects, that being remains concealed in the epistemic maneuvers of subjectivism and objectivism. Psychoanalysis, through the dialectic of repression, the return of the repressed, and the discursive reappropriation of the repressed, concretely demonstrates that the immobilized polarity of subject and object in epistemic conceptualization results in the curtailment and constraint of desire. In this respect, taken from afar, psychoanalytic discourse might be regarded as a vindication of Heideggerian critique. Against the disontologization of epistemic mentation, both psychoanalysis and contemporary hermeneutics require that the ontological question be granted a certain privilege.

Restoring ontology leads into discourse on the world-forming and truth-revealing nature of language. And here, too, there is, at least from afar, some semblance of an allegiance between psychoanalysis and contemporary hermeneutics. Both Freudian and Heideggerian hermeneutics present the knowing process as a movement within worlds that are semiotically constituted. What is similar is the acceptance of semiosis as the horizon within which human experience and understanding occurs—an admission that the prodigiousness of being is not captured by some subject's objectivations, but rather in the way in which the world "comes to stand" upon the ground of language. Hermeneutics rightly emphasizes the belongingness of patient and psychoanalyst within a common semiotic horizon, wherein the individuality of their experiences and understandings, "subjective" and "objective," is constituted as meaningful.

In contemporary hermeneutics, things must be allowed to speak, and, operating poetically and creatively, interpretation must provide an opening for being to disclose itself in this manner. To recapitulate, interpretation plays along the margin of ontological discourse; it must be an authentic questioning that retraces pathways of preunderstanding. Thinking is thus a manner of marking or memorializing the disclosure of things as they bring themselves into unconcealment. This Heideggerian account of discourse, which jettisons the reified notion of subject as substance or limit, as well as the ontic immobility of object conceptualization, bears a striking similarity to one dimension of psychoanalytic reflection and interrogation—namely, the relations between conscious and preconscious contents. The poetizing or playfulness advocated by contemporary hermeneutics resembles what is clinically designated "free association"; and the "structure" of pathways of preunderstanding resembles the "structure" of the preconscious, comprising the network of meanings or pathways along which conscious understanding is directed. "Insight" could then be defined, like Heideggerian thought, as a marking of pathways upon which being has already brought itself into unconcealment.

Behind such alluring resemblances, however, we come abruptly to the divergence between Heideggerian-Gadamerian philosophizing and psychoanalytic hermeneutics. Heidegger and Gadamer consistently forget to take seriously the possibility that semiosis may conceal being. Thus, they treat preunderstandings affirmatively for their revelatory potential, assuming that there is nothing to the world beyond or behind the structure of these preunderstandings as a hermeneutic whole. Rendering this structure into the interpretative awareness of a disclosure of being, they miss entirely the being that is repressed by such events of disclosure—the ubiquitous alienation that is the authentic discovery of psychoanalytic discourse. For contemporary hermeneutics, the nexus of pathways, as a totality, is inherently truth-revealing, and the problematic of the concealing of being within language is obligingly disregarded. For psychoanalytic hermeneutics, such "pathways" comprise the polysemous false consciousness of a totality that is contradictory. Contemporary hermeneutics and psychoanalysis may agree that "I-ness" and "world" meet semiotically, but this proves to be a rather superficial, initial convergence. It is one thing to promulgate a hermeneutic exposition based on the presumption of an identity between semiosis and human being-in-the-world, as a hermeneutic totality bounded only by nothingness or death. It is quite another to embark upon a hermeneutic discourse that discloses the nonidentity between semiosis and human being-in-the-world, within the contradictoriness of psychic reality. What we find here is the radical difference between hermeneutic ideology and hermeneutic science.

It is not that contemporary hermeneutics cannot make a contribution to the future of psychology. Indeed, against the dominant mode of operationalized investigation, contemporary hermeneutic scholars have often offered a richly evocative literature. Yet their contributions always operate within a notion of the whole that is preestablished as a horizon within which the world is given, and they appeal implicitly to the ground of language as a totality that is immutable, harmonious, and determinate. Hence, they are invariably partial and one-sided— "re-repressive"—and in this sense, false. Still, Heidegger's and Gadamer's exposition does open up the possibility of an altogether different notion of psychological inquiry and change, which should be noted.

As a study of mental life, contemporary hermeneutics might issue into the conduct of psychology as an aesthetics of human experience and understanding, with "research" as a hermeneutic responsiveness, a memorializing of the disclosures of psychic being. One might, for example, imagine the continued evolution of "personality" studies in this direction, as a mode of inquiry operating as conversation, participation, and inscription of the hermeneutics of individual life history. Psychobiography might then become the exemplar of all psychological research, with the psychologist as a sociocultural exegete, annunciating, elaborating, and translating the particularity of the individual's life passage of experiences and understandings. Such hermeneutic research could richly illuminate the stark one-dimensionality of our lives, even though its "conclusions" about this dimensionality would invariably be wrong. For hermeneutics of this sort, affirming the totality of our being-in-the-world, would necessarily accept this dimensionality as it finds it. Its conclusions would be "wrong," not in the ordinary sense of illogical or disconfirmed by "evidence," but in the sense that the acceptance of partial truth proves to be a falsity. Just as the hermeneutics of Schleiermacher and Dilthey assumed the coincidence or concordance of autobiographical speech, writing, and action, of understanding and expression, in order to justify its methods for the exposition of historical, cultural, and psychic events, so too must the hermeneutics of Heidegger and Gadamer assume the inherently truth-giving nature and the ultimate harmony of tradition, the romantic totalization of language, in order to render intelligible its semiotic exposition of our being-in-the-world. The psychological research founded by contemporary hermeneutics can only be as "true" as the tradition that generates it. By preempting the possibility that the conditions of its reality are fundamentally contradictory such hermeneutic research necessarily celebrates the existing sociocultural order, even when dressed as criticism. It is thus inherently a transmission of ideology, and only tenaciously avoids deterioration into a "psychology" of platitudinous common sense.

As a practice of change, contemporary hermeneutics might issue into the conduct of psychotherapy as a process of the individual's semiotic readjustment to the sociocultural order, a mode of sensitive and humane enculturation. One might, for example, imagine a therapeutic practice in which interpretation affirms the particular individual's being-in-the-world, allowing it to bring itself into unconcealment within the participatory discourse of the clinical relationship. Indeed, much contemporary therapy seems to operate in this manner. The patient's expressiveness in conversation, and other modes, is encouraged in a manner that rehabilitates this particularity within the wisdom of tradition, the *sensus communis*. The therapist *cares*, in the full Heideggerian sense, and this insistence upon belongingness, of the particular within the whole, evokes the patient's own affirmations of relatedness. This is the exegetic function of the shaman, who relocates the individual's experience and understanding within the normativity of the sociocultural system of signification, by the annunciation, elaboration, and translation of a mythology—a "personal" mythology that may be highly efficacious because it is essentially publicly endorsed yet, in a certain sense, privately customized (cf. Lévi-Strauss, 1949a, 1949b). Hermeneutically, it is not unlike a clinical version of Wittgenstein's (1933–1935) proposals for the "therapeutic" remedy of "language games."

Therapeutically, then, a psychology founded by contemporary hermeneutics would chart the boundaries of conscious and preconscious contents, realigning them within the sociocultural conventions of communication and exchange. In such a process, the patient might be lead interpretatively along previously unfamiliar pathways of preunderstanding, and the patient's access to familiar preunderstandings might be brought into the awareness of understanding, or even reordered and relocated. Thus, the patient's private modes of experience and understanding would be rehabilitated within the general semiotic system. Implicitly or explicitly, however, the criterion of such a hermeneutic therapy is always the normativity of the sociocultural system itself, within which the therapist, as an exegetic specialist, supposedly has a marginally wider and freer mode of ontic access than the patient. This normativity itself could never be altered by such hermeneutic therapies, because, as the everyday emblem of the semiotic totality within which all interpretative understanding occurs, it is an assumed absolute. Thus, the justification of such therapeutic processes is a sort of homeliness within the preexisting structures of language and the implications of such homeliness for the repression of desire are conveniently ignored.

Hermeneutic maneuvers of this sort are undoubtably important clinically, and may play a part within the everyday clinical practice of psychoanalysis. But they are definitely not the kerygma of psychoanalysis as a radically truthful and transformative discourse. They are not the dimension of psychoanalytic discourse that makes its odyssey so extraordinary and enigmatic. Indeed, it is a serious error to take such maneuvers as in any way characterizing the process of psychoanalysis, for this view misses all that is fundamentally radical and seminally unique in psychoanalytic hermeneutics—the dialectic of repression, the return of the repressed, and the ontologically transformative reappropriation of the repressed.

If psychoanalysis were a therapy of semiotic readjustment to the sociocultural order, if this were what its hermeneutics ultimately implied, it would be a process of ideological transmission, rather than a uniquely scientific mode of inquiry and change within the semiosis of psychic reality. For the purposes of my thesis, then, it is crucial to emphasize the epistemological and ontological distinction between a hermeneutic process that purports to erase the contradictoriness of discourse and one that sharpens contradictions and deploys them dialectically in order to reappropriate the being that semiosis curtails and constrains. A psychology founded on contemporary hermeneutics effectively prevents the patient and therapist from entering into a discourse that discovers alienated being contradictorily within and thence "behind" the homeliness of normative experiences and understandings. This is not psychoanalysis. Polemically, one might say that, having implicitly assumed the inherent harmony of "personhood" within the wholeness of the sociocultural order, this is an ideological hermeneutics that ignores the oppressive and exploitative conditions generated by this order, as blithely as it ignores the conditions of psychic reality as a locus of contradiction. Ultimately, a psychotherapy founded upon contemporary hermeneutics must perpetuate the psychic fragmentation of individuality, even if it appears to smooth out its wrinkles.

In sum, Heideggerian-Gadamerian hermeneutics never departs from the ideology of identitarianism. Psychoanalysis does. Identity thinking, the *sine qua non* of Western metaphysics and the epistemological tradition of subjectivism and objectivism, *appears* to be critically discarded by contemporary hermeneutics. But it reasserts itself in the ontological doctrine of being-in-the-world as a unitary, systemic whole, the parts of which are harmoniously and historically interrelated. Contemporary hermeneutics proceeds on the assumption that world and understanding are inseparable aspects of the ontological constitution of there-being as being-with. Hence, the movement of the thing may be assumed to be identical with the movement of interpretative thought. As we have seen, understanding is ontologically fundamental and in a certain sense prior to every act of existing. It is projective, in that it moves toward an anticipated completion in the finitude of the totality of human being-in-the-world as language. It is historicized, in that it always moves within the structure of already interpreted relations or meanings—within a relational whole, or "hermeneutic circle," entailing the ontological canon of meaning-in-itself. Thus, semiosis, as an identitarian totalization of human being-in-the-world, predetermines the possibility of particular hermeneutic events of disclosure.

In all this, contemporary hermeneutics requires the assumption of the identity of world and language, the metaphysics of its romanticized and traditionalist notion of totality, and the dogma of meaning-in-itself. These requirements are transported by a rhetoric of the "openness" of hermeneutic understanding to the unconcealing of being, and a doctrine of the accessibility of things through hermeneutic movements within the horizon of language. Against this, psychoanalytic interrogation and reflection signify the condition of psychic reality as polysemous contradiction, and thus demonstrate *in fieri* the *nonidentity* of such hermeneutic understanding and the being of things within this horizon of language. That is, *psychoanalysis discloses semiotically the nonidentity of semiosis and desire.* To be specific, the nonequivalence of the return of the repressed and the discursive reappropriation of the repressed demolishes the contemporary hermeneutic insistence on the lazy equivalence of the movement of things and the movement of interpretative thought. (Why such an equivalence is "lazy" will be discussed shortly in relation to the denigration of human praxis that contemporary hermeneutics entails.)

Whereas psychoanalysis discovers and operates on the contradictoriness of our realities, Heidegger and Gadamer never even inquire upon the serious questions that should be raised by their notion of the concealment of being. Psychoanalytic discourse concretely demonstrates that human reality *struggles*. In contrast, Heideggerian-Gadamerian hermeneutics ingenuously affirms a belief that human existence never has to contend with knowing and being; it must simply be open to the address of there-being as being-with. Here lies a significant flaw in the plausibility and intelligibility of their philosophizing—a flaw that provides the key to the ideological ramifications of the contemporary hermeneutic program.

Contemporary hermeneutics takes being as a movement of unconcealing and concealing. In this break with the epistemological tradition, Heidegger indicates that the thingness of things evades capture in the immobility of apophantic conceptualization, and he insists that things are immediately and affirmatively meaningful as events of hermeneutic disclosure. Yet, in his entire ontological exposition, Heidegger never gives a satisfactory account of concealment. It is never made clear why being may be concealed or why things may reconceal themselves after hermeneutic events of disclosure. As far as Heidegger is concerned, this is just a fundamental ontological statement about the way the world is—it is not something that can be questioned, nor could the world be otherwise. Similarly, it is never made clear whether, and in what sense, there can ever be such an event as hermeneutic *mis*-understanding. Although Gadamer (1960) does attend to this question in some detail, neither he nor Heidegger significantly modifies a doctrine in which being, when it is not unconcealing itself semiotically, may merely be indifferent to interpretation, and hence interpretation oblivious to it. And here again we see how the psychoanalytic dynamic of contradiction impugns such a doctrine.

As far as contemporary hermeneutics is concerned, the truth of being may reveal itself in language, or it may be indifferent to such revelation and remain concealed. But the notion of falsity is never seriously addressed. When being does appear to come into the open semiotically, Heidegger has neither the means nor any need to question its authenticity. He never considers that the apparent events of hermeneutic disclosure, in which there-being seems to unconceal itself semiotically as being-in-the-world, might also signify the distortion and deformation of being. Nor does he consider that affirmation of such hermeneutic understanding within the preestablished horizon of language might actually curtail or constrain the full potential of being. Moreover, when being does not appear to come into the open semiotically, Heidegger presumes that such concealment is merely the flux of there-being, indicative of the obliviousness of interpretative thought to its presencing, or of the indifference of such being to its semiotic disclosure as a hermeneutic event. He never confronts the possibility that the structure of semiotic preunderstandings, as pathways along which hermeneutic disclosure is projected, might also preclude the revelatory potential of being, that semiosis might collaborate ideologically in curtailing and constraining the being of things, or that "concealment" might signify hermeneutic exclusion from full disclosure. The very presumptions of the Heideggerian-Gadamerian program ignore the possibility of an ontological semiotics of false consciousness; thus, the enterprise readily enmeshes itself in a dynamic of mystification.

It should be clear by now how psychoanalysis gives the lie to the presumptions of the Heideggerian-Gadamerian program. For psychoanalysis shows that unconcealment is not univocally authentic and truthful, but must be treated with suspicion, as a condition of polysemous contradiction. And it shows that concealment is not an indifference of being, but its expulsion from the semiotic domain; that interpretation is not oblivious, but obfuscating and prohibitory. Consider, for example, the discourse on unconscious psychic being as "striving for expression" semiotically, against the directionality and intentionality of the "preunderstandings" of conscious and preconscious mentation, from which it has been exiled by repression, only to reassert itself in a disguised and disruptive "return." This disclosure of psychic reality, or "world," as the condition of polysemous contradiction, crushes the Heideggerian precept of authentic revelation or indifference as the nexus of being-in-the-world and its semiotic habilitation. Against contemporary hermeneutics, the negativity of psychoanalysis finds that the appearances of concealment and unconcealment intimate the contradictoriness of language and there-being, the potential for a dialectic of nonidentity between language and the thingness of things, and thus the fundamentality of polysemous contradiction within the horizon of language itself.

In other words, psychoanalytic discourse does not only demonstrate that apophantic thinking may be oblivious to being, with the thingness of things remaining indifferent to its categorical and inferential manipulations. More radically and fundamentally, psychoanalytic discourse demonstrates that semiosis, including both apophantic conceptualization and hermeneutic understanding, occludes being, preventing its full and authentic disclosure even while presenting it. The result is the distortion and deformation of knowing and being within the givenness of the semiotic horizon. For this reason, psychoanalytic discourse interrogates language as the condition of false consciousness, in order to call forth not just the latency of being that is suppressed, but the full potential of being that has been repressed within the preunderstandings of ordinary representation. In this way, psychoanalysis discovers that the very concordance upon which Heidegger and Gadamer operate—namely, the semiotic identity of there-being and hermeneutic disclosure as being-with—is wholly mistaken and untenable. The doctrine of concealment and unconcealment ideologically masks the fundamental reality of contradiction and the nonidentity of being and semiosis.

Thus, psychoanalytic discourse may be said to disocclude the ideological affirmations of hermeneutic understanding. Psychoanalysis is a way of knowing that is also a disclosure of being, and in this sense, as we shall see, it is a mode of praxis within and upon the grounds of semiosis. By discovering the nonidentity of language and human being-in-the-world, psychoanalysis finds its labor in the scientific pursuit that sets its discourse as the directionality of emancipation. And here we come to a further aspect of the Heideggerian-Gadamerian program with which psychoanalytic hermeneutics takes issue—the denigration of human labor within the coordinates of fundamental ontology. From all the foregoing discussion, it can be concluded that Heideggerian-Gadamerian hermeneutics is, in a certain sense, essentially passive and receptive. Because this ontological exposition disposes of epistemology and the intentionality of the human subject, the notion of praxis is disempowered.

Contemporary hermeneutics allows no work, other than the workings of a totality that is preestablished, immutable, and predeterminative. As we shall see, the notion of "care" scarcely substitutes for the intentionalities of labor and subjectivity. In this program, interpretation is essentially the projection of there-being as being-in-the-world. In this respect, it is merely responsive to the flux of there-being as concealment and unconcealment, and it is determined by the romantic totalization of being-in-the-world as language. For Heidegger and Gadamer, interpretation plays along the margins of the concealing and unconcealing of things themselves, as a retrieval and repetition of the pathways of prior disclosure. Even questioning, as a calling forth of events of hermeneutic disclosure, supposes "openness" yet is firmly set within the boundaries of tradition, as the embodiment of language. This totality furnishes the conditions of possibility for questioning; there is nothing outside the totality itself. Thus, questioning always *affirms* the totality, implicitly or explicitly. Moreover, contemporary hermeneutics asserts the "I-less-ness" of language and insists that interpretative thinking must always proceed "from the center" of language, which is a structure or system of "games" in which "everyone is at the center" (Gadamer, 1960–1972). Against this, psychoanalysis instates the locus of the subject, demonstrating a subjectivity that is not "at the center" of the semiotic system, and hence involving a mode of interpretative reflection and interrogation that is not an impotent endorsement of the structure of preexisting conditions.

Overall, the aesthetic "work" of interpretative thinking, as presented by Heidegger and Gadamer, remains contingent. Their ontological exposition permits neither a methodological mandate, nor any sort of statement about the more radical potentialities of human praxis. The assertion of concordance between being-in-the-world and language, of an identitarian equivalence of the movement of things and the movement of thought, advances a sort of lazy hermeneutics. Interpretation is moved willy-nilly from the particular event of disclosure toward the whole; the exegete has no way of making fundamental distinctions, such as that between shared and unshared experiences and understandings; and the potential negativity of reflection and interrogation is abandoned in favor of an affirmation of the tradition that supposedly generates such questioning. Heidegger and Gadamer presume that tradition either rests or moves anticipatorily toward the full revelation of being-in-the-world. Their "idealism of linguisticality," as Jürgen Habermas (1968) has called it, exhausts itself in an ideology that upholds hermeneutic events of sociocultural transmission (cf. Gadamer, 1960–1972). Discourse has been—if we may excuse such barbarous terminology—disepistemologized and desubjectivated. Through its suppression of contradiction, contemporary hermeneutics leaves nothing for the intentionality of the human subject, and hence the notion of praxis, as a way of knowing and an imperative for being, is emptied. Psychoanalytic hermeneutics shows how wrong this is. As a praxis of reflection and interrogation, in the persistent pursuit of nonidentity in the contradictory locus of human subjectivity, it indicts the Heideggerian-Gadamerian ideology. For it demonstrates truths that go beyond a proclamative redundancy of disclosure, and a potentiality for fundamental transformation that subverts the metaphysics of the contemporary hermeneutic totality.

What, then, may be we conclude about the configuration of truth, transformation, and totality within the Heideggerian-Gadamerian world-view? As has been stated, the *sine qua non* of this exposition is a romantic and traditionalist totalization, in which ontic discourse and hermeneutic understanding are one. And this totality delimits the possible conditions of truth and transformation. Language supposedly spans the ontological difference between there-being and being-with. Yet if every immediate and particular hermeneutic event is determined by and projected toward this totality of human being-in-the-world, then nothing forestalls an absolutization of these particulars.

The distinctions required for the subject's interpretative labor of being-in-the-world thus dissolve. Contemporary hermeneutics becomes lost in a celebration of presentness.

This romantic totalization of language is, as Hegel (1807, p. 19) wrote of Schelling's metaphysics, the "night in which all cows are black." With its dissolution of epistemology, subjectivity, and human praxis, might well ask whether the program of contemporary hermeneutics can ever arrive anywhere, can ever get beyond the apparent finality and circularity of its own ontological exposition. Truth, for Heidegger and Gadamer, is a redundancy of disclosure, a historicized revelation along preestablished pathways of understanding. It is conditioned by the totality of being-in-the-world, within which every hermeneutic event fits harmoniously. The historicity of discourse in contemporary hermeneutics is not something that can be deconstructed; it can only be endlessly repeated and reserialized. Similarly, transformation, for Heidegger and Gadamer, is possible only within the totality, determined by this structural whole. The only movement is preordained within its elements. Nothing can challenge or move the harmony of the whole, as semiosis or tradition. For there is nothing outside the unity of language and there-being, and no internal contradictoriness to instigate its transformation from within. Interpretation thus appeals to the tradition that constitutes it, and this tradition, semiosis as a whole, the dogma of meaning-in-itself, remains unmoved.

In their writings, Heidegger and Gadamer do try to offset the pungency of such basic criticisms with their rhetoric about "openness" to being in language and their references to the "self-renewing contemporaneousness" and even the "continually self-transcending" character of language. But the fundamental coordinates of their philosophy fail to vindicate this rhetoric. Again, the metaphysics of the romantic totalization of language and world balks the fundamentality of contradiction and the possibility of praxis as a movement of negation within and against the totality. A totality without the dialectical potential of contradiction and negativity cannot develop. It is ultimately an inert and empty abstraction.

In its totalization, Heideggerian-Gadamerian hermeneutics profoundly affirms the existent, assuming the priority and unity of human being-in-the-world over its hermeneutic particulars. The possibility that contradiction might be fundamental to the present conditions of human existence is thereby preempted. Moreover, as just noted, this assumption of the immutable totality of being-in-the-world becomes an empty abstraction. Heidegger and Gadamer can only retain some semblance of concreteness by insisting that language is not some ineffable structural whole, but is immediately accessible in the presentness of tradition as a sociocultural system of semiotic relations. Thus, the program of interpretation is either pushed toward the emptiness of its totality, or proclaims itself as a celebration of tradition, an affirmation of the preexisting conditions of the world. All too readily, contemporary hermeneutics achieves the pseudo-concreteness of a doctrine of contentment, romanticizing existential presentness, everyday life, and our "heritage." That contemporary hermeneutics is ideologically conservative is an understatement. Its romantic totalization installs a veritable tyranny of contentment, falsely obtained against the reality of human suffering, through its fundamental reassertion of identitarianism.

Once again, psychoanalytic discourse proves the falsity of this totalization, concretely disclosing its ultimate emptiness and immobility, as well as the pseudo-concreteness of its ideological operations. Psychoanalysis demystifies human reality; its discourse immerses itself in the fragmentation of the human condition as language and world. And it recuperates a praxis of reflection and interrogation that is emancipatorily directed. What psychoanalysis offers is a *science* of hermeneutics as a dialectical discipline, rather than an ideology of hermeneutics. In Heideggerian-Gadamerian hermeneutics, truth may be the whole, but the whole proves empty. Fundamental ontology, as Adorno (1966, p. 89) remarks, "promotes slave thinking."

AGAINST THE LACANIAN REFORMATION

It is precisely the power of a critique of fundamental ontology, such as Adorno's, that must be brought to bear upon Jacques Lacan's "psychoanalytic" reformation. Indeed, an examination of this reformation will not only amplify my critique of the Heideggerian program by bringing it within an arena that is manifestly "psychoanalytic," but also demonstrate how profoundly Freud's *Psychologie der Verdrängung*, as elaborated in this book, indicts the Lacanian enterprise. For Lacan's theorizing, despite certain apparent and perhaps misleading similarities in terminology, is fundamentally opposed to the science of psychoanalysis advanced by my thesis. And given this divergence, which is particularly articulated around the notions of the splitting of subjectivity, desire, and the conditions of semiosis, a critique of Lacan's program, and its apostasy, opens the way for my concluding arguments concerning the quality of genuinely psychoanalytic science.

With comparative ease, Lacan's "reading" of psychoanalysis, which is both a return to the Freudian texts and a reformulation of their precepts, may be judged both brilliant and bad. For brilliance, let it initially be said that, given the contemporary malaise in psychoanalytic thinking, Lacan's *Écrits* and some of his variously published *Séminaire* (which will eventually encompass a score of volumes) form an indispensable and richly rewarding study. For badness, it must be said, as I hope to demonstrate, that his thesis (if it can be called such) entrenches "psychoanalysis" in an ontology which is, in its most fundamental aspects, unmitigatedly Heideggerian.

Since his "Rapport de Rome" (1953a), Lacan has presented a series of papers that are often illuminating and insightful in their minutiae, even when they are profoundly mistaken in the overall thesis upon which they are constituted—usually by implication rather than explication. Lacan has written and talked on a wide range of topics—and he rarely fails to be interesting. Presenting himself aphoristically and without regard for systematization, coherence, or definitional consistency, his work is provocative and evocative, even when it suffers from its superfluity of allusions and elusions.

Indeed, there is much to be learned from Lacan's "reading," both in terms of its minutiae and, with considerable qualification and criticism, in terms of its general orientation. For Lacan rescues Freud's discipline from the errors of Cartesian-Kantian formulations, insisting that psychoanalysis concerns the truth of desire and the elaboration of the notion of the subject, that the search for truth concerns the subject in the field of the unconscious and is never to be equated with the subject of self-certainty. Lacan takes up psychoanalysis as the science of the unconscious, and focuses on the decentering of the subject in the Freudian "universe" (1953a, 1964). In so doing, he provides a thoroughgoing reformulation of Freud's seminal discovery in terms of structural linguistics. In this respect, it must be said that, even when Lacan is wrong, he is to be credited for opening psychoanalytic theorizing to the communicational and semiotic character of Freudian discourse; for insisting that the subject cannot be considered apart from words and speech, and that Freud's discoveries are founded upon a discipline in which the subject is taken by its discourse. Indeed, for many of these aspects of his work, Lacan must be studied appreciatively, for he has succeeded in reorienting the approach to Freud at a time when much of psychoanalysis is on the verge of losing sight of the fundamental questions of its discourse: the questions of the subject, the conditions of truth, and the systems of semiosis in which we live.

Lacan thus occupies a heuristically needed role within contemporary psychoanalysis. And, in terms of my argument, we must assess his "thesis" on the discovery of the unconscious, and on the concomitant issues of epistemology and ontology. Yet assessment of any "thesis" of Lacan's—and especially of his major reformulation, rather than the attendant minutiae—is notoriously difficult. For, eschewing systematization, Lacan deftly, even roguishly, defies systematic critique. Moreover, as is well known, his style almost wholly obliterates considerations of the content of his thought. For Lacan, style is everything, and the content of whatever thesis he might happen to be presenting becomes quite unnecessarily adumbrated. The best that can be said about this style is that it is, in Eugen Bär's words, "a consistent monument to his conception of the Freudian unconscious" (1974, p. 475). But it is also a consistent monument to Lacan's conception of the means by which the unconscious is to be "made known"— thus ultimately it reveals the poverty of his method.

What Adorno says of Heidegger's philosophy—that it "is like a highly developed credit system, one concept borrows from the other" (1966, p. 76)—entirely fits the Lacanian reformulation, with the most grievous of consequences. Too often, potentially critical concepts are cheerily, yet covertly, modified, attenuated, or even abandoned to suit the rhetorical moment. Upon scrutiny, what appears to be a "thesis" about the workings of the human mind is found to be sustained by Lacan's talent for hopping, aphoristically and even diagrammatically, from ambiguity to ambiguity. Although this certainly makes for the razzle-dazzle of compelling showmanship, it would sometimes seem to be a manner of argumentation that lacks integrity.

Thus it is that Lacan's work manages to be intensely heuristic even while the epistemological and ontological fundaments of his reformulation can be found to be bankrupt upon inspection. This ostensible paradox, which is the key to any equivocation over the merits of Lacan's work that may appear here, can conveniently be illustrated by brief references to two of the many facets of the Lacanian program: the theory of the three "registers" and the emphasis on epistemological considerations.

As early as an unpublished paper in 1953, Lacan proposed that "the symbolic, the imaginary, and the real" are the three categories of psychoanalytic composition, necessary to the comprehension of any symptomatological or characterological formation (cf. Wilden, 1968, 1972; Bär, 1974; Muller & Richardson, 1982). Descriptively, this is an enormously useful distinction, one that can empower the practicalities of clinical communication. Epistemologically, however, it rests on a theory that seems haphazardly hotchpotch. Each of the three terms is used by Lacan in at least two different senses, and the overall theory appears to be a most uneasy admixture of thoroughly Heideggerian propositions and quasi-Fichtean mythology. On the one hand, the symbolic, as the realm of signifiers, seems to constitute the world in an authentically Heideggerian fashion, leaving the real as the "impossible presupposition"—defined within language, yet outside it, as the stock of what is not articulated by signification. On the other hand, the imaginary is supposedly a register of identifications also beyond the symbolic, yet not to be counterposed to the real. Moreover, this imaginary comes to have the status of a sort of myth of the primordial and prepsychoanalytic origins of the "ego"; a realm of presymbolic experience which, if it is to be discussable, can only be articulated fictitiously by signification in discourse to which it is, definitionally, external by antecedence (see Lacan, 1936). Now, there is nothing intrinsically wrong with myth-making—indeed, it may be a necessary moment of psychoanalytic communication. But Lacan's three "registers," whatever their clinical utility, entail a realm of knowledge-constituting discourse, a more or less plausible mythology, and an "impossible presupposition." To call this epistemologically syncretic is, I think, absurdly charitable. And this brings us to my second brief illustration of the Lacanian paradox—his flamboyant emphasis on epistemological considerations.

Lacan is widely credited with providing an epistemology for psychoanalysis, but it is only in an extremely restricted sense that this credit is deserved. Lacan does unremittingly bring to the fore issues of psychoanalytic epistemology. As has been said, his stress on the splitting of the subject, its decentering within and through the constitutive domain of semiosis, has a highly salutary effect on theorizing within psychoanalysis. But we must ask whether this emphasis on the problematic of psychoanalytic knowing ever furnishes a cogent epistemology for psychoanalytic discourse. And here I would reply that Lacan's theorizing offers no epistemology at all, if "epistemology" implies *method* for the process of knowing.

We have seen how Heideggerian-Gadamerian hermeneutics sets forth the ontological horizon in a program that does not shift epistemological attitudes so much as displace the entire epistemological problematic by subordinating the question of the subject that knows to the hermeneutic exposition of the grounding of being. So too does Lacan demote, and in the final analysis dismiss, the epistemological question, despite his voluminous emphasis on the knowing of the decentered subject. That Lacan's writings never appear committed to the conclusion that in the final analysis they entail is due both to certain incogitancies in his theorizing and to a significant feat of legerdemain. What Lacan offers, in lieu of epistemology, is style, with hubris—a style by which, in his view, the voice of the unconscious may make itself known. In Lacan's work, style forever eclipses method. Indeed, the notions of method for mentation, of the active pursuit of truth in praxis, and of the negativity of conceptual labor, all hover on the margins of Lacan's theorizing, but only to be repeatedly pushed aside in favor of his style of ontology, matched by unexplicated concerns such as the totality of language, the vacillations of being-toward-death, and the dread of futility and emptiness in words. Thus, as we shall see, Lacan's epistemological "contribution" to psychoanalysis must, in the final analysis, be vigorously refuted.

Since Lacan's theorizing is not systematic, systematic critique is not at issue here. And since it is multifaceted, no comprehensive account of his work will be attempted. Rather, my intent is threefold: to suggest a proper appreciation for Lacan's contribution to the psychoanalytic literature by paying contentious respect to his theorizing; to demonstrate the extent to which Lacan's reformulation replicates the errors of hermeneutic ontology; and hence to show how this reformulation lapses from the dialectical reading of psychoanalytic discourse to which my argument leads. In short, I believe that, beneath the hoopla of "structuralism," Lacan is an unregenerate Heideggerian, and that, his protestations to the contrary, the same presumptions tacitly animate many of his aphoristic fragments of theorizing as do the more systematically developed expositions of hermeneutic ontology.

To accomplish my purpose here, then, I shall examine Lacan's "reading" of Freud quite narrowly in relation to the seminal discovery of the unconscious. And I shall confront only the writings of Lacan himself, not those of his colleagues or students, some of whom have turned toward deconstructionism (with which my thesis has somewhat more in common).

In actuality, Lacan's work started with a smattering of interest in Hegel (see Lacan, 1947). As it "progressed," it became increasingly Heideggerian, utterly rejecting Hegel, to the point where Lacan ended up styling himself, in his 1964 seminars, as anti-Hegelian. Moreover, although Lacan rarely cites Heidegger directly, and suggests that Heideggerian philosophy is only *"propaedeutic"* to his own theorizing (1964, p. 18), it needs be added that it is "propaedeutic" to the apprehension of the most fundamental tenets of Lacan's "reading": in the final analysis, Heidegger has, for Lacan, "sovereign significance" (1957a, p. 175).

Lacan's theorizing attempts to vindicate his now-famous dictum that "the unconscious is structured like a language" (e.g., 1964, p. 20), and thus to characterize the splitting of human subjectivity by its birth into the symbolic order—the latter being cast in a manner reminiscent of the work of Claude Lévi-Strauss. To accomplish this, Lacan is interested not so much in signs and signals, which purport to have a one-to-one relationship between the semiotic construct and that which it designates, but rather in the structure of signification inaugurated by Ferdinand de Saussure (1906–1911). And here it might be noted that when Lacan writes of "language," he intends the narrow sense implied by "natural languages"; he does not—regrettably—address the broader question of semiosis, as the general system of representations (see Lacan, 1953a, 1957a, 1964).

Following Saussure, Lacan employs the categories of signifier and signified, feeling free to use and abuse the Saussurean distinction in his equivocality, and modifying its terminology without specification. Thus, Lacan impresses upon psychoanalysis his depiction of two nonoverlapping networks of organized relations: those of the signifier that form the synchronic structure of language, in which each element depends on the nexus of all other elements for its signification; and those of the signified that form the diachrony of discourse, the signification of which is again realized only in its relation to the totality (1956a, p. 126). In this manner, no signification can be sustained except by reference to further signification (1957a). Lacan then makes of this a double argument. First, having followed Saussure in accepting that any relations between signifier and signified are arbitrary, Lacan further suggests that the networks of the former may "slide" over that of the latter. That is, he introduces a notion of "polysemy"—and it should be emphasized here that the notion of polysemy deployed in my thesis is radically different from Lacan's—to indicate that a signifier may have more than one signified, and vice versa. Second, Lacan gives privilege to the realm of the signifier, to the extent that the signified is virtually irrelevant to his theorizing. Arguing that the structure of the signifier precedes and determines the signified, Lacan twists around Saussure's premises (that relations between words furnish meanings and not the reverse) to suggest that only the properties of signifiers, notably their structuration, prevent the deterioration into complete meaninglessness that is potentially engendered by this "sliding" between signifiers and signifieds. Thus, it is the structure of signifiers that is all-important. Lacan holds that signifiers may be reduced to their ultimate differential elements, namely letters or phonemes; and that they operate according to the laws of a closed order, forming a totality of signifying chains in which elements may be arranged and rearranged by rules of selection or substitution, and combination or contexture (1956a, 1957a). For Lacan, it is not the signifier in and of itself that speaks, but its structure, and this, as we shall see, guarantees the totality necessary for the Lacanian ontology, effectively overshadowing the nonidentity that might have been implied in the notion of "sliding."

How, then, is Freud's discovery of the unconscious to be located within this structure of the signifier? Here Lacan plays further with the Saussurean distinction. Both conscious and unconscious discourse involve signifiers such that unconscious signifiers determine conscious signifiers, thereby making them their signifieds, and such that the conscious signifiers, which might by extrapolation be taken to be the general sociocultural system, are signifiers for what is repressed, making the latter their signifieds. Thus, for Lacan, "everything emerges from the structure of the signifier" (1964, p. 206), including the division between conscious and unconscious discourse, and hence "the psychoanalytic experience has rediscovered in man the imperative of the Word as the law that had formed him in its image" (1953a, p. 106).

The unconscious, then, is a hole, something nonrealized, that is "produced" by the laws of the signifier. This gap produced by the structuration of the signifier involves "an ontological function" that issues into "the function of the unconscious," rendering the latter "neither being, nor non-being, but the unrealized" (1964, pp. 29–30). Descriptively, "the unconscious is that part of the concrete discourse, in so far as it [i.e., discourse] is transindividual, that is not at the disposal of the subject in re-establishing the continuity of his conscious discourse" (1953a, p. 49). It is the "chapter" of the subject's "history that is marked by a blank or occupied by a falsehood . . . the censored chapter" (1953a, p. 50), forged, so to speak, "on the trace of that which operates to establish the subject" (1966, p. 830). The unconscious thus appears, in Freud, as discontinuity, and its discovery is that of a loss.

Lacan immediately connects this discovery with the notion of lack, a "want-to-be"—"lack of being," *manque-à-être*. And it is evident here, in more Heideggerian terminology, that this lack is structured by language, the "law of the symbolic order," which, at the price of a certain loss, brings being into world. Lacan is relatively adamant that the unconscious is not the subject as desire in the syncopation of discourse—a depiction which more closely approximates the argumentation of my thesis. Rather, it is a synchronic "structure" of lack by which "the subject of enunciation" loses itself in every act of speech (1964, p. 26), which is to say that the unconscious, while it has been said to involve signifiers, is also an oblivion that effaces the signifiers of conscious discourse. Thus, Lacan renders the unconscious at a primordial level vis-à-vis the structuration of the symbolic order, and this "structuring function of a lack"—connected, as we shall see, with his notions of the subject, the "function of its desire," and the "want-to-be" (1964, p. 29)—makes the unconscious more or less metaphysical, despite Lacan's disavowal of metaphysical intentions.

Needless to say, this metaphysical thrust inexorably vitiates the notions of repression and the return of the repressed in the concrete dialectic of human discourse. Interestingly enough, even as he sets up this account of what he takes to be Freud's discovery of the unconscious, Lacan rather desperately strives to preserve its concreteness, as dynamic and sexual. For example, he advances the proposition that "the reality of the unconscious is sexual reality" (1964, p. 150). To do this, he points to an inherent, and presumably autochthonous, "affinity between the enigmas of sexuality and the play of the signifier," and suggests that the unconscious might be "a remanence of that archaic junction between thought and sexual reality" (1964, pp. 151, 152). Such assertions that his notion of the unconscious is indeed "dynamic and sexual" make for a transparently weak defense against the charge that his theorizing is dominated by structuralist considerations, to say nothing of the considerations of language as a romantic and traditionalist totality that sets the world in place. Even more, the extravagant speculations that comprise this "defense" must be tied to Lacan's notion of death—a Heideggerian "being-toward-death" in Lacanian disguise, which we shall discuss later. For "the reality of the unconscious" in Lacan's theorizing is basically that of a "lacuna, cut, rupture inscribed in a certain lack" (1964, p. 153).

The ontic function of Lacan's unconscious is that of the slit (la fente) through which something vanishes even as it emerges "into the light of day" (1964, p. 31). This depiction would seem to repeat Heidegger's discussion of "earth" coming to stand as "world," within the ground of language, as the concealment and unconcealment of there-being as being-with. Lacan continues in this Heideggerian vein when he writes that the unconscious comes to have "the rhythmic structure of this pulsation of the slit," the function of which is linked, as we shall see, to his theorizing about desire and death. Thus, in Lacan's work, the totality of signifiers, as a lawful, logical, and closed system, as well as the unconscious, with its "pulsative function," constitute a temporality through which being-in-the-world appears and disappears (1964, pp. 29–52). This, of course, is almost purely Heideggerian ontology under another jargon; it presents the psychoanalytic pursuit of the unconscious as nothing more than a play along the concealing and unconcealing margins of human being-in-the-world, tracing back and forth in a mapping of the network of signifiers (1964, pp. 42–52). To the critique of this Lacanian "method," or lack thereof, we shall come later. Meanwhile, in order to comprehend more deeply Lacan's deployment of such ontological maxims, we must examine further his notion of the unconscious in the context of his theorizing about the subject, its relation to the "Other," its desires and its death.

It might be surmised that the notion of the subject is crucial to the Lacanian reformulation, and, in a certain sense, such a view would be correct, insofar as Lacan aptly insists that psychoanalysis be apprehended as the discourse of an "excentric" subjectivity. Yet is is precisely here that Lacan's theorizing reaches the acme of its rhetorical, problematic, and vacuous tendencies. Given that Heideggerian philosophy subordinates subject to being, treating the former as a nugatory issue, one might have hoped that Lacan would have something to say about the subject that would rescue his theorizing from the mire of hermeneutic ontology. Yet, on this issue, Lacan's texts everywhere seem to proclaim more and more about less and less. In his theorizing, it is made abundantly clear what the subject is not. And in the process, the character of this subjectivity becomes emptier and emptier, to the point where it would seem that Lacan's "theorizing" could dispense with the notion of the subject altogether, however much it may depend on this notion for propagandistic purposes.

With Lacan's reformulation, it is made very clear that the subject of the Freudian revolution is not that of the Cartesian-Kantian tradition, and for this critique, Lacan's work is to be applauded. Lacan's opposition to the *cogito* dates from his earliest work (1936), and he argues appropriately that the validity of Cartesian apodicticity is subverted by the sliding of signification under the impetus of desire (1960). Against the abortive "subject" of the *cogito*, which he characterizes as a monster or homunculus, Lacan argues that "the difference of status given to the subject by the discovered dimension of the Freudian unconscious derives from desire" (1964, p. 41); *desidero* thus displaces the *cogito* in the Freudian universe. This psychoanalytic subversion of the subject leads Lacan to an oblique attack on operationalist methods, and on the claim that empiricism could ever constitute the foundation for science (1956a). It also leads Lacan to his notorious break with ego psychology, in which he provides the rudiments of a critique of its epistemological presumptions. Lacan views the "ego" as a fictitious, distorting construct, based on imaginary and alienating oppositions and identifications—a static objectivation of *je* as *moi*. It is "frustration in its essence" (1953a, p. 42), and thus should be treated as no more than a special sort of symptom, for to treat it otherwise is to leave the subject trapped in an alienated condition of objectivation (1953–1954). Above all, Lacan is rightly convinced that the "ego" must not be equated with the subject—indeed, that the subject is misconceived in the positive analysis of self-observing, synthetic, or integrative functions, and in any similarly objectivating models (1956a, 1957a). Against this legacy of Cartesian-Kantian thinking and its intrusion upon "psychoanalytic" theorizing, Lacan's "subject" is cast into an irrevocable excentricity. It would seem to be vehemently antihumanistic, neither entity nor identity, but rather formed in the gaping of the "slit" that pertains between being and meaning, or being and nonbeing.

Having implied that both conscious and unconscious discourse involve signifiers, Lacan establishes the splitting of subjectivity in the rupture between the conscious and the unconscious; indeed, he argues that the subject alternately reveals and conceals itself by means of the pulsation of the unconscious. More, however, must be said about how and why such splitting occurs, and hence how and why there comes to be a rupture between consciousness and the Freudian unconscious. Here Lacan depicts the unconscious as "something that opens and closes . . . its essence is to mark that time by which, from the fact of being born with the signifier, the subject is born divided" (1964, p. 199). In other words, the division of the subject is a function of the order of the signifier. It is due to the subject's receiving definition by being born into and constituted by a field exterior to it (a field Lacan refers to as the "Other"). To say that the subject is split, is to say that it is always an uncertainty, divided by the effects of language. It is a subject only because it speaks, and yet, because the effects of speech are constituted elsewhere, the subject always realizes itself more in this Other (1964, p. 188). Along these lines, Lacan indicates that "the subject is born in so far as the signifier emerges in the field of the Other," and that the realization of the subject is in its "signifying dependence in the locus of the Other" (1964, pp. 199, 206). Thus, any coherence that Lacan's notions of the subject and of the unconscious may have would seem to pivot upon his theorizing about this Other in relation to the structure of signification.

Lacan uses his notion of the "Other" with great flexibility and ambiguity. He capitalizes "Other" to distinguish it from the notion of "others" (the latter approximately corresponding to the imaginary construct of an "object" in an "object relationship"—the representation of some person or thing other than the self). The capitalized "Other" refers to the Freudian unconscious, or "it," which governs the symbolic order. Lacan teaches "that the Other is the locus of that memory that [Freud] discovered and called the unconscious, a memory that he regards as the object of a question that has remained open in that it conditions the indestructibility of certain desires" (1959, p. 215). Thus, this notion emphasizes Freud's references to the unconscious as *ein anderer Schauplatz*, having supremacy over consciousness, and being intimately connected with desire (see Bär, 1974). To the questions surrounding Lacan's dubious notion of desire, we shall have reason to return later. For the moment, it should be noted that Lacan's "Other" is neither a person nor a collectivity, but a principle that transports, in a double sense, his idea about the relationship between being and language. His "Other" is both the locus of the "want-to-be," or "lack of being," and the locus of the signifier in the deployment of speech.

With respect to the Other as the locus of the "want-to-be," it should be noted that Lacan describes human being-in-the-world as organized around two lacks, the more significant of which "emerges from the central defect around which the dialectic [sic] of the advent of the subject of his own being in relation to the Other turns—by the fact that the subject depends on the signifier and that the signifier is first of all in the field of the Other" (1964, pp. 204–205). This lack develops an earlier, "real" lack, supposedly prior to language ontogenetically, and referring to Lacan's speculations on the conjunction of sexuality and death. It is these "lacks" and the notion of the Other as the locus of "want-to-be" that permit Lacan fancifully to portray the subject as choosing being and thence disappearing into the realm of nonmeaning, or choosing meaning and having its meaning survive only deprived of its nonmeaning which "constitutes in the realization of the subject, the unconscious" (1964, p. 211). These ideas wholly depend on Lacan's presumptions about the "death instinct," as the *sine qua non* of his "reading"—presumptions that will shortly be subjected to my critique.

With respect to the Other as locus of the signifier in the deployment of speech, it should be noted that Lacan describes all speech as being produced in the locus of this Other in a particular manner (1958a, 1960). Speech is, in a certain sense, the privileged medium of the unconscious, in that the unconscious is discourse by, for, and of the Other (1960, 1964), and "the unconscious of the subject is the discourse [of the] Other" (1953a, p. 55). Speech, however, is also addressed to the Other inasmuch as Lacan's consistent depiction of human communications is one in which "the sender receives his own message back from the receiver in an inverted form" (1953a, p. 85). Thus, in Lacan's reformulation, as Bär (1974) has stated, there is no genuine otherness, for his notion of the Other covers almost everything of any significance.

Before advancing a critique of Lacan's notion of the Other and its ontological interests, however, let us return to the question of the subject. Lacan suggests that his theorizing counterposes, "in relation to the entrance of the unconscious, the two fields of the subject and the Other" (1964, p. 203). He posits circular processes between subject and Other, from the subject "called to the Other, to the subject of that which he has himself seen appear in the field of the Other, from the Other returning to it" (1964, p. 207). This intimates Lacan's vision of the dilemma of the Freudian subject. On the one side, the being of the subject depends on what speaks in the locus of the Other, in that "the Other is the locus in which is situated the chain of the signifier that governs whatever may be made present of the subject—it is the field of that living being in which the subject has to appear" (1964, p. 203). On the other side, there is, so to speak, no other for the Other, and it is, allegedly, the signifier of this lack in the Other that constitutes the subject. Lacan's "subject" is thus placed in the limbo of language that has been ontologized, for this signifier of a lack in the Other will be "the signifier for which all the other signifiers represent the subject: that is to say, in the absence of this signifier, all other signifiers represent nothing since nothing is represented only *for* something else" (1960, p. 316).

These sorts of pronouncement bring Lacan to the principal condition of his "subject," namely, its continual "fading," in the pulsations of the unconscious, for "the relation of the subject to the Other is entirely produced in a process of gap" (1964, p. 206). This statement becomes a trifle more comprehensible if we consider Lacan's definition of a signifier—as that which represents a subject for another signifier (1960, 1964)—and his proposition that the subject is merely born of and within the organization of signyifying chains. The subject, "in so far as it is contituted as secondary in relation to the signifier" (1964, p. 141), is designated by Lacan as the *sujet-barré*—it can only be represented by another signifier for another signifier in the signifying chain; hence it is barred from representation as such. This means that while a signifier, producing itself in the field of the Other, makes manifest the subject of its signification, it also reduces this subject to being no more than a signifier. Here we may note again the complete hegemony of the structure of the signifying chains in Lacan's scheme: the "subject" attains signification only to find itself to be nothing but a signifier, and indeed to be that only for another signifier. In this respect, speech may be a "presence made of absence" in that it makes manifest the subject only to make it fade away. The subject is called into being by its lack of being, only to have this being abrogated at the very moment of its inception. In sum, Lacan's notion of the splitting of the subject is nothing more than this: that when the subject appears somewhere as meaning, it is only to be manifested elsewhere as "fading" or disappearance (see 1964, pp. 203–229).

This provides an exposition of Lacan's proposal that "the unconscious is the sum of the effects of speech on a subject, at the level at which the subject constitutes himself out of the effects of the signifier," and that "the unconscious is contituted by the effects of speech on the subject, it is the dimension in which the subject is determined in the development of the effects of speech, consequently the unconscious is structured like a language" (1964, pp. 126, 149). With Lacan, the "subject" is structured by language, which gives this subject its being and lack of being by continually representing it by a signifier for another signifier. The subject is also historicized by language, and this relates to Lacan's notion of desire, as we shall see.[4] Yet, for Lacan, the subject is merely an indeterminacy, forever "fading" as it seems to move toward reconciliation with its being: "I" as subject comes on the scene only as the "being of non-being" (1960, p. 300). Thus, it seems that Lacan's "subject" is nothing more than a style of talking about the "pulsative function" of his notion of the Freudian unconscious, for the subject "fades" in "the temporal pulsation in which is established that which is characteristic of the departure of the unconscious as such . . . the closing" (1964, p. 207).

At this point we face a conundrum. As just indicated, for Lacan, the subject is to be apprehended in terms of its "fading" in "the rhythmic structure of this pulsation of the slit." But the unconscious is also to be apprehended in terms of the "pulsative function" of this "slit" with the "fading of its subject," that is, as a synchronic structuring of lack, conditioned by the Other, in which the enunciative subject loses itself in the signifying chains of every act of speech. One gains here the inescapable impression that Lacan's notion of the unconscious and his notion of the subject collapse into each other, being merely stylish ways of designating the effects of the Other, the transmutation of signifiers, and its "slit." What we have is hermeneutic ontology in fancy dress, for Lacan's unconscious and his subject merely refer to discourse on the margins of the concealing and unconcealing of being— the Heideggerian notion in which being makes itself manifest in the setting forth of being-in-the-world as language, bounded by its finitude and futurity. With Lacan, this setting forth is conjured by the notion of

---

[4] It should, however, be noted here that the status of historicity, let alone historicality, is quite impoverished in the Lacanian "reading," being debased, as Wilden (1972) has suggested, to a hierarchy of synchronic functions.

lack, or "want-to-be," wherein the "slit" is both the opening for disclosure and the closing for a reclosure as being and nonbeing. And Lacan reinforces this ontology with his distinctive debasement of the Freudian nisus of desire, a debasement grounded upon the Heideggerian presumption of being-towards-death.

At first glance, Lacan seems to make the notion of desire crucial for his reformulation. But, again, one finds that this notion readily devolves into something else—in this instance, Lacan's foundational ideas about "want-to-be" and the "death instinct." Lacan suggests that, "whatever animates, that which any enunciation speaks of, belongs to desire" and that the subject's "desire is the desire of the Other" (1964, pp. 141, 38; cf. 1960). Here he posits the heuristically interesting distinction between needs, demands, and desire. Needs are biological, and may or may not be gratified. Demands, however, are endemic to speech; are ultimately addressed to the Other; are for some specific "object"; and may or may not receive a response. In contradistinction, desire is a fundamental effect of signification, arising, in a certain sense, because of the noncorrespondence of needs and demands imposed by language upon the subject (cf. 1958a). Desire is coordinated, not with any "object" that might seem to gratify it, but with the "object" that kindles it; in this respect, desire is excentric and insatiable, emerging from a primordial and ubiquitous absence or lack. Desire "ex-sists," to use the Lacanian neologism, in the yawning abyss *(béance)* of the lack or "want-to-be" given by the structuring of the signifier. It is thus unconscious, barred from full representation, and always taken as Other. It is "that which is manifested in the interval that demand hollows within itself, in as much as the subject, in articulating the signifying chain, brings to light the want-to-be, together with the appeal to receive the complement from the Other, if the Other, the locus of speech, is also the locus of this want, or lack" (1958a, p. 263). Lacan frequently illustrates this by pointing to the birth of the symbol in "the primary dyad of the signifying articulation," presented by Freud (1920a) in the *fort/da* game, and he suggests that it "is in the interval between these two signifiers that resides the desire offered to the mapping of the subject in the experience of the discourse of the Other (1964, p. 218). Thus, Lacan's notion of desire refers back to the notion of "want-to-be," propounding that the desire of the subject is that which is constituted at the point of lack (1964, p. 219).

Lacan writes that "the unconscious is always manifested as that which vacillates in a split in the subject, from which emerges a discovery that Freud *compares* with desire" (1964, p. 27, my italics). Here I must flatly disagree: the splitting of human subjectivity does not generate a discovery that Freud "compares" with desire. Rather, it involves the profound estrangements and alienations of the representational world from desire in all its fullness, concreteness, and vivacity—that is from desire as concretely subject of movement and syncopation in discourse. It is exactly this Freudian discovery that Lacan dismisses quite cavalierly. Instead, what the Lacanian reformulation would seem to achieve is the complete dehumanization of desire, rendering it into an impassable oscillation between presence and absence, inherent to the border of being and its lack.

Occasionally, Lacan's theorizing does bestow upon the notion of desire a pseudo-concreteness—when, rather desperately, he links desire with erogeneity and with interpretation. Yet such grab-bag speculation scarcely succeeds in remedying the emptiness and abstraction into which Lacan has cast human desire. For example, while holding to his opinion that the function of desire "is a last residuum of the effect of the signifier in the subject" (1964, p. 154), he throws in addenda to the effect that "libido is the effective presence, as such, of desire" (p. 153), that desire is "a locus of junction between the field of demand, in which the syncopes of the unconscious are made present, and sexual reality" (p. 156), and that is is a "nodal point by which the pulsation of the unconscious is linked to sexual reality" (p. 154). Lacan also manages to suggest not only that interpretation is directed toward desire, and might be grasped by it (1958a, p. 260)—a laudable argument in and of itself—but also that, in some entirely unspecified way, desire "is interpretation itself" (1964, p. 176).

All this, however, is a casuistic and thoroughly tendentious way of dealing with the criticism that desire, in Lacanian theorizing, is reduced to oscillations of presence and absence. Lacan insists upon some primordial "affinity between the enigma of sexuality and the play of the signifier" (1964, p. 151). And this mystic belief connects with his defense of the universality and inevitablity of phallocentricity, a point which will be criticized shortly (see 1964–1980). Ultimately, for Lacan, the notion of desire is an assertion of the insatiable "want-to-be" (1958a). The quest of desire is supposedly the function of the signifier, and yet desire is nothing that can be assumed by the "I" in speech. Rather, desire lacks, and this brings the subject into its fundamental relation with death.

As has already been intimated, the importance of the notion of death in Lacanian theorizing cannot be underestimated; it is its *sine qua non*. The theme of desire for death—conjoining Freud's "death instinct" and Heidegger's "being-toward-death"—permeates Lacan's reformulation, more or less holding it together. We find this theme in his earlier work, such as the "Rapport de Rome" (1953a), as well as in his more recent and lesser-known seminars, where it is often emphasized more overtly. Interestingly, Lacan rarely acknowledges adequately the extent of his debt to Heideggerian philosophy in general, and to the notion of "being-toward-death" in particular. Yet he is wholly candid about the importance of the "death instinct" in his "reading" of Freud's texts—writing that "to ignore the death instinct in his doctrine is to misunderstand that doctrine entirely" (1960, p. 301), and that in Freud's work life itself comes to have "only one meaning, that in which desire is borne by death" (1958a, p. 277). Ultimately, in Lacanian psychoanalysis, death expunges any notion of a dynamic as contradictoriness, and it even upstages oedipal conflicts specifically, together with Lacan's devotion to phallocentricity.

For Lacan, the notions of the subject, the unconscious, and desire are all ultimately referred to, and conjugated upon, the "want-to-be" and thence death itself (see 1960). For example, the Lacanian subject, with all its "fading," is constituted around a basic lack, and only in death does it become replete—the subject being brought to realization in the endless circularity of its assumption as being-toward-death (1953a, p. 105). In this sense, death is the ultimate notion of the subject, and each instance of the subject's "fading" is, in Lacan's words, "a matter of life and death" (1964, p. 218). Similarly, the Lacanian notion of the unconscious, as neither being nor nonbeing but the unrealized, is discovered only as the "structuring" or "pulsative function" of a loss, the "slit" of "want-to-be" that effaces the signifiers of being-in-the-world, casting the subject into vacillations of concealment and unconcealment, that is, into deathlike oblivion whenever and wherever it might attain meaning and being. Moreover, Lacanian desire, having its "origins" in an irreparable failure, or lack, meets the very limit of human possibility in the fundamental "want-to-be" (1964, p. 31). "Being-toward-death" is, in this respect, the ultimate assumption of desire (1953a).

Lacan mobilizes the "death instinct" to express the limit of Heideggerian humanity as "being-toward-death," in that death defines all human being-in-the-world by establishing its finitude and futurity. Lacanian theorizing is thus dissociated from any tendency toward an existentialist *Daseinanalyse*, which would emphasize and uphold "being" at the expense of the "fading of being," for Lacan makes superordinate the significance of disappearance and death (see 1964, p. 239). In Lacan's as in Heidegger's philosophy, death is the innermost, unconditional and insurmountable potential of this "subject" (1953a, p. 103). Moreover, in an act of myth-making essential to his work, Lacan repeatedly insists that the structuring of signifiers is originally evinced by death, in that "the symbol manifest itself first of all as the murder of the thing, and this death constitutes in the subject the eternalization of his desire" (1953a, p. 104). Death becomes the primordial "ground" for the "birth" of the symbolic order, and thence of any passage of articulations in speech. At bottom, then, Lacanian theorizing is held together by this more or less metaphysical presumption of a "profound relationship uniting the notion of the death instinct to the problems of speech" (1953a, p. 101). Language is circumscribed by its "outer darkness": semiosis, for Lacan, is a totality bounded by death, and any movement of the chaining of signifiers has death, via "want-to-be," in its interstices. Thus, it is from death that the existence of the "subject," of human being-in-the-world, "takes all the meaning it has"; it is "in effect as a desire for death that [this subject affirms itself] for others," by identifying with the Other, for no being is ever evoked by the subject "except among the shadows of death" (1953, p. 105).

The scaffolding of Lacanian theorizing is thus errected upon semiosis as "Other," human being-in-the-world vis-à-vis "being-toward-death," and the "slit" or "want-to-be"- that is, so to speak, constituted between the chaining of signifiers, nonmeaning, meaning, and nonbeing. With Lacan, as with Heidegger, death is the potentiality toward which all human being-in-the-world—embodied for Lacan by the "Other" of signification—is inexorably thrown. The subject as divided subject, the unconscious, and the vicissitudes of desire—despite all the commotion they engender in Lacan's theorizing—are merely derivative notions. For they are only comprehensible in terms of the "want-to-be" that "ex-sists" in the interstices of semiosis and its effacement. Desire is directly referred to this vacillation of presence, absence, and death; and both the Lacanian subject and the Lacanian unconscious turn out to be merely stylish ways of referring to the margins of the concealing and unconcealing of there-being as being-with.

Indeed, such a comparison of Lacanian theorizing with Heideggerian philosophy deflates much of the grandeur of "originality" claimed for Lacan. I have already hinted, several times, at the extent to which Lacan's "subject," let alone his notion of the unconscious, comprises, a rendering of Heideggerian being-in-the-world. Similarly, in the enigma of the Lacanian "Other," we cannot but hear a version of the "there-being" upon which hermeneutic ontology is founded, with what Lacan calls "psychoanalysis" being eventuated as the being-in-motion of this there-being. Only the position of language as ground is shifted. For Heidegger, humanity is at home in language, whereas for Lacan, with the Other as the locus of signifiers in the deployment of speech, the emphasis is on inaccessibility and excentricity. But this is the point: Lacan's distinctiveness vis-à-vis contemporary hermeneutic ontology is, in a certain sense, nothing more than a matter of "emphasis." Lacan's reformulation of psychoanalysis is decisively not Heideggerian philosophy, but only because of Lacan's stylistic persistence, his rhetoric of semiosis as "Other," and the legerdemain with which he imposes psychoanalytic jargon—not to mention pseudo-psychoanalytic jargon—upon the mandate of hermeneutic ontology.

We arrive here at a view of Lacanian theorizing as hermeneutic ontology askew. Heidegger and Gadamer grounded their ontology on the notions of death and language. With Lacanian theorizing, death and the Other are positively theologized. All too readily, such ontologies articulate a metaphysical anguish over death and, with it, the promotion of slave thinking. It is not too unfair to suggest that Lacan's reformulation is unmitigated hermeneutic ontology, and that the difference is so much posturing, a faithful yet quasi-psychoanalytic rhetoric about the "ex-sistence" of existence. Moreover, if this is so, we shall now find that the Lacanian reformulation is vulnerable to the same lines of psychoanalytic critique as was the Heideggerian-Gadamerian program, concerning the questions of totality, identity, contradiction, and praxis.

Lacan appeals to structuralism in presuming the romantic and traditionalist totalization of language. He thereby installs the metaphysical totality required by hermeneutic ontology, although displacing it as "Other." Asserting a sort of inaccessible and excentric *loquor ergo sumus*, he argues that Freud's discovery of the unconscious, which is a "different matter from everything that had previously been designated by that term," implies our "determination by symbolic law" (1956a, p. 141). This determination is complete, as the Other governs all. In order for this theorizing to maintain some semblance of coherence, Lacan must insistently invoke the laws of this totality—presumed to be entirely immutable and universal—as setting the horizon (that is, both the ground and the limit) for the ontology of human being-in-the-world. Repeatedly, in the Lacanian reformulation, the hegemony of the signifier and its chains, over all else, is evident.

Such signifying chains compose a structured, closed—and, as we shall see, logocentric, phallocentric, and hence identitarian—order, bound only by the perimeter of being-toward-death. The composite chains of this whole reserialize Heidegger's pathways of preunderstanding, which form the latter's totality of language. Accordingly, Lacan is found to offer some straightforwardly Heideggerian remarks on the predetermination of "knowledge," suggesting, for example, that "I can only be taught to the degree of my knowledge, and everybody always knew that teaching is to teach myself" (Lacan, quoted in Bär, 1974, p. 490n). The finality and circularity of the Other, as an absolutized totality, tacitly secures the Lacanian ontological exposition. Nothing can challenge this structuralized and temporalized whole, for, as Lacan makes plain, there is no other for this "Other," nor is the potentiality for inner contradictoriness to be treated as significant. By giving privilege to and even formalizing, such a totalization, Lacanian theorizing thus inevitably evacuates its own "subject" and attempts an expunction of the power of nonidentity.

With respect to the subject, we have already seen the vacuity of Lacan's reformulation and the vitiated version he offers of its "division." Certainly, Lacan is to be applauded for his endorsement of the psychoanalytic critique of the Cartesian-Kantian subject, which believes itself, illusorily, to have an absolute anchor in being. By drawing attention to Freud's ambiguous usage of *Ich* as *je* or as *moi*, and by pointing to the "sliding" of signifiers within the symbolic order, Lacan effectively presents his opposition to objectivism, as well as to subjectivism or phenomenology as pursuing the illusory goal of unity in meaning of subject with being, and to Cartesian-Kantian "science" in general as an "ideology of the suppression of the subject" (Lacan, quoted in Bär, 1974, p. 535.) It is in this critical facet that Lacan's work is, in my judgment, most successful, as summarized in his excellent aphorism concerning the kerygma of psychoanalytic discovery: "there is no truth that, in passing through awareness, does not lie" (1976, p. vii).

But even though Lacan's indictment of the *cogito* is apposite and trenchant, his notion of the subject is miserably depleted. Lacan's emphasis on "the word"—on the subject as being spoken by the word, and on the structuration and temporalization of the totality of signifying chains prior to any "constructive activity" of the subject, who is merely born of and within this totality—effectively demeans the question of the subject, even though this is the very question that Lacanian theorizing purports to reinstate within the psychoanalytic field. It is as if the Lacanian reformulation were caught within a spurious dichotomy: if psychoanalysis dispossesses the Cartesian subject, then its discourse either engages an inversion of the Cartesian subject, or deals with no significant subjectivity at all. Between such "alternatives," Lacanian theorizing oscillates. Given Lacan's emphasis on the supremacy of the unconscious, and on the determinative conditioning of the Other, it is not invalid to criticize Lacan for "abandoning" the Cartesian subject, only to readopt it in inverted form, assuming a "true" subject beyond and behind the falsity of self-consciousness.

Indeed, this line of criticism has been suggested by Anthony Wilden (1968, 1972) and others. Yet it may be even more valid to suggest that, beyond and behind Lacan's superabundant propaganda, the "subject" has been abolished in favor of the voicing of an ontic movement—epistemological activity being thereby entirely subordinated to ontology, and even rendered irrelevant by ontology, in an authentically Heideggerian fashion.

Presuming the givenness of the world as the linguistic structure of the Other, Lacan derogates human self-consciousness by formulating a "divided subject" that refers to nothing more than the unconcealing and concealing of human being-in-the-world. Fancifully garbed in the Lacanian rhetoric of presencing and "fading," the vacillation of this "subject" appears to be governed entirely by the signification of the Other amid the interstices of "want-to-be"—and this would seem to render ever more empty Lacan's proclamation that truth in general, and psychoanalytic truth in particular, concerns the relation of the subject to the signifier. In any case, the central issue here is not whether the Lacanian reformulation is better apprehended as an inverted Cartesianism, or simply as appending a rhetoric of the "subject" onto the tenets of Heidegger's ontological operations. (Indeed, it is hard to condemn Lacan for one or the other because his discussion of the "subject" is so enmuffled with equivocation.) Rather, the issue is that Lacan never takes seriously the "third alternative"—namely that, dispossessing the Cartesian-Kantian heritage, the splitting of subjectivity discovered in psychoanalysis demonstrates, *in fieri*, the concreteness of nonidentity as contradictoriness, epistemologically and ontologically. Regrettably, although Lacan's "subject" is actually a nonidentity, the potency of this is avoided by every foundational presumption of his theorizing.

In this respect, Lacan is found to reestablish identitarian ideology with every twist and turn of his reformulation—and here it must be said that Lacan often dissembles, reintroducing identity within "psychoanalysis" even while pronouncing it in quasi-nonidentitiarian style. Principally, identitarianism becomes evident in his presumptions of a romantic and traditionalist totality, in his notion of "anchoring points" that arrest the "sliding" of signifiers, and in his general attitude toward the sociocultural order. Each of these may be mentioned briefly in turn.

At various junctures in his work, Lacan might be seen as attempting to forestall the totalization of language. The theory of the three "registers" is perhaps one instance of such an effort. In the "Rapport de Rome," Lacan argues for a psychoanalytic identity of the particular and the universal "realized as disjunctive of the subject, and without appeal to any tomorrow," and he proceeds to object to any reference to totality within the individual, given this "division of the subject" (1953a, p. 80). Yet this disjuncture of the subject is, as we have seen, merely the margins of the unconcealing and concealing of human being-in-the-world. Nothing prevents the perpetual collapse of Lacanian theorizing into the totalization of language, even though it is rendered as "Other." Like the hermeneutic ontology of Heidegger and Gadamer, Lacan's formulation suggests the "nonidentity" of semiosis and being, yet there is nothing within the framework of his theorizing to hold them apart. To put it another way, his reformulation fails to indicate why the chaining of signifiers unconceals and conceals being. Although the crucial notion of lack or "want-to-be" supposedly comes into play here, it is, as we have shown, merely assumed as an inevitable and universal function of human being-in-the-world through being-toward-death. With repression and the return of the repressed given insufficient weight, Lacan's notion of the structuration and temporalization of signifying chains amounts to nothing other than an identitarian totality.

Identity also reasserts itself in Lacan's notion of "anchoring points." In his dalliance with Saussurean linguistics, Lacan suggests that the networks of the signifier may "slide" over the networks of the signified (the latter also effectively being that of signifiers), and that only the structuration of the signifier, as a totality, prevents the deterioration into complete meaningless made possible by such "sliding." Thus, for Lacan, such "sliding" must stop at certain "anchoring points," at certain privileged "nodes" of meaning (1956a, 1957a, 1964). Here we can see the extent to which Lacan is mesmerized by natural languages and their suggestive structuration, giving them privilege over semiosis and system. This, as Wilden (1968, 1972) and others have argued, is Lacan's logocentric prejudice, a fundament of Lacanian theorizing that has rightly been criticized by Jacques Derrida and certain of the deconstructionists.

With Lacan, structural anthropology and structural linguistics consistently preempt the nisus of deconstruction, as his formulation continually embraces a logocentric metaphysics, despite his ostensibly anti-logocentric style. It could be said that Lacan's work is very much caught in the contemporary French fetish of formalism and its attempted diremption. Again and again, Lacan purports to break with formalism, only to reinvent it at every moment of his theorizing—as can be seen in his mathematizations, or quasi-mathematizations, his diagrams, his reliance on spatial models of rings and knots, and his appeal for a strict calculus or algebration of the structuring of the Other (cf. 1956b and his later seminars). Formalization preempts the priority of movement and, as we shall see, of praxis. Nowhere is this more incontestable than in Lacan's idolatry of the phallus.

The prototype of the "nodes," by which the logocentric hegemony of linguistic structure asserts itself, is the phallus—in Lacan's words, the "signifier of signifiers" (1964–1980). According to Lacan, the "name-of-the-father," which is this privileged phallus signifier, sustains the structure of law and desire (1964, p. 34). Thus, the Other is the locus of this "law of desire" with its incest prohibition, its insignia of the symbolic father of *Totem und Tabu* (as well as all the other significations of this phallocentric discourse). Lacan's phallocentricity, for which he has been roundly and extensively criticized elsewhere, assumes the privilege of these significations to be insuperable and universal. It is a major aspect of his ubiquitous tendency toward the entrenchment of identitarian ideology—his phallocentricity being, in this respect, part of a piece with his logocentricity. As has already been intimated, in positing the notion of "sliding," Lacan made a promising start toward the discourse of nonidentity. This departure, however, proves spurious. For the notion of "anchoring points" and "nodes," with all its logocentric and phallocentric implications, bespeaks the restitution of identity. In line with my thesis, these points should have been treated as moments of contradiction. Instead, for Lacan, they express totality and identity as the dominance of structure, thus expunging the potentiality of nonidentity.

Totality and identity secure law and order in the Lacanian world. It might have been thought that Lacan, as someone who was taken to be one of the peripheral pundits of May 1968, would have avoided Heidegger's explicit obeisance to "authority" and "tradition" as the embodiment of hermeneutics. And indeed he does, but only insofar as the obeisance of Lacanian theorizing is perniciously inexplicit. Considerations of "law" and "order" hold together the Lacanian reformulation, in which the Heideggerian-Gadamerian emphasis on *Volkgeist* and the authority of tradition is replaced, more subtly, by assumptions of the logocentric, phallocentric, and identitarian Other as all-determinative, universalized, and insurmountable. (And presumably "psychoanalytic" discourse, in the Lacanian mode, must make the subject "at home" with these inevitabilities unto death.) These assumptions, together with Lacan's notable and somewhat paradoxical anti-culturalism, establish the fundamental immutability of the sociocultural order. Like hermeneutic ontology, Lacan's theorizing celebrates the existing order, even when it poses as criticism. The impetus of ontology, as

Adorno (1966) has warned, is again found to be the restoration of an unassailable order, against the deconstructivity of dialectical negation.

The ultimate test of identitarianism is the theoretical and methodological effort to eradicate the power and fundamentality of contradictoriness, and thus to contain and curtail the movement of dialectical negativity. Lacan's formulation of psychoanalysis is largely predicated upon such an effort. In this theorizing, the notion of contradiction is tellingly absent; indeed, in the final analysis, neither contradiction nor any other critical notion is inherent to the fundaments of his reformulation. The critical psychoanalytic notions of repression, the return of the repressed, and the reappropriation of the repressed are entirely disempowered in the Lacanian "reading." With the ineffability of the Lacanian unconscious, the deconcretization of his "subject," and the general treatment of content as nugatory, the epistemological and ontological contradictoriness, embodied as the splitting of the subject in the discourse of self-consciousness and the repressed unconscious, is deliberately ignored, and dialectic is concomitantly vitiated. As has been indicated, Lacan should have apprehended the polysemy of "sliding" as the polysemy of a movement of contradiction, and the "anchoring points" or "nodes" as concrete and frozen moments of contradiction, in which movement is arrested in the specific alienation of an affirmation of alleged identity. But Lacan avoids the psychoanalytic notion of polysemous contradiction for which I am arguing. In his view, the "dialectic" of the subject merely refers to its dual ontology as a presencing and fading (1964). The dynamic of contradictoriness, in all its fullness, concreteness, and determinacy, is thus overshadowed by the ontology of totality, identity, and death. Negation and semiosis are blithely assimilated to the generic notion of absence, so that the Lacanian "dialectic" becomes even less of a dialetic than that of the Aristotelian *Topics* (cf. Lacan, 1953a, p. 76). It is a kind of powerless duality of unconcealment and concealment, matched by an aimless "method" of systematization and formalization: "dialectic," in Lacan's debasement of psychoanalysis, will ultimately never be allowed to transgress the bounds of this respectability.

This brings us finally to a critique of Lacanian "method" and praxis. Here again, Lacan is moderately successful in his opposition to the Cartesian-Kantian heritage, yet bankrupt when it comes to his own proclamations. Lacanian theorizing does rescue psychoanalysis from the Anglo-American preoccupation with therapeutics and "orthopedics," but only to embroil it in the mystification of hermeneutic ontology. "Cure" is not the principal purpose of Lacan's discourse—at least manifestly—and insofar as adaptation must not take precedence over psychoanalytic truth, his discourse stands against the objectivating orientation of ego psychology. Lacan properly attacks the goal of the patient's identification with the psychoanalyst, pointing to the *méconnaissance* or falsity of all such identifications (1958a). Moreover, he argues against the objectivating notions of the "self-observing ego" and its "therapeutic split," in that practice based on such notions necessarily leads to a circle of misunderstandings (1956a). Indeed, Lacan heuristically suggests that psychoanalysis cannot be entered if the "ego" of the subject is equated with the presence that speaks to the psychoanalyst—this being the error fostered by objectivating practices derived from metapsychology (1953a, pp. 90–91). Dubbing psychoanalysis "the science of the mirages that appear within this field" of patient, psychoanalyst, and "intersubjectivity" (1953a, p. 119), Lacan forbids alliances with the ego, even though cognizance must be taken of the latter, as a "verbal nucleus" through which the subject poses its "question" (1953a, p. 89). In the effort to dissolve mirages, Lacan aptly suggests that psychoanalysis must, in a certain sense, work at cross-purposes to any unification in the here-and-now or reflective awareness in self-consciousness, treating the latter as *un discours trompeur*, a lie behind which the psychoanalytic process must reach (1953–1954).

Although Lacan's refusal of the cure prescribed by the Cartesian-Kantian tradition may be thoroughly laudable, beyond this, his theorizing makes innumerable pronouncements about what "psychoanalysis" does, rarely pausing to consider how and why. An example is Lacan's well-known dictum that the subject "begins the psychoanalysis speaking about himself without speaking to you, or speaking to you without speaking about himself—when he can speak to you about himself, the psychoanalysis will be terminated" (1954, p. 373n). For Lacan, it is "always in the relation between the subject's ego *(moi)* and the 'I' *(je)* of his discourse that you must understand the meaning of the discourse if you are to achieve the dealienation of the subject" (1953a, p. 90). "Dealienation," however, turns out to be a rather grandiose ambition, inasmuch as the Lacanian formulation specifies that the best that can be hoped for discourse is that the "barrier of silence" be overcome, as the subject "learns" [*sic*] to listen to what the Other is saying in itself—supposedly, the patient's "true desires" (cf., 1953a, 1964). It is in this way that the subject will be brought from the "imaginary" to the "symbolic," and from speech that is "empty" into speech that is "full." Yet these bold claims all seem inflated in the absence of any clear exposition of the *method* by which such praxis might be engaged.

When Lacanian theorizing does seem to approach the question of method, it refers, predictably, to the totality of language, its structuration, and its imposition of "anchoring points" or "nodes." Insofar as the Lacanian unconscious is transindividual, it is systematically inferrable on the basis of the general principles of linguistics—although Lacan is neither helpful nor detailed in specifying the operation of such "inferences." Insofar as the Lacanian unconscious is individual, it is a matter of the psychoanalyst's guesswork on the basis of each session's "nodal" structuring. This, then, is the psychoanalyst's "procedure": "nodes" are to be recognized as "points of intensity," the "absence of intensity," or as "hollows" in the patient's discourse. They are to be "followed backwards," and then treated reconstructively—not, it should be noted, deconstructively. In this task of reconstruction, the psychoanalyst may be aided by familiarity with the diversity of rhetorical devices necessary for listening to the unconscious (1953a, p. 58), and of these metaphor and metonymy are especially privileged, for reasons we need not reiterate here (see 1953–1954, 1957a). Nevertheless, reconstruction is ultimately the psychoanalyst's guesswork, in which the patient has no authority other than to bestow on the psychoanalyst a status both as other or "object" and as Other. Lacan occasionally has the audacity to suggest that this permits "systematic" interpretation of the unconscious, and compares the procedure to working one's way back and forth through a dictionary, in which reliability is secured only by extensive "cross-checking" (see 1953–1954, 1964). "Interpretation," however, is to be directed "not so much at the meaning as towards reducing the non-meaning of the signifiers" (1964, p. 212). The purported intent is to isolate a kernel of "non-sense" in the patient, in order to bring out the unconscious, irreducible, "nonsensical" (nonmeaning) signifying elements (1964, p. 250). But, again, a method by which this is to be achieved is scarcely discernible.

There is then, in the Lacanian reformulation, an almost complete denigration of the question of method, and this conforms to the presumption that hermeneutic ontology can replace the epistemological problematic. Given the totalization of language and the concomitant abrogation of contradiction as epistemologically and ontologically fundamental, "truth" can be proclaimed as simply a matter of "letting things speak" (1956a). In the Lacanian corpus, the Other and death hold together theorizing, in which being-toward-death and desire for death take precedence over considerations of method. For psychoanalytic discourse to proceed, Lacan suggests, the psychoanalyst must provide a setting in which "things speak," that is, in which one allows oneself to be determined by words to which, ultimately, one must accede anyway—a purely unconscious encounter of the "subject" with the symbolic order or Other. To do this, the psychoanalyst adopts the "role" of death itself, as a void or "dummy" *(le mort)*. The psychoanalyst must "cadaverize" his or her position as the silence of the Other, thus making "death present" as an abyss into which the subject's discourse may speak its "truth" (cf. 1953, 1956a, 1958a, 1964). Lacan's own style, which becomes equivalent to doctrine itself, thus brushes aside the question of method.

Lacanian discourse may succeed in tracing and retracing pathways within language, in authentic Heideggerian-Gadamerian fashion, but this is surely the sum of its achievement. Lacan would insist that "psychoanalytic truth" is against redundancy, yet—given his totalization of semiosis as Other—Lacan leaves the subject trapped either in the emptiness of its death or in the emptiness of a ceaseless redundancy. Whereas Heidegger and Gadamer gave privilege to conversation, art, and poetry, of certain sorts, as ways of "letting things speak," Lacanian theorizing emphasizes rhetoric, irony, and the mystique of "full speech." Yet the "procedure" of "cadaverizing" the psychoanalyst, and of maintaining an allegiance to the vicissitudes of rhetorical device and to Socratic irony, as the pretense of not knowing—to say nothing of Lacan's proximity to the debased eristic practices of the Sophists—is only evocative of the "unconscious" if nothing other than the vacillation of presence and absence prevents this "unconscious" from "voicing itself" within the chaining of signifiers. To put it another way, the Lacanian reformulation has no method at all, and no epistemology—despite Lacan's propagandizing in this area—precisely because it lacks a critical notion of the process by which unconscious mental life becomes concealed semiotically. It lacks the critical dialectic of repression, the return of the repressed, and a method for its epistemological and ontological reappropriation.

Lacanian theorizing never accepts the need for a means, a methodological procedure, by which the representational containment, constraint, and concealment of the truth of the unconscious may be actively undone or deconstructed. Again, given his presumption of semiosis as an ultimately noncontradictory totality, bounded only by death, Lacan's cultivation of ambiguity triumphs over the pursuit of nonidentity, and his rhetoric with irony substitutes for the labor of dialectic. In Lacan's writings, nonidentity is reduced to ambiguity rather than apprehended for its genuine negativity; negation becomes little more than gainsaying; and the power of contradiction is eclipsed by the ubiquitous "want-to-be." Dialectic, then, is supposedly obviated by rhetoric, as a merely preordained movement of speech with death at its interstices. With method and praxis derided, no work is possible against the alienation generated by the Other, given its determinacy. Rather, it is as if Lacan believed that, so long as one keeps talking riddles, "truth" or "desire" will—automatically—speak to us from the Other. Obviously, this is something of a caricature of anything Lacan actually proclaims, but more important, it is a caricature in which we can grasp Lacan's theorizing for what it is. Against such a reformulation, it must be said that there is nothing intrinsically emancipatory in the passage from one signifier to the next, even with the cultivation of ambiguity, rhetoric, and an ironical attitude in the "presence" of an "abyss." This passage is, according to Lacan's own tenets, mere dilly-dallying, the interstitial play or vacillation of being and nonbeing as the "subject" transfers from one meaning to the next, with the concomitant emerging and "fading" of its "desire." As far as Lacan is concerned, the subject is freed from this entrapment within the chaining of signifiers only at the expense of its life. In this respect, Lacan's reformulation would render "psychoanalysis" the pursuit of Sisyphus—an absurd task bounded, for its haplessly subjected subject, only by death.

With Lacan's death, the French "psychoanalytic" vogue has also died, dissolving into cultism and chaos. Lacan's brilliance has helped prevent the reduction of his brand of psychoanalysis to the banalities of common sense. Yet his claims that psychoanalysis concerns the truth of desire and the notion of the subject, while superficially correct, prove empty within his particular theorizing, given his totalization of language and death in the tradition of hermeneutic ontology. Lacan leaves the discovery of the unconscious enigmatic and extraordinary, but only by casting it into the abyss, rendering its discourse a thorough mystification of its truth. In 1977, in a moment of uncharacteristic forthrightness, Lacan declared that his psychoanalysis is not science, but a special mode of rhetoric (see Schneiderman, 1983, p. 169). Against Lacan, and all the equivocality, pseudo-concreteness, and emptiness of his hermeneutic ontology, it is my intent to establish unequivocally the scientificity of psychoanalytic discourse—by demonstrating the fundamentality, not of some totalization, nor of death, nor of some logocentric and phallocentric identitarianism, but of an epistemological and ontological contradictoriness, elucidated by dialectical negativity.

As Gadamer (1971) once suggested, only two responses to Hegel's self-apotheosis of the subject are possible: either a denial of its notion of truth by establishing an ontology grounded upon the temporality and finitude of human existence, or a reawakening of the power of dialectical negativity to the point of contradicting the fundamental presumptions of identity and totality. The first route is the one taken—disastrously—by Heidegger as well as Gadamer himself; the second is the one taken by Theodor Adorno, in the only theoretical and methological work in which we may today seriously take hope. Wrongly dismissing Hegel as a mere immanentist (1960), Lacan attempts to reformulate psychoanalysis within the horizon of Heideggerian-Gadamerian philosophy. And here his "reading" of Freud is demonstrably a failure, in many respects a bad failure at that. For, ultimately, it is not dialectical negativity but hermeneutic ontology that triumphs in the patchwork of Lacan's theorizing. Thus, in the final analysis, the Lacanian "reformation" of Freud's discourse is a cul-de-sac.

DIALECTICS AND DECONSTRUCTION

Psychoanalysis is a discipline *sui generis*. Yet its unique mode of knowing and being is also an exemplification of dialectics, in a certain specific sense. I have insisted that the odyssey of reflection and interrogation in which patient and psychoanalyst are engaged is both scientific and emancipatory. But what is meant by this? My thesis embarked with the working premise that psychoanalytic praxis *is* truthful and transformative as Freud proclaims—that there is indeed such a process as the discourse of repression, the return of the repressed, and the reappropriation of the repressed. The time has come to make good this proleptic starting point. And, anticipatorily, it may be said that we shall arrive at the point where it is necessary to read Freud through Adorno and Adorno through Freud: *psychoanalysis as negative dialectics*.

In Chapter 2, a particular reading of Freud's earlier writings provided a protatic discussion of the critical claims of psychoanalysis as *Psychologie der Verdrängung*, from which we have drawn conclusions about its relation to various world-views. *If* psychoanalytic reflection and interrogation indeed works as proclaimed, *then* it is neither a subjectivistic nor an objectivistic epistemology, nor is it the fundamental ontology of contemporary hermeneutics. Moreover, *if* psychoanalytic discourse is the sort of movement discussed, *then* it indicts such epistemological attitudes and ontological expositions in the most radical and fundamental manner. Psychoanalytic reflection and interrogation move against the metaphysical dogmas of things-in-themselves and the fixed finality of the subject, necessary to the epistemological tradition. Psychoanlytic discourse also moves against the metaphysical dogma of meaning-in-itself, necessary to contemporary hermeneutics. Against these dogmas, psychoanalysis, as we shall see, is dialectically deconstructive. It deconstructs the affirmativeness of the epistemological subject and the noncontradictory immutability of things-in-themselves. At the same time it deconstructs the affirmativeness of the ontologized hermeneutic totality. In this respect, psychoanalysis breaks with identitarianism, and shows itself as both an ontologized epistemology and an epistemologized ontology. Its discourse transgresses and thus demonstrates the ideological falsity, partiality, and limitation of the Cartesian-Kantian and Heideggerian-Gadamerian world-views.

To reiterate, psychoanalysis is the exemplification of dialectics. And as dialectics, this *Psychologie der Verdrängung* is alien to the established universe of discourse, a threat to the presumptions of the sociocultural order. As has been intimated, psychoanalytic discourse reopens the question of ideology, truth, and transformation in a manner that profoundly challenges and criticizes ordinary notions of reality, subject, and science. The discourse of patient and psychoanalyst, which has been our reference throughout, cannot be the affirmation of ideology, comprised as an epistemology or ontology born of identitarian metaphysics.

Of course, I am not suggesting that dialectics is all that psychoanalysis is, as a day-to-day and moment-by-moment clinical process. On an everyday level, the dialogue between patient and psychoanalyst may contain elements that are, or appear to be, subjectivistic, objectivistic, and hermeneutic. But these are not, and cannot be, quintessential. What is suggested here is that dialectics, in a certain specific sense, is what makes psychoanalysis authentically psychoanalytic, what distinguishes it from all other processes of psychological inquiry and change. And this dialectically deconstructive discourse is what makes psychoanalysis uniquely scientific and emancipatory, when other psychotherapies falter on both counts.

In arguing that psychoanalytic discourse is uniquely scientific and emancipatory, I am referring, as I have been all along, to psychoanalysis as a *method*, a particular mode of reflection and interrogation between patient and psychoanalyst. And, again, the uniqueness of this method, the manner in which it compels us to reconfront fundamental questions of reality, subject, and science, renders its discourse unavailable to prolegomenous exposition. The truth of the debate between patient and psychoanalyst cannot be apprehended without participation. Freud knew this very well, emphasizing this point in several publications (e.g., 1916–1917, 1925a, 1926a). "One can only know what psychoanalysis is about," he once wrote, "by experiencing it personally" (1933, p. 161). Psychoanalysis defies propaedeutics. It is with this in mind that we now turn to the question of how and in what sense psychoanalytic method is dialectical. At the same time we may ask how this particular mode of dialectics is scientific and emancipatory.

In looking at psychoanalytic discourse as a dialectical method, a preliminary caution is needed, given the recent vogue of "dialectical psychology" within the mainstream of Anglo-American investigation. Psychoanalytic dialectics has nothing whatever to do with the emptily affirmative "dialectics" recently promoted by several investigators as a new "model" for the explanation of developmental, cognitive, and psycholinguistic phenomena (e.g., Riegel, 1975; Rychlak, 1975). Often, this kind of "dialectics" would be more correctly regarded as hermeneutics in the traditions of Dilthey and Gadamer, for its method tacitly appeals to the givenness of the totality of truth-disclosing events, and the fundamental significance of negativity is consistently ignored. Dialectics of this sort amounts to nothing more than hermeneutic perspectivalism, adroitly jazzed up as a "solution" to the barren disjuncture of mentalism and behaviorism. The character of this "solution" is either a descriptive hermeneutics or an oscillation between subjectivistic and objectivistic procedures, newly billed as a "dialectical" way of looking at the world. It is important to realize that much of what passes under the rubric of "dialectics" preserves the metaphysics of identitarianism, and hence promotes an ideology of affirmation or positivity. Once again, in contrast, psychoanalytic discourse exemplifies the dialectics of negativity and thereby upsets the givenness of the established order.

But how is the discourse of patient and psychoanalyst scientific? From the beginning of this book, it has been argued that scientific discourse differs from all other epistemological and ontological programs by its readiness to call every belief practice into question, and most emphatically to call its own belief practices to account. Accordingly, the imperative of a psychology that is truly scientific must be to confront the fundamentally significant question of the subject who knows and of the "reality" from which such knowing proceeds. To do this, it must rigorously refuse to grant any aspect of reality privileged immunity from reflection, interrogation, or inquisition. It is in this sense that psychoanalytic praxis is the truly scientific psychology. For the negativity of its dialectic implies a rigorous and methodical process in which subject and reality are progressively called into account.

How, then, is the discourse of patient and psychoanalyst emancipatory? It has just been argued that for psychological inquiry and change to be scientific it must confront the double question of the subject who knows and of the "reality" from which such knowing proceeds. Differently expressed, this is the question of ideology and truth. Psychoanalysis is emancipatory insofar as it pursues the truth of the human subject against what it finds to be the ideological formation of human subjectivity. And this pursuit is possible only in a discourse that organizes itself around the nonidentity of semiosis and desire, as will become clear as we elaborate the implications of psychoanalysis as negative dialectics. For the moment, we need only note that the negativity of psychoanalytic discourse concords with its emancipatory directionality—even though it might appear not to do so. In this respect, two notions must be worked together in the course of our discussion—first, that psychic reality is contradictorious, and second, that psychoanalytic reflection and interrogation are indeed a liberation of the human spirit.

What needs to be reiterated here is that psychoanalysis proves the fundamentality of contradiction in human being-in-the-world. It operates as a method in which this contradictoriness is disclosed, inasmuch as psychoanalysis supposes that polysemous contradiction is fundamental in the knowing and being of psychic life and then vindicates this supposition through its odyssey of interrogation and reflection. It should also be emphasized here that psychoanalysis is inherently a recuperative and healing process—albeit sometimes in a paradoxical manner. I may have seemed to swerve from an interest in the healing properties of psychoanalysis in arguing that the notion of recuperation must be divorced from the pregiven sociocultural standards of adaptation and adjustment. But healing should not be presumed to imply that the breach between the individuality and the sociality of human discourse will immediately be salved. Indeed, the contrary may be more correct.

Before we go into this, however, more must be said about the emancipatory direction of psychoanalytic discourse. For although it is emancipatory, it operates without any articulated goal of emancipation. It is from this important point that my discussion of psychoanalytic dialectics unfolds, for it enables us to apprehend more fully the authentic negativity of its discourse. It leads into a critique of Jürgen Habermas' reading of Freud's psychology, and from there to the distinction between the implicit positivity of the Hegelian dialectic and the negativity of psychoanalytic reflection and interrogation.

The notion of psychoanalysis as dialectically deconstructive severely faults the currently popular but mistaken image of psychoanalysis as a teleology of emancipation. Specifically, we must take issue here with Habermas' transcendentalized depiction of the dialectics of Freudian discourse. Habermas (1968, 1971) presents a theory of knowledge in which three quasi-transcendental "cognitive interests" are operative in the constitution of epistemological programs. In a formulation which is, for me, uncomfortably reminiscent of Dilthey's tripartite typology of *Weltanschauungen*, Habermas posits three types of epistemological enterprise, each having a "medium" and each governed by a particular "cognitive interest." The first is empirical-analytic investigation, involving the medium of labor and guided by a technical interest in the manipulative control and instrumentalist domination of the physical world of things objectivated. This enterprise, of course, is the logical empiricism of naturalistic research by another name. The second is historical-hermeneutic investigation, involving the linguistic medium and guided by a practical interest in communication, the preservation and expansion of mutual understanding for the orientation of action possibilities. The third epistemological program involves reflection upon power relations within the media of labor and language, as in Habermas' (1970, 1973a) own style of ideological criticism, and it is guided by an "emancipatory interest."

This theme is both quaint and provocative. In the course of its presentation, Habermas (1968) offers a sporadically brilliant interpretation of a wide range of philosophizing about epistomelogical processes. Yet, for all this, Habermas' position seems fundamentally problematic, particularly with respect to the transcendentalized constitution of his three "cognitive interests." His 1968 book leaves unsatisfactorily vague the status of such knowledge-founding "interests," their interrelationships, and their implications for the notions of truth and transformation. The grounds upon which Habermas himself posits this scheme remain unclear. Moreover, the pursuit of a transcendentalized epistemology is, to my mind, suspect. The ideal of static systematization is, of course, anti-dialectical, even if it could be founded upon reflection and reconstruction in the manner of Habermas' claim. The transcendentalized pursuit of such an ideal all too readily serves, descriptively and typologically, to conceal the historicized and metamorphic conditions of human knowledge.[5]

---

[5] It is not the purpose of this book to elaborate such potential criticisms of Habermas' metatheory, which has stirred up an important debate; and, with regard to certain aspects of these questions, Habermas has already made an effort to defend his position against a multitude of criticisms (see Habermas,

For Habermas, "emancipatory interest"—the interest he associates with psychoanalysis—seems to refer to an ideal of enlightenment by which the prevailing authority of power may be modified. It entails reflection and action that is motivated or otherwise governed by an ideal of nonconflictual discourse and noncontradictory sociocultural relations (Habermas, 1968, 1976). If such an ideal is to guide the reflective and reconstructive task, there is an imminent danger that this task will devolve into the pursuit of goals that are already in some sense articulated, within a particular tradition of discourse, as the embodiment of "emancipation." Habermas' ego-psychological orientation, and his talk of the significance of autonomy and responsibility, would seem to court such a conceptualization. Methodologically, this can, all too easily, come to imply that the nonidentity of reality is to be held up to an identitarian image of possibility, with a concomitant neglect of suffering and hence of the negativity of genuinely emancipatory discourse. The advocacy of methods that erase contradictions rather than deploy them deconstructively ensues all too readily. This may not be the intention of Habermas' theorizing, yet his theorizing does not adequately close off the possibility of such an approach. Such reformist and utopian pursuits ultimately affirm the established and the existent, even when their reflections and reconstructions do not immediately and apparently seem to do so. For the image or goal pursued is ultimately nothing other than an aspect of the prevailing conditions of discourse, presenting itself as "news from nowhere."

Within the context of psychoanalysis, we have already had occasion several times to criticize any ameliorative formulations. Conducting psychotherapy with an implicit or explicit goal of reform incurs the limits within which the subject of consciousness and preconsciousness may affirmatively alter itself—that is, alter itself without actually negating itself in a dialectic of deconstruction. Psychotherapy often does operate on the basis of such goals, in the interests of sociocultural adaptation, but the psychology of the repressed cannot. Psychotherapy of this sort is closer to the scientistic psychologies of subjectivism and objectivism than to genuinely scientific psychoanalysis.

The danger is that an epistemology derived from an "emancipatory interest," which is allegedly grounded transcendentally, collapses into procedures directed toward an ideal of discourse. Nothing in Haber-

---

1973b; McCarthy, 1978). However, the "emancipatory interest" must be examined further here, since Habermas treats psychoanalysis as the exemplar of such an epistemological discourse.

mas' theorizing would seem to prevent such a collapse. In the course of a debate with Habermas, Gadamer (1960–1972) once referred to this ideal as a "fictitious goal"—a strange criticism, given that the category of totality could be said to operate as just such a goal in Gadamer's hermeneutics. In any case, the criticism here is not so much that Habermas' goal is fictitious, but that it can too easily be debased into a mirroring of the alienated immediate, the established and existent. Given the fundamental contradictoriness of our realities, science, unlike scientism, cannot appeal to the established and existent. Nor can it appeal to a guiding image that is generated from the established and existent. Hegel made this clear when he wrote that, in the context of alienation, "still less can science appeal to the hints of something better which may be found within false consciousness [knowing that is untrue], and which seem to indicate a route toward scientific cognition; for this would be the same sort of appeal [as the appeal to the immediate] to something that is merely existent, and it would be an appeal to itself, to its own mode of existence as false consciousness" (1807, p. 66).

The methods of Habermas' third "cognitive interest" seem potentially vulnerable to Hegel's criticism. Discourse governed by some notion of "emancipation" can all too readily lose the power and truth of its mode of critical reflection and action, and thence devolve into affirmation of a fragmented individuality and a fractured sociocultural order. And this danger is precisely due to Habermas' insistence on transcendental system-building, and his failure to address adequately the scientificity of dialectical negativity. "Emancipatory epistemology" in Habermas' affirmative mode could then achieve palliative changes, but, even in their most dramatic form, such changes are no more than a flipflop within the alienation of the established and existent discourse. They would be "changes" in which untruth affirms it untruthful mirror-opposite. Thus, Habermas' notion of "emancipatory interest" and his reading of Freud's psychology unwittingly perpetuate an ideology that the negativity of psychoanalysis itself discredits. The uniquely scientific discourse of psychoanalytic dialectics demonstrates the falsity of emancipation achieved by affirmatively goal-directed reflection and action within the conditions of alienation.

More specifically, the scientific work of negativity, its potential for truth, lies in its interpretative effort to contradict a reality that is contradictorious, a reality in which discourse is false to the extent that it is constructed upon the nonidentity of semiosis and desire. The emancipatory work of negativity, its potential for transformation, involves its interpretative effort to deconstruct "that-which-is" in terms of "that-which-is-not," to confront givenness and "I-ness" with the dynamic of "I-less-ness" that is excluded (cf. Marcuse, 1957–1967). As a negativity of reflection and interrogation within the established order of discourse, psychoanalysis is the rigorous and consistent pursuit of nonidentity. It is emancipatory without avowing an image of reconciliation, without espousing an identitarian thesis concerning the correspondence and unities of subject and thing-in-itself, or the harmony of human being-in-the-world as a totality. It is scientific without avowing a fixed and final reference point from which or toward which all discourse may proceed, for this, too, is an espousal of identitarianism which perpetuates the ideology of alienated conditions.

The argumentation leading to these conclusions depends significantly on G. W. F. Hegel. Yet there are philosophical and practicl differences between Freud's *Psychologie der Verdrängung* and Hegelian dialectics. As will become evident, the negative dialectic of psychoanalysis reflects and interrogates its own notion. To be more specific, it supposes the contradictions of the subject and its psychic reality, and then vindicates this supposition through its consistent, rigorous pursuit of nonidentity. Hegel, however, foreshortens the dialectic by his implicit tendency toward positivity. This tendency has given many commentators the idea that dialectics necessarily "knows" its destiny, that it is teleological or eschatological—almost a theodicy. Indeed, even the famous "left-wing" readings of Hegel do little to counter this impression (see Hyppolite, 1946; Kojève, 1933–1939).

For Hegel, identity and positivity ultimately coincide. Everything nonidentical is embraced and eventually subsumed under a "subjectivity," or *spirit*, that expands by the dialectical movement of "scientific cognition" until it absolutizes itself in the exalted resting point of complete reconciliation (see Adorno, 1966). With Hegel, as with psychoanalysis, dialectical reason respects that which is to be interpreted or thought—as distinct from that which has been given to thought. And in both cases, dialectical movement has ontological implications. Yet, unlike psychoanalysis, the Hegelian route tends to essentialize the direction of reflection toward a notion of the being of beings; Hegel's notion of essence thus gives his dialectics a somewhat transcendental quality (Marcuse, 1941, 1968). In this sense, the Hegelian dialectic is abstract, essentializing and absolutist, whereas psychoanalysis deals concretely and practically with the human subject. By its resolute pursuit of nonidentity, the psychoanalytic dialectic retains its critical and deconstructive impulse. It is not a positivity. Psychoanalysis as negative dialectics cannot come to rest in itself as if it were total; its discourse, in this sense, cannot be totalizing, but only deconstructive. This is what is meant when we argue that the discourse of patient and psychoanalyst cannot be and should not be "psychosynthetic." In the interest of the human subject and its repressed condition, psychoanalytic discourse must disavow any methodology that would lazily alleviate contradictions by espousing an image of unity and totality, or of future reconciliation in an absolute, toward which discourse supposedly progresses.

Psychoanalytic discourse may never attain the absolute, in the manner that Hegel imagines he does. But in another sense, psychoanalytic methodology goes well beyond the procedures of "scientific cognition" exemplified in Hegelian dialectics. To oversimplify, the Hegelian procedure is one of progressive differentiation and integration or organization, in which each newly achieved position sublates—that is, surpasses and subsumes—the givens of its predecessors. One might think that this movement of sublation is, with certain qualifications, rather like Jean Piaget's dialectic of assimilation and accommodation, and that the overall progression is not unlike Heinz Werner's account of orthogenetic development. Of course, as a day-to-day and moment-by-moment clinical practice, such processes of "scientific cognition" are a vital and necessary dimension to all psychoanalytic experience and understanding. Yet such processes are not sufficient to account for the extraordinary and enigmatic character of psychoanalytic discourse.

Precisely because it operates positively, the dialectical movement of "scientific cognition" leaves untouched the contradictoriness of repression and the return of the repressed. It expands the horizon of conscious and preconscious mentation without acting deconstructively within this horizon. Thus, it never adequately interrogates or reflects upon its own desirousness and contradictoriness. It never calls into question its own functioning in the exclusion of "I-less-ness," and cannot break from the hegemony of the established and existent over the dynamic of the repressed. Psychotherapy is often a movement of articulation, the division and connection of ideas held by the subject of conscious and preconscious mentation. Yet psychoanalysis is not merely articulatory. It is disocclusive. Similarly, psychotherapy is often a movement from commentary to metacommentary, a logical or quasi-logical progression fostering what is clinically called "psychological mindedness." Yet, again, psychoanalysis is not merely a metacommentary. It is revelatory and reintegrative. It is not just movement in which an attained moment gives way to higher-order comment, widening and deepening the sphere of discourse. In the interests of the revelation and reintegration of the repressed, restoring it to full subjectivity, psychoanalysis also dismantles and destructures the established domain of discourse. In these respects, the dialectic of psychoanalysis embraces but also goes beyond Hegelian "scientific cognition." For psychoanalytic discourse moves within conscious and preconscious mentation to disclose that which this domain actively excludes. It thus addresses the contradictoriness of its subject. And rather than developing the conscious-preconscious domain affirmatively, it proceeds negatively, as a dialectical movement that is deconstructive.

What does it mean to refer to a dialectic that is deconstructive? Here we must keep Freud's *Psychologie der Verdrängung* in focus. We must recall his notion of the splitting of the subject of psychic reality, and the five critical claims we adduced concerning repression, the return of the repressed, and the psychoanalytic reappropriation of the repressed. The cohesive domain of conscious, nonconscious, and preconscious mentation actively excludes certain contents from the "I-ness" that gives this domain its sense of unity, continuity, and organization. These contents are rendered "I-less," as *things* that are beyond the boundaries of the manifest subject's "object"-forming activity. Yet these repressed contents, the dynamic and desirous unconscious, do not remain mute and motionless. Rather, they persist, insist, and obtrude. They "return" in disguised and disruptive form, distorting and deforming the unity, continuity, and organized coherence of the domain of ordinary mentation. And here we come to the notion of false consciousness as the condition of polysemous contradiction. For this "return"—the distortions and deformations that are *in* the domain of self-consciousness but not *of* this domain—is an arrested and fixated condition of contradictoriness, bespeaking the alienated or immobilized state of the prepsychoanalyzed "I."

In this context, the nisus of psychoanalytic reflection and interrogation is *both* epistemic and ontic, a disocclusion of that which has been rendered opaque and a remobilization of that which has been immobilized. The dialectic of psychoanalytic discourse acts within and upon the semiotic domain of the subject's ordinary mentation in a particular way—so that the manifest subject's own dialectic, ideologically frozen in the state of polysemous contradiction or false consciousness, is restarted, and that which this state holds in exile is reappropriated. To reiterate, in psychoanalysis, the repressed is revealed and reintegrated. Thing-being is assimilated and accommodated within the horizon of ordinary mentation, the being of the manifest subject. Thing-being thus attains the "I-ness" of self- and other-representation, becoming human being-in-the-world. Desires are restored to the subject's semiosis. For this to occur, there must be a procedure by which the repressive activity of the domain of ordinary mentation is somehow modified or relinquished. The *negativity* of psychoanalytic discourse is necessary, truthful and transformative eduction of the repressed can only follow from a deconstruction of the givenness and "I-ness" of established discourse, of the arrested and fixated domain of ordinary mentation.

As has been argued, all other methods of psychological inquiry and change necessarily perpetuate the false consciousness of their subjectivistic and objectivistic starting points, or of the ontological totality of their discourse. Against the affirmativeness of identitarian epistemology and ontology, it is precisely the negativity of psychoanalytic discourse, within the horizons of psychic reality, that secures its truthful and transformative properties, and allows psychoanalysis to vindicate itself through its own movement of reflection and interrogation. It becomes evident that the dialectic of this *Psychologie der Verdrängung* cannot be a purely epistemological method, for it is equally a movement of psychic reality within itself. Nor can this dialectic be purely ontic. That is, it is neither a manner of dealing with being by succumbing to the established and existent order of things as they present themselves, nor is it a process of merely taking account of reality in the naive sense. For this dialectic is a method, a mode of praxis within and upon psychic reality.

Dialectical *reason* is such precisely because it *does* respond to the ontological need. Its praxis is shaped by the condition of the reality in which it finds itself, how this reality is and how it may become. Psychoanalysis is neither contemplative nor instrumental, but neither is it a passive or affirmative response to the voice of being-in-the-world. The need for ontology is fundamental, but remains empty unless there is the "epistemological" potential for dialectical praxis. Psychoanalysis is a labor of semiosis. But as such, it is a negativity within that semiotic totality defined by the established and existent subject. It deploys this subject, its "objects," and the there-being of things in a method that is thoroughly ontologized. For psychoanalysis responds to an alienation of psychic reality that is epistemically mediated and ontically surpassable by way of a deconstructive praxis.

It can be seen from this discussion that the dialectic of psychoanalytic inquiry and change stands upon the contradictoriness of the reality it reflects upon and interrogates, and within which it moves as a deconstructive discourse. If human reality were not contradictorious, the quality of science would be entirely different. Moreover, if the dialectical potential of this contradictoriness were not systematically foreclosed by the established order of discourse, the need for emancipation would not arise. Psychoanalytic discourse only makes sense given the contradictorious nature of psychic reality. Moreover, as I have argued throughout, if psychic reality is indeed fundamentally contradictorious then ultimately *only* psychoanalytic discourse makes sense. Freud's *Psychologie der Verdrängung* insists on the fundamentality of contradiction, and then vindicates this insistence in the course of the debate between patient and psychoanalyst (although we have yet to elaborate the character of this "vindication" and the method of the debate). As the emancipatory and scientific pursuit of the psychic unconscious, psychoanalysis is the way it is because of the falsity of prepsychoanalytic self-consciousness. And indeed, if this condition of false consciousness can be made to expose its falsity, then the dialectical negativity of psychoanalytic discourse vindicates an exclusive claim to reason, specifically to reason as praxis.

What is the contradictoriness of psychic reality? Earlier, I defined this in terms of both the five critical claims made about repression and the splitting of the subject of psychic reality. It was suggested that the key to psychoanalytic discipline is the fundamental contradiction between the cohesive "I-ness" of ordinary mentation and the repressed, split off from this "I." Repressed things are, so to speak, a subject that stands as the negation of the "I-ness" of conscious-preconscious semiosis. Repressed contents are "out of bounds," yet they are desirous and "strive for expression." The "return" in compromise formations—hypostatized contradictions that are located "in the midst" of conscious and preconscious mentation, yet do not issue from its subjectivity. To reemphasize, they are *in* it but not *of* it. Symptomatic and characterological formations may thus be apprehended as the ideologically arrested or fixated interlocution of "I" and the repressed, a frozen and falsified moment in the movement of subjectivity.

Psychoanalysis takes contradiction to be the fundamental condition of human mentation and existence. Contradictoriness may be unleashed as the dialectical movement of knowing and being, or it may be ideologically hypostatized. Indeed, what psychoanalysis demonstrates when it uncovers and recovers mental activity beyond the limit of the prepsychoanalyzed "I," is that ordinary self-consciousness represents an immobilization of the interlocutory dialectic of contradictions. The falsity of this self-consciousness, its ideological partiality and limitation, is due to this hypostatization of the dialectical potential of contradictions, and not to the contradictoriness of mentation and existence per se. Thus, to reiterate a point made earlier in a slightly different context, when we write of "false consciousness," and of psychoanalysis as a truthful and transformative discourse working within and upon this domain, it is not that there is some image of the "true," as a fixed and final condition of noncontradictory identity, to be found somewhere in the present, past, or future. With respect to the present, it is not that something fixedly and finally "true," such as an authentic personhood, simply lies dormant beneath masks and myths that have yet to be decoded, ready to emerge pristinely into the light of day. With respect to the past, it is not that some such "truth" pertained once-upon-a-time, in some primordialist mythology of a presemiotic and prealienated condition of human being-in-the-world. With respect to the future, it is not that some such "truth" will pertain as the teleological mythology of an anticipated resting point of human being-in-the-world, toward which all things must lead. Present, past, or future, the entire notion of the "true" as a condition of human being-in-the-world is an identitarian thesis, asserting that there is, was, or will be a noncontradictory condition to which mentation and existence may appeal.

For psychoanalysis, then, the fundamental question of mentation and existence is not the location of some spurious epistemological and ontological position wherein noncontradiction is allegedly to be found. In the interests of ideology, such identitarian aspirations pose the wrong question. Rather, for psychoanalysis, the fundamental question of mentation and existence is whether contradictoriness is dialectically engaged as a movement of knowing and being, or ideologically hypostatized by means of arrests and fixations within the semiotic practices of discourse. Here it becomes evident that identitarianism is itself the most fundamental way in which the dialectical potential of contradiction may be foreclosed. The assertion of identity, whether in the present, past, or future, serves to arrest or fixate contradictoriness by treating it as noncontradictory. Directly or indirectly, identitarianism thus legitimates or affirms the alienation of the established order of discourse. "Identity," as Adorno (1966, p. 148) has argued, "is the primal form of ideology," and it becomes "the authority for a doctrine of adjustment" to the alienation of human mentation and to the suffering of human existence. Against this, the scientific trajectory of psychoanalysis reflects and interrogates within and upon false consciousness in the methodical pursuit of its nonidentity.

When I write of false consciousness, it is implied that the givenness and "I-ness" of prepsychoanalytic self-consciousness is false inasmuch as it occludes to itself that it is itself excluding something from its domain. That is, the established order of discourse is false, not because contradiction is the fundamental nature of psychic reality, but because the semiotic structuring of this domain arrests or fixates its own dialectical potential vis-à-vis the desirousness of the unconscious. To put it another way, the symptomatic and characterological formations a patient presents, apprehended as an arrested or fixated interlocution of "I" and the repressed, are indeed the patient's truth. But they are a frozen and falsified truth inasmuch as their polysemous contradictions entail the partiality and limitation of dialectical potential, the constraint and curtailment of desire.

In this respect, psychoanalysis operates within and upon a semiotic system that presents itself as a totalization of the possible conditions of experience and understanding, despite the intrusive opacities, discontinuities, and deformations that are evident within it. It is a totality that is ideological in its barring of the realization of certain potential contents of its reality, that is, in its foreclosure of dialectical movement. Psychoanalysis embarks from the experiences and understandings of this false consciousness, beginning with those semiotic formations within the totality that it purports to present, which can be dialectically deployed for the negation of this totality. Psychoanalytic reflection and interrogation always start by deploying polysemy against identity, beginning with the manifest deformations and discontinuities of self-consciousness. This is what it means to say that psychoanalytic discourse moves deconstructively within and upon the domain of conscious and preconscious mentation, being the consistent and rigorous sense of its nonidentity. Psychoanalysis, as negative dialectics, does not attach itself to some identitarian point of reference outside of false consciousness, nor does it believe itself to have found such a point within. Rather, it breaks out of the falsity of false consciousness from within—deconstructively, by pursuing the contradictoriness of psychic reality and thus reactivating the dialectical potential of its subjectivity.

Again and again, psychoanalytic discourse demonstrates the way in which a movement of contradiction displaces and dispossesses the hypostatizing notions of totality, unity, and identity. Contradiction is to be apprehended both as a way of knowing and as the being of beings. The development of things themselves is determined by contradictoriness, as is the movement of thought. Psychoanalysis deals with a double contradiction, epistemically and ontically—for the contradiction between semiosis and desire issues into the polysemy of contradiction within semiosis. To put it more precisely, the nonidentity of meaning-in-itself within the "I-ness" of conscious and preconscious mentation intimates that the totalization of this semiotic system is false. The difference made by psychoanalytic reflection and interrogation is between the immobilization and the remobilization of contradictions, between identitarian construction and dialectical deconstruction.

Once again, the nisus of psychoanalytic reflection and interrogation is not to obliterate the contradictions, but to restart the dialectic of contradictoriness in the knowing and being of psychic reality. And at this point we might consider how the configuration of subject, object, and thing fits into the movement of psychoanalytic discourse. We may continue to speak of the subject of self-consciousness and of its semiotically formed objects (the representations of self and other). Yet the use of these terms is now thoroughly dialectical, for the methodology within which they are deployed is ontologized and transformative. It is thus neither subjectivistic nor objectivistic. Similarly, we may continue to speak of the there-being of things. But again, the usage is now thoroughly dialectical, for such things are no longer presumed to be a harmonious totality, as in the fundamental ontology of contemporary hermeneutics. Their contradictory nature is such that they need no longer disavow their subjectivity, nor need the truthfulness of scientific praxis be passive in relation to them.

As has been noted, any psychotherapy, grounding its method upon subjectivistic, objectivistic, or hermeneutic procedures, may bring about certain changes within the boundaries of the established and existent order—that is, within the limits to experience and understanding designated by the subject of the conscious-preconscious semiotic system. A self-representation may be altered with respect to an other-representation, for example, or vice versa. Such changes may chart the boundaries of conscious and preconscious mentation, but they do not involve any shift in the fixed givenness and apparent finality of its locus of subjectivity. They may reorder the contents within, differentiating and reorganizing these contents, but they cannot transform the horizon and ground of the subject with respect to the "I-less-ness" of the repressed. Psychoanalysis, as negative dialectics, radically transgresses the boundaries of such palliative therapeutic discourse. For in the course of psychoanalytic deconstruction, thing may become "I," and by this movement desire is restored to semiosis.

Here we come to the crux of all that is enigmatic and extraordinary in psychoanalytic discourse. In accordance with the dialectical tradition, the ontic nature of things is no longer immutably exterior to thought, and the epistemic subject is no longer an apodictic and unassailable point of reference, but a shifting locus (cf. Hegel, 1807). The "I-less-ness" of thing-being may be transmuted to the "I-ness" of subject-being, as the work of patient and psychoanalyst demonstrates. Moreover, psychoanalysis shows that the only way by which this may be brought about is the methodological negativity of an inquiry that moves against the manifest apodicticity and unassailability of the epistemic subject, the givenness and "I-ness" of ordinary mentation. Psychoanalytic discourse is only comprehensible if this fundamental discovery is grasped. And exposition of this is only possible through participation in the negativity of psychoanalytic debate. The truth of this discovery, which actually follows from the fundamental contradictoriness of human mentation and human existence, is that thing is also subject. And the psychoanalytic exposition of this, as we have said, does not proceed merely by allowing things to speak in self-consciousness. For in a certain sense, they already do so disguisedly and disruptively in the polysemous falsity or ordinary mentation. Rather, this exposition must proceed by a deconstruction of the subjectivity that would prevent things from speaking themselves.

More must be said here about the dialectic of split subjectivity. On the side of the there-being of things, it is evident that the manner in which psychoanalysis proceeds is due to the desirousness of the repressed. And as we discuss the deconstructive work of patient and psychoanalyst in more detail, it must be emphasized that this work justifies itself through the restoration of desire to semiosis, a movement of semiotic negativity. The repressed is cast beyond the limits of the "I-ness" of ordinary mentation; it is thus a thing precluded from expression within this totalizing semiotic system. Yet it also "strives for expression," both in the immobilized contradictions presented in the return of the repressed and in the remobilized contradictions freely developing as a dialectic in the psychoanalytic reappropriation of the repressed. In both the repressed's obtrusive "return" and its readiness for reappropriation, its subjectlessness becomes "subject." As has been suggested, the repressed subject stands as the negation of the "I-ness" of ordinary mentation. Desire is thus found to have a double nature, as thing-being and as subject-being of the repressed.

This psychoanalytic dialectic, in which the "I-less-ness" of the repressed unconscious is discovered and recovered not just as thing but as "I," radically transforms the notion of the subjectivity of mental life. The repressed subject, the there-being of repressed things, is active, insofar as it contradicts the subject of ordinary mentation. Its activity is not a reflectivity. It is animative—the desirousness of the repressed enters ordinary mentation either in the constructivity of dialectical movement, or disruptively in the falsifying form of symptomatic and characterological manifestations. Moreover, the repressed is not a contentless subject. The unconscious, when brought to consciousness, regularly appears to have been wishful, prototypically in some erotogenic or aggressive sense. The repressed subject has content in the sense that it transforms the significance of the semiotic system it enters, whether this entry is in the free development of a dialectical movement within the semiotic system, or in the opacity of an arrested contradictoriness. Psychoanalysis concretely demonstrates that the subjectivity of psychic reality is not unitary, and that totalizing the semiotic system of consciousness and preconsciousness is never truthful.

Thus, on the side of the subjectivity of the subject of ordinary mentation, Freud's *Psychologie der Verdrängung* also has radical implications. If the "I-less-ness" of the repressed stands as the negation of the "I-ness" of ordinary mentation, the subject cannot be apprehended as an identity, the fixed and final horizon within which the semiotic formation of objects occurs. Rather, it must now be apprehended as a shifting locus of becoming, an ontologization of the epistemic subject, in which the method of becoming is a dialectical deconstruction of its own object world, and in which the implication of "becoming" is both a restarting of a dialectical movement of contradictoriness and a restoring of lost desirousness.

The individual's subjectivity, the domain of conscious and preconscious mentation, is formed within the intersubjectivity of the general semiotic system. And because it is generated within this sociocultural totality, it gives the appearance, ideologically, of identity. Yet this "totality" is now approached as a totalization of false consciousness, and identity is now exposed as an ideological immobilization of contradictoriness. Dialectics must pass to the preponderance of things against the hegemony of ordinary subjectivity, to the precluded potential of the subject-being of things, to materiality and desire (see Adorno, 1966, p. 192ff.). The subject must, so to speak, become open to the possibility that its reality is insufficiently defined by its own apparent subjectivity, that there is, in a certain sense, a remainder excluded from its world of objects. The subject must act upon itself negatively, deconstructing its own givenness and "I-ness." Thus, the subject becomes a shifting locus, determined by the pursuit of its own nonidentity, and "in the unreconciled condition, nonidentity is experienced as negativity" (Adorno, 1966, p. 31).

This pursuit is mindful that the semiotic system of ordinary mentation is *not* a totality and cannot become one through its own affirmations. Thus, it is emphatically not that the subjectivity of ordinary mentation can adequately capture reality, nor that semiosis and reality were once one, nor that they will ultimately be so. Against these positions, the subject must experience and understand its own historicity, mobility, and even its inherent "excentricity," by means of a negative movement. To proceed dialectically in this manner means, as Adorno (1966, p. 145) argues, "to think in contradictions, for the sake of contradictions once experienced in the thing, and against that contradiction. A contradiction in reality, it is a contradiction against reality."

In psychoanalysis, self-consciousness deploys the contradictions in itself to remobilize the contradictoriness between itself and the repressed, to "reappropriate" that which it had excluded from itself. In this context, historicity and mobility are preeminent characteristics of a freely dialectical self-consciousness, in contrast to the stasis of false consciousness. And even the historicity of self-consciousness cannot be treated as an invariant—as has been done by György Lukács (1923) and certain existentialists in quite divergent ways. For to do so is typically to debase historicity into the epistemological and ontological stance of historicality, and thus attenuate the full dialectical development of discourse (an error all too frequently made in the day-to-day practice of psychotherapies informed by the psychoanalytic worldview). Rather than gearing treatment to such an invariance, the negativity of psychoanalytic discourse moves relentlessly across the boundaries of subjectivity, and hence along the margins of continuity and discontinuity, regaining the potential of contradictoriness between the thing-being of the repressed "subject" and the "I-ness" of the subject's semiotic world of "objects." Truth in psychoanalysis is a realizing movement of the subject, which—because repressed desirousness stands as the negation of semiotic subjectivity—can only proceed negatively and deconstructively. This is what it must mean when Freud (1933) characterizes the scientific and emancipatory direction of psychoanalytic discourse as dialectically reappropriative. "Wo Es war, soll Ich werden"—"Where It was, should I become."

PSYCHOANALYTIC NEGATIVITY, THERAPEUTIC DISCOURSES, AND THE QUESTION OF IDEOLOGY

How, then, does the work of patient and psychoanalyst actually proceed negatively and deconstructively? As a dialectically deconstructive praxis of discourse, psychoanalysis exhibits for us what Hegel calls "the seriousness, the suffering, the patience, and the labor of the negative." It is time now to be somewhat more specific and concrete about the significance of this, and to draw out some of its implications for the general questions of psychological inquiry and change—the questions of reality, representation, subject, and science.

As has been argued, psychoanalytic discourse is as it is because it addresses the alienated condition of psychic reality. It addresses the epistemic and ontic nonidentity of human semiosis and the desirousness of human being-in-the-world. And, as we have just seen, its trajectory issues from a double reversal of subject into thing. The marked subject (ordinary self-consciousness), by deconstructing itself, pursues its own nonidentity. And in so doing, the desirousness of the repressed may be reappropriated and remarked semiotically. Psychoanalysis vindicates itself only in its own movement, in the restarting of the dialectic of mental life and the restoration of desire to semiosis. And here we should note that the process of knowing and being may itself involve a movement of contradiction as the mobilization of estrangements *(Entfremdungen)* or "objectifications" (see Chapter 1, n. 7). But the alienation *(Entäusserung)* of false consciousness, against which psychoanalysis moves, is precisely an immobilization of this contradictoriness of psychic reality.

How does this psychoanalytic discourse start? Obviously, it has to start with the givenness and "I-ness" of the semiotic system, with the immediacy of ordinary mentation. But it does not principally involve a widening and deepening of this consciousness, in an affirmative, articulatory movement. Rather, psychoanalysis begins with the decision of common consciousness to treat itself as false. As Freud (1925c) indicates, neither the patient nor the psychoanalyst can publicly explain what the unconscious is. They cannot be assured of the solidity of their common experiences and understandings, and they cannot specify what experiences and understandings they are aiming to achieve. What the alienated condition of the system of common consciousness intimates is the existence of something else obtruding upon it. But it is no use simply to assert the existence of unconscious contents—the subject that has become thing. Instead, psychoanalysis starts with a negative reflection and a dispossessive interrogation of the presentness of the being of things that are ideologically precipitated as subject.

Psychoanalysis, then, is thoroughly dialectical from the moment it starts. There is no fixed starting point, nor any assumption about final resting point. Rather, dialectics starts with the nonidentity of the present. Initially, the notion of dialectics connotes no more than that the being of things does not enter the semiotic world of objects without leaving a remainder—a surplus of meaning—and that this remainder accounts for the frozen contradictions of the world as it presents itself semiotically (cf. Adorno, 1966). Thus, psychoanalytic dialectics begins with the untruth of identity, with the partiality of false consciousness as it is given in all that is immediate and familiar.

Psychoanalysis starts with the reality defined by the conscious-preconscious semiotic system, but it also starts with the proleptic tenet that this semiotic system, when reflected upon and interrogated dialectically, will be found not to exhaust the thingness of things. In other words, psychic reality may be more than that which belongs within the horizon of conscious and preconscious meanings. Still, the dialectic must start with this world of self- and other-representations as it is given. After all, although these "objects" may never attain the thingness of things, they are all that the patient, the psychoanalyst, or anyone else can actually know. But the psychoanalytic dialectic does not assume that this semiotic system is a totalizing unity. Any and every appearance of harmony, correspondence, or identity between semiosis and desire may be false and must be treated with suspicion.

In practice, this means that psychoanalysis initially focuses on aberrations and impairments in the text of conscious and preconscious meaning. Opacities, disruptions, discontinuities, symtomatic and characterological formations, these are the concrete but arrested contradictions that immediately impel negative dialectics. In this sense, Freud's psychology gives privilege to the maladjusted manifestations of mental life. However, the distinction between the psychically "normal" and "abnormal" is not scientific; it merely holds the status of convention (see Freud, 1938/1940). Freud insists that even the "common mental activities of normal people" exclude yet express disguised unconscious meanings (1923b, p. 216). Thus, psychoanalysis must eventually engage all manifestations of ordinary mentation and of human being-in-the-world in the negativity of its dialectics, whether such appearances are dystonic or syntonic to self-consciousness.

As was said, it is as if psychoanalytic discourse embraced Bloch's aphorism, "that which is cannot be true." Thus, Freud (1923a, p. 239) refers to the notion of repression as the "first shibboleth" of psychoanalytic discourse—it is a proleptic tenet that aids the patient and the psychoanalyst in reflecting and interrogating negatively, mindful that psychic reality will be found not to be exhausted within the limits of ordinary mentation. In this regard, one should note again that metapsychological concepts cannot prescribe the workings of the psychoanalytic process. Certain ideas, however, may operate proleptically within the engagement of patient and psychoanalyst as a sort of talisman or *aide memoire*, by which the participants remain faithful to the tenet that the perceptual and conceptual privileges of givenness and "I-ness" must be abused. And this tenet of negativity ensures that the discourse will be psychoanalytic rather than ordinarily conversational.

Against the allure of immediate givenness, Freud's psychology concurs with Hegel's argument that the most common way in which we deceive ourselves and others is to assume something as familiar and to accept it because of its familiarity. As was stated earlier, such knowing, for all its backing and forthing, never moves beyond its own boundaries, but does not realize that this is the case (see Hegel, 1807, pp. 28–29). This kind of knowing, bound by its own presumptions, is, of course, the ideological functioning of false consciousness. And Freud, with Marx and Nietszche, stands for a discipline that would dispossess and disocclude the ideology of everyday life.

As Adorno (1966, p. 40) indicates, "to dialectics, immediacy does not maintain its immediate pose. Instead of becoming ground, it becomes a moment." The familiarity of what Hegel calls "natural consciousness" and "self-consciousness" will show itself to be only an idea about knowledge, an epistemological attitude to be subsumed and surpassed. It cannot be true knowledge, although it erroneously takes itself in its immediacy to be so (cf. Hegel, 1807, p. 67). The dialectical path toward true knowledge, in which truth is a movement of knowing and being, thus has a negative significance for this attitude of consciousness, which thereby loses its "truth." Here we must note again that any affirmative reflection of self-consciousness upon itself, even an allegedly "transcendentalized" one, cannot possibly succeed in dispossessing itself as false. The radicalism of psychoanalytic method lies in what Hegel calls "the enormous power of the negative," implying a passage of reflection and interrogation in which the immediacy and familiarity of "I-ness" are jeopardized.

Psychoanalysis, then, places the immediacy and familiarity of ordinary mentation under suspicion and dispossesses its priority and authority. This method goes beyond some sort of Socratic *docta ignorantia*, and beyond the suspension of credence advocated by phenomenology. It is a thoroughgoing negation of credence. Negativity challenges the manifest to disclose the latent. What ordinary mentation took to be "true" experiences and understandings are found to be ideologically false, as they give way to "new" experiences and understandings. With respect to the "I-ness" of self-consciousness, such dialectical negativity implies the shifting locus of subjectivity in a movement of discourse that is, for such a subject, objectifying but not objectivating. In this movement, the frozen identity of the subject is repeatedly subverted and sublated, as it pursues its own nonidentity.

With respect to the givenness of "natural consciousness," dialectical negation of the manifest presentation (e.g., the semiotic construction of an "initial" symptom) evinces further personal meanings previously held latent by suppression and repression. Freud's case reports offer abundant retrospections of this aspect of the discursive process. For example, one patient complains of a dystonic obsessive fantasy in which rats burrow devouringly into the anus of his father and of an allegedly beloved woman friend (1909b). In the course of the debate between this patient and Freud, the givens of this fantasy, its contextuality as well as its imagism, are effectively jeopardized. Their apparent fixity, the patient's "truth" as the stasis of the symptom in the form of polysemous contradiction, is subverted and sublated. This devolution of the authority of the immediate and familiar permits the voicing of "new" semiotic constructions—descriptions and narrations concerning a syphilitic penis, florins, babies, marital relations, and sadistic punishment at the hands of father figures. Through the negativity of repeated reflection and interrogation of these successive and seemingly unrelated or nonsensical "new givens," the concealing function of semiotic construction is deconstructed, and the desirousness of the forgotten and the repressed may be immanently repossessed.

In psychoanalysis, self-consciousness can re-create itself as it negates itself precisely because the repressed becomes concretely apprehensible after the authority and priority of the immediate and familiar have been transgressed. Through negativity, the discourse of patient and psychoanalyst genuinely widens and deepens, from its reflection and interrogation of the "initial" symptomatic or characterological formation. The debate cannot stop with the subversion and sublation of this initial presentation of the conscious-preconscious domain, because this domain is inherently self-totalizing as the semiotic constitution of reality. The meaning of the particular formation implicates the entire fabric of the domain. As the initial presentation gives way to the emergence of further manifestations indicative of the significance of their predecessor, the entire trajectory of psychoanalytic discourse opens. The incidental appearance of a particular discontinuity within the semiotic whole is inevitably disabused. Placing the quasi-isolated aberration in jeopardy, calling it fundamentally into question, discloses the complicity of an entire network of meanings. Manifest presentations that were initially pellucid, as well as latent presentations that have been reordered and were previously assumed adequate, all become problematic.

Psychoanalysis is like the odyssey that Hegel (1807) calls "the pathway of doubt" or "the highway of despair." Indeed, it is not unusual for patient and psychoanalyst to have a sense of despair as they each realize that the "discrete" symptom or character manifestation is not to be treated in isolation, for it has profound implications for the entire conduct of each of their lives. This is the existential implication for all who have ever dreamed—regardless of their designated status as asymptomatic, "well-adjusted," or whatever. Neither the nonidentity of knowing and being, nor the fixation of this nonidentity in symptomatic or characterological formations, occurs insularly. The semiotic system of conscious, nonconscious, and preconscious mentation is indeed a system, a network that appears as a totality. The particular formation necessarily connects with all other parts of the whole. The quasi-insular aberration, a seemingly specific discontinuity, eventually implicates the fundamental mutilation of the whole, the hypostatized rupture of semiosis and desire.

The psychoanalytic odyssey may thus be apprehended as a widening and deepening movement of negativity against the hegemony of the apparent fixity and finality of semiotic constructions as they are given. In this movement, subject and objects are treated as moments in a discourse that progressively subverts and sublates. Moreover, although this debate takes into account its own earlier states of knowledge and its earlier conditions of its being, it does so in the same manner that it treats all givens. In this sense, psychoanalysis might be said to reprocess the preceding results of observation, inference, and interpretation, refusing to grant them authority or priority as fixed or final, but insisting on maintaining the tension of their potential for the disclosure of nonidentity. Thus, all manifestations of subjectivistic or objectivistic process, as well as all manifestations of things hermeneutic, must eventually come under the corrective reflection and interrogation of dialectical negativity. In the course of the work of patient and psychoanalyst, they will be treated as matters of rhetoric and logic—as a denial and disavowal of dialectical potential and an ideological foreclosure of the reality of psychic being. In this sense, the dialectic maintains itself against appearances of the transcendental, the apophantic, or the hermeneutic.

In discussing the seminal negativity of psychoanalytic methodology, it should be clear that this method involves neither theory nor technique in the ordinary sense of these terms. As has been argued, psychoanalytic discourse does not entail a formalized epistemology, being neither contemplative nor instrumental. Psychoanalysis does not, for instance, impose some formal model or ideal upon the events of mental life, subordinating content to form. It does not generate a set or rules about the lawfulness of the world, such as a theory of semantics, syntactics, and pragmatics—nor does it depend upon such a systematization. Indeed, it does not appeal to some higher aprioristic authority such as a notion of correspondence, unity, or the harmonious totality of human being-in-the-world. More precisely, psychoanalysis works against all tendencies toward such attitudes and their formalization, treating them as fixedness to be subsumed and surpassed. In this sense, psychoanalysis is anti-systemic, grounding itself upon the negative movement of its own discourse within the semiotic system upon which it operates. As dialectics, Freud's psychology *cannot* produce such a theoretical structure, nor does it subscribe to one (see Freud, 1923a). Its dialectical negativity implies the precedence of its own directionality and the transformative potential of deconstruction over systematization and stasis.

To say this, however, does not mean that psychoanalysis merely responds to the there-being of things as they are given, submitting itself passively to the way the world is. Psychoanalysis is a semiotic labor, a method or praxis. But this is not to say that psychoanalysis is a technique. It is a movement within the semiotic system—the world of concepts, as it might be called. Yet it is not a manipulation of concepts, as in logical empiricism. Nor is it an abandonment of conceptual work in favor of the ephemeral thingness of things, as in contemporary hermeneutics. In psychoanalysis, the notion of *praxis* becomes necessary to the notion of truth and transformation. The negativity of its praxis is formed by the contradictoriness of reality as it transforms it. In this sense, psychoanalytic discourse is not a technical matter that can be specified externally, or learned by formulas, just as it is not a matter of guidance, persuasion, advice-giving, or manipulation. It is a methodology of negativity within the relatedness of "care"—a methodology that can be learned in only one way, namely, by submitting oneself to it and participating in its process.

What, then, is the determinacy of psychoanalytic discourse as a methodological movement of negation? That psychoanalysis is not formalized, systematized, or technical, that it cannot generalize outside of its own widening and deepening movement, is not to imply that its dialectical hermeneutics is some sort of intellectual anarchy or irrationalism. The dialectics of psychoanalysis is a praxis of reason, epistemically, as well as an ontic responsiveness to the alienated reality in which it finds itself. Psychoanalysis apprehends each moment through a negativity of reflection and interrogation. This means that the moment is known only when it has been subverted and sublated. It also means that the being of each successive moment emerges, via negativity, from the nonidentity of its predecessor. Each of these implications requires some elaboration.

Although psychoanalytic discourse gradually moves forward, the patient and psychoanalyst never know the truth of the moment they are at, nor do they know the truth of the moment ahead of them. In a certain sense, they experience but do not understand the present, and anticipate the future only bewilderingly. Such is the thoroughly historicized and vigorously mobile character of the discourse itself. However, the patient and psychoanalyst do know the untruth of the preceding moment, for the falsity of this preceding moment has been treated negatively, its untruth unmasked in the emergence of the present. It is in this sense that psychoanalytic discourse is dialectically truthful and transformative. It is what Freud tries to express when he writes that "what emerges from the unconscious is to be apprehended not in terms of what goes before but in terms of what comes after" (1909a, p. 301). Truth is bound to transformation. It is not something attached to a proposition, a property of certain semiotic constructions. Truth is deconstructively inherent to a reality in process, a movement of interlocution. Thus, what must be given credence in the conduct of our lives is precisely *not* the apparent historicity of the present, the immediate experiences and understandings that lead into the sense of apodicticity and adequacy. Rather, we must hold to a discourse that unmasks the present in such a way that we may in the future take cognizance of its untruth: understand its partiality and limitation, and reexperience its lost desirousness. Freud approvingly quotes the man-servant's slogan in J. N. Nestroy's *Der Zerrissene*, whose only answer can be: "all will become clear in the course of further developments" (1937b, p. 52). My argument here is that the man-servant's aphorism is only true if the present is scientifically and emancipatorily treated by the praxis of negativity that the alienated condition of discourse deserves. Psychoanalysis, or more generally the deconstructive discourse of negative dialectics, is, in this sense, a way of life.

As a negativity implying the dialectical subversion and sublation of the "I-ness" and givenness of the present moment, psychoanalysis follows Hegel (1807) in deploying the ability of self-consciousness to cancel itself in such a way as to subsume what is thereby surpassed. The negativity of psychoanalytic discourse does not come from outside the semiotic domain, nor, of course, can it jump out of this domain. But as a movement of dispossession and disocclusion, it transgresses it in such a way that desire appears anew within the now-transformed horizons of conscious and preconscious mentation. Such negativity is, in a certain sense, a negation of a negation, as Freud (1925b) himself indicates in a short essay that is unusually blatant in its Hegelianism. Before psychoanalysis, the content of the repressed does make its way into ordinary mentation—on the condition that it appears as its negation, as disavowal or in the disguised form of polysemous contradiction. Given this inherent contradictoriness of psychic reality, negation becomes "a way of taking cognizance of the repressed" in a double sense: prepsychoanalytically, as the "return" of the repressed, and through psychoanalytic negativity, as the restoration of the repressed in the dialectic of subjectivity.

This, then, is the determinacy and historicity of psychoanalytic discourse—that the negativity of reflection and interrogation is not an arbitrary movement. Negation comes from the reality it negates. Each successive moment of the debate issues from the polysemy of the previous moment, the contradictoriness of its experiences and understandings. The exemplary rigor of psychoanalysis comes from its discovery of meanings that are, in a certain sense, already there. Freud's seriously inadequate—indeed anti-dialectical—analogy between psychoanalytic debate and archaelogical investigation does at least serve to signify that the process is at once mutative and loyal to its "material." Whatever their capacity to reveal anew something previously concealed, to reinstate the repressed, the experiences and understandings of the psychoanalytic process are also determined by semiotic conditions that precede them. What I have called deconstruction is also necessarily construction and reconstruction. Through negation, the untruth of the present moment discloses its partiality and limitation, its function in precluding and excluding certain content from itself. Concomitantly, what seemed like "truth" becomes unsure of itself, calls itself to account in a new process of reflection and interrogation. In this manner, psychoanalytic discourse does not evoke understanding from preunderstanding, but regresses back from understanding to preunderstanding in a movement of negativity in which every preunderstanding will be reworked.

Meaning is determined by the interrelationship of representations, implying not only that representations are built one upon another historically and systemically, but also that mentation may, in a certain sense, return to prior experiences and understandings, both in the repetitions of the return of the repressed and deconstructively in the recollection and reappropriation of the psychoanalytic dialectic. The antithetical moments of the negativity instated by this dialectical discourse are thus not arbitrary, but inhere to the contradictory conditions of that which is reflected and interrogated. Given the regressive dimension of this discourse, psychoanalytic reflection and interrogation are a determinate deconstruction of the fixity of polysemous contradiction in all that is given and "I," in such a manner that something held latent by suppression, and later something precluded and excluded by repression, may be progressively recollected and reappropriated. Whereas before psychoanalysis the desirous repressed disrupts and deforms the conditions of givenness and "I-ness," psychoanalytic praxis attends to this desire of a split subjectivity within the formation and transformation of its psychic reality.

The integrity of knowing and being in psychoanalysis lies in its negativity, a negativity that ensures the emancipatory and scientific quality of its discourse. Psychoanalytic praxis concretely demonstrates what Adorno (1966, p. 159) calls "the seriousness of unswerving negation," a refusal to endorse things as they are, given their conditions of alienation. Psychoanalysis refuses the complicity of identity thinking. Rather, it deconstructs the semiotic totalization of this ideological discourse of false consciousness, to reinstate the dialectic that restores desire.

An unswerving deconstruction is not destruction. The rigorous negativity of psychoanalytic discourse is completely different from some sort of *reductio ad nihilem*, for it reinstates and restores something that the falsity of prepsychoanalytic self-consciousness prevented. Its unremitting negativity is recuperative, actively transgressing the boundaries of concealment and unconcealment. Here it is easy to mistake psychoanalysis for a doctrine of the realism of the unconscious, to view the unconscious as a sort of thing-in-itself, or as meaning-in-itself. The movement of psychoanalysis is neither circular nor solipsistic. It arrives at something new at each moment of its odyssey. And thus it seems to imply the existence of reality "outside" of the horizons of the semiotic system of psychic reality. In a certain sense, this is correct, for psychoanalysis does indeed demonstrate that psychic reality is not exhausted by semiotic construction, that the totalization of the semiotic system is false. By pointing to the nonidentity of signification, psychoanalysis vindicates the authentic concreteness of desire and materiality that is not held captive in any hypostatized signifying practices.

But psychoanalysis is not a doctrine of essentialism, asserting the repressed as the stable essence of mental life—even if it often gives the impression of being close to such a doctrine. Its negativity, the notion of nonidentity and of the remainder unfulfilled by identity thinking, is the antinomy of essentializing thought. It does not make sense to assert the existence of a "free subject" exterior to discourse, yet at

the same time the repressed is found, through psychoanalytic deconstruction of self-consciousness, to be desirous and intrinsically meaningful. As has been shown, attempts to assert that the unconscious is a
pure essence, or that it is, with respect to self-consciousness, only
extrinsically meaningful and ontically irrevocably external, are fundamentally mistaken. Such erroneous readings of psychoanalytic discourse serve only to defuse its extraordinary and enigmatic dialectical
tension. For in psychoanalysis, the formative dialectic of desire and
self-consciousness is reopened. Freud's psychology, in its pursuit of
nonidentity, demonstrates the ideological error of asserting the direct
accessibility of reality outside of semiosis, but equally it demonstrates
the ideological error of asserting the totalization of the semiotic system.

A dialectic that is unswervingly deconstructive deploys the polysemy of semiotic practices, the arrested contradictoriness of the return of the repressed, and brings this into play, as a continual
renunciation and repositioning of the signifying process (cf. Kristeva,
1974). This play may be apprehended as an evocative psychopoetics of
semiotic functioning. It is what is achieved by the "free play" of so-
called associative thinking, which uses the tropological and allegorical
character of the preconscious for an inquiry upon the network of meanings surrounding each particular polysemous event. The semiotic play
of "free association" is a mode of reflection that facilitates the relations
between conscious awareness and preconsciousness within their common boundaries—a "working over" *(Verarbeitung)* of a certain sort. It
also functions expressively as a mode of cognitive understanding that
is also a conative and affective experience. And it illuminates the truly
nonidentitarian quality of the patient's ordinary mentation.

This playful reflectivity is, of course, punctuated by the interrogative mode of questioning, metacommentary, and "interpretation,"
which serves both as a negating and as a marking of the patient's
discourse. As a negating, psychoanalytic interrogation could be said to
operate as a maieutic clearing, disposing of the wrong questions
generated by spontaneous reflectivity. In this sense, the psychoanalytic dialectic exhibits a negativity unfamiliar to the Socratic method, in
which hermeneutic reflection arises from the ability of self-
consciousness to generate questions. (The affirmative generation of
questions by self-consciousness is not the same as the negativity by
which self-consciousness calls itself into question, and there is indeed
reason why Socrates did not discover the repressed unconscious.)
Psychoanalysis must negate, in order to transgress the boundaries of
ordinary mentation. Here it is also important to acknowledge that

silent listening may serve this commentatorial function of negativity, that the role of the caring but silent psychoanalyst may be as significant as that of the psychoanalyst who vocally calls meanings into question. As a marking, psychoanalytic interrogation facilitates the process of "working through" *(Durcharbeitung)*, by which the desirousness of repressed ideation, affect, and motive is progressively rehabilitated. Its play is thus not a matter of poetic license, but a historicization of truth in a movement by which desire is recollected and reappropriated.

In distinguishing moments in the psychoanalytic debate as play or commentary, I am not implying a division of labor between the performative patient and the constative psychoanalyst. Not only may the patient be engaged in commentary as well as play, but the psychoanalyst must be silently at play. Indeed, implied in this discussion of the negativity of psychoanalytic discourse is an odyssey wherein the psychoanalyst is moved as much as the patient. For, above and beyond all else, the discourse cannot function without their relatedness, the psychoanalyst's "care" in the Heideggerian sense. And it is a profoundly dialectical engagement—conatively, affectively, and cognitively.

The dialectical negativity of play and comment, in which both patient and psychoanlyst are engaged, is the only way in which the arrested contradictoriness of the patient's condition may be reworked. In this sense, psychoanalysis is like dreaming. It is both a freeing and marking of the "subject" who is precluded and excluded. Yet, unlike dreaming, the discourse of patient and psychoanalyst has the full intentionality, determinacy, and mobility of dialectical praxis. The dream is the return of the repressed, and psychoanalytic negativity educes and transmutes such mental events toward the recollection and reappropriation of the repressed.

Negativity, Hegel's "royal road" to science, is also Freud's "royal road" to the unconscious. When Freud (1900) writes that dreams are such a road, he cannot mean the dream in and of itself, so much as the trajectory of reflection and interrogation that conducts patient and psychoanalyst from the manifest toward that which the manifest conceals. This trajectory is truthful in that it authentically signifies the psychic reality in which it occurs. It is transformative as an eduction and transmutation of the return of the repressed toward its recollection and reappropriation.

The work of the patient and psychoanalyst can, of course, go astray. And it can do so in two ways. In the first place, the patient and psychoanalyst can lose their relatedness, the sense of belongingness or context of "care" necessary for their dialectical work to proceed. Given the inevitable vicissitudes of the patient's "transferences," the development and maintenance of this relatedness, the context of the psychoanalytic situation, are usually the responsibility of the psychoanalyst. It is the psychoanalyst, not the patient, who must create the context of "care" in this Heideggerian sense. For such "care" is the prerequisite of psychoanalytic process. In clinical terms, any breakdown in this context is usually a problem of the psychoanalyst's narcissism—a lapse in the task of reflecting and interrogating his or her own "material" in order to become adequately available to the patient's discourse.

The psychoanalyst prevents the psychoanalytic process from going astray by silently playing in response to the patient's discourse of play—the psychoanalyst's task is thus the continual freeing and marking of responsiveness to the patient's knowing and being. Nevertheless, the psychoanalyst will frequently fail at this task, and the second way in which psychoanalytic work can go astray is that the psychoanalyst will not say something that must be said, or will say something that is mistaken—the problem of erroneous, mistimed, or inappropriate interpretations. Such mistakes are a lapse in the determinate negativity of dialectical reflection and interrogation. As such, they halt the dialectical movement of the discourse between patient and psychoanalyst. These incorrect comments or incorrect silences, on the part of the psychoanalyst, may prove temporarily efficacious, but ultimately they inhibit the movement of reflection and interrogation, for they fail to emerge from the authentic contradictoriness of the psychic reality in which they are framed (see Freud, 1937b). They foreclose the widening and deepening of dialectical negativity, and they can only deform the dialogue of patient and psychoanalyst into a therapy that depends on a manipulation of semiotic constructions within the alienated conditions of conscious and preconscious mentation.

Negativity is thus the corrective function of psychoanalytic discourse. When people ask what is going to assure the truth of any particular practice, they usually mean what is going to secure the naive realism of everyday life. Psychoanalysis, however, works precisely against the naive realism of everyday life, demonstrating its ideological functioning. What the odyssey of negative dialectics tells us is that the true reality is never the most obvious. Indeed, all that purports to be obvious and whole, psychoanalysis unmasks as the state of false consciousness. As my argument has proceeded, three notions of correction, and three notions of truth, have been called into question: first, the objectivist belief that it can appeal to the experience of its objects as determined by a reality ontically outside of itself, the world of evidence and data; second, the subjectivist proclamation of the truth of its own experiences and understandings, of the subject's adequacy and apodicticity; and third, contemporary hermeneutics, insistence on truth as the enunciation or disclosure of a presumed totality of articulated meaning-events, an allegedly harmonious totality that balks contradiction. All these "truths" are variants of an identitarian ideology. What, then, is the quality of truth under the conditions of nonidentity?

Inasmuch as the corrective function of psychoanalytic discourse lies within the discourse itself, truth is not attached to finalized propositions, but inherent to reality in process. It is neither immutable, nor is it mystically disconnected from the concreteness of things given in the appearances of immediacy and familiarity. Thus, psychoanalysis is not a cumulative body of knowledge, but a historicized process of knowing and becoming. Its odyssey of play and comment is faithful to psychic reality as it concretely transforms itself by grasping its own fundamental contradictoriness. True reality, to borrow Hegel's words, "is its own becoming" as a purposive movement without any evident assurance of an identitarian beginning or ending: *"La verité marche."* Reality is thus a realizing, a movement impelled by its own contradictions, a developing of subjectivity through the dialectic of semiosis and desire. In this sense, under the conditions of nonidentity, the authenticity of the subject is as a negativity of its discourse. Truth is a becoming, but it is a becoming in the mode of a negative dialectic of discourse, in conditions where the being of psychic life is fundamentally alienated from itself.

The recollection and reappropriation achieved by psychoanalytic reflection and interrogation are not to be apprehended as a fixed and final truth, but as a reopening of the formative dialectic of desire and the semiosis of self-consciousness. The psychoanalytic itinerary of inquiry and change is forever anchored in the particular contingencies and determinations of discourse. Yet it is uniquely scientific in its uncompromising interrogation of the ideology of the established and existent mode of discourse. Overall, psychoanalysis might be described as an odyssey toward reconciliation via the disocclusive and dispossessive movement of negativity. Yet, whereas reconciliation is falsely attained in the ideology of an identitarian thesis, psychoanalysis makes no such proclamation of completion. Truth, as Freud (1936, p. 127) once wrote to Arnold Zweig in a slightly different context, "is unobtainable, mankind does not deserve it."

The negative dialectics of psychoanalytic debate is incessant and unassuaged. "Truth," in the sense of stasis, is not obtainable, although psychoanalysis indeed knows the untruth of what has gone before it, because of the truthfulness of its transformative work upon the present, in a creative and re-creative movement of deconstruction. In a certain sense, psychoanalysis is a method that both discovers what the world has been and moves toward making it what it ought to be. Against the alienation of psychic reality, the scientificity of negative dialectics takes up an imperative similar to that of Albert Camus' rebel: a hope for the emancipatory potential of the future, through an understanding of the untruth of the past, and an experiencing of the contradictoriness of the present. The "moral" attitude of patient and psychoanalyst, if we may call it this, is that of the greatest humility toward all the contradicting details of the "material" of psychic reality, toward their own relatedness, and toward the dialectical movement in which they are engaged.

Again, psychoanalysis is not a philosophy of stable essences existing beneath the appearances of semiotic construction. Rather, it is a *dynamic* account of desire. Desire enters self-consciousness in the repressed condition of polysemous contradictions. As a negative dialectic, psychoanalytic reflection and interrogation act within and upon this "return" of the repressed so that desire now enters self-consciousness as its own notion. This reappropriation of the repressed is not a static repossession, for, in emerging as its own notion, desire is neither formally possessed by semiotic construction nor fixedly self-certified within the semiotic system. Psychoanalytic knowing thus restores desire by restarting the dialectical movement of psychic reality. Such knowing is negative in that it pursues the nonidentity of semiotic construction, and in that it is a dialectic of knowing that restarts a dialectic of being. By thus recouping the dialectic of semiosis and desire, psychoanalysis must continually go beyond itself, aiming at the coincidence of knowing and being by pursuing their noncoincidences. In its discourse, reason creates itself as the movement of negation—a movement of the subjectivity of psychic reality, and against the pregivenness and stasis of this subjectivity. Psychoanalytic reason thus accords with the desirousness of the psychic reality within which it works.

As a praxis that, so to speak, turns the semiotic constitution of the world against itself, Freud's psychology exhibits the process of becoming of a dialectical discourse that negates the whole sphere in which it moves, thus imploding the Hegelian epithet *"das Wahre is das Ganze"*—the true is the whole *but* the whole is false (cf. Adorno, 1966).

Psychoanalysis, as the science of discourse, moves against the ideology of everyday life. Ideology is here defined as a semiotic closure, the fixating functioning of the subjectivity of psychic reality as an immobile point of self-reference, or as the frozen and final boundary of the possible conditions of knowing and being. This mode of functioning prevents the subject's entry as process into a historicized and mobilized dynamic of self-consciousness and the materiality of desire. In this sense, ideology is a dehistoricization and immobilization of discourse. Ideology includes the cooptation of beliefs that are in some sense critical of the established and existent order—as we have seen with the subjectivistic, objectivistic, and hermeneutic "readings" of Freud's psychology. But more profoundly, ideology entails every semiotic attenuation of reflection and interrogation as a potentially emancipatory praxis. And the scientific pursuit of the repressed unconscious is such an emancipatory praxis. Thus, not only do the issues of "psychopathology" fall under the rubric of questions about ideology and the semiotics of false consciousness, but so does every issue of significational practice. The movement of negative dialectics cannot single out specific meaning events as ideological, but must proceed toward an apprehension of the totality of meaning events as a semiotic system that is fundamentally contradictory, yet that generates a false consciousness by identitarian constructions which repress the potential of contradiction. Ideology functions semiotically as an incapacity to deconstruct and reconstruct ourselves and our worlds within the historicized context of our knowing and being. It is, above and beyond all else, the arrest of the dialectical potential of contradictoriness.

Against the ideology of identitarian and totalitarian thinking, psychoanalytic science demonstrates that, whereas the estrangement of objectification, of the semiotic construction of world representations, may be ubiquitous and indeed a necessary dimension of the dialectics of development, the anti-dialectical alienation of psychic reality may be surpassed. Freud's psychology asserts and demonstrates the fundamentality of contradiction. It is not a thesis of "total ideology" inasmuch as the notion of totality is retained merely as a manner of speaking, a methodological category rather than an ontological presumption—hence the possibility of a deconstructive praxis that seems to operate upon the conundrum, *the true is the whole but the whole is false*. Freud's psychology is a particularistic venture, a truthful and transformative discourse upon the fundamental contradictoriness of psychic reality—a discourse that perpetually subverts and sublates the stasis of identitarianism.

The work of patient and psychoanalyst is basically a private and particularistic odyssey, a therapy between two persons. The truths and transformations of psychoanalytic discourse are specific and idiographic—a remobilization of the subject of *psychic* reality in all its negativity and historicity. Unlike Hegelian dialectics, psychoanalytic dialectics offers no means for assuming that the particular and individual might legitimately be universalized. Given the historicity of the processes involved, a retrospective account of one psychoanalysis cannot provide information about another, except insofar as each psychoanalysis conducted becomes a part of the historicity of the particular psychoanalyst's experiences and understandings. The truths and transformations of psychoanalysis are such that they cannot be generalized beyond their own dialectical movement. Psychoanalysis offers little or nothing extrapsychoanalytically. Yet, in another sense, psychoanalysis does have implications for the entire realm of sociocultural discourse. Whatever its range of therapeutic implications, the scientific and emancipatory praxis of psychoanalysis works against the ideology of false consciousness in a way that engenders a process of sociocultural critique.

That the repressed can be recollected and reappropriated dialectically upsets the authority and priority of the sociocultural order of discourse. The move that psychoanalytic negativity makes against all ideology is not just a matter of therapeutic discourse, it is inherently an indictment of the established and existent order as it presents itself semiotically. To a certain extent, Freud realized this, as he tried to suggest that individual therapy must issue into a therapy for the communal disorder; for its participants, psychoanalysis comes to mean a vigorous and trenchant disclosure of the exploitative and oppressive conditions of the semiotically inscribed order of sociocultural relations (see Freud, 1909c, 1910b). Freud hinted at this when he said, "If we accomplish so little therapeutically, we at least learn why it is impossible to accomplish more" (1911b, p. 33). In this sense, the work of patient and psychoanalyst, if pursued scientifically, terminates not so much with some intimation of the sacred, as Ricoeur (1970, 1974) would have it, as with a materiality, a concrete challenge to the collective conduct of our lives (see Barratt, 1976).⁶ In psychoanalysis, the alienation of the individual and the particular points to the contradic-

---

⁶In citing my 1976 essay, I refer the reader only to those parts of this work which offer a critique of Paul Ricoeur's ideas about symbolism and the intimation of the sacred. Overall, this 1976 work is significantly flawed in its epistemological argument, and several of its main contentions must be abandoned in the light of the thesis presented herein.

tory conditions of the sociocultural order. The deconstruction of semiotic relations as an individuality necessarily issues into the deconstruction of semiosis as sociality. As Freud (1911c, p. 35) indicated to Ludwig Binswanger, it is the fate of psychoanalysis to "disturb the peace of the world."

Psychoanalytic negativity, as a discourse that reflects upon and interrogates the ideology of false consciousness, requires us to reorient radically our thinking and conduct with respect to the fundamental questions of reality, subject, and science. Psychoanalysis is indeed *eine entscheidende Neuorientierung in Welt und Wissenschaft*. In this book, I have tried to demonstrate the validity of this claim, first by disposing of all ideological variants of psychoanalysis (the world-views of subjectivistic or objectivistic epistemology and of hermeneutic ontology), and then by showing that the uniquely scientific and emancipatory quality of genuine psychoanalytic praxis, as the psychic pursuit of the repressed, is due to its movement as the discourse of dialectical negativity within and through the limits and conditions of semiotic construction. I believe this thesis suggests two directions for further work: first, a discussion of the semiotics of therapeutic discourse, developing the epistemological and ontological implications of psychoanalysis on a more practical, clinical level; and second, a consideration of the general issues of ideology, with an eye to the semiotic and material formation of human subjectivity. These, however, are directions for the future. Here the emphasis is on the knowing and being of mental processes, with the argument that psychoanalysis is the only valid approach to fundamental questions pertaining to all psychological inquiry and change.

Freud once told a student and patient that *all psychology is psychoanalysis* (Wortis, 1954). I have argued that if psychology is neither the ideological functioning of a descriptive account of everyday life, nor the ideological functioning of a behavioral technology, then it is indeed the science of psychoanalysis. If we define psychology as the study of psychic reality, a study that must perforce reflect upon and interrogate the epistemological and ontological conditions of its own discourse, then Freud's claim is valid. But this claim radically reorients our notion of reality and our notion of science. Psychoanalysis shows us the scientific and emancipatory power of the negative within the contradictory semiosis of psychic reality. It vindicates for us the excentricity, historicity, and mobility of human self-consciousness and of the worlds in which we live. In psychoanalysis, to know something is to change it, to pursue its nonidentity with itself and to find it to have been false. To know something is to deconstruct it, by developing the arrested potential of its contradictoriness. To know something is not merely to articulate a reality as it is given by the semiotic system, to unfold an identitarian thesis, but to operate negatively upon the experiences and understandings given in the "I-ness" of our realities in order to move against the ideology inherent in the discourse of false consciousness. To know something is thus not fixed, final, apodictic, or systematic, but a historicized movement that reappropriates the desirousness of human being-in-the-world by restarting the dialectic of human subjectivity.

Unfortunately, contemporary "psychoanalysis" may lose itself within the hegemony of ideological formulations. As Freud (1928) himself intimated, psychoanalysis must be defended from the ideologies of priests and physicians—its liberational potential protected from the machinations of magicians and technicians. If indeed psychoanalysis can be preserved as the exemplification of an anti-ideological discourse, then it sets the course for a critical new direction in the world and in science, and particularly for a critical new direction in the practices of psychological inquiry and change. As the psychic pursuit of the repressed, psychoanalysis remains an enigmatic and extraordinary discipline. It can exemplify for us a praxis of discourse both uniquely scientific and authentically emancipatory, the way knowing and being in the interests of liberating our alienated human potentialities.

REFERENCES

Adorno, T. W. (1966), *Negative dialectics*, trans. E. B. Ashton. New York: Seabury, 1973.

Alexander, F. (1933), The Relation of Structural and Instinctual Conflicts. *Psychoanalytic Quarterly*, 2:181–207.

Andreas-Salomé, L. (1912–1913), *The Freud journal of Lou Andreas-Salomé*, trans. S. A. Leavy. New York: Basic Books, 1964.

Bachelard, G. (1928), *Essai sur la connaissance approchée*. Paris: Vrin.

———— (1934), *Le Nouvel esprit scientifique*. Paris: Presses Universitaire de France.

———— (1938), *La Formation de l'esprit scientifique: Contribution à une psychanalyse de la connaissance objective*. Paris: Vrin.

———— (1940), *La Philosophie du non*. Paris: Presses Universitaire de France.

Bär, E. S. (1974), Understanding Lacan. In: *Psychoanalysis and contemporary science*, Vol. 3, ed. L. Goldberger & V. H. Rosen. New York: International Universities Press, 1975, pp. 473–544.

Barratt, B. B. (1976), Freud's Psychology as Interpretation. In: *Psychoanalysis and contemporary science*, Vol. 5, ed. T. Shapiro. New York: International Universities Press, pp. 443–478.

———— (1978), Critical Notes on Schafer's "Action Language." *The Annual of Psychoanalysis*, 6:287–303. New York: International Universities Press.

Binswanger, L. (1957), *Sigmund Freud: Reminiscences of a friendship*, trans. N. Guterman. New York: Grune & Stratton.

Boden, M. A. (1972), *Purpose explanation in psychology*. Cambridge, Mass.: Harvard University Press.

Boeckh, A. (1877), *Encyklopädie und Methodologie der philologische Wissenschaften*, ed. E. Bratuscheck. Leipzig: Teubner.

Brentano, F. (1874), *Psychology from an empirical standpoint*, trans. A. Rancurrello, D. Terrell, & L. McAlister. London: Routledge & Kegan Paul, 1973.

Breuer, J. & Freud, S. (1893–1895), Studien über Hysterie. *Gesammelte Werke*, 1:7–312. [Trans.: Studies on Hysteria. *Standard Edition, 2.*]

Canguilhem, G. (1952), *La Connaissance de la vie*. Paris: Hachette.

———— (1968), *Études d'histoire et de philosophie des sciences*. Paris: Vrin.

Descartes, R. (1637), Discourse on the Method of Rightly Conducting the Reason. In: *The philosophical works of Descartes*, Vol. *1*, trans. E. S. Haldane & G. R. T. Ross. London: Cambridge University Press, 1911, pp. 81–130.

—— (1641), Meditations on First Philosophy. In: *The philosophical works of Descartes*, Vol. *1*, trans. E. S. Haldane & G. R. T. Ross. London: Cambridge University Press, 1911, pp. 133–199.

—— (1644), The Principles of Philosophy. In: *The philosophical works of Descartes*, Vol. *1*, trans. E. S. Haldane & G. R. T. Ross. London: Cambridge University Press, 1911, pp. 203–302.

Feyerabend, P. K. (1970), *Against method: Outline for an anarchistic theory of knowledge*. London: New Left Books, 1975.

Fichte, J. G. (1974, et alia), *Fichte: Science of knowledge (Wissenschaftslehre)*, trans. P. Heath & J. Lachs. New York: Appleton-Century-Crofts, 1970.

Foucault, M. (1966), *Les Mots et les choses*. Paris: Gallimard.

—— (1969), *L'Archeologie du savoir*. Paris: Gallimard.

Freud, A. (1936), The Ego and the Mechanisms of Defense. *The writings of Anna Freud*, Vol. *2*. New York: International Universities Press, 1966.

Freud, S. (1887–1902), *Aus den anfangen der psychoanalyse*. London: Imago, 1950. [Trans.: *The Origins of Psychoanalysis*, ed. M. Bonaparte, A. Freud, & E. Kris. New York: Basic Books, 1954]

—— (1895a), Entwurf einer Psychologie. In: *Aus den anfangen der psychoanalyse* [1887–1902]. London: Imago, 1950, pp. 371–466. [Trans.: Project for a Scientific Psychology. *Standard Edition*, 1:295–397]

—— (1895b), Zur Kritik der 'Angstneurose.' *Gesammelte Werke*, *1*:357–376. [Trans.: A Reply to Criticisms of My Paper on Anxiety Neurosis. *Standard Edition*, *3*:123–139.]

—— (1896), Weitere Bemerkungen über die Abwehrneuropsychosen. *Gesammelte Werke*, *1*:379–403. [Trans.: Further Remarks on the Neuropsychoses of Defence. *Standard Edition*, *3*:162–185.]

—— (1898a), Zum psychischen Mechanismus der Vergesslichkeit. *Gesammelte Werke*, *1*:519–527. [Trans.: The Psychical Mechanism of Forgetfulness. *Standard Edition*, *3*:289–297.]

—— (1898b), Die Sexualität in der Ätiologie der Neurosen. *Gesammelte Werke*, *1*:491–516. [Trans.: Sexuality in the Aetiology of the Neuroses. *Standard Edition*, *3*:263–285.]

—— (1899), Über Deckerinnerungen. *Gesammelte Werke*, *1*:531–54. [Trans.: Screen Memories. *Standard Edition*, *3*:303–322.]

—— (1900), Die Traumdeutung. *Gesammelte Werke*, *2–3*:1–642.

[Trans.: The Interpretation of Dreams. *Standard Edition*, *4–5*:1–627.]

——— (1901a), Zur Psychopathologie des Altagslebens. *Gesammelte Werke*, *4*. [Trans.: The Psychopathology of Everyday Life. *Standard Edition*, *6*.]

——— (1901b), Über den Traum. *Gesammelte Werke*, *2–3*:645–700. [Trans.: On Dreams. *Standard Edition*, *5*:633–686.]

——— (1904), Die Freudsche psychoanalytische Methode. *Gesammelte Werke*, *5*:3–10. [Trans.: Freud's Psychoanalytic Procedure. *Standard Edition*, *7*:249–254.]

——— (1905a), Bruchstück einer Hysterie-Analyse. *Gesammelte Werke*, *5*:163–286. [Trans.: Fragment of an Analysis of a Case of Hysteria. *Standard Edition*, *7*:7–122.]

——— (1905b), Drei Abhandlungen zur Sexualtheorie. *Gesammelte Werke*, *5*:29–145. [Trans.: Three Essays on the Theory of Sexuality. *Standard Edition*, *7*:130–243.]

——— (1905c), Psychische Behandlung (Seelenbehandlung). *Gesammelte Werke*, *5*:287–315. [Trans.: Psychical (or Mental) Treatment. *Standard Edition*, *7*:283–302.]

——— (1905d), Über Psychotherapie. *Gesammelte Werke*, *5*:13–26. [Trans.: On Psychotherapy. *Standard Edition*, *7*:257–268.]

——— (1905e), Der Witz und seine Beziehung zum Unbewussten. *Gesammelte Werke*, *6*. [Trans.: Jokes and their Relation to the Unconscious. *Standard Edition*, *8*.]

——— (1906), Meine Ansichten über die Rolle der Sexualität in der Ätiologie der Neurosen. *Gesammelte Werke*, *5*:149–159. [Trans.: My Views on the Part Played by Sexuality in the Aetiology of the Neuroses. *Standard Edition*, *7*:271–279.]

——— (1907), Der Wahn und die Träume in W. Jensens "Gradiva." *Gesammelte Werke*, *7*:31–125. [Trans.: Delusions and Dreams in Jensen's "Gradiva." *Standard Edition*, *9*:7–95.]

——— (1909a), Analyse der Phobie eines Fünfjährigen Knaben. *Gesammelte Werke*, *7*:243–377. [Trans.: Analysis of a Phobia in a Five-Year-Old Boy. *Standard Edition*, *10*:5–149.]

——— (1909b), Bemerkungen über einen Fall von Zwangsneurose. *Gesammelte Werke*, *7*:381–463. [Trans.: Notes upon a Case of Obsessional Neurosis. *Standard Edition*, *10*:155–320.]

——— (1909c), Letter to James J. Putnam, December 5. In: *James Jackson Putnam and Psychoanalysis*, ed. N. G. Hale. Cambridge, Mass.: Harvard University Press, 1971, pp. 89–91.

——— (1910a), Über Psychoanalyse. *Gesammelte Werke*, *8*:3–60. [Trans.: Five Lectures on Psychoanalysis. *Standard Edition*, *11*:9–56.]

———— (1910b), Die zukünftigen Chancen der psychoanalytischen Therapie. *Gesammelte Werke, 8:*104–115. [Trans.: The Future Prospects of Psychoanalytic Therapy. *Standard Edition, 11:*141–151.]

———— (1911a), Formulierungen über die zwei Prinzipien des psychischen Geschehens. *Gesammelte Werke, 8:*230–239. [Trans.: Formulations on the Two Principles of Mental Functioning. *Standard Edition, 12:*218–226.]

———— (1911b), Letter to Ludwig Binswanger, May 28. In: L. Binswanger, *Sigmund Freud: Reminiscences of a friendship,* trans. N. Guterman. New York: Grune & Stratton, 1957, pp. 32–33.

———— (1911c), Letter to Ludwig Binswanger, September 10. In: L. Binswanger, *Sigmund Freud: Reminiscences of a friendship,* trans. N. Guterman. New York: Grune & Stratton, 1957, pp.. 35–36.

———— (1912), A Note on the Unconscious in Psychoanalysis. *Standard Edition, 12:*260–266.

———— (1912–1913), Totem und Tabu. *Gesammelte Werke, 9.* [Trans.: Totem and Taboo. *Standard Edition, 13:*1–162.]

———— (1913), Das Interesse an der Psychoanalyse. *Gesammelte Werke, 8:*390–420. [Trans.: The Claims of Psychoanalysis to Scientific Interest. *Standard Edition, 13:*165–190.]

———— (1914), Zur Einführung des Narzissmus. *Gessammelte Werke, 10:*138–170. [Trans.: On Narcissism: An Introduction. *Standard Edition, 14:*73–102.]

———— (1915a), Triebe und Triebschicksale. *Gesammelte Werke, 10:*210–232. [Trans.: Instincts and Their Vicissitudes. *Standard Edition, 14:*117–140.]

———— (1915b), Das Unbewusste. *Gesammelte Werke, 10:*264–303. [Trans.: The Unconscious. *Standard Edition, 14:*166–204.]

———— (1915c), Die Verdrängung. *Gesammelte Werke, 10:*248–261. [Trans.: Repression. *Standard Edition, 14:*146–158.]

———— (1916–1917), Vorlesungen zur Einführung in die Psychoanalyse. *Gesammelte Werke, 11.* [Trans.: Introductory Lectures on Psychoanalysis. *Standard Edition, 15 & 16.*]

———— (1917a), Metapsychologische Ergänzung zur Traumlehre. *Gesammelte Werke, 10:*412–426. [Trans.: A Metapsychological Supplement to the Theory of Dreams. *Standard Edition, 14:*222–235.]

———— (1917b), Eine Schwierigkeit der Psychoanalyse. *Gesammelte Werke, 12:*3–12. [Trans.: A Difficulty in the Path of Psychoanalysis. *Standard Edition, 17:*137–144.]

———— (1917c), Trauer und Melancholie. *Gesammelte Werke, 10:*428–446. [Trans.: Mourning and Melancholia. *Standard Edition, 14:*243–258.]

—————— (1918), Aus der Geschichte einer Infantilen Neurose. *Gesammelte Werke*, *12*:29–157. [Trans.: From the History of an Infantile Neurosis. *Standard Edition*, *17*:7–123.]

—————— (1920a), Jenseits des Lustprinzips. *Gesammelte Werke*, *13*:3–69. [Trans.: Beyond the Pleasure Principle. *Standard Edition*, *17*:7–64.]

—————— (1920b), Über die Psychogenese eines Falles von Weiblicher Homosexualität. *Gesammelte Werke*, *12*:271–302. [Trans.: The Psychogenesis of a Case of Homosexuality in a Woman. *Standard Edition*, *18*:147–172.]

—————— (1923a), Das Ich und das Es. *Gesammelte Werke*, *13*:237–289. [Trans.: The Ego and the Id. *Standard Edition*, *19*:12–66.]

—————— (1923b), "Psychoanalyse" und "Libidotheorie." *Gesammelte Werke*, *13*:211–233. [Trans.: Two Encyclopaedia Articles. *Standard Edition*, *18*:235–259.]

—————— (1925a), Selbdarstellung. *Gesammelte Wrke*, *14*:33–96. [Trans.: An Autobiographical Study. *Standard Edition*, *20*:7–74.]

—————— (1925b), Die Verneinung. *Gesammelte Werke*, *14*:11–15. [Trans.: Negation. *Standard Edition*, *19*:235–239.]

—————— (1925c), Die Widerstände gegen die Psychoanalyse. *Gesammelte Werke*, *14*:99–110. [Trans.: The Resistances to Psychoanalysis. *Standard Edition*, *19*: 213–222.]

—————— (1926a), Die Frage der Laienanalyse. *Gesammelte Werke*, *14*:209–286. [Trans.: The Question of Lay Analysis. *Standard Edition*, *20*:183–250.]

—————— (1926b), Hemmung, Symptom und Angst. *Gesammelte Werke*, *14*:113–205. [Trans.: Inhibitions, Symptoms and Anxiety. *Standard Edition*, *20*:87–172.]

——————(1926c), Psychoanalyse. *Gesammelte Werke*, *14*:299–307. [Trans.: Psychoanalysis. *Standard Edition*, *20*:263–270.]

—————— (1928), Letter to Oskar Pfister, November 25. In: *Psychoanalysis and faith*, ed. H. Meng & E. L. Freud, trans. E. Mosbacher. New York: Basic Books, 1963, pp. 125–126.

—————— (1933), Neue Folge der Vorlesungen zur Einführung in die Psychoanalyse. *Gesammelte Werke*, *15*. [Trans.: New Introductory Lectures on Psychoanalyis. *Standard Edition*, *22*:5–182.]

—————— (1936), Letter to Arnold Zweig, May 31. In: *The letters of Sigmund Freud and Arnold Zweig*, ed. E. L. Freud, trans. E. Robson-Scott & W. Robson-Scott. New York: Harcourt, Brace & World, 1970, pp. 127–128.

—————— (1937a), Die endliche und die unendliche Analyse. *Gesammelte Werke*, *16*:59–99. [Trans.: Analysis Terminable and Interminable. *Standard Edition*, *23*:216–253.]

—— (1937b), Konstruktionen in der Analyse. *Gesammelte Werke,* *16:*43–56. [Trans.: Constructions in Analysis. *Standard Edition,* *23:*257–269.]

—— (1938/1940), Abriss der Psychoanalyse. *Gesammelte Werke,* *17:*67–138. [Trans.: An Outline of Psychoanalysis. *Standard Edition, 23:*144–207.]

Gadamer, H.-G. (1960), *Truth and method.* New York: Seabury, 1975.

—— (1960–1972), *Philosophical hermeneutics,* trans. D. E. Linge. Berkeley: University of California Press, 1976.

—— (1971), *Hegels Dialektik: Fünf hermeneutische studien.* Tübingen: Mohr.

Gill, M. M. & Holzman, P. S., Eds. (1976), *Psychology versus meta-psychology [Psychological Issues,* Monogr. 36]. New York: International Universities Press.

Gillispie, C. C. (1960), *The edge of objectivity: An essay in the history of scientific ideas.* Princeton: Princeton University Press.

Goodman, N. (1978), *Ways of worldmaking.* Indianapolis: Hackett Publishing.

Guntrip, H. (1971), *Psychoanalytic theory, therapy, and the self.* New York: Basic Books.

Habermas, J. (1968), *Knowledge and human interests,* trans. J. J. Shapiro. London: Heinemann, 1972.

—— (1970), *Toward a rational society,* trans. J. J. Shapiro. Boston: Beacon Press.

—— (1971), *Theory and practice,* trans. J. Viertel. Boston: Beacon Press, 1973.

—— (1973a), *Legitimation crisis,* trans. T. McCarthy. Boston: Beacon Press, 1975.

—— (1973b), A Postscript to "Knowledge and Human Interests." *Philosophy of the Social Sciences, 3:*157–189.

—— (1976), *Communication and the evolution of society,* trans. T. McCarthy. Boston: Beacon Press, 1979.

Hartmann, H. (1924–1959), *Essays on ego psychology,* trans. D. Rapaport. New York: International Universities Press, 1964.

—— (1927), Understanding and Explanation. In: *Essays on ego psychology,* trans. D. Rapaport. New York: International Universities Press, 1964, pp. 369–403.

—— (1939), *Ego psychology and the problem of adaptation,* trans. D. Rapaport. New York: International Universities Press, 1958.

—— (1948), Comments on the Psychoanalytic Theory of Instinctual Drives. In: *Essays on ego psychology* trans. D. Rapaport. New York: International Universities Press, 1964, pp. 69–89.

—— (1950), Comments on the Psychoanalytic Theory of the Ego. In: *Essays on ego psychology*, trans. D. Rapaport. New York: International Universities Press, 1964, pp. 113–141.

—— (1951), Technical Implications of Ego Psychology. In: *Essays on ego psychology*, trans. D. Rapaport. New York: International Universities Press, 1964, pp. 142–154.

—— (1952), The Mutual Influences in the Development of Ego and Id. In: *Essays on ego psychology*, trans. D. Rapaport. New York: International Universities Press, 1964, pp. 155–181.

—— (1956), Notes on the Reality Principle. In: *Essays on ego psychology*, trans. D. Rapaport. New York: International Universities Press, 1964, pp. 241–267.

—— (1958), Comments on the Scientific Aspects of Psychoanalysis. In: *Essays on ego psychology*, trans. D. Rapaport. New York: International Universities Press, 1964, pp. 297–317.

—— (1959), Psychoanalysis as Scientific Theory. In: *Essays on ego psychology*, trans. D. Rapaport. New York: International Universities Press, 1964, pp. 318–350.

—— Kris. E., & Loewenstein, R. M. (1946), Comments on the Formation of Psychic Structure. *The Psychoanalytic Study of the Child*, 2:111–38. New York: International Universities Press.

Hegel, G. W. F. (1807), *Phänomenologie des geistes*. Hamburg: Meiner Verlag, 1952.

—— (1812),*Hegel's science of logic*, ed. & trans. A. V. Miller. London: Allen & Unwin, 1969.

—— (1817), *Hegel's philosophy of mind*, trans. W. Wallace. London: Oxford University Press, 1971.

Heidegger, M. (1927), *Being and time*, trans. J. Macquarrie & E. Robinson. New York: Harper & Row, 1962.

—— (1935–1936), *What is a thing?*, trans. W. B. Barton & V. Deutsch. South Bend, Ind.: Gateway Editions, 1967.

—— (1950), The Origin of the Work of Art. In: *Poetry, language, thought*, trans. A. Hofstadter. New York: Harper & Row, 1971, pp. 17–87.

—— (1951), The Thing. In: *Poetry, language, thought*, trans. A. Hofstadter. New York: Harper & Row, 1971, pp. 165–186.

—— (1953), *An introduction to metaphysics*, trans. R. Manheim. New Haven: Yale University Press, 1959.

—— (1954), *What is called thinking?*, trans. J. G. Gray. New York: Harper & Row, 1968.

—— (1959), *On the way to language*, trans. P. D. Hertz. New York: Harper & Row, 1971.

Horkheimer, M. (1968), *Kritische theorie*, Vols. 1 & 2. Frankfurt: Fischer Verlag.

Husserl, E. (1923), *Ideas: General introduction to pure phenomenology*, trans. W. R. B. Gibson. London: Allen & Unwin, 1969.

—— (1929), *Cartesian meditations*, trans. D. Cairns. The Hague: Nijhoff, 1960.

—— (1935), *The crisis of european sciences and transcendental phenomenology*, trans. D. Carr. Evanston, Ill.: Northwestern University Press, 1974.

Hyppolite, J. (1946), *Genesis and structure of Hegel's "phenomenology of spirit,"* trans. S. Cherniak & J. Heckman. Evanston, Ill.: Northwestern University Press, 1974.

Jacobi, F. H. (1787), David Hume über den Glauben, oder Idealismus und Realismus. In: *Friedrich Heinrich Jacobis werke*, Vol. 2. Leipzig: Fleischer, 1812–1825.

James, W. (1890), *The principles of psychology*, Vols. 1 & 2. New York: Holt, 1902.

Kant, I. (1770), Dissertation on the Form and Principles of the Sensible and Intellibible World. In: *Kant's inaugural dissertation and early writings on space*, ed. & trans. J. Handyside. Chicago: Open Court, 1929, pp. 31–85.

—— (1787), Kritik der reinen Vernunft. In: *Immanuel Kants Sammtliche Werke, 3:*1–470. Leipzig: Voss, 1867.

—— (1788), Kritik der practische Vernunft. In: *Immanuel Kants Sammtliche Werke, 5:*1–169. Leipzig: Voss, 1867.

Klumpner, G. H. & Wolf, E. S. (1971), A Pagination Converter Relating the "Gesammelte Werke" to the "Standard Edition of the Complete Psychological Works of Sigmund Freud." *International Journal of Psychoanalysis, 52:*207–224.

Kojève, A. (1933–1939), *Introduction to the reading of Hegel*, ed. A. Bloom, trans. J. H. Nichols. New York: Basic Books, 1969.

Kris, E. (1956). On Some Vicissitudes of Insight in Psychoanalysis. In: *Selected papers of Ernst Kris*. New Haven: Yale University Press, 1975, pp. 252–271.

Kristeva, J. (1974), *La révolution du langage poétique*. Paris: Éditions du Seuil.

Kuhn, T. S. (1962), *The structure of scientific revolutions*. Chicago: University of Chicago Press, 1970.

Lacan, J. (1936), Le Stade du miroir comme formateur de la fonction du Je, telle qu'elle nous a révélée dans l'expérience psychanlytique. *Revue française de psychanalyse, 13:*449–455, 1949.

—— (1947), Propos sur la causalité psychique. *Evolution psychiatrique, 1:*123–165.

——— (1953a), The Function and Field of Speech and Language in Psychoanalysis. In: *Écrits: A selection*, trans. A. Sheridan. London: Tavistock, 1977, pp. 30–113. [Often referred to as the "Rapport de Rome."]

——— (1953b), Some Reflections on the Ego. *International Journal of Psychoanalysis, 34:*11–17.

——— (1953–1954), *Le Séminaire, Livre 1: Les écrits techniques de Freud.* Paris: Éditions du Seuil, 1975.

——— (1954), Introduction au commentaire de Jean Hyppolite sur la "Verneinung" de Freud. In: *Écrits.* Paris: Éditions du Seuil, 1966, pp. 369–380.

——— (1956a), The Freudian Thing, or the Meaning of a Return to Freud in Psychoanalysis. In: *Écrits: A selection*, trans. A. Sheridan. London: Tavistock, 1977, pp. 114–145.

——— (1956b), Seminar on "The Purloined Letter," trans. J. Mehlman. *Yale French Studies, 48:*38–72, 1972.

——— (1957a), The Agency of the Letter in the Unconscious or Reason since Freud. In: *Écrits: A selection*, trans. A. Sheridan. London: Tavistock, 1977, pp. 146–178.

——— (1957b), La Psychanalyse et son enseignement. In: *Écrits.* Paris: Éditions du Seuil, 1966, pp. 437–458.

——— (1958a), The Direction of the Treatment and the Principles of its Power. In: *Écrits: A selection*, trans. A. Sheridan. London: Tavistock, 1977, pp. 226–280.

——— (1958b), The Signification of the Phallus. In: *Écrits: A selection*, trans. A. Sheridan. London: Tavistock, 1977, pp. 281–291.

——— (1959), On the Possible Treatment of Psychosis. In: *Écrits: A selection*, trans. A. Sheridan. London: Tavistock, 1977, pp. 179–225.

——— (1960), The Subversion of the Subject and the Dialectic of Desire in the Freudian Unconscious. In: *Écrits: A selection*, trans. A. Sheridan. London: Tavistock, 1977, pp. 292–325.

——— (1964), *The four fundamental concepts of psychoanalysis*, trans. A. Sheridan. London: Hogarth, 1977.

——— (1964–1980), *Feminine sexuality: Jacques Lacan and the école freudienne*, ed. J. Mitchell & J. Rose, trans. J. Rose. New York: Norton, 1982.

——— (1966), Position de l'inconscient. In: *Écrits.* Paris: Éditions du Seuil, 1966, pp. 829–850.

——— (1976), Preface to the English Language Edition. In: *The four fundamental concepts of psychoanalysis*, trans. A. Sheridan. London: Hogarth, 1977, pp. vii–ix.

Lecourt, D. (1969), *Marxism and epistemology: Bachelard, Can-*

guilhem and Foucault, trans. B. Brewster. London: New Left Books, 1975.

Lenin, V. I. (1908), *Materialism and empirio-criticism*. Peking: Foreign Languages Press, 1972.

Lévi-Strauss, C. (1949a), The Effectiveness of Symbols. In: *Structural anthropology*, trans. C. Jacobson & B. G. Schoepf. London: Penguin Books, 1972, pp. 186–205.

———— (1949b), The Sorcerer and His Magic. In: *Structural anthropology*, trans. C. Jacobson & B. G. Schoepf. London: Penguin Books, 1972, pp. 167–185.

Lukács, G. (1923), *History and class consciousness: Studies in Marxist dialectics*, trans. R. Livingstone. Cambridge, Mass.: MIT Press, 1971.

Marcuse, H. (1941), *Reason and revolution: Hegel and the rise of social theory*. London: Oxford University Press.

———— (1957–1967), *Five lectures: Psychoanalysis, politics and utopia*, trans. J. J. Shapiro & S. M. Weber. Boston: Beacon Press, 1970.

———— (1968), *Negations: Essays in critical theory*, trans. J. J. Shapiro. Boston: Beacon Press.

Marx, K., & Engels, F. (1845–1846), The German Ideology. In: *Karl Marx, Frederick Engels, collected works*, 5:19–539. New York: International Publishers, 1976.

McCarthy T. (1978), *The critical theory of Jürgen Habermas*. Cambridge, Mass.: MIT Press.

Monod, J. (1972), *Chance and necessity*. New York: Random House.

Muller, J. P., & Richardson, W. J. (1982), *Lacan and language: A reader's guide to "Écrits."* New York: International Universities Press.

Nagel, E. (1961), *The Structure of Science: Problems in the logic of scientific explanation*. New York: Harcourt, Brace & World.

Nunberg, H. (1931), The Synthetic Function of the Ego. *International Journal of Psychoanalysis*, 12:123–140.

Paci, E. (1963), *The function of the sciences and the meaning of man*, trans. P. Piccone & J. E. Hanson. Evanston, Ill.: Northwestern University Press, 1972.

Polanyi, M. (1958), *Personal knowledge: Towards a postcritical philosophy*. Chicago: University of Chicago Press.

Popper, K. (1935), *The logic of scientific discovery*. New York: Basic Books, 1959.

Rapaport, D. (1942a), *Emotions and memory*. Baltimore: Williams & Wilkins.

—— (1942b), The History of the Awakening of Insight. In: *The collected papers of David Rapaport*, ed. M. M. Gill. New York: Basic Books, 1967, pp. 100–112.

—— (1944), The Scientific Methodology of Psychoanalysis. In: *The collected papers of David Rapaport*, ed. M. M. Gill. New York: Basic Books 1967, pp. 165–220.

—— (1947), Dynamic Psychology and Kantian Epistemology. In: *The collected papers of David Rapaport*, ed. M. M. Gill. New York: Basic Books, 1967, pp. 289–298.

—— (1951a), Interpersonal Relationships, Communication, and Psychodynamics. In: *The collected papers of David Rapaport*, ed. M. M. Gill. New York: Basic Books, 1967, pp. 440–449.

—— Ed. (1951b), *Organization and pathology of thought.* New York: Columbia Unviersity Press.

—— (1951c), Toward a Theory of Thinking. In: *Organization and pathology of thought.* New York: Columbia University Press, pp. 689–730.

—— (1957), The Theory of Ego Autonomy: A Gernalization. In: *The collected papers of David Rapaport*, ed. M. M. Gill. New York: Basic Books, 1967, pp. 722–744.

—— (1958), A Historical Survey of Psychoanalytic Ego Psychology. In: *The collected papers of David Rapaport*, ed. M. M. Gill. New York: Basic Books, 1967, pp. 745–757.

—— (1960a), Psychoanalytic Developmental Psychology. In: *The collected papers of David Rapaport*, ed. M. M. Gill. New York: Basic Books, 1967, pp. 820–852.

—— (1960b), *The structure of psychoanalytic theory: A systematizing attempt [Psychological Issues*, Monogr. 6]. New York: International Universites Press.

—— & Gill, M. M. (1959), The Points of View and Assumptions of Metapsychology. In: *The collected papers of David Rapaport*, ed. M. M. Gill. New York: Basic Books, 1967, pp. 795–811.

—— & Weber, A. O. (1941), Teleology and the Emotions In: *The collected papers of David Rapaport*, ed. M. M. Gill. New York: Basic Books, 1967, pp. 80–90.

Ricoeur, P. (1967), *Husserl: An analysis of his phenomenology*, trans. E. G. Ballard & L. E. Embree. Evanston, Ill.: Northwestern University Press.

—— (1970), *Freud and philosophy: An essay on interpretation*, trans. D. Savage. New Haven: Yale University Press.

—— (1974), *The conflict of interpretations: Essays in hermeneutics*, ed. D. Ihde. Evanston, Ill.: Northwestern University Press.

Riegel, K. F., Ed. (1975), *The development of dialectical operations* [*Human Development*, Vol. 18, Issues 1–3]. New York: Karger.

Ronchi, V. (1963), *Critica dei fondamenti dell' Acustica e dell' Ottica.* Firenze: Marzo.

Rychlak, J. F., Ed. (1975), *Dialectic: Humanistic rationale for behavior and development* [*Contributions to Human Development*, Monogr. 2]. New York: Karger.

Sartre, J.-P. (1948), *Sketch for a theory of emotion*, trans. P. Mairet. London: Methuen, 1962.

———— (1943), *Being and nothingness: An essay on phenomenological ontology.* trans. H. E. Barnes. New York: Philosophical Library, 1956.

———— (1960), *Critique of dialectical reason*, trans. A. Sheridan-Smith. London: New Left Books, 1976.

Saussure, F. de (1906–1911), *Course in general linguistics*, ed. C. S. Bally & A. Sechehaye, trans. W. Baskin. New York: McGraw-Hill, 1966.

Scheffler, I. (1967), *Science and subjectivity.* Indianapolis: Bobbs-Merrill.

Schneiderman, S. (1983), *Jacques Lacan: The Death of an Intellectual Hero.* Cambridge, Mass.: Harvard University Press.

Wilden, A. (1968), *The language of the self.* London: Johns Hopkins University Press.

———— (1972), *System and structure: Essays in communication and exchange.* London: Tavistock.

Wittgenstein, L. (1933–1935), *The blue and brown books.* New York: Harper & Row, 1958.

———— (1945–1949), *Philosophical investigations*, trans. G. E. M. Anscombe. New York: Macmillan, 1953.

Wortis, J. (1954), *Fragments of an analysis with Freud.* New York: Simon & Schuster.

NAME INDEX

A

Adler, A. 138
Adorno, T. W. 116, 130, 187n, 212, 214, 234, 239, 246, 251, 255–256, 258–259, 265, 270
Alexander, F. 142
Allport, G. W. 140
Anaxagoras of Clazomenae 189
Andreas-Salomé, L. 137
Aquinas, St. Thomas 185
Aristotle 187, 234
Arlow, J. A. 142
Augustine, St. 195

B

Bachelard, G. 36n, 39, 47, 54
Bacon, F. 133, 150
Bär, E. S. 214, 222, 230
Barratt, B. B. 60, 272
Barthes, R. 15
Bataille, G. 29
Bergson, H. 175n, 190
Betti, E. 175n
Binswanger, L. 137, 273
Bloch, E. 180, 258
Boas, F. 138
Boden, M. A. 58
Boeckh, A. 195
Brenner C. 142

Brentano, F. 13, 70, 101, 126, 158
Breuer, J. 20, 58
Bridgman, P. W. 35
Brücke, E. 57
Bruner, J. S. 14

C

Camus, A. 270
Canguilhem, G. 39, 54
Carus, C. G. 72
Cassirer, E. 15
Charcot, J. M. 58
Chomsky, N. 77
Cohen, H. 37
Cooley, C. H. 46n, 138
Copernicus, N. 2, 69

D

Darwin, C. R. 69, 143
Derrida, J. 15, 232
Descartes, R. 2, 10–12, 23, 47, 79, 91–101, 105–106, 116–118, 132, 138–140, 150, 171, 174, 179, 181, 183, 185, 187, 189, 193, 213, 220–221, 230–231, 234–235, 240
Dewey, J. 138
Dilthey, W. 3, 46n, 106, 173,

175–178, 181–182, 190, 203, 241, 243
Droysen, J. 190
Durkheim, E. 15

E

Einstein, A. 35, 38
Engels, F. 29
Erikson, E. H. 150
Exner, S. 57
Eysenck, H. J. 29

F

Fairbairn, W. R. D. 139
Festinger, L. 29
Feyerabend, P. K. 36n
Fichte, J. G. 6, 10, 26, 94, 189, 215
Fleiss, W. 57
Foucault, M. 23, 36n, 39, 54
Freud, A. 142, 152–153, 165
Freud, S. 3–4, 7, 10–12, 15, 19–20, 32, 50–80, 82–87, 91, 95–98, 111–113, 115, 119, 124–142, 144–146, 148–154, 156–159, 161–165, 167–168, 170–175, 179–181, 191, 201, 213–214, 218–227, 229–230, 239–243, 245–246, 248, 250, 255–260, 262–264, 266–269, 271–274
Fromm, E. 139

G

Gadamer, H.-G. 23, 173, 183–186, 190–192, 194–200, 202–203, 205–212, 215, 229, 232–233, 237–241, 245
Galanter, E. 14
Galileo, G. 2, 92, 99, 132
Gendlin, E. T. 41
Gill, M. M. 60, 150
Gillispie, C. C. 31, 39
Goethe, J. W. von 2, 6, 29, 35
Goffman, E. 46n
Goodman, N. 36
Guntrip, H. 139

H

Habermas, J. 48, 58, 176, 210, 242–245
Hartmann, E. von 72
Hartmann, H. 142–143, 149–150, 152–155, 158–166
Hegel, G. W. F. 6, 7, 10, 22n, 24, 26, 34, 36, 38, 41–44, 48, 60, 120–121, 130, 174, 185, 187, 211, 216, 238–239, 242, 245–248, 253, 256, 259–260, 263, 267, 269–270, 272
Heidegger, M. 15, 23, 35, 106, 115, 173, 175n, 183–198, 200–203, 205–216, 219–220, 224, 226–227, 231–233, 237, 239–240, 267–268
Helmholtz, H. 57
Henrich, D. 24n
Heraclitus of Ephesus 2, 189
Hering, E. 57
Hobbes, T. 2, 150
Hölderlin, F. 197
Holzman, P. S. 60
Horkheimer, M. 33, 130
Horney, K. 139
Hume, D. 2, 23, 32, 36, 48, 63, 148, 150

Husserl, E. 3, 23, 98–117, 119–
    120, 130, 175n, 182, 184–
    187, 189–190
Huxley, A. 5
Hyppolite, J. 246

J

Jacobi, F. H. 6, 32
Jacobson, E. 142
James, W. 1–2, 17, 27, 46
Janet, P. 95
Jaspers, K. 176
Jung, C. G. 176

K

Kant, I. 2, 6, 8–9, 12, 14, 17,
    23–26, 32, 34, 36–37, 47–48,
    79, 91, 94, 100–101, 104,
    122–129, 132–133, 137, 150–
    151, 154–155, 162n, 163,
    171, 174, 177, 179, 181, 183,
    185, 187–188, 190, 193, 213,
    220–221, 230–231, 234–235,
    240
Kelly, G. A. 10
Kepler, J. 2
Kernberg, O. F. 139
Kierkegaard, S. A. 190
Klein, M. 135
Klumpner, G. H. 3
Kohut, H. 139
Kojève, A. 246
Kris, E. 142, 150, 164
Kristeva, J. 266
Kuhn, T. S. 35, 38–39, 47, 54

L

Lacan, J. 22, 106, 168, 191, 201,
    212–239
Langer, S. 15
Lecourt, D. 39
Leibniz, G. W. von 2, 23, 37,
    105–106, 151, 182
Lenin, V. I. 47
Lévi-Strauss, C. 15, 204, 217
Locke, J. 36, 150
Loewenstein, R. M. 142, 149
Lukács, G. 47, 94, 256

M

Mahler, M. S. 142
Marcuse, M. 50
Marcuse, H. 246
Marx, K. 15, 29, 49, 259
Maslow, A. 140
McCarthy, T. 243–244n
McDougall, W. 176
Mead, G. H. 46n, 138
Merleau-Ponty, M. 115
Meynert, T. 57
Miller, G. A. 14
Monod, J. 30
Moore, G. E. 37
Muller, J. P. 214

N

Nagel, E. 36
Natorp, P. 37
Nestroy, J. N. 263
Neurath, O. 34
Newton, I. 2, 35, 38
Nietzsche, F. 3, 32, 190, 259

Novalis, (Hardenberg, F. L. F. von) 32
Nunberg, H. 142

P

Paci, E. 47
Parmenides of Elea 189
Peirce, C. S. 14–15, 39
Piaget, J. 10, 14, 54, 150, 247
Plato 104, 185, 193
Polanyi, M. 32
Popper, K. 11n, 39, 90
Pribram, K. 14
Proust, M. 29

R

Ranke, L. von 190
Rapaport, D. 57, 142–143, 149–155, 157–166
Reichenbach, H. 36
Richardson, W. J. 214
Rickert, H. 37, 174
Ricoeur, P. 108, 115–116, 119, 272
Riegel, K. F. 241
Rogers, C. R. 41, 140
Ronchi, V. 33
Rousseau, J. -J. 6
Russell, B. A. W. 37
Rychlak, J. F. 241

S

Sapir, E. 138
Sartre, J. -P. 44–45, 115, 144–145
Saussure, F. de 15, 217, 232

Schafer, R. 60
Scheffler, I. 30, 40
Scheler, M. 189
Schelling, F. W. J. von 6, 72, 200, 211
Schilder, P. 151
Schiller, F. 3
Schlegel, F. von 32
Schleiermacher, F. D. E. 6, 32, 173–178, 203
Schlick, M. 34
Schneiderman, S. 238
Schopenhauer, A. 6, 32, 72, 151
Schütz, A. 46n
Simmel, G. 175n, 189
Socrates 237, 259, 266
Spitz, R. A. 142
Spranger, E. 176
Strachey, J. 20, 87
Sullivan, H. S. 139

T

Thompson, C. 139

U

Uexküll, J. von 3

W

Weber, A. O. 161
Weber, M. 46n
Werner, H. 10, 150, 247
Whitehead, A. N. 15
Wilden, A. 224n, 231–232

Winch, P. 46n
Windelband, W. 37, 174
Winnicott, D. W. 139
Wittgenstein, L. 14–15, 23, 37,
    204
Wolf, E. S. 3
Wolff, C. von 37

Wortis, J. 273

Z

Zajonc, R. B. 29
Zweig, A. 269

SUBJECT INDEX

A

Adaptation and adjustment, 4–
5, 51–52, 138–141, 143–
144, 151–153, 159–160,
165–168, 242, 261
Affirmative "dialectics" (critique of), 241–248
"Analytic" epistemology, *see*
Cartesian-Kantian for-
mulations, Logical em-
piricism, Objectivism,
Subjectivism.
*Analytische Wissenschaft-
theorie, see* Logical em-
piricism.
Autobiography, *see* Life history.

B

Being-in-the-world, *see* Dialectics and deconstruction,
Heideggerian-Gadame-
rian formulations, Laca-
nian reformation, Life
history, Negativity of
psychoanalysis, Psychic
reality, Representational
worlds, Subject, Thing-
being and "objects."
"Being-towards-death," *see also*
Heideggerian-Gadame-
rian formulations, His-
toricity and historicality,
Lacanian reformation,
Temporality; 191, 199,
202, 219, 222, 225–229,
233–234, 236–237

C

Cartesian-Kantian formulations,
ego psychology, 141–166
empiricism (in relation to), 2,
36–37
hermeneutic ontology as critique, 183–188, 193
Husserlian phenomenology,
98–101, 104–105, 118–120
Lacanian critique, 169, 213,
221, 230–231, 234–245
neo-Kantianism and *verstehen*
philosophy, 37–38
psychoanalytic critique, 168,
213, 221, 230–231, 234–
235
psychologies of selfhood, 138–
141

rationalism (in relation to), 2, 36–37
subject in Descartes, 23, 47–48, 79, 91–98, 100–101, 104–105, 118–119, 138–141
subject in Kant, 23–27, 47–48, 79, 94, 100–101
thing-being and "objects," 8–9, 32, 34, 36–37, 100–101, 122–125
Compromise formation, see Unconscious mental processes.
Contradiction, see Negativity of psychoanalysis, Psychic reality, Unconscious mental processes.

D

Death, see "Being-towards-death."
"Defenses," see also Ego psychology, Unconscious mental processes; 80–81, 145–147, 152–153, 165–166
Desire,
   historicity and historicality of mentation, 9–10, 12–14
   investment in representation, 12–13, 16, 19–21, 32, 70–85
   Lacanian reformation, 220, 225–228
   repressed unconscious and splitting of subject, 70–85
   restoration in psychoanalysis, 242, 252, 254–256, 265–

267, 269–271
Development, see Historicity and historicality, Life history.
Dialectics and deconstruction, see also Affirmative dialectics (critique of), Negativity of psychoanalysis, Psychoanalytic psychology;
   adaptation (critique of), 242, 261
   being-in-the-world and thing-being, 248, 251, 254–258, 265, 273–274
   desire (restoration of), 242, 252, 254–256, 265–267, 269–271
   hermeneutic ontology (in relation to), 239–241, 253
   method and the ontic in reflection and interrogation, 118–121, 125–130, 240–274
   negativity of method, 85–88, 245–246, 249–250, 252, 255–274
   nonidentity of psychic reality (in relation to), 242, 245–252, 254–259, 264–267, 271
   objectivism (in relation to), 239–241, 253
   repression and the dynamic unconscious, 239, 244, 247–250, 252, 264, 266–267
   semiotics (and discourse), 242, 249, 251, 254–256, 258, 263–267, 270–271
   subject, 239, 247–257, 259

subjectivism (in relation to),
76–88, 166–170, 239–241,
253, 269
therapeutics (in contradistinction to), 244, 247–248,
253, 272
totality and identity, 240,
245–246, 251–252, 255,
265, 270–271
truth and transformation, 70–
88, 263, 267–270
Dilthey's formulations, see
Schleiermacher-Dilthey
formulations.
Discourse as therapy, see also
Dialectics and decon-
struction, Lacanian re-
formation, Negativity of
psychoanalysis, Psychic
reality, Truth and trans-
formation;
conceptual manipulation (critique of), 262
determinacy, 262–264, 268–
269
Heideggerian-Gadamerian
formulations, 203–205
historicity and historicality,
264, 269, 271–274
instrumentalism of ego objectivist psychologies (cri-
tique of), 64–65, 158–166
play and metacomment, 266–
267
psychoanalysis defined as
method, 66–68, 70–88
psychologies of selfhood, 138–
141
Schleiermacher-Dilthey formulations, 178–180
Dominant psychology, 7–8, 27–
30, 40–49

E

Ego cogito, see Subject.
Ego psychology, 55, 57, 62–65,
77, 141–166, 168, 235
Empiricism, see Cartesian-Kantian formulations, Log-
ical empiricism.
Essentialism, see also Husserlian phenomenology; 84,
116, 118, 265
Existentialism, 99–100, 190, 227
Extrapsychoanalytic research,
51, 55–56, 58–60

G

Gadamerian formulations, see
Heideggerian-Gadame-
rian formulations.

H

Heideggerian-Gadamerian formulations,
background, 106, 171–173,
183–186
being (concealment and unconcealment thereof),
188–197, 201–202, 207–
209
being-in-the-world, 184–212
"being-towards-death," 191,
199, 202
Cartesian-Kantian formulations (critique of), 183–
188, 193
epistemological critique, 184–
189, 192–194

historicity and historicality, 190–191, 194
identitarianism, 199, 205–206, 212
Lacanian reformation (in relation to), 191, 201, 212, 215–216, 224–231, 233, 236–239
"language" and being, 184–186, 191, 194–212
mysticism (in relation to), 193–194
psychoanalytic hermeneutics (in relation to), 200–202, 205–209, 212, 239–241, 253, 269
subject (critique of), 185–189, 192–196, 198, 210
temporality, 184, 187, 190–191, 194, 198–199
therapeutic possibilities, 203–205
totality and identity, 191–192, 195, 197–200, 202–206, 209–212
"understanding" (hermeneutically), 35, 184, 188–190, 192–212
Hermeneutics, see Dialectics and deconstruction, Heideggerian-Gadamerian formulations, Negativity of psychoanalysis, Schleiermacher-Dilthey formulations.
Historicity and historicality, see also Life history, Temporality;
    evolutionism in science, 39–40
    Heideggerian-Gadamerian formulations, 190–191, 194

Lacanian reformation, 224
progressive movement of psychoanalytic inquiry, 264, 267, 269, 271–274
progressive movement of mentation, 9–10, 12–14
regressive movement of mentation, 10, 12–14
therapeutic discourse, 264, 267, 269, 271–274
transcendental methods (in relation to), 108–110, 117–121
"Humanistic" therapies, 140
Husserlian phenomenology (transcendental subjectivism),
Cartesian-Kantian formulations (in relation to), 98–101, 104–105, 118–119
historicity and historicality, 108–110, 117–121
language (semiosis and the Lebenswelt), 103, 106–112, 115–117
Lebenswelt and intersubjectivity, 3, 101, 103, 106–112
Leibnizian philosophy (in relation to), 105–106
methods of "reduction" (epoché), 101–113
naturalistic objectivism (critique of), 99–101, 108–110, 113, 130
"phenomenological Marxism," 109
psychoanalysis (convergence with), 114–118
psychoanalytic critique of phenomenology, 118–121
subject and reflection, 100–

107, 109–121
transformation (problem of),
    118–121
truth and identity, 118–121
"unconscious" in phenomenol-
    ogy, 115–117

I

Identitarianism, *see also*
    Dialectics and decon-
    struction, Negativity of
    psychoanalysis, Psychic
    reality, Truth and iden-
    tity; 118–121, 199, 205–
    206, 212, 231, 233–234,
    238, 240–241, 246, 251,
    253, 269, 271
Identity, *see* Totality and iden-
    tity, Truth and identity
Ideology, *see also* Identitarian-
    ism;
    cooptations of psychoanalysis,
        134–138, 166–168
    dominant psychology as ideol-
        ogy, 27–30, 40–49
    psychoanalysis as anti-
        ideological discourse,
        166–170, 256–274
    scientificity, 27–30
    stasis of mentation, 40–49,
        82–83, 256–274
Individuality, *see also* Psychic
    reality; 5–8, 16–17, 45–46
Intentionality (Brentano,
    Freud, Husserl), *see also*
    Desire; 13, 70, 101, 105–
    106, 111, 115, 126, 158
Intersubjectivity, *see* Sociality
    and intersubjectivity.

K

Kantian formulations, *see*
    Cartesian-Kantian for-
    mulations.

L

Lacanian reformation,
    background, 22, 106, 168,
        191, 201, 212–216
    being (concealment and un-
        concealment thereof),
        219, 221, 223, 227, 231,
        238
    "being-towards-death," 219,
        222, 225–229, 233–234,
        236–237
    Cartesian-Kantian formula-
        tions (critique of), 168,
        213, 221, 230–231, 234–
        235
    desire, 220, 225–228
    Heideggerian-Gadamerian
        formulations (in relation
        to), 191, 201, 212, 215–
        216, 224–231, 233, 236–
        239
    historicity and historicality,
        224
    identitarianism, 231, 233–234,
        238
    "methodology" and claims to
        epistemology, 215, 234–
        239
    "Other," 221–225, 228–230,
        233, 236–238
    phallocentricity, 226–227,
        229, 233, 238
    registers (symbolic, imagi-
        nary, real), 214, 231

repression, 219, 232, 234
structural linguistics (use
    thereof), 216–218, 223–
    224, 228–230, 232–233,
    236
subject, 168, 220–228, 230–
    232, 234–235, 238
totality and identity, 228–234,
    237
unconscious, 216–223, 227,
    234
"want-to-be" (lack), 218–219,
    222, 224–225, 227, 231–
    232
Language, see Representational
    worlds.
Lebenswelt, see Sociality and
    Intersubjectivity.
Life history (autobiography),
    see also Historicity and
    historicality; 6, 16–17,
    40, 44–46
"Life philosophies"
    (Lebensphilosophie), 6,
    56, 175n, 189
Logical empiricism, see also
    Cartesian-Kantian for-
    mulations, Objectivism,
    Subjectivism;
    "data" and theorizing, 31, 33–
        39, 42–46, 130–134
    definition, 11n, 28
    dominant psychology, 28–30,
        40–49
    evolutionism and historicity,
        33, 39–40
    objectivity (critique of), 30–
        49
    operationalism and in-
        strumentalism, 28, 32–
        40, 44–46
    psychic reality (foreclosure
        thereof), 40–49
    theoretical adjudication, 31,
        34–40, 130–134
    thing-being and "objects"
        (problem of realism), 31–
        49
    types of logical empiricist dis-
        course, 36–40, 90

M

Meaning, see Representational
    worlds.
Metapsychology, see also
    Psychoanalytic psychol-
    ogy; 55, 57–62, 68–69,
    136, 142–143, 145–166,
    258–259
Mysticism, 11, 49, 56, 193–194

N

Natural science, see Logical em-
    piricism.
Naturalistic Objectivism, see
    Logical empiricism, Ob-
    jectivism.
Negativity of psychoanalysis,
    being-in-the-world and thing-
        being, 248, 251, 254–258,
        · 265, 273–274
    desire (restoration of), 242,
        252, 254–256, 365–367,
        369–371
    dialectics and deconstruction
        (in relation to), 85–88,
        245–246, 249–250, 252,
        255–274
    essentialism, (critique of), 84,
        116, 118, 265
    facticity, 130–134

historicity and historicality,
264, 267, 269, 271–274
method and the ontic in
reflection and interroga-
tion, 81–85, 118–121,
168–170, 240–274
nonidentity of psychic reality
(in relation to), 168–170,
242, 245–252, 254–259,
264–267, 271
phenomenology (critique of),
118–121
semiotics (and discourse),
242, 249–251, 254–258,
263–267, 270–271
subject, 119–120, 239, 247–
257, 259, 274
temporality, 263
truth and correction, 130–
134, 263, 267–270
Neo-Fichtean philosophy, *see*
Neo-Kantian, neo-Fich-
tean and *verstehen*
philosophies.
"Neo-Freudianism," 138–141,
167
Neo-Kantian, neo-Fichtean and
verstehen philosophies,
37–38, 46n, 86–87, 173–
183
Nonidentity, *see* Dialectics and
deconstruction, Iden-
titarianism, Negativity
of psychoanalysis, Psy-
chic reality, Totality and
identity, Truth and iden-
tity, Unconscious mental
processes.
Normativity and pathology, *see*
Adaptation and adjust-
ment.

O

Object, *see* Thing-being and
"objects."
Object relations theory (British), 139–140
Objectification (definition
vis-à-vis objectivation),
22n
Objectivism, *see also* Cartesian-
Kantian formulations,
Logical empiricism, Sub-
jectivism, Thing-being
and "objects."
ego psychology, 141–166
Heideggerian-Gadamerian
critique, 184–189, 192–
194
Husserlian critique, 99–100,
108–110, 113, 130
logical empiricist discourse,
30–49, 89–91, 121–134
psychoanalysis as dialectical
critique, 85–88, 121–134,
141–170, 239–241, 253,
269
Schleiermacher-Dilthey formulations, 175–183
Ontogenesis, *see* Historicity and
historicality, Life his-
tory.
Ontology vis-à-vis ontic
(definition), 18n

P

Phallocentricity, *see* Identitarianism, Lacanian re-
formation.
"Phenomenological Marxism,"
109

Phenomenology, *see* Husserlian phenomenology.

Polysemous contradiction, *see* Psychic reality, Unconscious mental processes.

"Post-Freudianism," 138–141, 167.

Psychic reality, *see also* Individuality, Representational worlds, Self-consciousness, Sociality and intersubjectivity, Subject;
adaptation and normality/pathology, 4–5, 143–144
definition, 1–8, 12–14
dominant psychology (foreclosure by), 7–8, 10–12, 27–28, 40–49
ego psychology and suppression of subject, 62–65
individuality, 6–8, 16–17, 45–46
nonidentity, 13–14, 70–74, 76–85, 95–98, 118–121, 168–170, 242, 245–252, 254–259, 264–267, 271
scientific inquiry, 27, 40–49, 85–88

Psychoanalysis (six revolutionary tenets), *see also* Psychoanalytic psychology; 13–14

Psychoanalytic psychology, *see also* Dialectics and deconstruction, Ego psychology, Lacanian reformation, Metapsychology, Negativity of psychoanalysis, Psychic reality, Reading Freud, Representational worlds,
Unconscious mental processes;
background and definitional discussions, 7–8, 12–14, 50–56, 65–76, 85–88
Cartesian-Kantian formulations, 91–98, 117–119, 121–134, 141–170, 240
cooptations and domestication, 50–56, 85–88, 134–138, 167–168, 273, 274
hermeneutic ontology (critique of), 85–88, 200–212, 239–241, 253, 269
Husserlian phenomenology (convergences and divergences), 114–121
method and the ontic in reflection and interrogation, 66–68, 70–74, 76–88, 118–121, 125–134, 240–274
objectivism (critique of), 85–88, 121–134, 141–170, 239–241, 253, 269
psychologies of ego objectivity (critique of), 62–65, 141–166
psychologies of selfhood (critique of), 138–141
revolutioary science, 50–56, 85–88, 166–170
subjectivism (critique of), 85–88, 138–141, 166–170, 239–241, 253, 269

Praxis, 209–212, 240–274

R

Rationalism, *see* Cartesian-Kantian formulations.

Realism/Idealism, *see* Representational worlds.
Reading Freud, 50–60, 68–76
"Reduction" (phenomenological method of), *see* Husserlian phenomenology.
Reductionism, 58
Reflection and interrogation, *see* Dialectis and deconstruction, Husserlain phenomenology, Negativity of psychoanalysis, Subject, Truth and transformation.
Regression, *see* Historicity and historicality.
Repetition compulsion, *see* Historicity and historicality.
Representational worlds, *see* *also* Desire, Individuality, Psychic reality, Sociality and intersubjectivity, Subject, Totality and identity, Unconscious mental processes;
background and definitional discussions, 8–22
being-in-the-world and thing-being, 8–9, 32, 184–212, 219–237, 248, 251, 254–258, 265, 273–273
Cartesian-Kantian formulations, 8–9, 12, 32–37, 100–101, 122–125
dominant psychology (foreclosure by), 7–8, 10–12, 27–28, 40–49
ego psychology and "language," 160–161
Heideggerian-Gadamerian formulations and "language," 184–186, 191, 194–212
Husserlian phenomenology and "language," 103, 106–112, 115–117
Lacanian reformation and "language," 214, 216–219, 223–224, 228–234
psychoanalytic approach, 11–14, 65–85, 242, 249–251, 254–258, 263–267, 270–271
referentiality and figurativity, 16–19
self and other, 16, 21–22
semiotic theories and terminologies, 14–22
Repressed unconscious (five critical claims), *see* *also* Psychic reality, Psychoanalytic psychology, Unconscious mental processes; 70–74, 79–85, 145–146
Repression, the "return of the repressed" and the reappropriation of the repressed, *see* Unconscious mental processes.

S

Schleiermacher-Dilthey formulations, *see* *also* Cartesian-Kantian formulations, Neo-Kantian, neo-Fichtean and *verstehen* philosophies, Objectivism, Subjectivism;

background, 106, 171–175
Cartesian-Kantian formulations (in relation to), 181–182
Husserlian phenomenology (in relation to), 182–183
life history, 176–183
"lived experience," 176–183
objectivism, 175–183
subjectivism, 175–183
textual hermeneutics, 173–174, 177–183
therapeutic possibilities, 178–180
"understanding" (hermeneutically), 175–183
Scientificity and scientism (definition), *see also* Truth and correction, Truth and identity, Truth and tranformation; 27–28, 30n.
Self-consciousness (Hegelian), *see also* Subject; 6–7, 24–27, 34–36, 41–46, 48, 60–61, 120–121, 130, 245–248, 259–260, 263–264, 269–270.
Selfhood (psychologies of), 138–141
Semiosis, see Representational worlds.
Sociality and intersubjectivity, *see also* Heideggerian-Gadamerian formulations, Husserlian phenomenology, Psychic reality, Representational worlds, Schleiermacher-Dilthey formulations;
shared and unshared repre-
sentations, 15–19
psychoanalysis and semiotic deconstruction, 242, 249, 251, 254–256, 258, 263–267, 270–271
Subject, *see also* Desire, Identitarianism, Individuality, Objectivism, Psychic reality, Representational worlds, Self-consciousness, Sociality and intersubjectivity, Subjectivism, Totality and identity, Truth and identity, Unconscious mental processes;
Cartesian-Kantian formulations, 23–27, 47–48, 79, 91–98, 100–101, 104–105, 118–119, 138–141
dispossession by psychoanalytic negativity, 119–120, 239, 247–257, 259, 274
dominant psychology and logical empiricism, 23, 40–49, 94–95
ego psychology and suppression of subject, 62–65, 145–166
Heideggerian-Gadamerian critique, 23–24, 185–189, 192–196, 198, 210
Husserlian phenomenology, 100–121
Lacanian reformation, 168, 220–228, 230–232, 234–235, 238
psychologies of selfhood, 138–141
representational world (general considerations), 6–8, 12–14, 16–17, 23–27, 46–

49, 70–74, 76–85
splitting of subject (repressed
    unconscious and the
    nonidentity of psychic re-
    ality), 12–14, 26–27, 67–
    85, 95–98, 118–121,
    123–130, 139–141, 157–
    158, 219, 232–234, 239,
    242, 245–259, 264–267,
    271, 274
Subjectivism,
    Cartesian-Kantian formula-
        tions, 89–121
    psychoanalysis as dialectical
        critique, 76–88, 166–170,
        239–241, 253, 269
    Schleiermacher-Dilthey for-
        mulations, 175–183
    selfhood (psychologies of),
        138–141
    transcendental subjectivism
        (Husserlian phenomenol-
        ogy), 98–121
Suppression, see Unconscious
    mental processes.
Symbol systems, see Repre-
    sentational worlds.
Symptomatology and charac-
    terology, see Adapta-
    tionand adjustment,
    Unconscious mental
    processes.

T

Temporality, 9, 44–46, 132, 184,
    187–192, 194, 198–199,
    263
Textual hermeneutics, see
    Dialectics and decon-
    struction,

Heideggerian-Gadame-
    rian formulations,
    Negativity of
    psychoanalysis, Repre-
    sentational worlds,
    Schleiermacher-Dilthey
    formulations.
Thing-being and "objects," see
    also Objectivism;
    Cartesian-Kantian formula-
        tions, 8–9, 32, 34, 36–37,
        100–101, 122–125, 187
    Heideggerian-Gadamerian
        formulations, 184–212
    logical empiricism, 31–49,
        130–134
    psychoanalytic dialectics, 248,
        251, 254–258, 265, 273–
        274
Totality and identity, see also
    Identitarianism, Truth
    and identity; 9–10, 12–13,
    16–17, 177–183, 191–212,
    228–234, 237, 240, 245–
    246, 251–252, 255, 265,
    270–271
Trieb, see also Desire; 20–21
Truth and correction, see also
    Truth and identity,
    Truth and trans-
    formation; 27–28, 130–
    134, 263, 267–270
Truth and identity, see also
    Identitarianism, Totality
    and identity, Truth and
    correction, Truth and
    transformation; 93–98,
    117–121, 177–183, 228–
    234, 237, 245–246, 251–
    252, 265, 270–271
Truth and transformation
    (method and the ontic in

reflection and interrogation), *see also* Truth and correction, Truth and identity; 70–88, 118–121, 125–134, 168–170, 240–274

U

Unconscious mental processes, *see also* Metapsychology, Psychoanalytic, psychology, Representational worlds, Subject;
background and definitional discussions, 11–13, 50
compromise formation, (*see also* polysemous contradiction), 74–76, 81–85
desire and semiosis, 70–85, 242, 252, 254–256, 265–267, 269–271
dominant psychology, 11–12
dynamic notions, 11–13, 65–76, 95–98, 118–121, 125–134, 139–141, 157–158, 219, 232, 234, 239, 245–252, 264, 266–267
ego psychology, 145–166
Lacanian reformation 216–223, 227, 234
nonconscious (in contradistinction to), 13–14, 70–74, 76–82

nonidentity of psychic reality, 13–14, 70–74, 76–85, 95–98, 118–121, 168–170, 242, 245–252, 254–259, 264–267, 271
phenomenology and "unconscious" meaning, 115–117
polysemous contradiction, 74–76, 81–85, 130–134, 139–141, 157–158, 168–170, 219, 232, 234, 242, 245–252, 254–259, 264–267, 271
preconscious (in contradistinction to), 13–14, 70–74, 77–82
repression, the "return of the repressed" and the reappropriation of the repressed, 61, 65–85, 95–98, 118–121, 125–134, 139–141, 157–158, 219, 232, 234, 239, 245–252, 264, 266–267
psychologies of selfhood, 138–141
symptomatology and characterology, 74–75

V

Verstehen philosophy, *see* Neo-Kantian, neo-Fichtean and *verstehen* philosophies.

—